MODERN JAPANESE LAW SERIES

INTERNATIONAL TRADE AND COMPETITION LAW IN JAPAN

MODERN JAPANESE LAW SERIES

The aim of this series of monographs is to provide first-rate introductions to various branches of Japanese Law for academics, legal practitioners, and businessmen and women. Particular prominence is given to subjects which are of some commercial importance. The monographs are by Japanese experts and are published in English.

International Trade and Competition Law in Japan

MITSUO MATSUSHITA
Professor of Law, The University of Tokyo

OXFORD UNIVERSITY PRESS
1993

Oxford University Press, Walton Street, Oxford OX2 6DP
Oxford New York Toronto
Delhi Bombay Calcutta Madras Karachi
Kuala Lumpur Singapore Hong Kong Tokyo
Nairobi Dar es Salaam Cape Town
Melbourne Auckland Madrid
and associated companies in
Berlin Ibadan

Oxford is a trade mark of Oxford University Press

Published in the United States
by Oxford University Press Inc., New York

British Library Cataloguing in Publication Data
Data available

Library of Congress Cataloging in Publication Data
Matsushita, Mitsuo, 1933–
International trade and competition law in Japan / Mitsuo Matsushita.
p. cm.—(Modern Japanese law)
ISBN 0-19-825440-7
1. Antitrust law—Japan. 2. Foreign Trade regulation—Japan.
I. Title. II. Series.
KNX3242.M36 1993
343.52'087—dc20
[345.20387] 93-15359

1 3 5 7 9 10 8 6 4 2

Typeset by Best-set Typesetter Ltd., Hong Kong

Printed in Great Britain
on acid-free paper by
Bookcraft Ltd, Midsomer Norton, Bath

Preface

The Meiji Restoration which occurred in 1868 was a turning-point in Japanese history in that it was the beginning of modern Japan. Until this time the Japanese political and social system was one of medieval feudalism in which the country was divided into small principalities or clans (which were called 'Han') with feudal lords and in which the loyalty of the subjects was directed not so much to the country as the whole as to the clan to which they belonged. Tokugawa was the largest clan and dominated the other clans for more than 250 years. Although there was the Emperor as a symbol of the country, his power was nominal and political power was in fact held by the largest clan—the Tokugawa Clan. In this system, the Tokugawa were the government.

The visit of an American fleet (the 'Black Ships') under Commodore Matthew Perry to the port of Uraga (in the present Kanagawa Prefecture) in 1853 and the request by the government of the United States for Japan to be open for commerce with the world was received in feudal Japan as a sign that the country would be ruled by foreign powers if this ancient regime continued any longer. Nationalistic sentiments arose among lesser *samurai* (the ruling class) and this was exacerbated by incidents in foreign countries which had been overrun by Western powers such as the Opium War in China. It was urgently felt that the country should be unified under the banner of one Emperor in order to avoid domination by foreign powers.

Young *samurai* in clans in southern Japan, notably the Satsuma (in present Kagoshima Prefecture) and the Choshu (in present Yamaguchi Prefecture), which had become powerful at that time, succeeded in forming an alliance between their clans to strike down the rule of the Tokugawa Clan. With the fall of the Tokugawa rule, the feudal system was abolished and a new regime was created. This was the Meiji Restoration.

Under the new regime, a central government was created, the clan system was abolished, and clans were turned into prefectures which were, unlike the old clans, mere administrative subdivisions of the country. The Emperor was named the 'Meiji Empereor' and was elevated to the position of a divine being who was the centre of the unity of the nation. In this way the country was unified as a modern state.

The most important task of the government after the Meiji Restoration was to introduce the modern military system, to promote industries and commerce, to adopt modern institutions into Japan, and convert the country from a feudalistic state to a modern state. The goal was, in short, to 'catch up the West'. In 1885 the Cabinet system was established and Hirobumi Itoh, who was one of the activists in the Meiji Restoration, was nominated as the Prime Minister. In 1889 the Constitution of Imperial Japan was promulgated. This constitution incorporated some modern principles, such as the separation of powers, and provided for the basic state organs such as the Executive, the Legislature, and the Judiciary although the protection of civil rights was insufficient and some old remnants stayed such as discrimination against women. In this Constitution, the Emperor was sanctified as 'sacred and inviolable'. In 1890 the House of Nobles and the House of Representatives were established.

Another important task of the government in introducing modern institutions was the introduction of civil law. The French Napoleonic Code was used as a model and French scholars were invited to help in drafting a civil code. Later the influence of the German Civil Code became important. The Civil Code was enacted in 1896. The enactment of other codes such as the Commercial Code and the Criminal Code then ensued. This system, which was established in the early Meiji Period, basically persisted until the end of the Second World War.

The end of the Second World War in 1945 was another big turning-point in the history of modern Japan. Japan was occupied by the Allied Occupation Forces in which the central role was played by the Forces of the United States. Various reform programmes were introduced. In 1946 a new Constitution was enacted in which the status of the Emperor was changed from divine to that of 'symbol' of the nation. Sovereignty was declared to be vested in the people. The new constitution which is in force today contains, *inter alia*, provisions for the peoples' sovereignty, the renunciation of war as a means of settling international disputes, the equality of the sexes, and civil rights. The Criminal Procedure Code was modified largely by introducing concepts of American criminal procedure. Parts of the Civil Code such as inheritance and marriage were changed to match such new principles as equality of the sexes. The Commercial Code was modified to facilitate the introduction of foreign capital into Japan.

Various new laws were transplanted from the United States to Japan such as Securities Exchange Law, the Anti-monopoly Law, labour laws, and a new set of tax laws based on US tax-law concepts.

By reviewing the history of Japan since 1868, one can recognize that the Japanese legal system is a hybrid of three elements, namely, the continental European systems (such as in the Civil Code), the American system (such as the Constitution), and the traditional Japanese system (such as emphasis on the practice of extra-legal dispute settlement).

Today this system is faced with new challenges coming from a rapid internationalization of the Japanese economy and the country as a whole. The legal system in Japan will have to undergo a fundamental change. However, the new direction to which this system will be oriented in future is not yet certain.

Contents

List of Figures

Abbreviations

Gyōsai Reishū	*Gyōsei Jiken Saiban Reishū* (*Administrative Cases Reporter*)
Haijo Meireishū	*Kōsei Torihiki Iinkai Haijo Meireishū* (*Fair Trade Commission Excluding Orders Reporter*)
Hanrei Jihō	(*Current Cases Reporter*)
Hanrei Taimuzu	(*Current Cases Times*)
Kakyū Keishū	*Kakyū Saibansho Keiji Saiban Reishū* (*Lower Court Criminal Cases Reporter*)
Kakyū Minshū	*Kakyū Saibansho Minji Saiban Reishū* (*Lower Court Civil Cases Reporter*)
Keishū	*Saikō Saibansho Keiji Hanreishū* (*Supreme Court Criminal Cases Reporter*)
Kōsai Minshū	*Kōtō Saibansho Minji Hanreishū* (*High Court Civil Cases Reporter*)
Minshū	*Saikō Saibansho Minji Hanreishū* (*Supreme Court Civil Cases Reporter*)
Mutai Reishū	*Mutaizaisanken Kankei Minji Gyōsei Saiban Reishū* (*Civil and Administrative Cases on Intellectual Property Rights Reporter*)
Shinketksushū	*Kōsei Torihiki Iinkai Shinketsushū* (*Fair Trade Commission Decisions Reporter*)

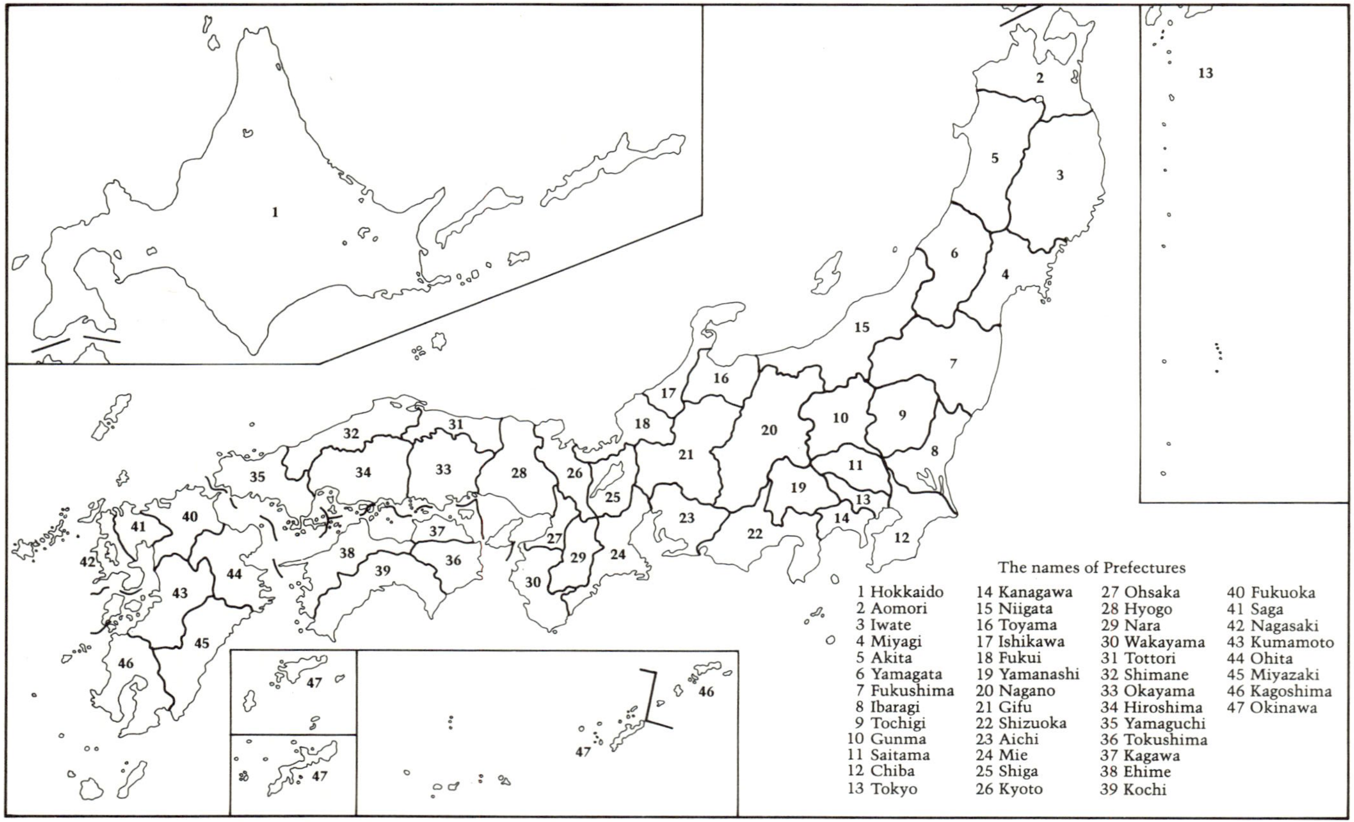

Japan: with Prefectures reserved

1
The Legal Framework of Government Regulation of Business

1.1 A Bird's-Eye View of Japanese Laws

The Japanese legal system consists of six basic codes and several other important areas of law. The six basic codes are: (1) the Constitution, (2) the Civil Code, (3) the Commercial Code, (4) the Civil Procedure Code, (5) the Criminal Code, and (6) the Criminal Procedure Code. There are several important areas of law other than those six codes, of which the major ones are: (1) administrative law, (2) tax law, (3) labour and employment law, (4) social security law, (5) international law, (6) law on conflict of laws (international private law), and (7) economic law.[1] Although the purpose of this book is not to engage in a detailed analysis of every aspect of the Japanese legal system, a brief explanation of the major areas of law is probably useful.

The Constitution, which was enacted in 1946, establishes the basic framework of the government by providing for the Emperor, the renunciation of war, the basic civil rights of citizens, the National Diet, the Cabinet, the Judiciary, budgetary matters, local government, the amendment procedure, the supremacy of the Constitution, and some supplementary rules. Under the Constitution, the basic organs of the state are the National Diet (the legislature), the Cabinet (the administration or executive), and the Judiciary (the Supreme Court and lower courts). The Constitution provides for the civil rights of citizens such as, *inter alia*, equality under the law, the right to petition the government, the liability of the state in cases of tort by a government official, freedom of thought, freedom of religion, freedom of association and expression, freedom of occupation, freedom of learning, and equality of the sexes. Some aspects of the Constitution will be dealt with in greater detail later.

The Civil Code was enacted in 1896. It was originally modelled after the French Napoleonic Code and later strongly influenced by the German

[1] See, in general, Noda, *Introduction to Japanese Law* (Tokyo, 1976), 187–211; also Matsushita (ed.), *CCH Japan Transactions Guide*, i and ii (North Ryde, NSW, 1988).

Civil Code (the BGB).[2] The Civil Code, which has more than 1,000 articles, is the basic law for private rights and the relationship between citizens. It provides for: (1) the general rules (such as, for example, expression of will, natural and juristic persons, juristic acts, and time duration of rights and obligations), (2) real rights (such as ownership and related rights), (3) claims and obligations (such as contracts, undue enrichment, and torts), (4) domestic relations (such as marriage, divorce, and adoption), and (5) inheritance. Many special laws clarify and modify the Civil Code.

The Commercial Code was enacted in 1899. Since then the Code has been amended many times and, after the Second World War, major amendments were made to the Code based on American law. Originally drawn up along the lines of Germany's commercial law system, the Commercial Code is now a hybrid of German, American, and traditional Japanese rules. Title 1 of the Code provides for such matters as merchant and commercial registration, trade names, commercial books and documents, commercial employees, and commercial agencies. Title 2 is the corporation law and provides for several forms of corporation among which stock corporation is the most important form. Title 3 contains provisions for commercial transactions such as sale, transportation, warehousing, and insurance. Title 4 is the section on the admiralty. The Commercial Code is supplemented by numerous special laws such as the Law on Bills and Notes and the Law on Limited Liability Companies.

The Civil Procedure Code was enacted in 1890 based on the German civil procedure law. It provides for rules for civil litigation and related matters like jurisdiction of the courts, parties, oral arguments, evidence, and appeals. Civil suits under the Civil Code, the Commercial Code, and any other laws of a civil nature must be carried out according to the rules incorporated in the Civil Procedure Code. Several important laws supplement the Civil Procedure Code.

The Criminal Code, enacted in 1908, provides for the general rules governing crime and punishment such as the construction of crime, self-defence, emergency, and various forms of crimes and the punishment thereof. The Criminal Procedure Code, which was originally enacted in 1891 and modified after the Second World War, provides for the provisions governing the trial of crimes under the Criminal Code and also supplementary laws.

Among these six Codes, the Constitution, the Civil Code, and the Criminal Code are probably the most basic codes and others provide either special rules applied in a special area (such as the Commercial Code in relation to the Civil Code) or procedural rules to be used in the

[2] See Noda, n. 1, above, pp. 197–202.

enforcement of the basic codes (such as the Civil Procedure Code and the Criminal Procedure Code in relation to the Civil Code and the Criminal Code).

Beside the six Codes, there are several other important areas of law. We will briefly touch upon some of the major ones. Administrative law is an aggregate of laws establishing the organization of the government and governing the relationship between the government and the citizen. There are many laws which can be classified as administrative law.[3] We will only mention the major ones.

The National Diet Law provides for rules governing the operation of the National Diet such as Diet committees, ministers, political ethics, and impeachment. The Public Election Law provides for various rules for election to public office. The Administrative Organizations Law establishes the structure of the offices such as ministers and special agencies. The Civil Service Law provides for rules governing government officials and employees. The Local Autonomy Law incorporates provisions for prefectures, cities, towns, inhabitants, and related matters. The Administrative Appeals Examination Law and the Administrative Cases Litigation Law provide for recourse against the government when the legal interest of a private party is adversely affected by an official act of the government. The State Redress Law provides for tort liability of the government when the property of an individual is unlawfully damaged by an official act of the government.

Tax law is in a sense part of administrative law. However, there are some features in tax law which make it distinct from other laws which belong to administrative law, and it is more appropriate to treat tax law as a separate area of law. Tax law consists of several important laws such as the Individual Income Tax Law and the Corporate Income Tax Law. There are also laws for the procedure for collecting taxes. In 1989, consumption tax was introduced by the Consumption Tax Law. There are special laws providing for tax exemptions in various areas for the purpose of promoting some industrial sectors.

Another important area is labour and employment law. Labour law is a post Second World War phenomenon. As part of the Economic Democratization Policy introduced to Japan by the Allied Occupation Forces, the Labour Standard Law, the Labour Union Law, and the Labour Relations Adjustment Law were enacted. At present, these three labour laws are supplemented by many other laws.

Social security law is the area of law in which laws concerning unemployment insurance, old age pensions, health insurance, and related

[3] See articles incorporated in Tsuji (ed.), *Public Administration in Japan* (Tokyo, 1984).

matters are included. With the advent of the 'welfare state', this area of law is becoming more and more important.

As discussed in greater detail later, Article 98(2) of the Constitution declares that treaties and established international law shall be faithfully observed. It is generally accepted that treaties and the international customary law have the force of law in Japan,[4] and, in this sense, international law is a source of law.

The Law Concerning the Application of Laws, enacted in 1898 and which is usually referred to as 'international private law', provides for several rules to be applied to the choice of law questions such as determination of applicable law in contract, torts, domestic relations and inheritance, the enforcement of foreign judgment, and exclusion of foreign laws on the basis of public order.

Economic law is the major subject of this book and details must be left to later sections. Here it suffices to say that laws such as the Antimonopoly Law, various laws regulating foreign trade and investment, and laws governing industrial policy are involved.

As high technology becomes more and more important in the economy, intellectual property law is gaining in importance. The Patent Law, the Utility Model Law, the Trade Mark Law, the Design Law, the Copyright Law, the Maskwork Law, and related laws are included in this area. Some aspects of intellectual law will be dealt with later.

1.2 The Structure of the Government and Regulatory Agencies

There are three main organs of the state. One is the National Diet (the legislative branch), the other is the Cabinet with ministers (the administrative or executive branch), and the third is the Supreme Court and lower courts (the judiciary). Details of each will follow.

A. THE NATIONAL DIET AND THE LEGISLATIVE PROCESS

The National Diet and the Legislative Process under the Constitution

Article 41 of the Constitution states that the National Diet is the highest organ of the state and the sole legislature. The National Diet is composed of the House of Representatives (the lower house) and the House of Councillors (the upper house), and the members of both houses are elected from among the people by the popular vote. The number of members of both houses is determined by law. The term for members

[4] Decision of the Great Court of Judicature (predecessor of the Supreme Court), 28 Dec. 1928, *Daihan Minshū*, 7 (1929), 1128 *et seq*.

of the House of Representatives is four years unless the House of Representatives is dissolved before the term expires. The term for members of the House of Councillors is six years, and half the members are elected every three years.

A legislative bill may be introduced into the National Diet either by members of both houses or by the Cabinet. A bill can be introduced either in the House of Representatives or in the House of Councillors, is voted on in both Houses by majority, and becomes law when approved by both Houses. If a bill passes the House of Representatives and the House of Councillors votes differently, then the bill becomes law when the House of Representatives approves it by a two-thirds majority vote. However, in a case of difference between both Houses, the House of Representatives can request the establishment of a joint conference with the House of Councillors. A revenue bill must be introduced into the House of Representatives first. When a bill passes both houses, the Emperor promulgates it as a law.

In revenue or budgetary matters, the supremacy of the House of Representatives is recognized. If the House of Concillors votes differently from the House of Representatives on a revenue bill and no agreement between both Houses can be ironed out after the joint conference, or the House of Councillors does not vote on a revenue bill which has been approved by the House of Representatives within thirty days, the decision of the House of Representatives is deemed to be the decision of the National Diet.

The above is a brief description of the formal legislative process under the Constitution. As noted above, a bill can be introduced into the National Diet either by the Cabinet or members of both Houses. In actuality, however, many bills that pass both houses and become laws are introduced into the National Diet by the Cabinet.

The Role of Ministries and the Liberal Democratic Party in the Legislative Process

As stated before, although legislative bills can be introduced into the National Diet either by the Cabinet or members of either house, the majority of bills that pass both houses are prepared by ministries and introduced by the Cabinet. Let us briefly review this process.[5]

The idea for a bill (especially a bill which promotes or regulates an industrial sector) is often conceived within the ministry of the government

[5] See Jackson, Louis, and Matsushita, *Implementing the Tokyo Round-National Constitutions and International Economic Rules* (Ann Arbor, Mich., 1984), 80–1; Fukushima, 'The Rise of Liberal Democratic Party in the Policy-making Process in Japan', in Schoenbaum, Matsushita, and Dallmeyer (eds.), *Dynamics of Japanese—United States Trade Relations* (Athens, Ga., 1986), 57–95.

which is in charge of the matter. The idea may have been suggested by an enterprise, enterprises, or a trade association in the industrial sector. Sometimes the ministry and the industry form a task force to study ways to deal with a problem and, as the result of such a study, the idea for a bill may come up. Then the idea is discussed within the ministry and the basic outline for a legislative bill is formed. During this process of formulating the bill, officials of the ministry contact key persons of the Liberal Democratic Party which has a committee within the Policy Research Council which corresponds to each ministry, discussions are held among the members of the Liberal Democratic Party and the ministry, differences are reduced, and a compromise is reached.

The bill is drafted by officials of the ministry in charge, is reviewed by the Cabinet Legislation Bureau for its constitutionality and compatibility with existing laws, and the Cabinet formally decides to introduce it into the National Diet. As long as the Liberal Democratic Party controls the National Diet, such a bill is almost certain to be passed and become law, since the prior agreement of the controlling party in the National Diet has already been obtained. The Liberal Democratic Party (or its predecessor) held the majority in both Houses from the end of the Second World War (except for a short period of time) until 1989 when it lost its majority in the House of Councillors.

At present, therefore, bills formulated by a ministry and introduced by the Cabinet into the National Diet with the prior informal consent of the Liberal Democratic Party may not automatically pass the National Diet since they may be blocked in the House of Councillors or by political parties other than the Liberal Democratic Party. However, the above description of the legislative process, in which the role of ministries in formulating bills is very important, still applies in many situations.

B. THE EXECUTIVE POWER AND THE MINISTRIES

The Power and Responsibility of the Cabinet

Under Article 65 of the Constitution, the executive powers are vested in the Cabinet. The Cabinet is organized according to the Cabinet Law and composed of the Prime Minister and other ministers, all of whom must be civilians. In exercising executive power, the Cabinet is jointly responsible to the National Diet. The Prime Minister is nominated by a resolution of the National Diet from among the members of the National Diet. In practice, however, the head of the political party which controls the National Diet is nominated as the Prime Minster. Ministers are nominated by the Prime Minister, and the majority of them must be nominated from among the members of the National Diet. The Cabinet

Law stipulates that the number of ministers is twenty persons or fewer. The Prime Minister can fire any minister.

The Cabinet must resign when the House of Representatives adopts a resolution of no-confidence or refuses to adopt a resolution of confidence unless the House of Representatives is dissolved within ten days. Also the Cabinet must resign when the Prime Minister is lacking or the National Diet is called for the first time after a general election for the House of Representatives. In those cases, the Cabinet continues to execute its powers until the new Prime Minister is appointed.

The Prime Minister, representing the Cabinet, introduces legislative bills and other proposals for resolutions to the National Diet, reports to the National Diet important domestic and international matters and supervises the different branches of the executive branch. In addition to general administrative responsibility, the Cabinet is responsible for the following matters: (1) to execute laws, (2) to manage diplomatic relations, (3) to conclude treaties (but, it is necessary to obtain a prior consent, and, if it is not convenient to do so, a post consent, of the National Diet), (4) to execute matters concerning government officials in accordance with the law, (5) to prepare a budget proposal and introduce it to the National Diet, (6) to promulgate cabinet decrees to execute the Constitution and laws, and (7) to declare clemency. Laws and cabinet decrees must be signed by the relevant minister and the Prime Minister.

The Organization of the Executive Branch

The organization of the executive branch of the government is based on the National Government Organization Law.[6] Under this law, there are the Prime Minister's Office (*Fu*), the Ministry (*Shō*), the Commission (*Iinkai*), and the Agency (*Chō*). This organization is shown in Fig. 1.1. The head of the Prime Minister's Office is the Prime Minister. The head of a ministry is the Minister, and ministers of various ministries are appointed by the Prime Minister from among the ministers of state.

There are establishment laws which establish each agency and which provide for the powers and responsibilities of the agency covered by the law. For example, the Law Establishing the Ministry of International Trade and Industry (the MITI) provides for the powers and responsibilities of the MITI. There are similar laws for the other ministries and agencies.

As shown in Fig. 1.1, there is one Prime Minister's Office and twelve ministries in the executive branch. Even though it is hard to state which ministries are more important in economic regulation, ministries such as the MITI, the Ministry of Finance (MOF), the Ministry of Agriculture,

[6] Kokka Gyosei Soshiki Ho, Law 120, 1947.

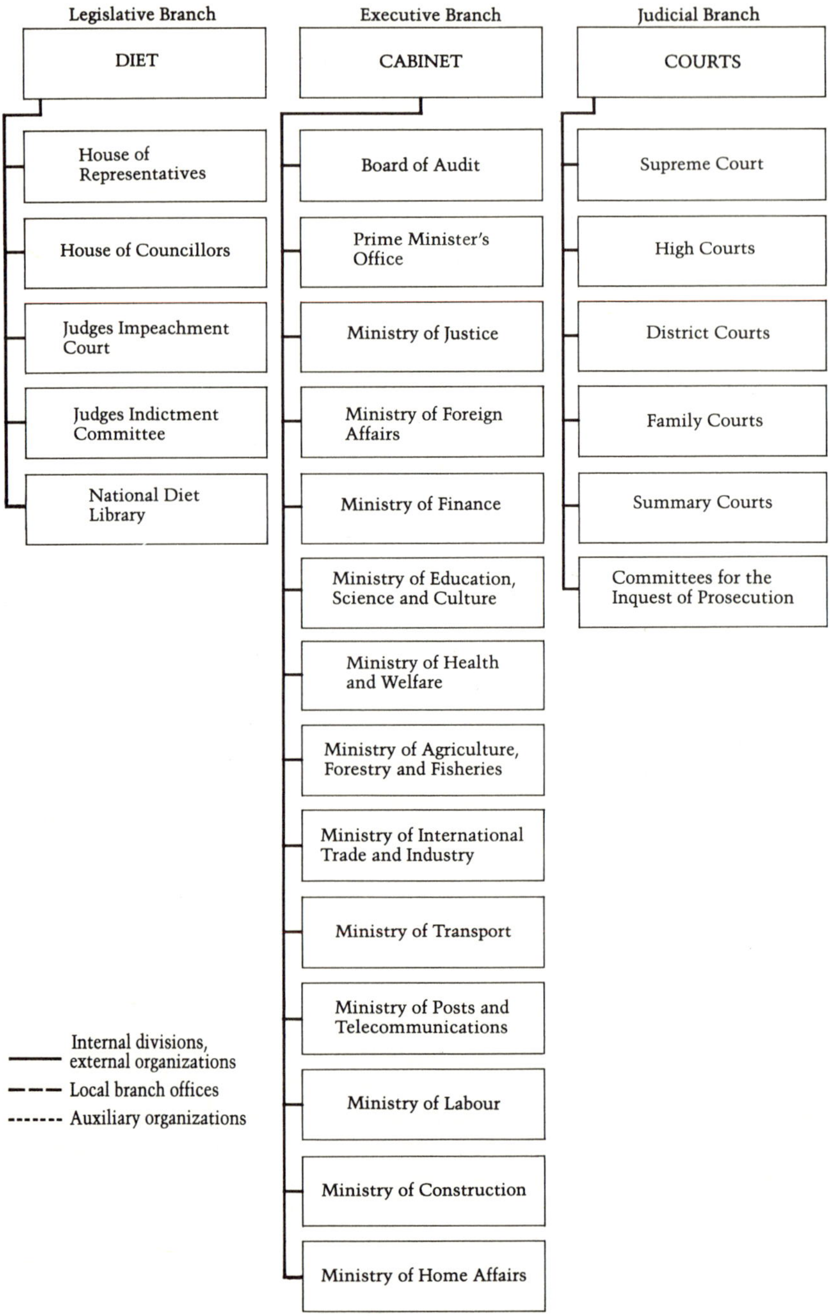

FIG. 1.1 Organization Chart of the Government

Source: Matsushita and Schoenbaum, *Japanese International Trade and Investment Law* (Tokyo, 1989).

Forestry, and Fisheries (MAFF), and the Ministry of Posts and Telecommunications (MPT) are probably most important. Most of the ministries are vested with the power to enforce laws and they grant licences to enterprises and individuals, enact ministerial decrees to enforce laws and cabinet decrees, collect information on the matters which are under their charge, and give advice to enterprises and individuals.

Let us briefly review the powers of the MITI and the MOF as examples. The MITI is responsible for promoting and supervising industrial policy concerning manufacturing industries and small business, granting industrial property rights such as patents through the Patent Office, licensing and regulating public utilities such as electricity and gas through laws such as the Electricity Business Law and the Gas Business Law, and enforcing foreign trade policy, for such things as export and import, under the Foreign Exchange and Foreign Trade Control Law. The organization of the MITI is shown in Fig. 1.2.

The MOF is responsible for preparing the budget for the government, securing governmental revenue by taxation, supervising tariffs under the Customs and Tariff Law, regulating foreign investment and foreign exchange under the Foreign Exchange and Foreign Trade Control Law, and promoting and regulating such business sectors as banking, insurance, and securities under the relevant laws. The organization of the MOF is shown in Fig. 1.3.

The Fair Trade Commission (FTC), which is the enforcement agency of the Anti-monopoly Law, the National Public Safety Commission and the Environmental Disputes Co-ordination Commission, the Defence Agency, the Economic Planning Agency, the Science and Technology Agency, and the National Land Agency are some of the agencies which belong to the Prime Minister's Office. Some of them are external organs of the Prime Minister's Office and are headed by ministers.

Some of them are important in economic regulation. The FTC, which will be fully explained later, enforces the Anti-monopoly Law which is regarded as the basic law for the regulation of industries. The Economic Planning Agency is responsible for co-ordinating activities of various parts of the executive branch, promoting the welfare of consumers, and engaging in economic research. The Science and Technology Agency formulates programmes for promoting basic research in science and technology. The National Land Agency formulates the basic policy for utilization of land in Japan.

C. COURTS AND OTHER ADJUDICATORY AGENCIES

Regular Courts

Chapter 6 of the Constitution (Articles 76–82) is devoted to the establishment of the judiciary. Under Article 76, judicial power is vested

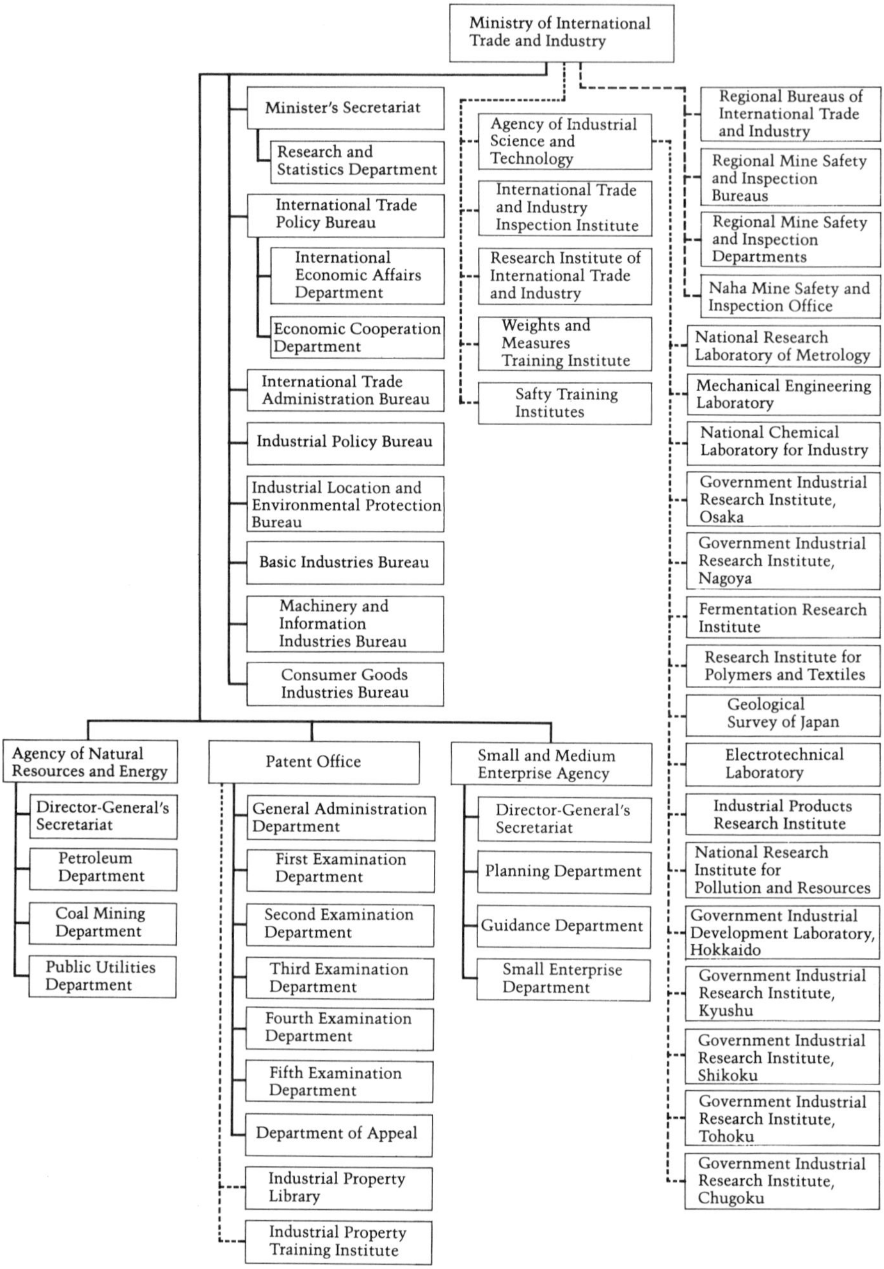

FIG. 1.2 Organization Chart of the Ministry of International Trade and Industry

Source: Matsushita and Schoenbaum, *Japanese International Trade and Investment Law* (Tokyo, 1989).

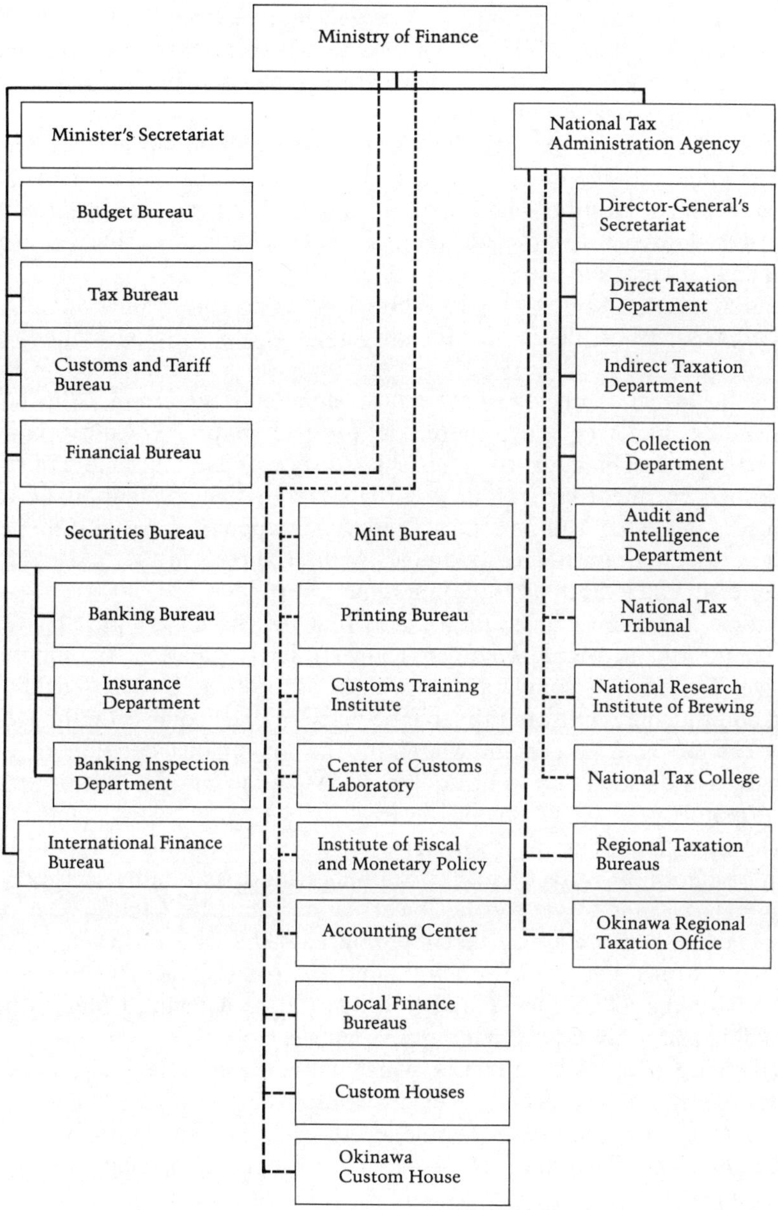

FIG. 1.3 Organization Chart of the Ministry of Finance

Source: Matsushita and Schoenbaum, *Japanese International Trade and Investment Law* (Tokyo, 1989).

in the Supreme Court and lower courts which are established by law. The independence of the judiciary from the other branches of the government is recognized, judges exercise their powers independently from other agencies and they are bound only by the Constitution and laws.

The establishment of a special court (such as an administrative court where administrative cases are handled and a constitutional court where cases in which constitutional issues are involved are tried) is prohibited, and the Supreme Court and regular lower courts are charged with handling all kinds of cases.

The Supreme Court is empowered to enact rules concerning the procedure of trials, disciplines for lawyers, and other matters related to the administration of justice. The Supreme Court is composed of the Chief Justice and other justices whose number is determined by law. Under the Judiciary Law, there are fourteen Supreme Court judges other than the Chief Justice. The Chief Justice of the Supreme Court is appointed by the Emperor in accordance with the nomination of the Cabinet, and other Supreme Court judges are appointed by the Cabinet. Judges of lower courts are appointed by the Cabinet on the basis of the list of candidates drafted by the Supreme Court.

Article 81 of the Constitution states that the Supreme Court has the final authority to decide whether a law, order, regulation, or administrative disposition is compatible with the Constitution. Under Article 82, trial and judgment must in principle be made in open court even though a trial can be held *in camera* when, by the unanimous decision of the judges, it is decided that to do so is necessary to maintain public order or good morals.

The Supreme Court passes judgment only on questions of law rather than on questions of fact, and the Supreme Court is bound to accept the facts of a case as found by the lower court from which the appeal has been taken. Depending on the importance of the case in question, the Supreme Court sits either in a full court or in divisions. The full court consists of the Chief Justice and fourteen judges with the Chief Justice presiding and a division is made of five judges.

There are eight superior courts, which are generally called 'high courts' as the courts of the second level divisions. At present, there are eight courts and a division in the jurisdiction of each, and so eight courts and eight divisions. The number of judges of superior or high courts is determined by the Judiciary Law but the distribution of judges can be determined by the Supreme Court. There are chambers in each superior court, and the number of judges in each chamber is three or five. Superior courts hear appeal cases from the decisions of district courts.

Courts of the first instance are district courts. They hear all civil and criminal cases except for certain matters which come under the exclusive jurisdiction of a superior court and summary courts. There is a district court in each prefecture and four in Hokkaido. The total number of district courts is fifty. A district court is composed of a number of judges and assistant judges as decided by the Supreme Court. There are chambers in a district court. Generally one judge decides a case in a district court proceeding although in more important cases, such as those involving offences punishable by death or imprisonment for more than one year, a bench of judges is necessary.

Special Courts

There are family courts at the same level as district courts but their jursidiction is limited to cases of domestic relations and juvenile delinquency. There are fifty family courts—the same number as district courts.

Summary courts have the jurisdiction on civil claims whose value does not exceed 300,000 yen and criminal cases in which minor offences are at issue. They are at the lowest level in the judicial hierarchy and appeals can be taken from their decisions to district courts. There are 570 of them. Cases before summary courts are heard by judges or by judicial commissioners who are lay persons appointed by district courts.

Other Adjudicatory Agencies

Besides the regular courts as outlined above, there are several agencies which are charged to deal with specific legal areas. The Labour Relations Adjustment Law provides for labour mediation boards. There is a central labour mediation board and local labour mediation boards. When one of the parties (i.e. a trade union or the management) requests mediation, a proceeding is instituted by either the central or a local mediation board. A decision of the board has the same effect as that of a labour–management agreement.

Under the Pollution Disputes Adjustment Law, the Adjustment Commission is established which is empowered to mediate and to decide cases involving disputes over pollution, public nuisance, and the mining laws.

The Maritime Collisions Tribunal Law provides for the establishment of the primary maritime collisions tribunal and the higher maritime collisions tribunal. They handle cases involving collisions of ships at sea. They are quasi-judicial agencies, and they have powers including revoking a licence to operate a ship. The decision of the primary tribunal can be taken to the higher tribunal and a further appeal can be taken from the decision of the higher tribunal to a superior court.

Besides the above, the Fair Trade Commission handles cases in which a violation of the Anti-monopoly Law is involved. Also the Office of Trade and Investments Ombudsman (OTO) deals with cases in which foreign exporters, foreign governments, or a domestic importer complain about the enforcement of trade statutes.[7] They are considered in greater detail later.

1.3 The Constitution and the Freedom of Business Activities

A. GUARANTEE OF PRIVATE ENTERPRISES UNDER THE CONSTITUTION

The Japanese economy is basically a market economy in which private enterprises are mainly responsible for producing and distributing goods and services. As in other countries which adopt a market economy, in Japan the price mechanism is the most basic economic institution. As we will examine later, even though there is some government involvement in economic activities, it is generally accepted that the role of the government in the economy should be kept to a minimum so that private initiatives are not unduly hampered. In this sense, we can say that private enterprises are the most important factors in the Japanese economy.

However, there is no country in the world which adopts a market economy in which the philosophy of '*laissez-faire*' is maintained in its pure form. Every market economy is inevitably a mixture of the market and government involvement in the economy up to a certain point. In this sense, the Japanese economy is also a hybrid of the market and government involvement. This is a subject of great interest among economists and political scientists, and there are extensive writings on this subject.[8] Even though we must refrain from a detailed discussion of the economic advantages and disadvantages of this hybrid system in Japan, we will make an analysis of this hybrid system from a legal standpoint.

The most important dimension in such a legal analysis is the constitutional framework for private enterprises, that is, the question as to how much the government can control by laws the activities of enterprises under the Constitution, or conversely the extent to which private enterprises are guaranteed freedom of activity under the Constitution.

There are two constitutional provisions which guarantee the existence and activities of private enterprises. One is Article 22 and the other is Article 29 of the Constitution. Detailed discussions of the interpretations

[7] Matsushita and Schoenbaum, *Japanese International Trade and Investment Law* (Tokyo, 1987), 44–5.

[8] See e.g. Komiya *et al.* (eds.), *Nihonno Sangyo Seisaku* (*Japanese Industrial Policy*) (Tokyo,1984), and Johnson, *MITI and the Japanese Miracle* (Stanford, Calif., 1982).

of these provisions are given in the following sections. Here we will briefly look at the structure of these two constitutional provisions.

Article 22 of the Constitution declares that the freedom of occupation is guaranteed. It also states that the freedom of occupation can be restricted for the purpose of promoting public welfare. The activities of private enterprises are included within the scope of the freedom of occupation as provided for in Article 22 of the Constitution. Therefore, the freedom of activity of private enterprises is guaranteed and can be restricted by law only when necessary for promoting public welfare.

Article 29 of the Constitution declares that private property is guaranteed. Private property is the basis for private enterprises, without which no private enterprise can exist. Article 29 guarantees that no private property can be taken away or restricted unless to do so is necessary for promoting public welfare.

Both Articles 22 and 29 of the Constitution form the constitutional basis for the private enterprise system in Japan.

B. THE RULE OF LAW AND THE REGULATION OF BUSINESS ACTIVITIES

As explained above, the freedom of private enterprise business activities is guaranteed under Articles 22 and 29 of the Constitution. However, that freedom is not without limitation. It can be restricted if necessary for the purpose of promoting public welfare. An important question is the meaning of 'public welfare'. There are several aspects of the public welfare concept which need to be discussed, and they are considered in the following sections. Here we will discuss one aspect of it, that is, the rule of law and government regulation of business activities.

As a general principle, public welfare must be explicitly declared in the form of legislation. Since the freedom of business activities is a constitutional right expressed in the Constitution, in order to restrict it for the purpose of promoting public welfare, there must be a clear declaration of it by the legislature. A mere statement of policy by the Executive Branch is not sufficient. Legislation is an expression of the will of the people, and it can be regarded as a sufficient ground for restricting the freedom.

The decision handed down in the *COCOM* case[9] in 1969 by the Tokyo District Court is a good expression of this principle. In this case, an export ban applied on some electronic devices under the Foreign Exchange and Foreign Trade Control Law (hereafter referred to as 'the

[9] The 1969 Peking–Shanghai Nihon Kogyo Tenrankai Case, Decision of Tokyo District Court, 8 July 1969, *Gyōsai Reishū*, 20 (1969), 842 *et seq*.

Control Law') was held to be unconstitutional. A group of business persons in Japan wished to export electronic devices to the People's Republic of China and exhibit them in a trade show held there. At this time, the products in question were listed as controlled items under the Control Law since they were part of the products whose export to Communist countries was prohibited under the COCOM agreement and, in exporting such items, the exporter needed to file an application with the MITI and obtain an export approval.

When an application for approval of export was filed with the MITI, the MITI refused and the persons who wished to export filed a suit with the Tokyo District Court for an injunction restraining the MITI from refusing an approval of export. In the proceedings, the plaintiffs argued that the freedom to export was part of the freedom of business activities (the freedom of occupation) guaranteed by Article 22 of the Constitution and could be restricted only if such a restriction was necessary to promote public welfare, and that in this case the prohibition of export did not come into this catogory.

The Tokyo District Court held that the refusal by the MITI to grant an approval in this case was unconstitutional for the following reason. Whereas Article 22 of the Constitution permits the restriction of the freedom of business activities for the reason of promoting public welfare, the public welfare must be expressed in the form of legislation. The legislation in question here is the Control Law, and the basic nature of this law is expressed in Article 1 in which the objective of the law is declared as the maintenance of the balance of international payments and the promotion of sound development of international trade.

The court reasoned that, as expressed in Article 1, the objectives of the Control Law were of an economic nature but the refusal to grant an approval to export the products in the case in question was based on the COCOM agreement whose purpose was to prohibit and restrict the exportation of strategic products to Communist countries in order to slow down the military build-up in those countries. In the opinion of the court, this objective was of a political or strategic nature but not of an economic nature as envisaged in Article 1 of the Control Law.

Therefore, the court held that to refuse to grant an export approval for the purpose of implementing the COCOM agreement was not included in the scope of the Control Law and, consequently, the MITI was not authorized to prohibit the export of commodities under the Control Law if the purpose of such a prohibition was to carry out the mandate of the COCOM agreement. Therefore, the Tokyo District Court held that the MITI's refusal to grant approval in this case was *ultra vires* and so unconstitutional.

The court admitted that whether or not the export of some

commodities should be prohibited, the implementation of the COCOM agreement was a matter of policy decision and that there could be such a policy decision. However, the court stressed that there must be a clear indication to that effect in the form of legislation if such a policy was to involve the restriction of activities of private enterprises.

The defendant (the government) argued that if the prohibition of export in this case was held to be invalid and could not be enforced, it would be a great disappointment to the Allies, especially the United States. It maintained that if the implementation of the COCOM agreement was frustrated, then there would be repercussions in the United States by way of some retaliation against Japan such as import restrictions or some other economic measures and that, for this reason, the implementation of the COCOM agreement had a strong economic implication. In this way, the government tried to persuade the court that the prohibition of items covered by the COCOM list was within the objective of the Control Law.

However, the court refused to accept this argument by pointing out that the cause-and-result relationship between the non-enforcement of the COCOM agreement in Japan and a possible retaliation by the United States against Japan was too remote and was not sufficient to convince the court of the validity of such an argument.

During the proceedings of this trial, the trade show in China ended and, therefore, the issue of whether or not an injunction restraining the MITI from prohibiting the export of the items in question should be issued became hypothetical. Consequently, the plaintiffs modified their action and asked for the recovery of damages sustained by the prohibition of export under the State Redress law which authorized the recovery of damages sustained by private individuals caused by the wrongful conduct of government officials.

The court denied such redress to the plaitiffs. The ground relied upon by the court was that the State Redress Law required proof of malicious intent or negligent conduct on the part of a government official in order for the injured individual to recover damages. Under the circumstance of this case, the interpretation of the Control Law in this regard had not been an issue. There had been several possibilities for the interpretation of the Control Law. One such possibility being that the Control Law could be used to implement the COCOM agreement. The court reasoned that even if the MITI officials in charge of the enforcement of the Control Law had taken this interpretation and prohibited import, it could not be held that they had acted with malicious intent or through negligence. For this reason, relief was denied.

Even though the relief sought by the plaintiffs in this case was denied and the result was somewhat anti-climactic, the implication of the case is quite important. It established the legal precedent that there must be clear statutary wording in legislation which authorizes the restriction of private enterprise activities by the government, if such restriction is to be interpreted as within the scope of the public welfare under Article 22 of the Constitution. The above conclusion is nothing but an expression of the principle that the excercise of government powers in restricting activities of private enterprises must be done under the rule of law.

Despite this decision, however, the Control Law was not amended for a long time. The MITI stated that it would object to the interpretation of the Control Law by the Tokyo District Court and continued to use this law to implement the COCOM agreement. In 1979, there were major revisions of the Control Law, and, on this occasion, a new wording was incorporated in the provisions dealing with international capital transactions and trade in services to the effect that they could be restricted for the purpose of 'preserving international peace'. The incorporation of this new wording was designed to expand the scope of the Control Law to include in its jurisdiction restrictions based on international-political and strategic considerations.

Curiously, however, no amendment was made on this occasion to Article 48 of the Control Law which authorized the MITI to impose export restrictions and was used to implement the COCOM agreement. Finally, in 1987, when the *Toshiba Machinery* case occurred and a bill was introduced into the United States Congress[10] which would have imposed sanctions on not only the Toshiba Machinery Company but also its parent the Toshiba Company, the Japanese government moved to amend the Control Law and incorporated a phrase in Article 48 which stated that this law could be used to preserve international peace as well as increasing the penalty for violations of the Law.

The decision of the Tokyo District Court in the *COCOM* case stressed that the objective and character of the Control law should be determined by Article 1 of this law which stated the objective of it. One may argue that, as long as Article 1 has not been changed, the basic objective of the Control Law is unchanged and the constitutional doubt has not been completely wiped out. However, now that there are provisions in the Control Law with regard to international capital transactions, trade in services, and also trade in goods which state that control can be imposed on them when it is necessary to do so to maintain international peace, the authority of the MITI, or the MOF as the case may be, is established to implement export control policies of a non-economic nature such as the COCOM agreement or the United Nations decision.

[10] See, on this subject, US Congress, House of Representatives, Report 100–576, *Omnibus Trade and Competitiveness Act of 1988*, Conference Report to Accompany HR. 3 (1988), 830–7.

C. THE FREEDOM OF BUSINESS ACTIVITIES AND THEIR RESTRICTIONS

An Overview

As mentioned before, Article 22 of the Constitution permits restrictions of business activities if it is necessary for the purpose of promoting public welfare. It has been mentioned already that, under the doctrine enunciated in the decision in the *COCOM* case, such a restriction should be based on legislation. Is there any constitutional constraint imposed on the legislature to enact a law which defines the extent to which legislation can restrict business activities? There are several important Supreme Court cases on this issue, and we will examine the major ones. However, before that, it is useful to review the legal propositions.

There are a variety of laws which restrict business activities. There is diversity in the purpose of such restrictions. Some of them are aimed at controlling business activities for the purpose of maintaining public order and good morals. Prohibitions on the manufacture and sale of narcotics, weapons, obscene literature, and strict licensing requirements for some amusement businesses (such as bars and cabaret) are some examples.

Others are designed to accomplish socio-economic policies, such as the protection of agriculture, small enterprises, or declining industries. As discussed in a later section, there are many laws which promote and protect specific agricultural and industrial sectors.

Again there are some laws which regulate public utilities such as those supplying electric power, gas, telecommunications services, and transportation.[11] Generally there are licensing requirements in such industries and enterprises intending to enter into such areas must obtain a licence from the relevant ministry to begin business. In some laws which regulate such industries, there are provisions stating that, in deciding whether to give a licence to a newcomer, the ministry in charge should consider the supply and demand conditions existing in the industry with the view of not creating over-supply.[12] In considering the constitutional issue, the nature of the law in question must be carefully studied and evaluated.

[11] See e.g. Denki Jigyo Hō (Electric Power Business Law), Law 170, 1964; Gasu Jigyō Hō (Gas Business Law), Law 51, 1954; Denki Tsūshin Jigyō Hō (Telecommunications Business Law), Law 86, 1986; and Dōro Unsō Hō (Road Transportation Law), Law 183, 1951.

[12] e.g. Art. 5(1) of the Electric Power Business Law states that the Minister of the MITI shall not grant a licence to operate an electric power business unless the initiation of such business is suitable in relation to the general demand for electricity.

Major Constitutional Cases Dealing with the Freedom of Business Activities

The *Public Bathhouse* case[13] is one of the important cases in which the Supreme Court dealt with the relationship between a regulatory law which restricted the activities of private enterprises and the freedom of business activities. Involved in this case was the Public Bathhouse Law which required a person who intended to operate a bathhouse to obtain a licence from the prefectural government. It provided that a person who operated a public bathhouse without a licence should suffer a criminal penalty. It provided further that when giving a licence to a new person intending to operate a public bathhouse, the prefectural government could take into consideration the geographical distribution of public bathhouses and that when it was asked to grant a licence to a newcomer in a location in which a new bathhouse would create 'excessive competition' among public bathhouses, the prefectural government could decide not to grant a licence. A person who operated a public bathhouse without a licence was indicted and put on criminal trial.

The defendant argued that the provision incorporated in the Public Bathhouse Law which authorized the prefectural government to regulate the bathhouse business and to attach consideration of the geographical distribution of public bathhouses in a certain area as a condition to a licence contravened Article 22 of the Constitution.

The Supreme Court, however, refused to accept this argument and held that to allow new operators to open new public bathhouses without any control might lead to maldistribution of public bathhouses and excessive competition among them. It argued that this would deprive citizens living in remote places of access to public bathhouses since operators would open new bathhouses only in areas where the population was heavily concentrated and that excessive competition among bathhouses would lower the profit of public bathhouses. It argued further that the lowered profit would mean deterioration of sanitary conditions of public bathhouses, a situation highly undesirable from the public hygiene standpoint. For these reasons, the Supreme Court rejected the argument of the defendant and upheld the constitutionality of the provision of the Public Bathhouse Law in question which required a licence to operate public bathhouses and authorized the prefectural government to attach conditions when granting a licence such as making the licence contingent upon the proper geographical distribution of public bathhouses.

The *Retail Market* case[14] is a case in which the licensing system for building a retail market and leasing space to tenants under the Retail

[13] Decision of the Supreme Court, 26 Jan. 1955, *Keishū*, 9/91 (1959), 89 *et seq*.

[14] Decision of the Supreme Court, 11 Nov. 1972, *Keishū*, 26/9 (1972), 586 *et seq*.

Business Adjustment Special Measures Law (hereafter referred to as 'the Special Measures Law') was challenged as incompatible with Article 22 of the Constitution. Under the Special Measures Law, a person who intends to build a retail market complex and lease it to tenants who operate retail stores must obtain a licence from the prefectural government. A retail market complex under the Special Measures Law is not a large-scale retail market such as a supermarket. It is a building or buildings built adjacent to each other in which small shops (mostly 'Mom and Pop stores'—stores operated by wife and husband without employees) are located.

The pronounced purpose of the Special Measures Law is to prevent 'excessive competition' among small stores and to protect the interests of small storekeepers. For this purpose, the prefectural government is given the discretion to attach conditions to a licence to build a shopping complex. In this sense, the Special Measures Law is a piece of legislation specifically designed to protect the interest of small enterprises.

When the *Retail Market* case arose, the Prefecture of Osaka ruled that a licence to build a new retail market complex would be given on condition that the distance between the existing retail market complex and the newly built complex was at least 700 metres. A complex was built inside the 700-metre range from an existing complex without a licence and store units were leased to tenants. The Osaka Prefecture brought a criminal claim to the prosecutor's office against the person responsible. The defendant was tried for a violation of the Special Measures law, lost in the lower courts, and brought an appeal to the Supreme Court.

The defendant argued before the Supreme Court that the control by the Special Measures Law on the distribution of retail markets was an undue interference with the freedom of business activities protected by Article 22 of the Constitution. The Supreme Court rejected this argument and held the defendant guilty of a violation of the Special Measures Law. The Supreme Court stated that the Special Measures Law was designed to protect small shops from cutthroat competition and, in this sense, it was a piece of law based on socio-economic policy to protect small enterprises. In the view of the Court, the National Diet (the legislature) had the power and ability to investigate socio-economic problems and formulate a policy to deal with them, whereas courts had no comparable capabilities in such matters. Therefore, courts should in principle adhere to the judgment of the National Diet as regards the policy dealing with socio-economic matters and should not lightly pass judgment on the wisdom of a law which incorporated such a policy unless the law in question clearly overstepped the limit of the discretion given to the National Diet or the methods of enforcement used were unreasonable. The Court went on to say that, in the Special Measures Law, there was nothing which indicated that the National Diet overstepped its discretionary power or the methods of enforcement were unreasonable.

In the *Pharmaceutical Affairs Law* case,[15] the power given to the prefectural government under the Pharmaceutical Affairs Law (hereafter referred to as 'the Pharmaceutical Law') to restrict the distance between existing pharmaceutical stores and a new store was nullified by its unconstitutionality. The Pharmaceutical Law was originally designed to authorize the Minister of Public Welfare to license new pharmaceutical products and related matters. Under the Law, a person who intended to operate a pharmaceutical store had to obtain a licence from the prefectural government, and, under an amendment of the law, the prefectural government was authorized to attach conditions to licensing a new pharmaceutical store.

The Governor of Hiroshima Prefecture enacted a rule to the effect that a new pharmaceutical store must be located at least 200 metres away from any existing pharmaceutical store. This restriction was designed to protect pharmaceutical stores from cutthroat competition.

A person who wished to open a new pharmaceutical store within 200 metres of an existing store applied for a licence but his application was rejected on the ground that the intended establishment was within the restricted distance. The applicant brought a suit against the Governor of the Prefecture of Hiroshima and argued that the said restriction unduly limited the freedom to open a new store and violated Article 22 of the Constitution.

The Supreme Court upheld the argument of the plaintiff for the following reasons. The Pharmaceutical Law is designed to protect and promote public health and safety, and it is not designed to promote a particular socio-economic policy to protect the interests of one group or industry. In this respect, the Pharmaceutical Law is different from the Special Measures Law which is specifically designed to protect the interests of small storekeepers. If the Pharmaceutical Law is characterized in the above way, for the purpose of achieving its legislative objective it is not necessary to impose a geographical restriction on the distribution of pharmaceutical stores.

Today pharmaceutical products are manufactured in large factories, packed there, and distributed to consumers through pharmaceutical stores. In this way, the role of pharmaceutical stores is to pass on pharmaceutical products from manufacturers to the consumers. Generally pharmaceutical products are not mixed or processed at pharmaceutical stores. Therefore, no matter how hard competition among pharmacetucial stores may be, and how low the profit rate of stores is, that does not

[15] Decision of the Supreme Court, 30 Apr. 1975, *Minshū*, 29/4 (1975), 572 *et seq*.

affect the quality of pharmaceutical products since the role of pharmaceutical stores is merely to distribute the products without processing the contents of the products. Therefore, as long as the purpose of the Pharmaceutical Law is to protect public health and safety, the provision in the Law in question which authorizes the prefectural government to attach a condition to a licence for the purpose of protecting pharmaceutical stores should be held as excessive intervention into the freedom of business activities, contrary to Article 22 of the Constitution.

Under the above reasoning, the Supreme Court stated that the provision in question in the Pharmaceutical Law was null and void due to its unconstitutionality. As a consequence, the Japanese government amended the Pharmaceutical Law (as well as some related laws) and deleted the provision which authorized the prefectural government to attach such a condition.

The cases examined above are ones in which the freedom of business activities guaranteed under Article 22 of the Constitution was at issue. The *Forestry Law* case,[16] which will be touched upon in this part, is a case in which the guarantee of private property under Article 29 of the Constitution was at issue. A brief account has been given of Article 29 of the Constitution. This provision guarantees that private property shall not be taken away nor its use restricted by the government unless to do so is necessary to promote public welfare. Therefore, there are similar interpretational problems with regard to Article 29 as there are with regard to Article 22.

The Forestry Law whose constitutionality was challenged was enacted to conserve forest from devastation. For this purpose, a provision in the law provided that when a piece of woodland was owned by a plural number of persons, none of them could ask for his share of the land unless the requesting party owned at least a half of the total land in question. The purpose of this provision was to prevent a piece of land from being segmented out into small pieces owned by a number of individuals and to maintain woodland in large units. The rationale of this legislation was that if a piece of land was parcelled into smaller units owned by different individuals, it would be more difficult to conserve the forest.

A piece of land was owned by several brothers and one of them requested the partitioning of his share. When his request was denied, he brought a suit against the brother who refused. The brother argued that the request could not be granted since the Forestry Law prohibited the partition of a piece of jointly owned woodland unless the party requesting partition owned at least a half of the whole land, and, in this case,

[16] Decision of the Supreme Court, 22 Apr. 1987, *Minshū*, 41/3 (1987), 408 *et seq*.

the requesting brother did not own that much land. The requesting brother argued that the provision of the Forestry Law in question was unconstitutional as it unreasonably interfered with the use of private property guaranteed by Article 29 of the Constitution.

The Supreme Court agreed with the argument raised by the brother seeking the partition of the land and held that the provision in the Forestry Law which provided a restriction on partition of a jointly owned piece of land did not serve the promotion of public welfare and was contrary to the guarantee of private property under Article 29 of the Constitution.

The Forestry Law was a piece of legislation designed to conserve forestry and, therefore, was a law based on a specific economic policy. Nevertheless, the Supreme Court stated that the law could not be justified by legislative discretion. The Court reasoned that if a piece of jointly owned woodland could not be parcelled out to individual owners, then it would deprive the owners of the incentive to exert efforts to conserve the forest. If none of the owners wanted to take care of the forest, then the woodland would deteriorate through lack of care. This would produce the opposite result from what had been intended when the Forestry Law was enacted, and, in this sense, could not be held as promoting public welfare.

The Supreme Court held that there was no reasonable linkage between the objective of the Forestry Law and the provision in question. It also noted that the Forestry Law allowed segmentation of a piece of woodland in different ways and to prohibit segmentation only in cases where joint ownership was involved should be regarded as an unreasonable restriction.

A review of the Supreme Court decisions on the freedom of business activities under Article 22 of the Constitution reveals that there are two doctrines as regards this issue. One is that courts will in principle refrain from passing a judgment on the wisdom and validity of a law which incorporates a socio-economic policy. Included in this category are, *inter alia*, laws whose objectives are to protect and promote small businesses, agriculture, consumers, and any other specific groups in society. This type of legislation may be termed 'policy law' since it is based on policy.

In the view of the Supreme Court, it is the task of the National Diet (the legislature) to decide upon policy and to enact a law which incorporates it, and the National Diet is invested with the powers to investigate, hold debates, and come to a policy decision on the matter. Courts are not a suitable agency to deal with policy matters. Therefore, in the view of the Supreme Court, courts should in principle refrain from examining the validity of a policy adopted by the National Diet and incorporated in a law. Under this doctrine, the judicial review by courts of a piece of legislation is limited to examining whether the law in question involves a clearly excessive control and the methods used to implement the law are unreasonable. We may call this interpretational doctrine 'the judicial passivity doctrine'.

On the other hand, under the Supreme Court decisions as examined above, courts may (and should) examine the validity of a law when the law in question is based on the need to protect public order and safety. Laws for such purposes include, *inter alia*, those providing a licensing system for products in order to maintain product safety, the level of sanitary conditions, good morals, and any other conditions necessary for the maintenance of a good society. Laws prohibiting the manufacture of weapons, drugs, and other dangerous objects belong to this category also. Such laws are not based on a socio-economic policy to promote a specific group or individuals. They are aimed at maintaining the conditions necessary for the maintenance of a sound and healthy society. The essence of regulation under such laws is to supervise and control the activities of enterprises and individuals for police purposes and, therefore, such laws may be called 'police law'.

The Supreme Court has enunciated the doctrine that if the law in question is police law rather than policy law, then courts should examine the validity of it to see if it contains control above the necessary minimum for the purpose of achieving the objective of the law and that if, as the result of such review, it is clear to the court that the law exerts an excessive control, then the court should hold that law as unreasonably intervening into the freedom of business activities as declared in Article 22 of the Constitution, and unconstitutional. This doctrine may be called 'the judicial activity doctrine'.

This dualism as expressed in Supreme Court decisions seems to have resulted from the Supreme Court's interpretation of the separation of powers. The Supreme Court interprets the separation of powers as the principle dividing and allocating powers of the government into different branches and requiring that each branch respects decisions made by other branches in their own jurisdiction.

It may be observed also that this dualism to some extent reflects the fact that courts in Japan, including the Supreme Court, are not comfortable in handling socio-economic policy matters. The Supreme Court mentions in one of its decisions that it is not equipped with the necessary powers and capacities to decide whether a socio-economic policy is wise or not.[17] This applies especially to economic policy matters.

Although this dualism is, to a degree an inevitable result of the doctrine of separation of powers, we must also state that it causes a paradoxical result. Policy laws are often the result of active lobbying by specific

[17] See the decision cited in n. 14, above.

interest groups. They protect specific groups whose interests may be (and often are) adverse to other groups and to the public in general. Under the judicial passivity doctrine, however, courts should refrain from passing judgment upon the validity of them unless they are clearly unreasonable in their content and methods of enforcement.

On the other hand, police laws are generally those designed to protect and promote the interest of the general public rather than specific groups or sectors in society. In the above constitutional doctrine, police laws are closely scrutinized by the courts and if they are found to have transgressed the necessary minimum limit, they are held as unconstitutional and struck down. This means that police laws whose purpose is to protect the general public are more closely reviewed by courts and held unconstitutional than policy laws whose objective is often to protect specific interests.

The Supreme Court tried to correct this paradoxical situation in the *Pharmaceutical Law* case. As noted before, the Pharmaceutical Law was originally a piece of legislation designed to protect the general public and, under the classification mentioned above, was a police law. Later an amendment was made to this law and a new provision was added which authorized the prefectural government to attach conditions when it granted a licence to operate a pharmaceutical store. This provision for the geographical distribution of pharmaceutical stores was a policy law regulation in substance. However, formally the provision was declared to be a police law regulation, and therefore there was a contradiction between the substance and the form in this amendment. In a way, the National Diet introduced the provision for the protection of specific interests under the subterfuge of protecting the general public and the provision for the geographical distribution of pharmaceutical stores in the Pharmaceutical Law was a policy law type regulation under the disguise of police law.

The Supreme Court recognized this contradiction and held the provision in the Pharmaceutical Law unconstitutional as long as it was a police law regulation. If the legislative intent of the provision in question had made clear that it was planned as a regulation to protect small pharmaceutical stores from cutthroat competition, then the Supreme Court would have had to state that it was compatible with Article 22 of the Constitution since it would have been at the legislative discretion of the National Diet to enact a law protecting small enterprises from cutthroat competition. The hidden purpose of the Supreme Court may have been to remedy the anomaly resulting from the doctrine that a policy law should be generally outside the scope of a close judicial review by utilizing the contradiction involved in the Pharmaceutical Law.

In the *Forestry Law* case, the Supreme Court went one step closer to modifying this paradoxical result. This case was not concerned with

Article 22 of the Constitution but with Article 29 which guarantees private property. However, in Article 29 there is a similar wording to that in Article 22 stating that private property can be restricted only for the purpose of promoting public welfare. Therefore, an analogy can be drawn from this case and applied to situations involving the freedom of business activities under Article 22. As touched upon earlier, in the *Forestry Law* case, the Supreme Court struck down a provision in the law which provided that a piece of woodland owned by a plural number of individuals could not be parcelled out unless the owner requesting partition owned at least 50 per cent of the whole land.

This provision in the Forestry Law was clearly a policy law type regulation since the purpose of this legislation was the protection of natural resources. The Supreme Court held that this provision in the Forestry Law was not appropriate for achieving the purpose of this law (that is, conservation) and held that it was an unnecessary restriction. We may observe that the Supreme Court looked into the substance of a policy law and scrutinized the compatibility between the objective of the law and the substance of this provision.

We should also note that the Supreme Court did not pass a judgment on the wisdom of the conservation policy which lay behind this legislation. It merely examined the usefulness of the provision in question in achieving the purpose of the law. Nevertheless, it should be stressed that we can discern a slight shift of direction as regards the attitude of the Supreme Court when dealing with cases in which the public welfare issue in relation to private enterprise activities is at issue.

1.4 International Trade Agreements

A. DIFFERENT KINDS OF INTERNATIONAL AGREEMENTS

Japan is a party to many multilateral and bilateral international trade agreements such as the General Agreement on Tariffs and Trade (GATT) and the Friendship, Commerce and Navigation Treaty between the United States and Japan. The purpose of this section is to enquire what status international trade agreements have in the context of Japanese law.

In Japanese law, the most formal type of international agreements are treaties. Article 73(3) of the Constitution declares that the Cabinet is vested with the power to conclude treaties with foreign nations. However, the Cabinet must obtain a prior, or if the circumstances demand, subsequent, approval of the National Diet when it concludes a treaty with a foreign nation. If an international agreement is a treaty, it enjoys, under Article 98(2) of the Constitution, higher status than domestic laws. It is generally agreed that an international agreement is a treaty under Article 73(3) of the Constitution if it affects the rights and obligations of private individuals in Japan.[18] If, therefore, an international agreement contains provisions such as the restriction of an individual's conduct, it is a treaty and must be approved by the National Diet in order for it to have legal force domestically.

If an international agreement is concluded between the Japanese government and a foreign country but the agreement is not approved by the National Diet, then the agreement is regarded as an executive agreement. An executive agreement duly concluded by the Japanese government with a foreign country is part of the Japanese legal order and posesses a certain level of legal effect, even though the status and effect of an executive agreement is somewhat lower than those of a treaty. There will be a detailed discussion of the status and effect of treaties and executive agreements in a later section.

There are many types of international agreements to which the Japanese government is a party. They include: *jōhyaku* (treaty), *kyōyaku* (convention), *kyōtei* (agreement), *torikime* (arrangement), *sengen* (declaration), *giteisho* (protocol), *ketteisho* (act), *kōkanbunsho* (exchange of notes), *kōkanshokan* (exchange of letters), and *oboegaki* (memorandum). Whether an agreement falls under the category of treaties as provided in Article 73(3) of the Constitution or executive agreements depends on the substance of the agreement in question rather than the formal name for it.

Some important international trade agreements have been approved by the National Diet and are, therefore, international treaties. Prominent examples include the GATT, the IMF Treaty, and the World Bank Treaty. The Protocol of Terms of Accession of Japan to the GATT was drafted and signed on 7 June 1955 and approved by the National Diet on 29 July of the same year.

There is no need for an approval of the National Diet with regard to certain international trade agreements. They are: (1) an international agreement concerning technical details of diplomacy, (2) an international agreement concluded to provide for detailed rules of implementing a treaty that has already been approved by the National Diet, and (3) an international executive agreement within the scope of the powers authorized to the Cabinet by legislation.[19]

Often the Executive Branch takes a relaxed interpretation of the requirement for obtaining approval of the National Diet and does not

[18] A comprehensive treatise in Japan on this subject is: Iwasawa, *Joyakuno Kokunaihōteki Kōryoku* (*Domestic Law Effect of Treaties*) (Tokyo, 1985).
[19] See n. 5, above, pp. 83–4.

introduce international agreements into the National Diet for approval on the grounds that they belong to one or other of the categories mentioned above.[20]

Also the Executive Branch takes a view that as long as an international agreement is not self-executing and requires domestic legislation to implement it, the Cabinet need not submit the agreement to the National Diet for approval since implementation takes place through domestic legislation enacted by the National Diet. In 1974, the United States and Japan entered into the United States–Japan Textile Agreement in which the Japanese government promised to impose a quantitative restriction on the export of textile products directed from Japan to the United States. The implementation of this agreement required the restriction of the export of textile products to the United States and, therefore, involved a restraint imposed on individuals' activities. However, this agreement was never submitted to the National Diet for approval.

Questions were posed by the opposition parties in the National Diet about why the agreement had not been submitted to the National Diet for approval. The Director General of the Cabinet Legislation Bureau answered the questions and stated that the agreement in question was no more than an executive agreement which did not directly impose obligations on private individuals and, therefore, there was no need to bring it before the National Diet.[21] According to this rationale, the agreement would have no effects on Japanese exporters of textile products. However, in reality, the government invoked the export licensing requirement under the Control Law and imposed export restraint on the export of textile products to the United States. Again the rationale used by the government was that the government had been authorized by the Control Law to impose such restrictions.

B. TREATY-MAKING POWER

Treaty-Making Process

As stated earlier, the Cabinet has the power to conclude treaties with foreign nations under Article 73(3) of the Constitution subject to the approval of the National Diet. In the language of Article 73(3), prior approval is required in principle and subsequent approval is permitted only exceptionally. In practice, however, international trade agreements are often submitted to the National Diet for approval subsequent to their conclusion. So far there have been eleven cases in which the Cabinet

[20] See ibid. 84–5.
[21] See ibid. 85.

sought the subsequent approval of the National Diet including the Protocol of Terms of Accession of Japan to the GATT.

Under Article 61 of the Constitution, in approving a treaty, the Lower House votes first, and, in cases of disagreement between the Lower House and the Upper House with regard to approving or not approving, the Lower House prevails.

As mentioned before, if an international agreement imposes restrictions on the rights and obligations of individuals, that is, if it changes an existing law, requires enactment of a new law, or abolishes an existing law, then it is necessary for the Cabinet to introduce it to the National Diet and obtain its approval.

Validity of a Treaty and Executive Agreement

The question of the validity of a treaty in Japanese law should be distinguished from that of the direct applicability. The question of validity is concerned with whether or not a treaty has the force of law in Japan whereas that of direct applicability is concerned with whether or not a treaty applies as a law without implementing legislation. Article 98(2) of the Constitution declares: 'Treaties concluded by Japan and established laws of nations shall be faithfully observed.' This provision is couched in generalities and the exact content is not immediately clear. However, it states that the government and citizens are obligated to respect treaties. From this, it follows that treaties are part of Japanese law and have the force of law.

The natural interpretation is that an executive agreement also has the force of law under Article 98(2) of the Constitution. This should be the correct interpretation of Article 98(2) which states that 'established laws of nations' shall be faithfully observed. Established laws of nations means customary international law and Article 98(2) requires that customary international law be faithfully observed. An executive agreement duly concluded by the Japanese government with a foreign nation should be at least equated with established customary international law which consists of cases, practices, understandings, and usages among nations. Compared with customary international law, an executive agreement provides for more formal and clear rights and obligations between the Japanese government and a foreign nation.

Direct Applicability of a Treaty

The question of whether or not treaties are directly applicable is separate from the question of their validity as discussed above. The validity question requires an inquiry into whether treaties are part of Japanese law and have the force of law in Japan. On the other hand, the question of direct applicability of treaties is that of whether treaties are self-executing or not. If a treaty is self-executing, then it can be applied without any implementing domestic legislation. However, if it is not self-executing, in order for it to be domestically applicable, it needs implementing domestic legislation.

Whether or not a treaty is self-executing is determined by the wording employed, the intent of the contracting parties, and the circumstances under which the treaty came into force. Generally speaking, it should be maintained that treaties are applicable as law in Japan since their observance is mandated by Article 98(2) of the Constitution and, from this constitutional command, it can be inferred that treaties are applicable as law.

However, sometimes there are phrases in a treaty which can be interpreted as not having been intended to be self-executing. If so, the treaty in question should be held as not self-executing. A good example is the decision of the Supreme Court in the *Shiomi* case[22] which was handed down in 1989. In this case, the petitioner was a disabled person who had been naturalized to Japan. She was born in Korea when Korea was part of Japan. Her naturalization took place in 1970. She applied for a welfare pension under the Welfare Pension Law which came into effect in 1959 but was denied for the reason that pensions could be granted only to Japanese citizens and when the law in question came into effect she was not a citizen of Japan. She argued that the International Covenant on Economic, Social, and Cultural Rights (ICESC), to which Japan was a party and which stated in Article 9: 'The State Parties . . . recognize the right of everyone to social security', required the Japanese government to grant pension rights to her.

The Supreme Court rejected the argument of the petitioner on the ground that Article 2(1) of the Convention stated that the member states 'take steps with a view to achieving progressively the full realization of the rights . . .'. This clause indicated that the Convention did not confer a right on individuals but merely imposed an obligation on the member states progressively to take steps to realize the content of the Convention.

In the ICESC, there were clauses which clearly stated that the member states were obligated progressively to take steps to realize the rights of individuals to social security. However, courts may rule that even an international agreement which contains no clear wording indicating that it is not self-executing has no direct applicability.

C. TREATIES AND DOMESTIC LAWS

An Overview

When the requirement under a treaty and that under a domestic law are in conflict, which prevails over the other? This question is directly related

[22] Decision of the Supreme Court, 2 Mar. 1989, *Shomu Geppo*, 35 (1989), 1754 *et seq.*

to that of the applicability of treaties, since no question arises as to whether a treaty or a domestic law prevails when they are in conflict if a treaty is not directly applicable because then there would be no clash between the two requirements or obligations to be reconciled. However, if a treaty is directly applicable and provides for certain rights or obligations and if a law exists which carries conflicting rights and obligations, then one or the other should prevail.

Many commentators in Japan maintain that a treaty should override a conflicting domestic law.[23] Among the reasons given by the commentators, that based on Article 98(2) of the Constitution is probably the most important. Article 98(2) declares that treaties and the established laws of nations shall be faithfully observed. Under this article, treaties are given a special constitutional status as compared with regular domestic laws. From this constitutional provision, it follows that the National Diet is obligated to enact a law which would not conflict with the requirement of a treaty. If the National Diet did enact a law which conflicted with a treaty, then the legislation would be contrary to the constitutional requirement and should be overridden.

However, there is no court decision yet in which a domestic law which was in conflict with a treaty obligation was held invalid for that reason. In the *Jewellery Smuggling* case (1961),[24] the Kobe District Court dealt with a violation of the Customs Law. A foreigner smuggled jewellery into Japan declaring that the jewellery he possessed was his 'personal effects' although in fact it was for sale in Japan. The court found him guilty of evasion of the Customs Law.

The defendant argued that Article 8(3) of the GATT, which stated that the Contracting Party shall not impose a penalty for minor breaches of customs regulations, restrained the Japanese government from imposing any penalty in this case. The court rejected the defence on the ground that the defendant's conduct was more than a minor offence. However, in referring to Article 98(2) of the Constitution, the court stated: 'the principle of faithful observance of treaties . . . is understood to proclaim superiority of treaties [over domestic law].'

The Kyoto Necktie *Decision*

The *Kyoto Necktie* decision is probably the most important decision with regard to the relationship between treaties and domestic laws. There are three decisions with regard to the *Kyoto Necktie* case: the decision of the

[23] See e.g. Sato, *Nihonkoku Kenpo Gaisetsu* (*A General Explanation of the Constitution of Japan*) (Tokyo, 1980), 467–9; Takano, *Kokusaiho Gairon* (*A General Theory of International Law*) (Tokyo, 1969), 84.

[24] Decision of the Kobe District Court, 30 May 1961, *Kakyū Keishū*, 3/5–6 (1961), 519 *et seq*.

Kyoto District Court,[25] that of the Osaka High Court,[26] and that of the Supreme Court.[27] The background to this case is rather complicated, and an account is given below.

Japan was at one time the major producer and exporter of raw silk. However, in recent decades, Japanese raw silk farmers have lost their international competitiveness because of the spiralling costs of production in Japan compared with those in neighbouring countries, especially Korea and the People's Republic of China.

To deal with this situation, the National Diet enacted the Silk Price Stabilization Law which established a price stabilization programme. Under this law and its regulations, the government set upper and lower price limits within which the domestic price of raw silk should stay. When the market price went above the upper limit, the Silk Business Agency (Sanshi Jigyodan, a government corporation) sold raw silk from the stockpile it held and brought the price down to within the predetermined limits. If the price of raw silk went below the lower limit, then the Agency purchased raw silk to make the price go above the lower limit. In this way, the price was manipulated to stay within the predetermined range.

So, under the stabilization programme, the government was authorized to engage in either selling or buying operations depending on the market situation. However, the real problem with which silk growers in Japan were faced was that of over-production and falling prices. Consequently, the main function of the Agency was to engage in the purchase of raw silk and to support of the market price in Japan. If low-priced foreign raw silk had been allowed to enter the Japanese market freely, then the price stabilization programme under the Silk Price Stabilization Law would have been disrupted since the imported silk would have pushed the domestic price below the lower limit even though the Agency bought up domestically produced raw silk.

An amendment was made to the Silk Price Stabilization Law and, under this amendment, the Silk Business Agency was given the exclusive right to import raw silk from abroad. Under the law, the Agency imported raw silk from abroad but was prohibited from selling it in the domestic market when the domestic price was below the price limit described above. When it sold imported silk in the domestic market, it had to sell it at a price within the price band determined by the Minister of Agriculture. Under this price-stabilization programme, the exclusive import of foreign-

[25] Decision of the Kyoto District Court, 29 June 1984, *Hanrei Taimuzu*, 530 (1984), 265 *et seq*.

[26] Decision of the Osaka High Court, 25 Nov. 1986, *Hanrei Taimuzu*, 634 (1986), 186 *et seq*.

[27] Decision of the Supreme Court, 2 Feb. 1990, *Soshō Geppō*, 36/12 (1990), 242 *et seq*.

produced silk by the Agency and the restricted price at which imported silk was sold, meant the price of raw silk in Japan was much higher than the international price of this product. Japanese producers of neckties in the Kyoto area had to use fabrics made of this high-priced raw silk. In Europe, raw silk is not produced and there are no protective measures for raw silk production and imports of raw silk are freely accepted. The price of raw silk in Europe was much lower than in Japan. Producers in Korea and Mainland China exported raw silk to the European countries. European necktie producers produced ties using fabrics made of inexpensive raw silk, and they exported the ties to Japan. Even though 17 per cent *ad valorem* tariff was imposed on imported ties in Japan, Japanese tie producers had difficulty in competing with imported ties from Europe because of the differences in costs.

Tie producers in the Kyoto area brought a legal action in the Kyoto District Court against the government and claimed that their interests were adversely affected by the restrictions on the import and the high price of raw silk. They maintained that this measure of the government protected silk growers at the expense of tie producers, unreasonably restricted the right of tie producers freely to import silk from abroad, and violated Article 22(1) of the Constitution.

The plaintiffs also alleged that the measure was in violation of Article 2(4) of the GATT, which stipulated that whenever a tariff concession under the GATT had been made for a commodity which was an object of state trading, a contracting party should not sell the commodity in the domestic market at a price which was above the actual import price plus tariff, i.e. earn a profit, and in violation of Article 17 of the GATT which required that state trading agencies operate on commercial considerations only in terms of price, quality, and availability. Their argument was that the Silk Business Agency was required by law to sell imported raw silk at the price which was artificially determined by the government and this was contrary to those articles of the GATT, and, since the GATT had been ratified by the National Diet as a treaty, it should override a conflicting law under Article 98(2) of the Constitution.

The Kyoto District Court held that the freedom of business activities guaranteed under Article 22(1) of the Constitution was subject to restriction for the public welfare and that courts should refrain from lightly passing judgment on the wisdom of legislation designed to achieve a socio-economic policy objective. This is nothing but a repetition of the doctrine which had been enunciated by the Supreme Court, as we have already seen in a previous section.[28]

The court also held that the tariff imposed on imported ties protected

[28] See 1.3, below.

domestic producers of ties, that the government could invoke Article 19 of the GATT and take safeguarding measures if the condition of Japanese tie producers had seriously deteriorated, and that, for the above reasons, the plaintiffs had not been disproportionately disadvantaged by the government protection of silk growers.

With regard to the compatibility of the exclusive import system under this law with the GATT, the court rejected the arguments of the plaintiffs and upheld the validity of this law and measure. The court stated that the exclusive right to import and the price stabilization system in this case were designed to protect raw silk producers from the pressure of imports for a while and this had the same effect as the emergency measures permitted under Article 19 of the GATT;[29] that although there should be a limit to the period for the exclusive right to import judging it as an emergency measure, such a limit should be determined flexibly depending on the situation; and that, since this period should be decided in relation to the duration of the pressure of imports, the provision of the law for the exclusive right to import could not be regarded as unreasonable.

As above, the court argued that, as an emergency measure, the exclusive right to import was not incompatible with the GATT which would permit this under Article 19 of the GATT. As long as the exclusive right to import was lawful under the GATT, it was not necessary for the court to decide the effectiveness of the Silk Price Stabilization Law and the exclusive right to import raw silk as a domestic law. However, the court went on to state its position on this matter in the form of a dicta.

The court stated that, following a violation of a provision of the GATT, it would pressure the country to rectify the violation by confronting that country with a request from another member country for consultation and retalitatory measures. However, it further stated that it would have no more power than that and, therefore, it would not necessarily follow that the legislation in question was invalid as a domestic law simply because it was contrary to the GATT.

The position expounded by the court was that a violation of the GATT should be remedied by resorting to the dispute settlement procedure provided in Article 23 of the GATT and that even though a domestic law was contrary to the GATT, it would not be deprived of its legal effectiveness by that reason alone.

The case was taken to appeal in the Osaka High Court which handed down a decision on 25 November 1986. With regard to the issue of whether the exclusive right to import in question was contrary to the freedom of business activities as guaranteed under Article 22(1) of the

[29] Article 19 of the GATT permits contracting parties to take emergency measures to protect a domestic industry from the impact of an increase in imports by way of import quotas or tariffs when a domestic industry is suffering serious injury from it.

Constitution, the Court upheld its compatibility by simply reiterating the doctrine pronounced by the Supreme Court in previous cases.

As to the issue of the compatibility of the exclusive right to import with the GATT and the validity of this law, the Osaka High Court distorted the issue by stating that the appellants argued that the sale price of imported raw silk was contrary to Article 2(4) and Article 17 of the GATT and that the sale price was determiend by the Silk Business Agency on the basis of the standard price established by the Minister of Agriculture. The Court held that the argument of the appellants did nothing but use the action of the Silk Price Agency as the basis for the illegality of the legislation and, therefore, was wrong.

An appeal was taken by the petitioners to the Supreme Court. The petitioners presented a detailed petition. An account of the part of the petition which deals with the relationship between the Silk Price Stabilization Law and the GATT is made below since its contents are relevant to our discussion. The petitioners argued that under Article 2(4) of the GATT, a state trading agency shall not sell imported products in the domestic market at a price above the import price plus the amount of tariff and earned extra profit when the imported product in question is subject to tariff concession under the GATT. Also under Article 17(1) of the GATT, each Contracting Party promises that its state trading agency operates on commercial considerations only. The exclusive right to import is established under Articles 12.13.2 and Article 12.13.3 of the Silk Price Stabilization Law. These provisions of the law are contrary to Articles 2(4) and 17(1) of the GATT and the enactment of those provisions is illegal in that the Diet passed provisions of law which violate the GATT. The petitioners argued that the damage had been caused by this illegal legislation and did not argue that the actions of the Silk Business Agency were contrary to the GATT.

The Osaka High Court, however, was mistaken in its understanding of this legal issue and decided the matter on a wrong basis. If the arguments of the petitioners in the Osaka High Court had been unclear, then the Osaka High Court should have used its power for requesting explanation of the meaning and come up with the correct interpretation of the issue.

The Osaka District Court did not touch upon the question of whether the exclusive right to import and the price stabilization programme violated Articles 2(4) and 17(1) of the GATT and the measures granted under those provisions amounted to a safeguard measure as permitted under Article 19 of the GATT. Article 19 of the GATT permits a safeguard measure when there is an increase of imports due to unpredictable circumstances. However, in this case, an increase of imports of raw silk from abroad had been long anticipated and, therefore, the measures did not satisfy the requirements of Article 19.

Also, Article 19 permits a safeguard measure within the necessary limit and time period. However, the exclusive right to import provides an excessive protection to domestic growers of raw silk and a permanent system for import control. Therefore, such measures cannot be permitted under Article 19 of the GATT.

Moreover, the decision of the Kyoto District Court states that the effect of a violation of a GATT provision is simply that the violating country will be faced with the request for consultation under Article 23 of the GATT or with a retaliation and that there is no legal effect other than this. However, in the view of the petitioners, the measures designed to guarantee the effectiveness of treaty observance are an entirely separate issue from the validity of a domestic statute in violation of the GATT and, therefore, cannot provide the grounds for holding that a domestic law in violation of the GATT is valid.

The Supreme Court handed down a decision in this case on 6 February 1990. The decision consisted of only twenty-five lines and said very little. The Supreme Court briefly touched on the constitutionality of the exclusive right to import under the Silk Price Stabilization Law, cited the previous decisions rendered by the Supreme Court, and noted that, in view of the precedents, the judgment as to whether domestic silk growers should be protected belonged to the realm of legislative discretion which should not be lightly interfered with by courts and that the decision of the National Diet to protect domestic silk growers by means of the price stabilization programme and the exclusive right to import could not be legally challenged unless the law provided protection to one group to the undue detriment to other members of the society or the means for achieving the legislative objective was unreasonable. For this reason, the Supreme Court upheld the decisions of the lower courts.

With regard to the issue of whether or not the exclusive right to import and the price stabilization programme violated articles in the GATT and was, for this reason, invalid, the Supreme Court merely stated: 'In light of the reasoning given by the original court, the judgment of that court can be approved. Therefore, there is no illegality in the decision as claimed by the petitioners.'

An Evaluation of the Case Law with regard to the Relationship between Treaties and Domestic Laws

There is a wide gap between the legal doctrine with regard to the superiority of treaties over conflicting domestic laws propounded by commentators and some court decisions on the one hand, and the consequences of the decisions which deal with this relationship on the other. In brief, treaties are given a very high status in the legal order in the

Japanese legal system but, in actuality, courts have never nullified domestic laws on account of their incompatibility with treaties.

The only court case in which this issue was squarely dealt with is the *Kyoto Necktie* case. In this case, the Kyoto District Court recognized that there was a possibility of conflict between the treaty obligation under the GATT and the domestic regulation incorporated in the Silk Price Stabilization Law. But, after examining the issues, the court held that there was no conflict between the articles of the GATT and the provisions of the law. One of the reasonings given by the court for holding that the exclusive right to import and the price stabilization programme did not violate Article 2(4) and Article 17(1) of the GATT was that the import measures in question could be justified under Article 19 of the GATT, which recognizes the power of Contracting Parties to use import quotas and other import measures temporarily and with compensations to other Contracting Parties when an increase in imports is causing serious injury to the domestic industry producing the same or competing products.

The reasoning of the Kyoto District Court in this regard is hardly persuasive. Whereas Article 19 of the GATT requires that there be serious injury to the domestic industry, that relief measures be temporary, and compensation be granted to other Contracting Parties, the measures provided in the Silk Price Stabilization Law do not require serious injury to be found nor is there any procedure in the law to determine serious injury. The exclusive right to import under the Silk Price Stabilization Law should last 'for a while' but, in actuality, it has lasted since its enactment (i.e. for seventeen years) and there is no prospect of its being revoked. This hardly satisfies the requirement that the relief be temporary. Furthermore, there is no provision for compensation. The Supreme Court could have given a close look at this issue and stated its legal position with regard to it.

The Kyoto District Court further stated that the provisions in the Silk Price Stabilization Law for the exclusive right to import and the price stabilization programme would not be denied validity as domestic laws for the reason that they were incompatible with the provisions of the GATT even if they *were* contrary to those provisions. The reason given by the Kyoto District Court is that the GATT provided in Article 23 as relief to violations of its provisions, that the violating party would be confronted with the possibility of consultation or retaliation, and that relief in the GATT should be sought in this dispute-settlement mechanism.

As argued by the petitioners, however, the simple fact that the GATT provides for the dispute-settlement process does not mean that there should be no remedy in the domestic legal order if a domestic law is in violation of the GATT and a party is suffering from this violation. Moreover, private parties cannot utilize the dispute-settlement process as provided by Article 23 of the GATT. It is only the government of a Contracting Party which can make use of this process. Viewed in this way, the rationale, used by the Kyoto District Court for denying relief to the plaintiffs, that the remedy provided in Article 23 of the GATT for violations of provisions of the GATT precludes other relief in domestic law is hardly persuasive, since the private plaintiffs could not have utilized the procedure under Article 23 of the GATT. Also, in this case, it was the Japanese government which exercised the restrictions of imports which were alleged to be in violation of the GATT and, therefore, the private plaintiffs could not have petitioned the Japanese government to invoke the dispute-settlement procedure under Article 23 of the GATT. In any event, the Japanese government is not obligated to bring a claim under Article 23 of the GATT even though private parties have petitioned the government to that effect.

As stated earlier, Article 98(2) of the Constitution provides for the supremacy of treaties over domestic laws. Also, as some commentators argue, it follows logically that the National Diet is obligated not to pass laws which contravene treaties and that, if the National Diet does enact a law which violates a treaty, then that domestic law should be overridden by the treaty.[30]

It may be observed that this high constitutional status of treaties may have had the paradoxical effect of inhibiting courts from closely examining the relationship between treaties and domestic laws when they come into conflict and declaring the domestic laws as invalid. And this may have serious political consequences. For example, if the Supreme Court decided that a law setting up the import quotas on agricultural products (say 'rice') was in violation of Article 11 of the GATT and, for this reason, null and void, then all the laws and regulations which establish such quotas or restrictions may have to be held invalid as the matter of domestic law in Japan. Even though this may be a desirable consequence in the long run, the political impact of such decisions is far-reaching and is going to produce strong reactions from interest groups, at least in the short run. Yet the Supreme Court and lower courts may have no choice but to hold that a domestic law in violation of the GATT and other international trade agreements is null and void under Article 98(2) of the Constitution. The only alternative is to avoid the issue.

As examined earlier, there are some court decisions which confirmed the supremacy of treaties over domestic laws but such statements were made as *dicta* and in situations in which courts did not have to invalidate the domestic laws in question. The Kyoto District Court did squarely face the question of whether or not a domestic law was in violation of the

[30] See writings cited in n. 23, above.

GATT and, if so, whether the domestic law should be held invalid. The Court decided against those questions but with dubious reasonings. As we saw, the Osaka High Court distorted the issue and, in effect, avoided facing such questions. The Supreme Court simply did not take up the question.

As we have seen, the petitioners in the *Kyoto Necktie* case brought forth detailed arguments as to the relationship between the GATT and the exclusive right to import and the price-stabilization programme under the Silk Price Stabilization Law, and distinguished the legal points they wished to bring up from the decision of the Osaka High Court. From simply reading the briefs of the petitioners, it is clear that they clarified their positions with regard to this issue. In light of this, it is quite strange that the Supreme Court dismissed the argument of the petitioners simply declaring that there was no fault in the decision of the Osaka High Court. A possible explanation for the attitude of the Supreme Court is that the Supreme Court did not want to take up this issue and wished to avoid answering the question as to whether the provisions in the Silk Price Stabilization Law were in violation of the GATT and, if the provisions were in violation of the GATT, the domestic law effects of such provisions.

D. TREATIES AND THE CONSTITUTION

An Overview (Two Schools of Thought)

The question here is whether the Constitution is superior to treaties or the other way round. This question may look absurd. However, there have been some controversies with regard to this issue. In short, there are two schools of thought. One school, which may be termed 'the treaties supremacy school', holds that treaties are superior to provisions of the Constitution. The school which may be termed 'the Constitution supremacy school' maintains that the Constitution is superior to treaties.[31]

The treaties supremacy school was quite popular shortly after the Second World War and it brings up the following grounds for its validity. Article 98(1) of the Constitution states the supremacy of the Constitution over 'law, ordinance, imperial decree or other acts of the government' and that 'treaties' are not included in this wording. Article 98(2) of the Constitution declares that treaties should be faithfully observed, and so if those two constitutional provisions are read together it would follow that treaties are superior to the provisions in the Constitution. Article 81 of the Constitution empowers the Supreme Court to review the constitutionality of 'law, order, regulation or official act', but here again

[31] Sato, n. 23, above, pp. 467–9.

treaties are not included. This school points out that the basic tenets of the Constitution are 'internationalism' and that treaties which incorporate agreements and consensus should be regarded more highly than the Constitution which incorporates only the consensus in one country.

On the other hand, the Constitution supremacy school bases its beliefs on the following grounds. Article 81 of the Constitution, which provides for the power of the Supreme Court to exercise judicial review on law, order, regulation, or official act, does not explicitly exclude treaties from its scope, and therefore there is reason to infer that treaties are included. Article 98(2) of the Constitution, which declares the obligation faithfully to observe treaties, refers to the domestic legal order only. This may be taken to mean that treaties are supreme over domestic laws but it does not refer to the relationship between treaties and the Constitution. Therefore, this provision does not necessarily exclude treaties from the scope of a judicial review to be exercised by the Supreme Court.

The treaty-making process is similar to the legislative process and, in this sense, treaties are equated with domestic laws. It follows, therefore, that treaties are subject to judicial review as much as regular domestic laws.

Also the amendment process of the Constitution is much more stringent than the treaty-making process. In amending a provision of the Constitution, there must be a National Diet initiative, approval by two-thirds or more votes of all members of the House of Representatives and the House of Councillors, and a referendum. On the other hand, a treaty can be made if the Cabinet concludes it with a foreign nation and the National Diet gives prior or subsequent approval to it—a much lighter requirement compared with the constitutional amendment.

If a treaty is given supremacy over the provisions of the Constitution, then the requirement of a provision in the Constitution can be *de facto* amended easily by concluding a treaty whose content is inconsistent with that of the constitutional provision without resorting to the constitutional amendment process provided for in the Constitution. Important provisions in the Constitution such as the basic human rights provisions could then be changed simply by making a treaty which denies them: an absurd proposition. The above is an outline of the arguments brought up by the school of thought which advocates the supremacy of the Constitution over treaties.

The Sunagawa *Case*

There is no court decision yet in which a treaty was held void due to its conflict with the Constitution. Nor is there any case in which a court exercised the power of judicial review over a treaty in light of the constitutional principles. However, the decision of the Supreme Court in the *Sunagawa* case[32] is relevant here, and an account is made of this case below.

Based on the Security Treaty between the United States and Japan, the governments of both countries entered into the Administrative Agreement (the Status of Forces Agreement). To implement this agreement, the Japanese government enacted a law entitled the Criminal Special Measures Law which made it a criminal offence to trespass on the properties used by the United States Forces in Japan. There was an anti-American demonstration organized by a political group near the Sunagawa Air Base used by the United States Air Force, and some members of the demonstrating group broke into property used by the United States Air Force. They were arrested, tried under the Criminal Special Measures Law, and found guilty. An appeal was made by the defendants and the case was tried in the Supreme Court.

An argument was put forward by the defendants that the Security Treaty, which was the basis of the Administrative Agreement and the Criminal Special Measures Law, was contrary to Article 9 of the Constitution, which renunciated war as a means of settling international disputes, and was void.

The Supreme Court held that it would not exercise its power of judicial review over the Security Treaty since this treaty was highly political in nature. Therefore, as far as the solution of this particular case was concerned, the Supreme Court relied on 'the political questions doctrine' and stated that the Supreme Court was barred from reviewing the treaty in light of its constitutionality. However, there is an important phrase in its decision which implied that the Supreme Court *would* in certain circumstances exercise its power of judicial review over the constitutionality of a treaty. It stated: 'The Security Treaty . . . must be regarded as having a highly political nature. . . . Consequently, the legal decision concerning its constitutionality has a character unsuitable in principle for review by the Supreme Court, *unless its unconstitutionality or invalidity is obvious*' (emphasis added).

It is generally understood that, in this decision, the Supreme Court admitted in the form of a *dicta* the possibility that a treaty could be reviewed regarding its unconstitutionality if its unconstitutionality or invalidity was obvious. What the circumstance is under which such a review can be made is not clear yet. This question is still open to future determination. However, this statement of the Supreme Court seems to reinforce the position of the Constitution supremacy school as opposed to the Treaties supremacy school.

[32] Decision of the Supreme Court, 16 Dec. 1959, *Keishū*, 13/13 (1959), 3225 *et seq.*

E. JUDICIAL REVIEW OF TREATIES

According to the preceding discussions, the Supreme Court and lower courts can exercise judicial review on treaties on certain occasions. Since, in the judicial review process, treaties are equated with laws, the grounds for judicial review would be similar to those which are used in reviewing regular domestic laws. Generally speaking, therefore, courts examine whether provisions in a treaty violate constitutional principles. In the realm of economic regulation, the relevant constitutional principles include, *inter alia*, the freedom of business activities (Art. 22(1)) and the guarantee of private property (Art. 29). The same principles apply here as those which are applied when examining the relationship between the constitutional principles and domestic laws.

As we have already examined, there are two principles which have developed from previous Supreme Court decisions on this matter: when the domestic law in question is 'policy law type', then courts examine closely whether the law in question does not exceed the necessary minimum regulation and, if it does, courts do not hesitate to hold it as unconstitutional. On the other hand, if a law is 'policy law type', then courts in principle refrain from passing a judgment on the wisdom of the legislation and from holding it as unconstitutional, unless the law in question clearly provides an excessive control or the methods employed are unreasonable.

In treaties concerning international trade, it is possible to identify those two types of agreements. One of them is that type of international trade agreement in which measures based on socio-economic policies are incorporated and the other is where measures for public order, safety, maintenance of health, and related matters are included. If a treaty belongs to the former type, then the scope for judicial review is rather limited, whereas courts can exercise wider powers on a treaty which incorporates measures of 'policy law type'.

1.5 Different Regulatory Methods

A. THE LEGAL FRAMEWORK FOR ECONOMIC PLANNING

Programme Laws

Although the Japanese economy is basically a market economy, there are various governmental acts which affect business activities. What legal methods are used to achieve government policy objectives? In this section, we will briefly survey such legal forms and methods. Of course, the forms of government involvement in today's economy are many and diverse. It would be impossible to undertake a thorough survey of all the legal areas. Nor would it be very meaningful to present an encyclopaedic picture of all the laws in Japan which are used as instruments to achieve government objectives. We must be satisfied with an illustrative study of them rather than an exhaustive one.

Economic policies can be achieved through legislative or non-legislative means. They can be carried out either by legally binding means on individuals or means which are more informal and non-binding. Generally speaking, legislation is deeply involved in many aspects of economic policies—in areas such as monetary policy and fiscal policy, for example, with laws which authorize market operations. The Bank of Japan is the central agency employed to carry out government monetary policy and the Bank of Japan Law,[33] which established the Bank and bestowed on it the power to engage in selling and buying operations, provides the basis for this policy. Laws which exempt, reduce, or increase tax burdens on some economic activities in order to float the economy so that it can recover from recession or to restrain the economy from overheating, form the basis of government fiscal policy.

Among those laws which provide the basis of the economic policies of the government, are laws called 'the basic laws'.[34] They are economic policies embodied in the form of law. They require the government to formulate concrete measures in a specified area, enact the necessary laws to implement them and to carry them out. The Small and Medium Enterprises Basic Law,[35] the Agricultural Basic Law,[36] the Environmental Protection Basic Law,[37] and the Consumers Basic Law[38] are important examples of such laws. They set up the framework for specific economic, industrial, and social policies. When the government has decided that the creation of a system for promoting an economic goal (such as the promotion of small and medium enterprises) is necessary or desirable, then it establishes the basic framework for the policy in the form of a law. This type of law may be termed 'framework law'.

'Framework laws' are not binding on individuals as such and are not enforceable through the courts. Moreover, private individuals cannot use provisions incorporated in such laws to bring actions against the government for not putting the mandates of the laws into practice. Yet such laws are more than a mere declaration of policies. They require the government to implement the programme contained in them. It is not clear what

[33] Nihon Ginkō Hō, Law 17, 1942.
[34] In Japanese it is called 'kihon hō'.
[35] Chūshokigyō Kihon Hō, Law 154, 1963.
[36] Nogyō Kihon Hō, Law 127, 1962.
[37] Kōgai Taisaku Kihon Hō, Law 132, 1967.
[38] Shōhisha Hogo Kihon Hō, Law 78, 1967.

the legal consequences might be for non-performance of the requirements. Non-performance would probably not create legal liability on the part of the government. However, since the contents of the policies are contained in the form of law, they are regarded as being of a higher ranking than mere policy statements. If the government neglected the mandate of such a law for a long time, it would certainly incur serious political opprobrium.

Since such laws provide 'legal programmes' for the government to put into practice, they are sometimes called 'programme laws'. In the pages that follow, we will limit ourselves to examining the basic laws which have bearings on business activities, namely, the Small and Medium Enterprises Basic Law and the Agricultural Basic Law.

The Small and Medium Enterprises Basic Law

This is one of the most important programme laws and we will briefly review the contents of it. Enacted in 1963, it provides the framework of governmental measures to promote the interests of small and medium enterprises. Article 1 of the law states that it is designed:

> to provide remedies to economic and social limitations surrounding small and medium enterprises, to promote their self-help efforts, and to improve their productivity and terms of trade with the view to rectifying the differences in the productivity among enterprises as well as contributing to the raising of the economic and social positions of employees of small and medium enterprises.

In order to accomplish this basic objective, the law provides: (1) a definition of small and medium enterprises, (2) government policies, and (3) legal measures. 'Small or medium enterprise' in this definition is an entity whose employees number 300 or fewer with capital of 100 million yen or less. Governmental policies towards small and medium enterprises are stipulated in Article 3. Included in the governmental policies are the modernization of facilities, the promotion of research and development, and the introduction of modern management techniques and related matters. Article 5 of the law states: 'The government should take necessary legal and financial measures in order to accomplish the measures provided for in Article 3.' From this structure, we can see that this law does not provide the details of governmental measures as such. It provides the basic legal framework within which the government is required to take the necessary steps.

The government has enacted more than twenty laws to promote and protect small and medium enterprises within the framework of this law. Details of those laws and their actual enforcement are touched upon in a latter chapter.[39] Such major laws fall into the following categories:

[39] See Chap. 4, 4.5, below.

1. Laws designed to provide financial assistance through loans at a preferential rate and providing guarantees for loans.

2. Laws which authorize enterprises to organize themselves in the forms of co-operatives and associations thereby creating economies of scale for operations and providing a countervailing power to larger enterprises when they are engaged in transactions with them.

3. Laws designed to facilitate research and development by authorizing research associations and providing financial assistance.

4. Laws providing for adjustment assistance in the form of, *inter alia*, funds when enterprises decide to shift from the business area in which they are engaged to a new area.

5. Laws protecting enterprises from abusive conduct by large enterprises when they supply parts and components to them as subcontractors.

6. Laws securing business areas by restricting the entry of large enterprises (such as the Large-Scale Retail Stores Law which restricts the entry of supermarkets into local markets).

The Agricultural Basic Law

The Agricultural Basic Law was enacted in 1961 and it formulates the basic agricultural policies which the government should pursue. In its Preamble, it recognized that Japanese agriculture is in difficulties since there is a wide gap between the agricultural and the industrial sectors in terms of productivity and the standard of living of workers in favour of the industrial sectors, and that the work-force is shifting from agriculture to industry. It states that the objectives of the law are to promote agriculture through modernization and rationalization.

This law is divided into: (1) the general rules (Arts. 1–7), (2) agricultural production (Arts. 8–10), (3) pricing and distribution of agricultural products (Arts. 11–14), and (4) the improvement of the structure of agriculture (Arts. 15–22).

Article 1 states that the government should adopt measures to rectify the disadvantages which agriculture has incurred from natural, economic, and social limitations, to promote productivity in agriculture with a view to correcting the differences between the agricultural and industrial sectors in terms of productivity, and to raise the income of workers in agriculture. In order to achieve this purpose, Article 2 stipulates some specific objectives such as: (1) the selective expansion of agricultural production, (2) the increase of productivity by way of the development of land and water, and related matters, (3) the increase of the scale of farm operations, (4) the improvement of the distribution of agricultural products, (5) the stabilization of prices of agricultural products and the maintenance of the income of those engaged in agriculture, (6) the rationalization of the distribution of agricultural tools and the stabilization of their prices, (7) the education of those who will be engaged in agriculture, and (8) the promotion of the welfare of those engaged in agriculture by means of improving transportation, sanitation, and working environments.

Article 6 obligates the government annually to report to the National Diet the trends in agriculture and measures taken by the government concerning agriculture.

Under Articles 8 and 9, the government must make a forecast of the demand and supply with regard to major agricultural products, announce it, and take the necessary steps to increase, on a selective basis, agricultural productivity, and total agricultural production.

The price stabilization programme is stipulated in Article 11 which states that the government should take the necessary measures to stabilize the prices of agricultural products. Also the government should encourage improvement programmes engaged in by agricultural co-operatives. Important among the measures stipulated is import restriction. Article 13 of the law states that, whenever the prices of agricultural products are conspicuously depressed by the import of competing products and the production of such products may be hampered due to the decline of the price, the government should restrain the import of such agricultural products by raising tariffs or by imposing quantitative restrictions.

As seen above, the Agricultural Basic Law only sets out the general outline of the agricultural policies which the government should pursue. There are several dozen laws which put them into effect. It is probably not very useful to enumerate all those laws, so we will only note a few of the most important ones.

The Agricultural Land Law[40] establishes rules with regard to the ownership of agricultural land. The basic purpose of this law is to establish the system in which each farmer owns his/her own land and cultivates it. Recently, however, the regulation of this law has been relaxed a little to allow the leasing of agricultural land so that farmers can engage in agricultural activities on large-scale farms. The Agricultural Co-operative Law[41] provides for co-operatives and associations in which farmers organize themselves and engage in joint purchasing, selling, research, and other related matters. The Agricultural Central Fund Law[42] establishes a governmental financial institution which issues loans and other financial assistance to farmers at preferential interest rates. The Foodstuffs Control Law[43] provides for the purchase and selling of rice and the prohibition of

[40] Nochi Hō, Law 229, 1952.
[41] Nōgyō Kyōdō Kumiai Hō, Law 132, 1947.
[42] Nōrin Chūo Kinko Hō, Law 42, 1923.
[43] Shokuryō Kanri Hō, Law 40, 1942.

rice imports. There are similar laws in the areas of fisheries and the fishing industry.

B. MASTER PLAN BY THE GOVERNMENT

From time to time the government sets up a general framework for a specific industrial sector in which private enterprises are urged to formulate their own business plans. In such cases, the government acts as the formulator of a master plan within which private enterprises make specific business plans. Some examples are given below.

The Petroleum Business Law[44] is one such example, and we will briefly look at this law and its operation. The Petroleum Business Law, which was enacted in 1962, is the basis of the petroleum policy of the Ministry of International Trade and Industry (the MITI). One of the basic objectives of the petroleum policy is to import crude oil from abroad and refine it in Japan. Another objective is to ensure the 'stable' supply of petroleum products.

Under the Petroleum Business Law, the Minister of the MITI is required to formulate 'the stable supply plan' for petroleum products and implement it. The Minister formulates a programme for the supply of petroleum products for the next five years based on a forecast of demand and supply of the products. The aim is to avoid over-production and consequent depression of prices. To achieve this objective, it is necessary to control production in some way.

Since it is private enterprises which import crude oil and produce petroleum products, government tools forcing private enterprises to go along with government policies are required. For this purpose, the law provides that the Minister of the MITI has the power to license the building of refining facilities. Any enterprise which intends to establish a new refinery must obtain a licence from the MITI before it can do so. The MITI utilizes this licensing power to control the increase of production facilities in private enterprises. Another provision enforces enterprises engaged in the production of petroleum products to report to the MITI their plans for production.

The law also gives the MITI the power to recommend to private enterprises that they change or modify their production plans, thus ensuring that the industry reduces total production when over-production is anticipated.

A combination of the above is used effectively to control production. Enterprises file their production plans, and, if the MITI finds that their plans, if carried out, would cause over-production, it invokes the power

[44] Sekiyugyō Hō, Law 128, 1962.

to recommend modification or change of production plans. The fact that the MITI possesses the power to license the building of refineries is a strong weapon for the MITI to exert an influence over the industry.

What is interesting in the above regime is that an informal, rather than a formal and legalistic, means is used to implement the policy. In actuality, however, the MITI has never utilized this recommendation power. The MITI has always used more informal means called 'administrative guidance' to achieve its policy objectives. A detailed examination will be made of administrative guidance in a later section. Here it suffices to state that the MITI has avoided using *formalized* administrative guidance but utilizes an informal administrative guidance to achieve the policy goals.

This law does not authorize private enterprises to agree among themselves jointly to determine the quantity of petroleum products to be produced. In fact, however, such agreements or 'cartels' have been made and have been held as a violation of the Anti-monopoly Law. This will be discussed in a later chapter.[45]

Another similar type of government programme was found in the law concerning structurally depressed industries. This law was in force from 1983 to 1988 and then abolished. It does not exist any more, but it provides a good example of how the government formulates a master plan and private enterprises come up with their own plans within this master plan. In the scheme established by the Structurally Depressed Industries Law, the MITI designated some structurally depressed industries as 'specific industries' and formulated a reorganization plan for each of them in which it indicated the general direction of how to cut back excess facility and to direct the whole industry to more promising business areas. Private enterprises in a designated industry were urged to establish a business co-operation programme in which they agreed on mergers and acquisitions, joint buying and selling and joint venture in production, research and development, as well as related matters.

This business co-operation plan had to be approved by the MITI. The MITI consulted with the Fair Trade Commission when aproving any plan to ensure that it would not run counter to provisions of the Anti-monopoly Law. Enterprises which were engaged in a business co-operation plan approved by the MITI were provided with a guarantee by a fund established by the government with respect to the repayment of borrowings from banks.

In this scheme, the role of the government was to set up a general master plan within which private enterprises made a concrete business co-operation plan for their own betterment. In such situations, the acts of

[45] See Chap. 2, 2.7, below.

private enterprises were private acts as well as being instrumental to the implementation of a governmental purpose.

C. UTILIZATION OF PRIVATE ASSOCIATIONS FOR GOVERNMENTAL POLICIES

Often the government utilizes private initiatives and private associations for the purpose of achieving governmental policy objectives. In areas such as the promotion of small and medium enterprises, sometimes the law authorizes the government to announce a framework within which private enterprises are expected to form associations for the improvement of management, production, or for some other purposes. Such associations are of a private nature in the sense that they are designed to promote the interests of the members. The activities of such associations are usually for the benefit of the members, and, in this sense, they are privately motivated. However, such associations are used by the government to achieve government purposes and, therefore, their activities are not entirely private since they are originally planned by the government and encouraged by the government. Indeed private associations in such situations are a policy instrument for the government. In this way, there is a mixture of government policies and private efforts.

Private associations are often utilized by the government as an important policy instrument for exercising 'industrial policy'. We will review the legal aspects of industrial policy in a later chapter and so detailed examination of this subject will be reserved for that chapter. However, we will briefly note some of the important laws which authorize such private associations.

Articles 667–88 of the Civil Code recognize the right of individuals and corporations to enter into a private association or to form a co-operative. However, an association or co-operative formed under the Civil Code is seldom used as a policy instrument. Beside the Civil Code, there are a number of laws which authorize the formation of associations or co-operatives in specified areas. Associations and co-operatives formed under those laws are private combinations since membership is not compulsory and entry and withdrawal are generally made on the free will of individuals or corporations. However, they are more than purely private combinations since the authorization laws usually specify the purposes and limitations for their activities and often government subsidies are given to such associations.

Private associations are recognized especially in the area of promoting and protecting small and medium enterprises. In this area, the Small and

Medium Enterprises Organizations Law[46] and the Small and Medium Enterprises Co-operatives Law,[47] *inter alia*, provide for associations and organizations for small and medium enterprises. They are designed to organize them into larger business units so as to achieve economies of scale in operations and to acquire countervailing bargaining-powers *vis-à-vis* large enterprises.

In foreign trade, the Export and Import Transactions Law[48] authorizes exporters to enter into an export agreement and also an import agreement. The law also authorizes the formation of export and import associations. Such agreements and associations are expected to restrain 'excessive competition' in exports which may cause trade frictions with the importing countries. Import agreements and associations, which are much less utilized, are designed to allow importers to combine themselves to form coutervailing powers to exporters in the country of export when the export trade in the country of export is monopolized by the government or private enterprises in the form of an export cartel.

Also in areas such as agriculture, fisheries, insurance, and research and development, similar associations and co-operatives are allowed. Some of them will be dealt with later.

C. LICENSING OF BUSINESS ACTIVITIES

Two Types of Licensing

Business activities are subject to licensing by the government for a variety of reasons. Some are subject to licensing because of the public nature of the business or the need for supervision. Such licensing powers are vested by law in the national government (usually in ministries) or in the local authorities (such as prefectural governments and their subdivisions).

Traditionally, according to the theory of administrative law, the licensing powers and the laws which authorize the licensing system have been classified into two categories.[49] It has been maintained that, in some business areas which are characterized as highly public in nature, the power to carry out business activities is originally vested in the hands of the government and that private enterprises have no freedom to engage in such business activities. The reason for this monopoly is that the absolute need to provide goods or services to secure the minimum level of

[46] Chūshō Kigyō Dantai Hō, Law 185, 1957.
[47] Chūsho Kigyōtoh Kyōdokumiai Hō, Law 181, 1949.
[48] Yushutsunyū Torihiki Hō, Law 299, 1952.
[49] See Kisugi, *Keizaikatsudō To Hō* (*Economic Activities and Law*) (Tokyo, 1987), 34 *et seq*.

civilized life regardless of profitability, the large requirement for capital investment, the limited demand, and related matters necessitate that the execution of the businesses be entrusted to the government. It has been argued that the nature of the businesses involved is such that the economic performance would be uncertain or inferior if private enterprises were allowed freely to enter into the areas without any government control.

The supply of electricity, gas, and water, and the provision of telecommunications are regarded as belonging to this category. In those areas, however, the government can delegate by licence under law the power to carry out the business to private enterprises. In those areas, the government grants by licence to private enterprises the special 'privilege' to engage in business, and the licence given in such cases is a 'privilege licence'.

The traditional theory holds that there are some other business areas in which private enterprises are originally vested with the right to engage in business but that the government imposes prohibitions on private enterprises to do business for the sake of maintaining public order, safety, public health, and related matters, and, when it becomes clear that an enterprise intending to enter one of these businesses is qualified to do so, and that no harm will be caused to society, the government gives permission to the enterprise to engage in the business. In those business areas, the right to engage in business by private enterprises is temporarily suspended by the prohibition under law and, when the government certifies that an enterprise is qualified to engage in the business, a licence given by the government restores the original right of the enterprise.

For example, in the restaurant business, private enterprises basically enjoy the freedom to engage in business. However, in order to maintain public health and safety, there are requirements in the relevant regulatory law which enterprises intending to do business must meet.[50] Therefore, the law controlling this business prohibits or suspends the right of a private enterprise to engage in business until a licence is given. A licence must be obtained from the relevant authority when an enterprise begins business in this area and the licence confirms that the enterprise is well qualified to operate a restaurant and cause no danger to the public.

In this category, the prohibition by law imposed on business activities and permission granted to enterprises to engage in those activities by licence under law are designed to maintain order in society and this type of regulation is an exercise of police power. A licence of this type may thus be called a 'police power licence'.

[50] e.g. Art. 14(1) of Shokuhin Eisei Hō (The Food Hygiene Law, Law 303, 1950) prohibits anyone from selling specified foods and additives unless tested and permitted by the Minister of Health and Welfare or the Governor of the prefectural, as the case may be.

Licence Granting Privilege to Engage in Business

Examples of business activities in which the power to carry out business is given to private enterprises by a privilege licence are: the supply of water, the postal service, the supply of electricity, public transportation, telecommunications, and some others. In fact, some of the services which belong to this category are supplied by the government itself. The supply of water is one example and the postal service is another. However, since it is not practicable for the government to engage in all such business activities, it delegates the power to operate some businesses to private enterprises by law. The laws which authorize such businesses provide strict requirements which the private enterprises so authorized must meet in terms of capital requirements, conditions for entry into those business areas, withdrawal from the business concerned, and other terms.

The theory holds that, in those business areas, although private enterprises are delegated the power to engage in business, the power is originally vested in the government and it is a privilege (not a right) for private enterprises to enter into those areas. Often-cited examples are business activities granted under the Electricity Power Business Law,[51] the Gas Business Law,[52] the Railroad Operations Law,[53] the Road Transportation Law,[54] and others.

There are several features which are common to all such laws. New entry of enterprises is allowed only when a licence is given by the ministry in charge, and the ministry in charge is regarded as having 'free discretion' to decide whether to grant a licence to a new entrant or not. Often there is a provision in the authorization law that, in granting a licence to a new entrant, the ministry in charge must take into consideration the supply and demand conditions in the relevant market, and, when it seems to the ministry that supply is sufficient or there is a threat of over-supply, it should not grant a licence.

Recently, however, this supply and demand provision has been criticized by commentators who say that it has unduly restricted new entries and that thereby competition in the relevant market has been restrained.[55] There is a slight sign of change in this respect. For example, in the Freight Trucking Business Law,[56] which was enacted in 1990 and replaced that part of the Road Transportation Law which dealt with trucking, there is no provision which states that the Ministry of Transportation

[51] Denki Jigyō Hō, Law 170, 1964.
[52] Gasu Jigyō Hō, Law 51, 1954.
[53] Tetsudō Jigyō Hō, Law 92, 1986.
[54] Dōro Unsō Hō, Law 183, 1951.
[55] See, in general, Kisugi, n. 49, above.
[56] Kamotsu Jidōsha Unsōjigyo Hō, Law 83, 1989.

should take into consideration supply and demand conditions in the trucking business when considering whether to grant a licence to a new entrant. This law abolished a prior-examination system with regard to licensing based on the supply and demand conditions and introduced a post-examination system in which the Ministry of Transportation examines the supply and demand conditions in a particular area after the licence is given. If the Ministry of Transportation finds that there is over-supply of services in a particular area, the enterprises in the area can be restrained from increasing the capacity for services. This is a somewhat more relaxed regulation.

In those areas covered by the laws, a market is not necessarily monopolized by an enterprise. It is legally possible to grant a plural number of licences to operate in one area. However, there often is a monopolistic situation in those areas due to the restriction of the entry of new enterprises by the ministry in charge. Here again there is a trend for change. In the telecommunications area, the business was once monopolized by the Nippon Telephone and Telegram Company. However, now there are several competing companies in the long-distance telephone business.

Under these laws, there is generally a restriction on withdrawal from the market. This means that a withdrawal is subject to approval by the ministry in charge. Also there is usually price regulation of some kind. The most common type of such regulation is that the price charged by enterprises must be licensed by the ministry in charge, as in the Electric Power Business Law. The licensing of price by the ministry is usually based on the principle of fair return; namely that the ministry gives the licence to a price which recovers the cost and yields a reasonable profit.

Recently, in some laws, there is a system of price reporting instead of price licensing. In the Freight Trucking Business Law to which a reference has been made earlier, enterprises engaged in the business are required to file their tariffs with the Ministry of Transportation. Although the Ministry of Transportation has the power to order a change in the tariff filed by an enterprise when it judges that the tariff in question would cause serious problems in the business, enterprises are free to set their own prices, at least in the initial period of their operations.

Often such laws stipulate that there is the duty to supply on the part of licensed enterprises. Therefore, the enterprises cannot refuse to supply services to those who request them. For example, in the Electric Power Business Law, the Gas Business Law, the Road Transportation Law, and others, there is a provision which states that the licensed enterprises must supply services when requested. In this sense, therefore, there is no freedom of contract or freedom to refuse to contract as far as licensed enterprises are concerned.

Police Power Licence

As noted before, there are some business areas in which enterprises are basically free to engage. However, even in those areas, an enterprise which intends to do business must obtain a licence from the government. The purpose of the requirement that an enterprise intending to do business in the area must obtain a licence is to ensure that the enterprise is fully qualified and equipped to do business and to observe the conditions necessary for maintaining public safety, health standards, good morals, and the like. In those laws which provide this licensing system, there are usually legal requirements which enterprises must meet if a licence is to be given.

Many kinds of businesses fall into this category. Examples include, *inter alia*, restaurants, hotels, bars and night clubs, cleaning stores, sports and amusement centres, pawn shops, banking, insurance.

In these areas, the government must give a licence to an enterprise which intends to do business as long as the enterprise meets the requirements since essentially there is the freedom of an enterprise to do business. The licensing law cannot infringe this fundamental freedom. All it can do is to exercise the power to make sure that the applying enterprise satisfies the legal requirements. If the applicant satisfies these requirements, the government is bound to give a licence.

The theory in administrative law states that the government's discretion in those areas is 'bound discretion' or 'restricted discretion', since the government is not free to decide whether to grant a licence or not but is obligated to grant a licence as long as the legal requirements incorporated in those laws are satisfied.

The New Theory

In recent decades, the traditional classification of the regulatory laws into the two types described above has come under criticism from commentators.[57] They maintain that the difference between 'free discretion' and 'restricted discretion' is at best a matter of degree and not that of kind. Even in the areas in which the government enjoys 'free discretion' to grant a licence to a business or not, the government is bound by the language of the relevant law and so does not have complete freedom as to whether to grant a licence or not. On the other hand, in the areas in which the government's discretion is restricted, the provisions of the law which set forth the licensing requirements may be couched in broad terms and, through interpretation, the government may, in fact, possess some discretion. Commentators argue that the dualism which the

[57] See, in general, Kisugi, n. 44, above.

traditional theory maintains is unrealistic in the light of the present economic regulations.

Commentators also maintain that nowadays there are many regulatory powers of the government which do not belong to either of these types. For example, the regulation under the Petroleum Business Law (to which reference has been made) does not incorporate a licence for the privilege to do business. Nor does it incorporate the power of the government to grant a licence for the maintenance of public order, good morals, and health standards.

Likewise, under the Large-Scale Retail Stores Law,[58] which provides for the restriction of new entry of large-scale retail stores (like supermarkets), the power of the government cannot be classified as either one or the other. In those new areas, the purpose of the regulation is to achieve policy objectives or to reconcile conflicting interests.

It is true that laws which belong to this middle ground are increasing tremendously in number and the traditional dualism is quickly becoming obsolete. Perhaps it is better to examine each piece of legislation on its own merits rather than to apply abstract criteria indiscriminately.

D. FORMS OF GOVERNMENT ORDERS AND REGULATIONS

Under some laws, the government is authorized to issue an order that commands the party to whom it is addressed to refrain from doing something (such as refraining from using materials which would cause environmental pollution) or to perform something (such as paying administrative fines). Government orders issued by the Executive Branch are generally called 'administrative dispositions' whose enforceability is usually backed up by the criminal penalty which will be imposed on the violating party.

In the areas of economic regulation, laws often state the general principles and delegate the authority to enforce them to administrative agencies through Cabinet decrees and ministerial orders. The Cabinet enacts Cabinet decrees, and administrative agencies (often ministries) are empowered to promulgate the regulations and issue orders (administrative dispositions) to enforce the content of the law and the Cabinet decrees. Often ministries announce guidelines in which the ministry shows its own interpretation of the law and regulation.

For example, under the Foreign Exchange and Foreign Trade Control Law,[59] Cabinet decrees entitled 'the Foreign Exchange Control Decree'[60]

[58] Daikibo Kouri Tenpo Hō, Law 109, 1973.
[59] Gaikoku Kawase Oyobi Gaikoku Bōeki Kanri Hō, Law 228, 1949.
[60] Gaikoku Kawase Kanre Rei, Decree 260, 1980.

and 'the Foreign Investment Control Decree'[61] authorize the Ministry of Finance to issue regulations in areas such as foreign exchange control and foreign investment control. The MOF has issued many ministerial orders which implement the details of the law and decrees.

In some laws, the administering authority is empowered to issue 'recommendations' prior to resorting to an order. For example, in the Large-Scale Retail Stores Law, the MITI or the prefectural government, as the case may be, is authorized to issue a recommendation to a large store which intends to make a new entry into a local market to put off the time of entry or to reduce the floor space of the store if it judges that new store would endanger the business of existing small shops in that local market, before resorting to an order commanding the large store to abide by it. As will be touched on in more detail, the Fair Trade Commission (FTC) can issue a recommendation to the party which is suspected of a violation of the Anti-monopoly Law advising the party to cease and desist from the conduct in question. If the party accepts the recommendation, then the FTC can enter a decision without a hearing or trial. If not, usually an administrative proceeding is initiated.

Other laws provide for a different way of enforcement. In the Law to Provide for Emergency Measures to Stabilize National Life[62] which was enacted in the Oil Crisis to cope with sky-rocketing prices, it is provided that the government can announce 'the standard price' for a designated commodity. This is the maximum price above which no enterprise is supposed to sell. However, any enterprise which sells the designated commodity above this standard price is not punished by criminal penalty. The only remedy provided is the publication by the government of the name of the enterprise in violation. This is a device to control the conduct of enterprises through bad publicity.

E. RECOURSE AGAINST THE GOVERNMENT

What kind of remedy is available when the person to whom an administrative disposition is directed wishes to challenge it? We will touch briefly on the general laws on this matter. Under the Administrative Appeals Law,[63] a person to whom an administrative disposition is directed may appeal to a higher office in the administrative agency which has issued the disposition and request a review of it. For example, if the Customs House issued an order to block the entry of a commodity in to Japan by reason of a violation of a law, the importer could bring an appeal to the higher office in the MOF to which the Customs House belongs.

[61] Tainai Chokusetsutōshi Nikansuru Seirei, Decree 261, 1980.
[62] Kokumin Seikatsu Antei Kinkyusochi Hō, Law 121, 1973.
[63] Gyōsei Fufuku Shinsa Hō, Law 160, 1962.

The Administrative Cases Litigation Law[64] provides for the right of an individual to bring a suit in court against the government when he/she feels that a disposition by the administrative agency has adversely affected his/her interests. Under this law, the requirement for standing to sue must be satisfied. This means that the person who brings a suit against the government must show that his/her legal interests are adversely affected by the disposition in question. Court decisions have interpreted this standing narrowly and generally the right to sue the government is limited to the person to whom the administrative disposition in question has been addressed. Although there may be a third person whose interests may have been adversely affected by an administrative disposition directed to a person, the standing to sue is not likely to be granted to that third person.

A famous decision which has some bearings on this issue is the *Juice Representation* case.[65] In this case, the FTC approved of a fair competition code entered into among producers of juice. Under the Law Prohibiting Unreasonable Premiums and Unreasonable Representation,[66] the FTC is empowered to approve of a fair competition code concluded among enterprises which contains rules regulating the contents of representations of the products in question or the amount of premium which is offered with sale of the products. In this case, producers of juice concluded a fair competition code which stated that they would use the representation which merely said 'coloured by synthetic additives' to represent juice which did not contain any fruit juice rather than saying 'without fruit juice'. This code was approved by the FTC. The Housewives Union and also the President of the Union initiated proceedings in the FTC arguing that the approval (an administrative disposition) was likely to mislead consumers and should be withdrawn.

The case was tried first in the FTC. The FTC denied the claim of the Union and the President on the ground that they did not have the standing to bring the case before the FTC since the law in question was not designed to protect each individual consumer, and the administrative disposition in question (the approval of the representation) did not deprive each consumer of any legal benefit which the law should provide. This decision of the FTC was approved in the Tokyo High Court and also in the Supreme Court.

The *Novo* case,[67] in which the issue was whether or not a foreign party to an international contract could bring an action against the FTC when the FTC issued an order commanding the domestic party to the contract

[64] Gyōsei Jiken Soshō Hō, Law 139, 1962.

[65] Decision of the Supreme Court, 14 Mar. 1978, *Minshū*, 32/2 (1978), 211 *et seq*.

[66] Futō Keihinrui Oyobi Futō Hyōji Bōshi Hō, Law 134, 1962.

[67] Decision of the Supreme Court, 28 Nov. 1975, *Minshū*, 29/10 (1975), 1592 *et seq*.

to cancel it on the ground of its illegality under the Anti-monopoly Law, is another important example of how courts would deal with this issue. The Supreme Court ruled that the foreign party did not have the standing to sue the FTC.

In principle, all suits must be brought in regular courts. There is no general administrative court which exists side by side with regular judicial courts. However, in some specific areas there are specialized administrative tribunals. A good example is the Tax Appeals Board to which claims against tax decisions made by the Tax Offices may be appealed. Judicial review is available after the decision of the Board has been rendered.

The State Redress Law[68] authorizes a private individual to bring a tort claim against the government when his/her property has been unreasonably damaged by a tort act of a government official in the course of exercising his/her official power. A remedy is available when the conduct which has caused the damage was done in the course of the exercise of official power. If the conduct was of a purely private nature, then the suit should be directed to the official as an individual. Also, in order for the plaintiff to recover, the illegality of the conduct in question whether in the form of a violation of the Constitution, treaties, laws and regulations, or *ultra vires* must be established, the intent or negligence on the part of the government official must be proved, and also the causal relationship between the illegal conduct of the official and the damage must be established.

In the *COCOM* case,[69] to which reference has already been made, the Tokyo District Court denied a relief to the plaintiffs on the ground that there had been no intention or negligence on the part of the MITI officials who had decided to disapprove the exportation in question even though the court held that the disapproval of the export in question under the Foreign Exchange and Foreign Trade Control Law was unconstitutional for the reason that the law did not authorize the control of export for the purpose of international political or strategic objectives.

1.6 Administrative Guidance

A. DEFINITION OF ADMINISTRATIVE GUIDANCE

No explanation of the Japanese governmental process is complete without some discussions of administrative guidance.[70] Although informal ways of

[68] Kokka Baishō Hō, Law 125, 1947.

[69] Decision of the Tokyo District Court, 8 July 1969, *Gyōsai Reishū*, 20/7 (1969), 84 *et seq*.

[70] For writings in the English language, see the following: Young, 'Administrative Guidance in the Courts; A Case Study in Doctrinal Adaptation', *Law in Japan*, 17 (1984),

carrying out government policies such as administrative guidance are not necessarily unique to Japan, the degree of pervasiveness and the importance of administrative guidance in the Japanese governmental process is probably unique to Japan. In Japan, economic regulations must ultimately be based on legislation as the source of their authority and legitimacy. However, government agencies in Japan often choose not to use laws directly to accomplish their policy goals but to utilize the more informal process of persuasion when they wish to control the conduct of private enterprises. This informal process of persuasion is often called 'administrative guidance'.

Administrative guidance is vague and flexible by its own nature, and, therefore, it is not easy to give a precise definition of administrative guidance. However, a high-ranking official of the Cabinet Legislation Bureau, when asked in the National Diet for the definition of administrative guidance, provided the following:[71]

> [Administrative guidance] is not legal compulsion restricting the rights of individuals and imposing obligations on citizens. It is a request or guidance on the part of the government within the limit of the task and administrative responsibility of each agency as provided for in the establishment laws, asking for a specific action or inaction for the purpose of achieving some administrative objective through co-operation on the part of the parties who are the object of the administration.

The above statement is regarded as an official definition of administrative guidance by the Japanese government. Although this definition is abstract, hard to understand, and susceptible of different interpretations, it does contain several salient features in administrative guidance. (1) Compliance is voluntary. Administrative guidance is not a legal order with penalties for disobedience and, therefore, the party to whom it is addressed has the *legal* freedom of non-compliance. (2) Administrative guidance is a *de facto*, rather than *de jure*, directive issued by government officials and, even if an administrative guidance is issued, it does not make it automatically a legal order. (3) Administrative guidance should, however, be distinguished from the personal conduct of government officials issuing it. It is often an expression of government policy of some kind. (4) In a broad sense, administrative guidance is a form of government regulation which imposes some kinds of rules of conduct on private individuals or enterprises. (5) Even though administrative guidance is informal and has no legally binding power, it is different from a request

120 *et seq*.; Smith, 'Prices and Petroleum in Japan: 1973–1974—A Study of Administrative Guidance', ibid. 10 (1977), 81 *et seq*.; Yamanouchi, 'Administrative Guidance and the Rule of Law', ibid. 7 (1974), 22 *et seq*.; Narita, 'Administrative Guidance', ibid. 2 (1974), 45 *et seq*.; Yoemans, 'Administrative Guidance', ibid. 19 (1986), 125 *et seq*.

[71] Cited in Matsushita and Schoenbaum, n. 7, above, p. 32.

made by an individual to another individual. The relationship between the party requesting (the government) and the party to whom it is addressed is often not equal. In many cases, the government has more bargaining power, resources, and influence than the private individual or enterprise which has been made the object of administrative guidance. (6) In exercising administrative guidance to impose a rule of conduct on private enterprises, the government often represents the consensus of the industry in which the rule of conduct should be enforced. (7) Generally speaking, no precise procedure is required nor is a delineated scope defined. Often administrative guidance is made orally rather than in document form. (8) Administrative guidance is often used before a law is invoked in a situation when the government can invoke the law to impose discipline on the conduct in question. Used in this way, administrative guidance may be a preliminary stage of invoking a law.

B. TYPES OF ADMINISTRATIVE GUIDANCE

Administrative guidance can be classified into different types, among which the following three types seem to be most common: (1) promotional administrative guidance, (2) regulatory administrative guidance, and (3) adjudicatory or conciliatory administrative guidance.

Promotional Administrative Guidance

Often government agencies provide advice to enterprises in order to promote their business activities. In agriculture, the offices of the Ministry of Agriculture and of the prefectural governments operate governmental research institutes and disseminate agricultural technology produced by those institutes to farmers and, when necessary, officials give advice to farmers and assist them to improve production, storage, and processing of agricultural products.

Also, in small and medium enterprise areas, government agencies often render assistance to small enterprises to try to improve their production, management, transportation, research and development, and other matters. Often financial assistance through government financial institutions like the Medium and Small Enterprises Financial Bank, the Commerce and Industries Central Finance Bank, and the People's Bank is given. They issue loans at interest rates much lower than the market rates. Often government officials engage in advising the management personnel of small and medium enterprises, who have borrowed money from those institutions, how to improve their production and other business operations.

This type of administrative guidance can be called 'promotional' administrative guidance whose main function is to promote or protect enterprises or persons who are recipients of such advice.

Regulatory Administrative Guidance

Often government agencies use administrative guidance to regulate the conduct of enterprises and persons, and, when used in this way, it serves as a substitute for an order under law. There are many examples of administrative guidance of this type, particularly in the area of foreign trade, i.e., export and import controls. However, we will deal with examples of regulatory administrative guidance in export and import controls in a later chapter.[72] Here we will limit ourselves to explaining regulatory administrative guidance in domestic regulation.

A well-known example is that of the *Sumitomo Metal* case[73] in 1965, in which the MITI used administrative guidance to cut back production of steel. In 1965, there was an economic recession and there was a general agreement among the producers of steel to cut back production in order to avoid a further decline in prices. The MITI applied administrative guidance to the steel industry to reduce the amount of steel to a certain level. Most of the companies in the industry complied with this advice and agreed to reduce production. However, the Sumitomo Metal Company was dissatisfied with the quota of production which had been allocated to it and denied compliance.

In those days, the MITI had the power to allocate foreign currency to importers and, without such allocation it was impossible for the company to import the necessary coal and iron ore for production. The company stated that it would bring a legal action against the MITI if the MITI suspended its allocation of foreign currency.

The dispute was finally settled by a compromise between the company and the MITI to the effect that the company would comply with the MITI's request, with some reservations.

Another example is that of the *Price Control* case in 1973.[74] In the year of the Oil Crisis prices in Japan sky-rocketed. The Cabinet decided to establish the price-reporting system in which each ministry would issue directives to enterprises producing products in its charge to report when they intended to raise prices. The ministries often pressured the enterprises to refrain from raising their prices or to reduce the level of price rises. Sometimes ministries set a maximum price above which enterprises could not raise their prices.

[72] See Chap. 3, 3.2, below.

[73] Okumiya, 'The Role of the Administrative Branch in Trade: Government Order and Administrative Guidance Concerning Trade Problems', in Schoenbaum, Matsushita, and Dallmyer (eds.), n. 5, above, pp. 917–121.

[74] Cited in Yamanouchi, *Gyoseishido* (*Administrative Guidance*) (Tokyo, 1977), 37–47.

The government could have invoked the price control decree[75] and fixed the price by law. However, the government decided not to use the price control order because of some questions about the interpretation of the order, and chose instead to use administrative guidance to deal with price hikes.

When used in this way, administrative guidance imposes rules of conduct on enterprises. As long as it is guidance, there is no compulsory power to enforce it in the event of non-compliance. However, government agencies try to utilize different types of persuasion techniques to secure compliance by enterprises.

There are several cases in which a regulatory administrative guidance caused the recipient enterprises to engage in collusive arrangements or cartels. There was an antitrust problem in those cases which will be touched on in a later chapter.

Adjudicatory Administrative Guidance

Government agencies sometimes use administrative guidance to help private enterprises settle disputes among themselves. Of course, legal disputes among enterprises must ultimately be settled by the courts. However, there are disputes which are not suitable for court proceedings and also there is a general desire among enterprises and among the public to avoid confrontation in the courts. For these and other reasons, there is a role for government agencies which belong to the Executive Branch to engage in dispute settlements.

A dispute between enterprises may have some impact on industrial policy matters too, and, in such a situation, the involvement of administrative agencies in mediating the dispute is probably justified as part of industrial policy.

Perhaps the best examples of the role of government agencies in dispute settlement are found in the solving of conflicts between large and small enterprises. As discussed in a later chapter, small and medium enterprises are given various types of protection and promotion due to their sheer number and their importance in the Japanese economy. However, because of a difference in scale of operations and in competitiveness between large and small enterprises, there are many conflicts and disputes between them when they are engaged in competition and also when they are in such transactional relationships as assemblers (like car manufacturers) and suppliers of parts and components (like subcontractors).

In the retail industry, there have been many disputes between supermarkets and small shopkeepers when a supermarket attempts to enter a

[75] Bukka Tosei Rei, Decree 118, 1946. Under emergency circumstances, the government is authorized to establish the maximum price of a commodity.

local market. Small shopkeepers in the locality fear that their business will be seriously damaged when a larger supermarket enters the market. Similar disputes have arisen in the manufacturing and wholesale industries. For example, in some parts of the food industry such as bean curds and bean sprouts, the undertaking industry, and some light manufacturing industries which have been traditionally regarded as the areas for small and medium enterprises, disputes arise when large enterprises intend new entries.

There are several laws which are designed to deal with such problems. In the retail industry, the Large-Scale Retail Stores Law[76] provides the mechanism for dispute settlements at the initiative of the government whereas, in the manufacturing and wholesale industries, it is the Medium and Small Business Areas Adjustment Law.[77] Generally, in those laws, there is the provision for the government (in the form of the MITI and the prefectural governments) to issue recommendations to parties in dispute to come to terms. However, usually neither the MITI nor prefectural governments utilize this formal power for dispute settlement but engage in a more 'informal' persuasion. For example, the MITI or prefectural governments would informally urge a large supermarket intending to make a new entry into a local market to delay opening a new store or to reduce the floor space so as to mitigate its impact on the existing business of small retail stores in the locality.

In the above situations, the role of the government is that of an informal mediator, advising and suggesting to the parties in the controversy ways of resolving a dispute. This has proved to be effective and many disputes which the parties would never have solved themselves have been resolved without utilizing court proceedings.

C. LEGAL BASIS FOR ADMINISTRATIVE GUIDANCE

As explained earlier, administrative guidance is not a legal action and has no legally binding effect on the party to whom it is addressed. However, administrative guidance is sometimes based on a provision in a law. Sometimes it is authorized by a specific clause in a law and sometimes no such legal basis is found. As noted earlier, even though a law authorizes a government agency to engage in administrative guidance in the form of 'recommendation' and 'warning', the government agency often chooses not to utilize this power but engages in *de facto* advice to the recipient party.

[76] Daikibo Kouri Tenpo Hō, Law 109, 1973.
[77] Chūsho Kigyō Jigyōbunya Chōsei Hō, Law 52, 1982.

Administrative Guidance without a Specific Statutory Authorization

Sometimes government agencies engage in administrative guidance without any specific statutory authorization. The *Sumitomo Metal* case, to which reference has been made, is one such case. In such cases, there is no wording in law which authorizes government agencies to render administrative guidance. Government agencies, especially the MITI, have emphasized that administrative guidance is allowed by 'establishment law' even though there is no specific provision in the authorization law. For example, the Law to Establish the MITI gives general powers and responsibilities to the MITI to supervise specified industries. The law, however, contains no wording which unequivocally sets out the power to give administrative guidance.

Even though administrative guidance is not based on a specific provision in a law authorizing the agency, it creates little problem when it is promotional administrative guidance. In such situations, the recipients of the guidance have little reason to complain since the nature of such guidance is to give benefit to the recipient by promoting its business, providing financial assistance, and so on.

However, if regulatory administrative guidance is utilized without any specific authorization by law, then the validity of it may be questionable since one inevitable aspect of regulatory administrative guidance is to impose a restriction on conduct or prohibition of conduct on the receiving party and, therefore, to infringe upon the rights and freedom of individuals.

Administrative Guidance based on Specific Statutory Language

There are laws which contain a provision that a government agency can issue administrative guidance. The terms used in those laws to describe administrative guidance vary from one law to another. Terms such as 'recommendation' (*kankoku*), 'warning' (*keikoku*), are used. If administrative guidance is issued on the basis of one of these laws, the administrative guidance is a legal act even though there is no power to enforce it by penalty.

The Marine Transportation Law[78] authorizes the Ministry of Transportation to issue a recommendation to enterprises engaged in the ocean freight business to take the necessary measures when it deems that cutthroat competition exists and the sound development of the industry is likely to be impaired. Such measures include agreements among enterprises to limit competition. As we have seen already, in the Petroleum Business Law, there is a provision which states that the MITI can establish the standard price at which the petroleum companies are expected to sell

[78] Art. 32, Kaijō Unsō Hō, Law 121, 1956.

petroleum products. The standard price has no binding power over the companies and is, therefore, a recommendation by the government.

As we have touched upon already, the National Life Stabilization Emergency Measures Law authorizes the government in a state of emergency to set the standard price for commodities designated by the government. Here again, the standard price has no binding effect on enterprises which sell the commodities. Non-compliance incurs only the publication of the names of the non-complying parties. In the Architects Law,[79] the Ministry of Construction is authorized to announce a standard for the fees which architects charge to their clients and recommend it to them.

Aministrative Guidance Combined with Other Promotional or Regulatory Measures

Sometimes, administrative guidance is not based on a provision of law but is combined with other measures to ensure its effectiveness. The Medium and Small Business Modernization Promotion Law[80] and the Agricultural Products Price Stabilization law,[81] which respectively authorize the government agency in charge to give advice to enterprises or farmers with regard to improving their management and operations, provide for financial assistance combined with such advice.

More importantly, however, regulatory guidance may be combined with some legal or extra-legal measures to ensure their effectiveness. The *Sumitomo Metal* case[82] is a case in point. As we have seen, the administrative guidance of the MITI was backed by the power of the MITI to allocate foreign currency to importers. There are many cases in which the MITI advised exporters to engage in 'voluntary export restraint' by way of administrative guidance with the compulsory power incorporated in law as the background. References will be made to those cases later.[83]

In the Large-Scale Retail Stores Law, there is a provision which states that the agency in charge (the MITI or the prefectural government, as the case may be) can issue an order to a large supermarket entering the local market to delay the opening of the store or to reduce the floor space after the agency has issued advice to the same effect and the advice has not been complied with. There is a similar provision in the Medium and Small Business Areas Adjustment Law. In such cases, the agency is required to use administrative guidance in the form of 'advice' before invoking compulsion by law.

[79] Art. 25, Kenchikushi Hō, Law 202, 1950.
[80] Chūsho Kigyō Kindaika Sokushin Hō, Law 64, 1963.
[81] Nōsanbutsu Kakaku Antei Hō, Law 225, 1953.
[82] See Okumiya, n. 73, above, pp. 106–8.
[83] See Chap. 3, 3.3, below.

As noted earlier, the agency, in enforcing those laws, often does not utilize even the provision authorizing it to engage in administrative guidance but exercises a *de facto* administrative guidance. However, even in such a situation, the fact that the government can ultimately resort to the provision in law which would achieve the same purpose if the *de facto* guidance is not respected enhances the effectiveness of the administrative guidance since the agency can utilize it as a tacit threat to make the party comply.

D. EFFECTIVENESS OF ADMINISTRATIVE GUIDANCE

Although the effectiveness of administrative guidance has somewhat declined compared with some decades ago, it is still an important policy tool for the Japanese government. Our enquiry turns to the reasons why guidance is effective. The effectiveness of administrative guidance depends on the types of administrative guidance and the circumstances under which it is made. However, as a general proposition, we can state the following.

When the government engages in administrative guidance, it often reflects the consensus in the industry to which the guidance is applied. An example is, again, the *Sumitomo Metal* case. Administrative guidance is never effective if the industry which is the object of the guidance opposes it as a whole. An important task for the government officials who exercise administrative guidance is to engage in effective persuasion and to create a spirit of co-operation among the recipients of the guidance. Often ex-officials of the government are in key positions in companies or trade associations of the industry to which the guidance is applied and they may play a crucial role in it.

There is a strong desire among the business community to avoid confrontation with the government even if the business community feels that the administrative agency has acted without legal authority in exercising *de facto* control by way of administrative guidance. This somewhat 'submissive attitude' of business communities towards the government may be a factor which makes administrative guidance effective.

When administrative guidance is supported by public opinion as in the cases of price control during the intensive inflation in the Oil Crisis, government agencies often publicize the fact that guidance has not been complied with in the event of non-compliance. In such a case, the effect of publicity is utilized as a technique of control. To give one example, consumer centres attached to local governments receive complaints from consumers regarding defects in commodities, and, when they think those complaints are not frivolous, they advise the manufacturers or vendors of such defective products to replace them with new goods or else take other appropriate measures to remedy the situation. This advice is not compulsory. However, if this advice is not respected, this is publicized. This has a considerable effect, and, whenever such advice is given, companies usually comply with it without questioning the legal authority behind it.

In view of this, some laws authorize recommendations to be issued by the administrative agencies and provide for publication as the sanction for non-compliance with such recommendations. The Law against Hoarding and Unreasonable Speculation,[84] the Land Utilization Planning Law,[85] and the National Life Stabilization Emergency Measures Law,[86] *inter alia*, all provide for advice to be given by the agencies in charge and for publication of the fact of non-compliance.

The wide range of powers possessed by some agencies may account for the effectiveness of administrative guidance. Although the legal powers of the MITI have declined in recent decades, it still has powers in areas such as international trade, safety and other standards, pollution control, mining and petroleum, electricity supply, gas supply, and industrial properties. The MOF has the power, *inter alia*, to control banking, securities, and insurance as well as to impose taxes. An enterprise with a wide range of operations (which is a feature of enterprises today) is likely to be affected by one or other of those powers possessed by the agency which has the supervisory authority over its activities. The enterprise which has been made the subject of administrative guidance takes into consideration possible consequences at present or in the future of ignoring the administrative guidance and generally judges that to comply with the guidance is a wise business policy.

In foreign trade, enterprises often need assistance from the government when faced with trade conflicts with other nations. For example, if Japanese enterprises are challenged in the United States on account of a violation of United States antitrust laws, they need the support of the Japanese government when they argue in a United States court that the activities in question have been imposed upon them by the government.[87] Also, if Japanese enterprises are unduly discriminated against in a foreign country, the enterprises may wish to complain to the Japanese government and request appropriate action (such as a complaint to the GATT) on the part of the government. Therefore, it is a good policy for enterprises to keep a good relationship with the government and avoid any

[84] Kaishime Urioshimi Bōshi Hō, Law 48, 1973.

[85] Kokudo Riyō Keikaku Hō, Law 92, 1974.

[86] Kokumin Seikatsu Antei Kinkyȳ Sochi Hō, Law 121, 1973.

[87] The case in point in this context is: *Matsushita Electric Industrial Co.* v. *Zenith Radio Corp.*, 475 US 574 (1986).

confrontation with it. This type of consideration may be another reason why administrative guidance has worked relatively well in Japan.

E. EVALUATION OF AMDINISTRATIVE GUIDANCE

In spite of what has been said above, it must be emphasized that administrative guidance is by no means sacrosanct. It is often effective only if it is based on a consensus within the industry as regards the reasonableness of the guidance. In other cases it is effective only if it is backed up by law. Indeed, the effectiveness of administrative guidance is, in a sense, proportionate to the powerfulness of the agency exercising it. In the post-war period when the economy had been badly shattered by the war, enterprises needed help and assistance from the government, and, under such circumstances, administrative guidance could be very effective. However, now that many enterprises have acquired economic power and independence, they may not need assistance from the government any more. In this situation, the effectiveness of administrative guidance tends to decline. It is probably accurate to say that the golden age of administrative guidance has passed or, at least, is passing.

Administrative guidance can be of great value both to the government and to citizens and enterprises, and there is nothing inherently sinister about it. Administrative guidance, generally speaking, is more flexible than the formal enforcement of law. In emergencies like the Oil Crisis of 1973, economic regulation by law may be too inflexible; it may take too long before a law is invoked, and the scope of a law may be too limited to cope with changing situations. In contrast to the enforcement of law, administrative guidance is much more flexible, and the response of the government to the situation is much more prompt. This should be regarded as the advantage of administrative guidance. Usually negotiations and persuasion are used before administrative guidance is invoked, and economic regulation is accomplished in a more amicable way than unilateral imposition of a legal order by the government which may create tension between the government and business.

However, the advantages of administrative guidance, viewed from a different angle, are also its shortcomings. The flexibility of administrative guidance may mean that its exercise is not circumscribed by any limits. Since, as explained before, administrative guidance can put irresistible pressure upon the addressee, the lack of a clearly defined area within which it can operate may lead to an arbitrary and capricious exercise of *de facto* governmental power and to infringement of individual rights.

Another shortcoming of administrative guidance is a lack of transparency of the process through which it is executed. In enforcement of a law, the procedures are usually provided for in the law, and everyone can see the process of enforcement. In administrative guidance, however, there is no clearly defined procedure, and even if a compromise is reached between the government and the enterprise which has received the administrative guidance, it may adversely affect the interests of outsiders, and yet there is no standard procedure through which they can raise their objections. Also the general public is deprived of the opportunity of knowing what is under consideration by the government and of participating in the formulation of policy.

In the Structural Impediments Initiative (the SII), a bilateral trade negotiation between the United States government and the Japanese government concluded in 1990, the Japanese government promised to improve the process of administrative guidance by using written documents instead of just oral presentations.[88] The idea involved here is to increase the transparency of the process. Perhaps a law should be enacted which generally provides for the process which the government must utilize when using administrative guidance and in which the rights of third parties to know the contents of administrative guidance and make their views known to the party receiving the guidance and to the government too are fixed.

F. REMEDY AGAINST ADMINISTRATIVE GUIDANCE

By definition, administrative guidance is an informal act of the government and has no binding power on the person receiving it. As such, compliance with administrative guidance is voluntary. As long as administrative guidance remains in such a pure form and non-compliance incurs no legal or *de facto* disadvantage, there is no legal remedy to it. Nor is it necessary to provide a remedy since non-compliance incurs no consequence. As we have seen already, however, administrative guidance is often a substitute for the enforcement of law. Sometimes the receiving party has little choice but to comply with it. If used in this way, it has almost the same effect as an order by law. In such a circumstance, it would be unjust and unreasonable to deny the party to whom it has been applied any relief even though the party has been seriously disadvantaged by it.

Under the Administrative Cases Litigation Law and the State Redress Law, the party whose interest has been adversely affected by the act of a government official can respectively seek for a cancellation of the act in question or for the recovery of damages caused by it. Under both laws, there must be an action by a state official in the exercise of the official

[88] On the SII, see Matsushita, 'The Structrual Impediments Initiative: An Example of Bilateral Trade Negotiation', *Michigan Journal of International Law*, 12/2 (1991), 346 *et seq.*

power of the government which has caused a hardship on the party to whom it has been applied before the party can seek for a cancellation of the action or for the recovery of damages. An administrative guidance is by definition advice of a government official issuing it compliance to which is voluntary for the party receiving it and, to that extent, a legal action in the above laws is not possible, since it is not regarded as an action in the exercise of official power of the government.

However, in exceptional situations, administrative guidance can be regarded as an act of an official in the course of exercising the official power of the government and, therefore, a remedy is available. A case in point is the decision in the *Model Gun* case decided by the Tokyo District Court.[89] Involved in this case was the following set of facts.

A person intended to import a model gun (a toy gun) and sell it. He imported and sold it. The police decided that the model gun in question was a weapon whose importation and sale was prohibited by the Law to Control Weapons.[90] The police could have invoked this law and prohibited the importation and sale of the gun. However, the police chose not to invoke an order by this law but utilized an administrative guidance requesting the party not to import and sell the gun. The police sent the records of the case to the Public Prosecutor's Office and the Prosecutor's Office decided to indict the person for illegal importation and sale of a weapon.

The case was tried by the Tokyo District Court. The court held the defendant not guilty since, after a series of experiments, the court had come to the conclusion that the model gun in question was not powerful enough to be classified as a weapon and, therefore, the importation and sale of the gun did not amount to an importation and sale of a weapon.

Meanwhile the person (the defendant in the criminal trial) went bankrupt and brought an action against the government (the police) on the basis of the State Redress Law. The plaintiff argued that the business of the plaintiff was wrongfully damaged by the administrative guidance which had been based on a wrong assumption that the model gun was a weapon.

The Tokyo District Court held that the plaintif could not recover damages since the plaintiff must prove the malicious intent or negligence on the part of the government official whose conduct had been alleged to cause the damage and there was no proof in this case that the act of the government official (the police officer) was done with malicious intent or negligence.

[89] 23 Aug. 1976, *Kakyū Minshū*, 27 (1976), 493 *et seq*. See, on this case, Matsushita, 'The Legal Framework of Trade and Investment in Japan', *Harvard International Law Journal,* 27, Special Issue (1987), 361 *et seq*.

[90] Jūhō Tōkenrui Shoji Torishimari Hō, Law 6, 1958.

The Tokyo District Court, however, noted in a *dictum* that the administrative guidance in this case was an act in the course of exercising the official power of the government; that is to say, the administrative guidance in this case was a substitute of an official act in the from of legal order. This means that the court characterized the administrative guidance in the case in question as an official act of the government subject to the State Redress Law even if the guidance involved in this case was not an order by law at least as far as the form of it was concerned.

Judging from this case, we can conclude that a remedy in the form of recovery of damage caused by an administrative guidance is available under some specific circumstances. However, this is a limitation to such a remedy. First, in the *Model Gun* case, the administrative guidance was used in lieu of invoking a law when the administrative agency could have invoked the law to prohibit it. In this type of situation, there is a high degree of likelihood that there would be a legal action by the agency if the administrative guidance was not complied with.

As we have seen already, however, administrative guidance is often exercised without any law which would accomplish the same purpose. Often administrative guidance is merely informal advice from the agency. It may indeed have a *de facto* coercive impact on the party to whom it is applied. For example, a subsidy to a person may be withheld if the guidance is rejected by that person. This prospect of withholding a subsidy may be a strong incentive for the party to whom the guidance is applied to obey it. If a causal linkage is established between the rejection of the guidance and the withholding of the subsidy, it is possible for the person to bring a legal action utilizing the rationale stated by the Tokyo District Court in the *Model Gun* case under the State Redress Law that the guidance in question is an exercise of the official power of the government. Often, however, it is hard (or impossible) to establish that linkage and, as long as no such linkage is established, the administrative guidance is nothing but an informal admonition by the government no matter how strong a pressure it may have exerted in actuality, and is not subject to a legal remedy.

Furthermore, adminstrative guidance is often issued orally. For example, a government official merely announces the content of administrative guidance in a private meeting. In such a case, it is hard to prove that there was an administrative guidance.

Recently there have been growing criticisms against excessive use of administrative guidance. As we have touched upon already, one such example is the Structural Impediments Initiative negotiated between the United States government and the Japanese government. The United States government raised an objection to administrative guidance to the effect that, because of its informality, it lacks transparency, and may lead to an infringement of the due process of law. The Japanese government promised to put administrative guidance in writing, to secure transparency.

In sum, administrative guidance is still a useful tool for the government to use for the variety of reasons mentioned above. However, it is perhaps necessary to bring in a little more 'legalism' in the process. To put it in writing in principle is an improvement in this respect since it increases transparency. It is also necessary to enact a law which establishes some rules for administrative guidance in general, such as the opportunity of third parties to be heard and the remedy which would be available. In Japan, there is no such law as the Administrative Procedure Act in the United States which provides general rules for actions by the United States government. Perhaps there is need for a law of this nature in which some rules on administrative guidance can be incorporated, such as those which require the government agency to publish administrative guidance to guarantee opportunities for third parties to participate in the process in some ways, including presenting their views on it and also to provide some procedure for remedy when the party which has been made the subject of administrative guidance is unreasonably disadvantaged.

2
Competition Law

2.1 Introduction

In this chapter, we will examine Japanese competition law (the Anti-monopoly Law). Since the scope of this law is so wide, some specific problems are dealt with in other chapters. For example, patent licensing will be dealt with elsewhere[1] and the legal problems with regard to exemption from the Anti-monopoly Law, which authorizes private associations and combinations, are dealt with in another chapter.[2]

In countries which have adopted a market economy, 'the market mechanism' is the central economic institution in which the price of products is determined by the balance of supply and demand. In this economic system, it is vitally important that the price mechanism operates effectively. If the demand for a product increases, enterprises in this product market increase investment and build new production facilities which in turn promote production and supply. On the other hand, if the demand for a product declines due to a recession or over-supply of the product, enterprises withdraw from production and supply decreases. In this way, those products which are needed are supplied effectively and the production of those products which are not needed any more declines and so the optimum allocation of resources in a society is achieved.

The effective operation of the economy is made possible through the quick response of numerous private enterprises engaged in the production and distribution of a product to the increase or decrease in demand. Private enterprises decide whether to increase or decrease production on the basis of upward or downward trends in prices.

In the above system, it is important to maintain competition. If an enterprise has a monopoly in a market or several enterprises combine through a cartel arrangement and so gain a monopolistic influence over a market, the enterprises can determine price by controlling production or

[1] See Chap. 3, 3.5, C, below.
[2] See Chap. 4, below.

by price-fixing. Through such anti-competitive conduct private enterprise can control supply and demand conditions, to a certain degree. And if such anti-competitive conduct is allowed to continue without legal constraint, the smooth operation of the market and of the price mechanism is jeopardized. As a consequence, the rigidity and inflexibility would increase in the economy and this would ultimately be detrimental to society in general.

In order to preserve the effectiveness of the market mechanism, those countries which adopt a market economy have enacted competition laws. Competition law is called by a variety of names, such as antitrust laws, restrictive business practices legislation, and anti-monopoly laws. It was in the United States that antitrust laws (the name unique to the United States) came to be enforced first on a massive basis. In 1890, the Sherman Antitrust Law was enacted and this legislation was soon followed by the Clayton Act and the Federal Trade Commission Act, both enacted in 1914. After the Second World War, in many countries which had a market economy, a piece of legislation for the purpose of maintaining competition was adopted under the strong leadership of the United States.

At present, there are about forty countries in the world in which competition law of some sort is enforced. They are countries in which the central economic system is that of market economy. Major countries are the United States, Canada, Australia, Germany, France, UK, Italy, Spain, Japan, and the Scandinavian countries. In the European Community, the European authorities (the EC Commission, the Council of Ministers, and the European Court of Justice) enforce Articles 85 and 86 of the Treaty of Rome and also the Merger Regulation enacted in 1990 which constitute the 'supra-national competition rules'. Indeed, the competition rules of the European Community are the most actively enforced rules in Europe beside the Law Against the Restraint of Competition enforced in Germany and the first supra-national competition rules applied directly to private enterprises.

Competition law is also enforced in Korea, Thailand, and India. Even in those countries with a non-market economy, there is movement towards legislation on competition law as they move from a non-market or socialistic economy to a market economy. In the People's Republic of China, draft legislation on competition has been presented. It seems that some kind of legislation on competition is necessary wherever a country adopts a market economy and operates economic institutions on the basis of the market principle.

2.2 A History of the Anti-monopoly Law

Competition law in Japan goes under the title of 'the Anti-monopoly Law' (hereafter referred to as 'the AML').[3] It is useful to know the historical development of this law.

A. BEFORE THE SECOND WORLD WAR

Before the Second World War, there was no anti-monopoly legislation in Japan.[4] The concepts of free enterprise and 'laissez-faire' had not developed. When Japan was opened up to the World in 1868 (the year in which the Meiji Restoration took place), Japan was a relatively backward agrarian society. The urgent task for the new government was to catch up with the West in industrial and military strength as soon as possible, and, for this purpose, the government took a strong role in developing the economy in various ways, for example, through the operation of government factories in industrial sectors such as iron and steel, and tight regimentation of industries by way of trade associations under government mandate. In short, economic development was achieved under strong government control and influence in which the guiding principle was not 'competition'.

Moreover, there were many large industrial combines called 'zaibatsu'. They were large industrial conglomerates composed of many enterprises engaged in various industries controlled by a head company and linked through mutual stock holdings and interlocking directorates. For example, in the Mitsui Zaibatsu, there was the Mitsui Headquarter Company which owned the stocks of various companies such as the Mitsui Trading Company, the Mitsui Bank, the Mitsui Shipbuilding Company, and so on. The headquarter company was a holding company which bound all the affiliated companies together in a group and they formed the Mitsui group. There were similar organizations in the Mitsubishi group, the Sumitomo group, and some others. In 1942, there were seventeen such *zaibatsu* conglomerates in Japan. Under the circumstances where such large industrial conglomerates dominated the economy, there was little room for free enterprise and competition to plan a role. Therefore, the period before the Second World War may be termed the age of government control and *zaibatsu*.

[3] There are a number of books and articles on the AML, including: Iyori and Uesugi, *Anti-monopoly Law of Japan* (Washington, DC, 1983); Nakagawa, *Anti-monopoly Legislation of Japan* (Tokyo, 1984); Matsushita, *Introduction to Japanese Anti-monopoly Law* (Tokyo, 1990).

[4] Yamamura. 'The Development of Anti-monopoly Policy in Japan: The Erosion of Japanese Anti-monopoly Policy, 1947–67', *Studies in Law and Economic Development*, 2 (1967), 1–22.

B. THE ECONOMIC DEMOCRATIZATION POLICY

The end of the Second World War drastically changed the situation. When the War ended, the Occupation Forces, in which the United States played a vital role, governed Japan for several years. Under the sponsorship of the Occupation Forces, the economic democratization policy was introduced. There were three dimensions in this policy and the anti-monopoly legislation grew out of it.[5]

The first dimension was the agrarian land reform by which the absentee landownership of farmland was abolished. Farmland was taken away from absentee landowners and was given to the farmers who had been tenants. The basic idea here was to introduce the system in which each farmer owned his own land and cultivated it.

The second dimension was labour reform in which three basic laws (the Labour Standard Law, the Labour Adjustment Law, and the Labour Union Law) for the protection of workers were enacted.

The third dimension, which paved the way to the enactment of the AML, was the dissolution of *zaibatsu* and the deconcentration of economic powers.[6] The measures included the following. First the headquarter companies (the holding companies) of the *zaibatsu* conglomerates which held stocks of the various companies which belonged to the group were dissolved and the ownership of stocks was widely dispersed. Many large companies were split up into smaller companies to decrease the concentration of economic power and create more independent enterprise units. For example, the Mitsubishi Heavy Industrial Company (MHI) was broken up into three companies, the Japan Steel Corporation was split into two companies, the Toyo Can Company was divided into two entities, and the Nihon Beer Company was separated into two companies. This deconcentration measure was carried out quite ruthlessly and it may be observed that this created the opportunities for new enterprises to rise. Some of the companies which are now actively engaged in international operations emerged in this 'power vacuum' period including Sony, Panasonic, and Honda.

The goal of the Economic Democratization Policy was to introduce the system of free enterprise into Japan, and, in this regard, deconcentration was only a preparation for the future economic system in Japan. The natural step which followed was to enact a law which would be the basis for a free enterprise system and the Occupation Forces recommended that the Japanese government enact a law which would serve as the basic law of competition.

[5] A good source of the subject is Kōseitorihiki Iinkai (The Fair Trade Commission), *Dokusenkinshi Seisaku Nijūnenshi* (*A Twenty-Year History of Japanese Anti-monopoly Policy*) (1967).

[6] On 'zaibatsu', see Bisson, *Dissolution of Zeibatsu in Japan* (Berkeley, Calif., 1954).

In response to this, the Japanese government prepared a draft of the AML. In the process of preparation, there was interaction between the Japanese government and the Occupation Forces. In the United States, antitrust policy had emerged as an integral part of the New Deal Policy in the late 1930s and enforcement had increased under the name of 'the New Sherman Act'. After interruption during the War, it resumed its upward surge from 1945. United States antitrust enforcers attempted to introduce into Japan an 'ideal type' of antitrust law which meant a law with stringent prohibitions on cartels, monopolies, mergers, and even the very existence of a large enterprise as such.

C. THE ENACTMENT OF THE ORIGINAL ANTI-MONOPOLY LAW

A draft of the AML was prepared in 1947, and, after some revisions, it passed the last Imperial National Diet in the same year. This new law was generally modelled after United States antitrust laws but, as we will see later, it was even more stringent than its counterpart in the United States in some respects. This law was entitled: 'The Law to Prohibit Private Monopolization and to Maintain Fair Trade'. The AML is, therefore, an abbreviated name. At the same time, the Trade Associations Law was enacted which imposed stringent prohibitions on restrictive conduct by trade associations. This law also established the Fair Trade Commission of Japan.

The AML as originally enacted in 1947 was a strict one. The salient features of it are illustrated below. In Article 4, it generally prohibited agreements among enterprises in competitive relationship (cartels) as regards price, territory of activities, quantity of production, and other terms of business except for the cases where the effect on competition of such agreements was negligible. This strict prohibition of cartels was modelled after United States antitrust laws in which the *per se* illegality rule had been adopted.

In Article 8, it prohibited 'undue imbalance in business powers', that is, if there was an imbalance in terms of productive capacity among enterprises, this imbalance was regarded as improper. For example, if an enterprise in a market owned 80 per cent of the productive capacity and four other enterprises shared 5 per cent of the capacity each, there would be an undue imbalance in business powers. The remedy would be to order the enterprise with the 80 per cent productive capacity to give up a part of the capacity and assign it to other enterprises, to license technology it owned to other enterprises, or otherwise take measures to restore competition, or, in extreme cases, to break up the enterprise into several smaller competitive units.

This apsect of the original AML was a 'structure control'. It was intended to apply the prohibition to the structure of the enterprise or the market rather than prohibiting specific conduct of enterprises. This prohibition went even further than the prohibition of monopolization in United States antitrust laws.

This may have been a reflection of the desire on the part of persons in the United States who pushed forward the enactment of the AML in Japan to establish an 'ideal type' of antitrust laws. Acquisition and ownership of stocks of a company by another company in competitive relationship was prohibited. Mergers of companies were prohibited unless permitted by the FTC.

In the above way, the original AML was quite stringent in prohibiting restrictive conduct by private enterprises as well as controlling the structure of markets.

This law was strongly enforced by the FTC for several years at least after its enactment. The Occupation Forces exerted strong pressure on the FTC to do so. This initial period of strong enforcement of the AML lasted until about 1950.

D. THE RELAXATION OF THE LAW AND THE AMENDMENT OF 1953

Soon, however, the enforcement became loose and dormant. This relaxation can be attributed to various causes, among which we can point out the following. In 1950, the Korean War broke out and the policy of the United States towards Japan shifted from that of establishing in Japan an economy in which no huge concentration of economic power would be allowed to exist to that of rebuilding heavy industries in Japan so that Japan would be a bulwark against Communist infiltration. Therefore, even in the late stages of the Occupation, the support of the Occupation Forces for the enforcement of the AML decreased and enforcement was already relaxed. With the conclusion of the Treaty of San Francisco of 1952, the Occupation ended.

At this time, the Japanese economy was still devastated by the War and its rehabilitation had barely begun. The AML was little known among the people, and it was detested by the business community as a result of the drastic measures against large businesses taken in the Occupation Period. With the support of the Occupation Forces gone with the end of the Occupation, it was inevitable that enforcement of the AML was relaxed.

In 1953, an amendment was adopted which established the present structure of the AML. First, Article 4 of the original AML, which had declared that cartels were prohibited *per se*, was deleted. Cartels were now prohibited only if they caused substantial restraint of competition in a particular field of trade. The amendment introduced two types of authorized cartels, that is, 'depression cartels' and 'rationalization cartels'. Under the amendment, these two types of cartels were given exemption from the application of the AML when they were licensed by the FTC, and enterprises could enter into agreements among themselves for the purpose of overcoming a depression and also in order to rationalize their business operations. This aspect of the amendment signified a change in policy towards cartels in the sense that under this amendment there were 'good cartels' and 'bad cartels', whereas in the orginal AML all cartels were regarded as basically bad.

Secondly, Article 8 of the original AML, which stated that an undue imbalance in economic power was unlawful, was deleted. This provision had never been invoked. Since, as touched upon earlier, large-scale deconcentration and reorganization measures had been taken under the Economic Democratization Policy and numerous large enterprises had been broken up into smaller units, there was little room for this provision to operate. This provision, however, was re-enacted in a different formula when an amendment was made to the AML in 1977.

Thirdly, the stringent controls that had existed in the original AML with regard to mergers and acquisitions were relaxed by this amendment, and now mergers and acquisitions were prohibited only when they tended substantially to restrain competition in a particular field of trade.

Fourthly, this amendment introduced the exemption of resale price maintenance. Resale price maintenance is the practice in which the manufacturer of a product directs, by way of contracts or otherwise, the wholesale price to wholesalers and/or the retail price to retailers of the product. In the orginal AML, this practice was regarded as unlawful. Under this amendment, resale price maintenance with regard to books, magazines, and other published materials and other objects which were covered by copyright (such as records) were given exemption from the application of the AML. Also when the FTC designated commodities for exemption, those commodities were given exemption.

In these ways, the 1953 amendment relaxed the enforcement of the AML. Furthermore, the activities of the FTC in the investigation and prohibition of cartels and other restrictive conduct of enterprises were relaxed. This period in which the AML was dormant lasted until approximately 1960. This was the period in which the industrial policy exercised by the MITI was very strong.

There is one aspect of the AML which was strengthened by the amendment of 1953, and this was the control of unfair business practices. The original AML stated that 'unfair methods of competition'[7] were prohibited.

[7] Art. 2(7) of the original law stated that 'fukōseina kyōsō hōhō' (unfair methods of competition) were prohibited.

The amendment of 1953 widened the scope of prohibition from unfair methods of competition to 'unfair business practices'.[8] This signified that those practices which were not unfair methods of competition but which were unfair practices came to be subjected to the control of the AML.

The aim of this part of the 1953 amendment in practice was to control abusive conduct by large enterprises *vis-à-vis* small enterprises when large and small enterprises were in transactional relationships such as purchasers and suppliers of parts and components. Because of the imbalance in bargaining power between large and small enterprises, large enterprises often imposed harsh conditions on small-scale suppliers of parts and components, like requiring smaller enterprises to accept the return of goods as a result of any reduction of production in a recession, or suppressing purchase prices unduly by threatening that there would be no purchase in future if the small supplier refused to accept this low price.

Such practices are not strictly speaking 'unfair methods of competition', since purchasers and suppliers of parts and components are not in competition with each other. Since there is no competition, there is no room for unfair methods of competition. However, those practices are clearly 'unfair business practices'. In this way, the amendment of 1953 widened the scope of control by the AML as far as unfair business practices were concerned.

It should be stressed that, although the amendment of 1953 weakened the enforcement of the AML, on the whole, the provisions for the control of unfair business practices were strengthened. This means that the antitrust principles introduced from the United States were weakened but the control of abusive conduct by large enterprises against small enterprises, which were not part of United States antitrust laws, was strengthened. This amendment signified that the AML had begun to reflect the needs of Japanese society rather than blindly following the example of the United States antitrust laws.

E. THE REVITALIZATION OF THE ENFORCEMENT

The AML was again revitalized from about 1960. Several factors explain this renewed enforcement.[9] The first one was inflation. Although consumer prices in Japan were stable in the 1950s, they began to take an upward swing in 1960. In a period of several years beginning in 1960, consumer prices went up by more than 6 per cent each year and government policy towards consumer prices became politically important.

[8] The amended law states that 'fukōseina torihiki hōhō' (unfair business practices) are prohibited and thus widens the coverage of prohibition.

[9] Matsushita, *Introduction on Japanese Anti-monopoly Law* (Tokyo, 1990), 2–5.

To deal with this inflation, the government organized a task force to investigate the causes. It reported that, among other measures, a stronger enforcement of the AML would be desirable since price-fixing cartels and resale price maintenance imposed on retailers by manufacturers may have contributed to the upward movement of consumer prices. In response to this, the FTC's activities increased, more cases were investigated, and more decisions enforced.

The second factor was the liberalization of trade and investment. This reduced the number of commodity items under the import quota system and eased licence requirements under the Foreign Investment Law for foreign enterprises intending to establish subsidiaries in Japan and to license foreign technology to Japanese companies. As the market became more and more open, the role of the AML as the basic rules of competition became more and more important.

The third factor was the protection of small enterprises. The Japanese economy was characterized by a dualistic structure in which a handful of large enterprises and numerous small enterprises coexisted, sometimes competing with each other and sometimes operating transactional relationships in the same way as purchasers of parts and components and their suppliers. Due to the sheer number of small enterprises, their protection *vis-à-vis* large enterprises was (and still is today) a very important political problem. An effective use of the AML in controlling abusive conduct by large enterprises to small enterprises was called for.

Last (but not the least) was the rise of the need for consumer protection. As Japanese society became an 'affluent society' in the late 1960s, the needs and demands of consumers became more and more diversified, companies tended to engage in excessive advertising and marketing activities, and the need to strengthen the enforcement of the AML was felt strongly in areas such as the control of false and misleading advertisements and the prohibition of price cartels and resale price maintenance.

When the Oil Crisis occurred in 1973, prices sky-rocketed and price-fixing cartels in the oil industry, which took advantage of the Crisis, surfaced. There was strong public reaction against such cartels. Utilizing this situation effectively, the FTC organized a task force to strengthen the AML, which came up with a report that recommended amendment of the AML in several areas. The recommendations of the task force were adopted by the government. The bill was drafted and passed the National Diet as the amendment of 1977.

F. THE AMENDMENT OF 1977

The amendment of 1977 is significant in the sense that it was the first amendment made to the AML which strengthened its enforcement—

previous amendments had relaxed enforcement in one way or another. There are numerous clauses to the amendment, but we will examine the three which are regarded as most important.

Prior to this amendment, the FTC could only order enterprises which had been engaged in price cartel agreements to cancel the agreements and to discontinue the collusive practices. Although there were criminal provisions which could be employed against price cartels, they were rarely used. Enterprises would engage in cartels and, when the cartels were detected, they would discontinue the practice following an order issued by the FTC, without incurring any financial disadvantages. This encouraged enterprises to re-establish cartels since they could reap extra profits during the period in which they were engaged in cartel activities.

In order to remedy this situation, the amendment of 1977 introduced an administrative surcharge[10] which could be imposed by the FTC on enterprises which participated in price cartels, or other cartels which affected prices (mainly production cut-back cartels), to an amount of approximately 2 per cent of total sales during the period in which they participated in the cartel activity in question.[11]

Secondly, control of monopolistic situations was implemented. As touched on earlier, the original AML contained the provision (Article 8) which stated that there would be a remedial measure to an undue imbalance among enterprises in terms of economic power. This was a 'structure control'. The 1977 amendment revived this provision in a different form. Under the 1977 amendment, when one enterprise occupies a market share of 50 per cent or above or two enterprises occupy a market share of 75 per cent or above, new entry into this market is difficult, and the profit rate and prices are excessively high or general expenses are excessively large, then the enterprise or enterprises are subject to an order in which measures to restore competition are included. In extreme cases, a deconcentration order is imposed whereby the enterprise can be split into several separate entities.

Thirdly, the price reporting system was introduced whereby the FTC could apply prohibition to a price cartel agreement as long as the existence of the cartel was proved by direct or indirect evidence. Often it happened, however, that different companies' prices went up simultaneously but there was no evidence to indicate that the prices were fixed by collusion. This type of situation could not be handled by the provision in the AML which prohibited cartel agreements since the provision which prohibited

[10] Art. 7.2 of the AML. In 1991, this provision was revised to raise the amount of administrative fine. A detailed explanation of the revision will be made later in this chapter.

[11] By the revision of 1991, the figure was raised to 6% in industries other than wholesale and retail businesses such as manufacturing industries.

cartels required that there be 'communication' of intentions among the participating enterprises.

To cope with this situation, the 1977 amendment introduced the system that, whenever prices of a product went up simultaneously (within three months), the FTC could order the major enterprises in the market which had raised their prices to report to the FTC the reasons why the prices had been raised. The FTC was authorized to demand enterprises to turn in business data including costs of production and other matters.

This was nothing but a reporting duty and, as long as the enterprises reported the reasons, that was sufficient. However, since enterprises are reluctant to submit to the FTC sensitive business data concerning costs of production and related matters, this provision has operated as an effective deterrent to simultaneous and parallel price raisings engaged in by enterprises.

The amendment of 1977 was an epoch-making event in the history of the AML. It introduced not only new provisions which strengthened the enforcement of the AML but also the control of monopolistic situations. This provision was modelled after some reports and bills published and introduced in the United States in the early 1970s which were aimed at industrial reorganization. In the United States, however, the movement towards structure control quickly died down from around the mid-1970s. The AML adopted some of these ideas and incorporated them into the 1977 amendment.

G. THE STRUCTURAL IMPEDIMENTS INITIATIVE AND THE ANTI-MONOPOLY LAW

The Structural Impediments Initiative (referred to as 'the SII') is a bilateral trade agreement between the United States and Japan whereby both parties agreed to reduce trade barriers. A task force composed of representatives from the United States government and the Japanese government submitted a report to President Bush and Prime Minister Kaifu in June 1990. Both governments pledged that they would implement the proposals in the report. One important proposal of the SII with regard to reducing Japanese trade barriers was reform of the AML.[12]

The SII report stated that some Japanese trade barriers were not legal or institutional impediments so much as the collusive or anti-competitive behaviour of enterprises. The report emphasized that situations such as interlocking relationships among enterprises through stock-ownership and interlocking personnel, long-standing relationships between purchasers and sellers, and collusive practices engaged in through trade associa-

[12] See generally Matsushita, 'The Structural Impediments Initiative: An Example of Bilateral Trade Negotiation', *Michigan Journal of International Law*, 12/2 (1991), 436 *et seq*.

tions or otherwise have hindered new entry of foreign commodities and enterprises into the Japanese market. The report recommended that some measures be taken to remedy the situation. The recommendations included measures to reform the enforcement of the AML including an increase of administrative fines, an active utilization of criminal prosecutions and private damage suits, and new guidelines on the enforcement policy to be issued by the FTC on such items as group boycott, exclusive dealings, stock-holding, and other related matters.

The FTC organized a task force to investigate the possibility of increasing administrative surcharge. The task force submitted a report which recommended that the administrative surcharge be calculated on the basis of the profit of enterprises during any period in which they participated in cartel activity. In early 1991, the AML was amended so that the level of administrative surcharge was raised to 6 per cent of sales during the period in which manufacturing businesses participated in cartel activity.

The FTC also announced draft guidelines on the enforcement of the AML which included: (1) rules on continuous and exclusive transactions among enterprises, and (2) rules of conduct in the distribution of products. Details of the guidelines will be discussed in later sections. Here we will only list the major items covered by the guidelines.

The rules on continuous and exclusive transactions cover items such as a group boycott, refusal to deal by a single enterprise, exclusive dealing arrangements, unreasonable reciprocal dealing, other conduct with the background of continuous transactional relationships which adversely affects competition, and ownership of stocks of the enterprises which are parties to transactions and its effect on competition. The rules of conduct in the distribution of products contain such items as resale price maintenance, non-price restriction, offering of rebates, manufacturer's participation in the management of distributors, and abuse of a dominant position by a retailer.

As we have seen in this section, the way in which the AML has been enforced in Japan has been by no means straight and plain. The route has been tortuous. However, through its forty-five-year history, the AML has been gradually strengthened through the amendment of 1977, the increase of administrative fines in 1991, and the enforcement of guidelines issued by the FTC. The AML has established itself as the basic law which governs the conduct of enterprises.

The problem which the AML will have to tackle in the 1990s will be the harmonization of competition law in the world. As the economic relationships among nations become closer and closer, differences in competition laws and policies will work as an impediment and disturbance to the operation of international enterprises. There will be an attempt at a harmonization of competition laws either in the OECD or in the GATT. It may be said that the reform of the AML on the basis of the SII is only a forerunner of such harmonization.[13]

2.3 An Overview of the Anti-monopoly Law

The major provisions of the AML are applied to the following three categories of conduct: (1) private monopoly, (2) unreasonable restraint of trade, and (3) unfair business practices. The purpose of this section is to provide a detailed analysis of these three categories. However, it is useful to give an overview before examining them in detail.

A. PRIVATE MONOPOLY

Private monopoly is defined in Article 2(5) of the AML. Under this article, if a powerful enterprise either 'controls' or 'excludes' the business activities of another enterprise or other enterprises and thereby brings about the condition in a market where competition is substantially restrained, the enterprise is regarded as committing a private monopoly. Private monopoly is prohibited under the former part of Article 3. Examples of private monopoly include the acquisition by a powerful enterprise of stocks or assets of another enterprise in competitive relationship whereby the acquiring enterprise controls the business activities of the acquired enterprise, and the contractual terms imposed by a powerful manufacturer on distributors of the product it produces thereby exclude competing manufacturers from the distribution network. If conduct such as the above is carried out by a powerful enterprise and competition in the relevant market is substantially restrained, the enterprise would be accused of having monopolized the relevant market.

There are several provisions which are related to the prohibition of private monopoly. Provisions contained in Articles 9–18 of Chapter 4 of the AML are devoted to the control of mergers and acquisitions. Article 9 prohibits the establishment of holding companies which are defined as companies whose main business is to own stocks of other companies to control them, Article 9.2 sets an upper limit to the value of the stocks of companies which a large-scale company can acquire and hold, and Article 11 prohibits, with some exceptions, financial companies (companies in banking, securities, and insurance) from acquiring and owning more than 5 per cent of the outstanding stocks of another company.

Article 11 prohibits companies from acquiring and owning stocks of

[13] See generally Matsushita, 'The Structural Impediments Initiative: An Example of Bilateral Trade Negotiation', *Michigan Journal of International Law*, 12/2 (1991), 436 *et seq*.

another company or other companies if, as the result of such acquisition and holding, competition in a market tends to be substantially restrained. Article 13 prohibits interlocking directorates if they tend substantially to restrain competition in a market. Article 15 prohibits a merger between companies if by such a merger competition in a market tends to be substantially restrained.

The purpose of these provisions is to arrest the tendency towards concentration of economic power in a market and, in this sense, it may be said that the provisions in Chapter 4 of the AML are designed to operate as 'precautionary measures' in relation to the prohibition of private monopolies.

Article 2(7) of the AML defines a 'monopolistic situation'. In this, a monopolistic situation exists if an enterprise occupies a market share of 50 per cent or above, or two enterprises 75 per cent or more in a product market, new entry into this market is difficult, and the price and profit rate of these enterprises or their general expenses and other expenses are excessively high. The FTC can issue an order to a monopolistic enterprise to restore competition in a market including, in extreme cases, a deconcentration measure whereby the enterprise is broken up into several competing units.

The control of a monopolistic situation is not premissed on 'a wrongful conduct' of an enterprise. As long as there is the monopolistic structure and other requirements as above described, a deconcentration order may be issued. Therefore, this control is a control of structure rather than a control of conduct. This can be regarded as a supplementary measure to the prohibition of private monopolies in the sense that there may be a monopolistic situation without any wrongful conduct which amounts to a private monopoly and yet competition in a market may not exist any more due to a monopolistic or oligopolistic market structure.

B. UNREASONABLE RESTRAINT OF TRADE

Article 2(6) of the AML defines unreasonable restraint of trade as an agreement or arrangement among enterprises to the effect that they mutually refrain from competing with each other with regard to a product or service. By definition, an unreasonable restraint of trade is a cartel. A cartel is prohibited by the latter part of Article 3. Cartels can be created through the decisions of trade associations as well as by agreements among enterprises. Therefore, the AML provides in Article 8(1) for the prohibition of restrictive conduct engaged in by a trade association.

When a cartel fixes prices or otherwise affects prices, the FTC must impose on the parties concerned an administrative surcharge. Similarly, when enterprises in a market simultaneously raise their prices, the FTC can demand the reasons. Although this is not a control of cartels as such, it is a measure related to the prohibition of cartels.

Some cartels are exempted and authorized by law. They include depression cartels, rationalization cartels, export and import cartels, small business cartels, and ocean freight conferences. Some of these cartels will be more closely examined when we look at legal aspects of industrial policy. When we study the law on cartels, it is necessary to examine the legal rules that permit cartels by way of exemption as well as those which prohibit them since there are many such authorized cartels.

C. UNFAIR BUSINESS PRACTICES

The third category of conduct which is prohibited by the AML is unfair business practices. They are defined in Article 2(9) and prohibited by Article 19. According to Article 2(9), the FTC is required to designate unfair business practices. In Notification 15 of 1982, the FTC designated sixteen items. They will be covered in subsequent sections so we will only lightly touch on them here.

Article 2(9) states that the FTC shall designate unfair business practices within six basic categories: (1) unreasonable discrimination, (2) a transaction with unreasonable pricing, (3) unreasonable inducement of customers or coercion of customers, (4) unreasonable restriction imposed on the other party to the transaction, (5) abuse of a dominant position in the transaction, and (6) unreasonable interference in the internal matters of competitors.

Unreasonable discrimination includes conduct such as a boycott, a refusal to deal by a single enterprise, and price discrimination. A transaction with unreasonable pricing is typically a sale below the cost of production or of purchasing. Unreasonable inducement of customers is exemplified by a false or misleading advertisement or representation and offering excessive premiums when an enterprise sells a product. Unreasonable coercion of customers is generally a tie-in sale whereby the seller of a product sells the product with the condition that the purchaser purchases another product or other products. Unreasonable restriction imposed on the other party to the transaction includes various conducts of which the typical ones are a resale price maintenance, an exclusive dealing arrangement, a vertical territorial restriction, and customer restriction. Abuse of a dominant position means that an enterprise with a stronger position *vis-à-vis* the other party to the transaction imposes harsh conditions on the other party. Unreasonable interference in the internal matters of competitors includes interfering with transactions between a competitor and its customers and inducing stockholders of a competitor to act against its interests.

It can be stated that the importance of the prohibition of unfair business practices lies in the following two areas. First, the control of unfair business practices is regarded as a precautionary measure in relation to the prohibition of private monopolies. The theory is that, if unfair business practices were allowed to continue with impunity, there would be a gradual concentration of economic power in the hands of those who practise them and the concentration of economic power would be the seed-bed of private monopolies. Therefore, it maintains that it is necessary to apply the prohibition on unfair business practices with the view to preventing private monopolies.

Beside the above, however, prohibition of unfair business practices is part of the law of consumer protection. For that matter, the whole AML is part of the law of consumer protection. However, this is especially true with the control of such unfair business practices as the prohibition of false and misleading advertisements, resale price maintenance, and a tie-in deal whereby consumers are forced to buy products tied to the product which is the main object of the transaction. Also the prohibition of unfair business practices is part of the law of small business protection. This is especially true with regard to the prohibition of the abuse of a dominant position in which the party to a transaction with superior bargaining power imposes harsh conditions on the other party to the transaction. Of course, the small business protection law has a much wider scope. However, the prohibition of unfair business practices by the AML is an important part of it.

There are two supplementary laws. One is the Law to Prevent Unreasonable Representation and Unreasonable Premiums[14] and the other is the Law to Prevent Unreasonable Delay in Payment to Subcontractors and Related Matters.[15] The contents of those two supplementary laws will be touched upon in a later section of this chapter. It is sufficient here to mention that, while the provisions of the AML are general, they specifically designate conduct which should be prohibited and provide for a more expedited procedure for enforcement.

2.4 The Basic Concepts of the Anti-monopoly Law

There are several important concepts in the AML which are common to different types of regulation under the AML. To avoid repetition in later sections, these basic concepts are explained below all together.

[14] Futōkeihinrui Oyobi Futōhyōuji Bōshi Hō, Law 134, 1962.
[15] Shitaukedaikin Shiharai Chien Boshi Hō, Law 120, 1956.

A. ENTERPPRISE

In principle, the AML is applied to an 'enterprise'.[16] Article 3, which prohibits private monopoly and unreasonable restraint of trade, states that enterprises shall not engage in private monopoly or unreasonable restraint of trade. Similarly, Article 19, which prohibits unfair business practices, also states that an enterprise shall not engage in unfair business practices. There are some exceptions, such as Article 10, which controls the acquisition by a company of stocks of another company and Article 15 which controls a merger between companies, which states that 'companies' are the object of regulation. Likewise, Article 13 prohibits directors and employees of a company from being in the position of director of another company, if to do so would tend substantially to restrain competition in a market. However, generally, enterprises are the object of regulation under the AML.

An 'enterprise' is defined in Article 2(1) as 'person who carries on business of a commercial, industrial, financial, or any other nature'. Commercial, industrial and financial businesses are but a few examples of business enterprises. Activities of 'any other nature' include agriculture, services, and research and development. In short, business engaged in by an enterprise comprises a wide variety of activities. Although the major parts of such business activities are profit-making activities, they are not necessarily limited to such. As long as an enterprise is an active participant in a market, the business activity engaged in by such business is regarded as coming under the definition of Article 2(1).

Of course, profit-making companies are central to the concept of enterprise as defined in Article 2(1). However, an enterprise in this Article is not necessarily limited to a profit-making enterprise. For example, co-operatives established by laws such as the Agricultural Co-operatives Law[17] and the Medium and Small Enterprises Organizations Law[18] are prohibited from engaging in profit-making activities. However, they do engage in continuously buying and selling products and are active participants in a market. Therefore, they are enterprises under the definition of Article 2(1). As long as an entity participates in a market by way of selling, buying, or otherwise, regularly, continuously, and repeatedly, the entity is qualified as an enterprise in the sense of Article 2(1).

Recently some questions were raised as to whether or not activities of professionals and educational institutions are business activities in the sense of Article 2(1). The FTC decisions answered them in the affirmative. Some examples are given. There are a number of FTC decisions in

[16] In Japanese, it is 'jigyōsha'.
[17] Nogyō Kyōdō Kumiai Hō, Law 132, 1947.
[18] Chūshōkigyō Dantai Hō, Law 185, 1958.

which the issue was a restrictive condition imposed by medical associations on newly opened medical clinics, such as the restriction of the location of a newly established clinic to the effect that the new clinic must be located a certain distance away from existing ones. The FTC held such a restriction as unlawful on the ground that medical associations were trade associations and the move on the part of medical associations stated above violated Article 8(1) of the AML, which prohibits trade associations from engaging in activities which restrain competition substantially.[19] The premiss of these decisions was that medical doctors and clinics which made up the medical associations were enterprises in the sense of Article 2(1).

In the *Architect Association* case,[20] an association composed of architects was accused by the FTC of establishing a minimum fee schedule. The FTC proceeded against this association on the theory that it was a trade association. Here again the premiss of the FTC's challenge was that architects who made up the Association were enterprises in the sense of Article 2(1). This case was settled between the FTC and the respondents.

Once it is established that medical doctors and architects are enterprises in the sense of Article 2(1), other professionals such as lawyers, accountants, and independent business consultants also become enterprises. This extends to educational institutions and vocational schools.

Enterprise is a functional concept and the form of enterprise does not matter. So it makes little difference whether a given enterprise is a joint-stock corporation, a non-profit making entity, or an individual. As long as an enterprise is actively participating in a market, it qualifies as an enterprise in the sense of Article 2(1) of the AML.

B. TRADE ASSOCIATIONS

Trade associations play a very important role in business activities in the Japanese economy. There are trade associations in virtually all fields of business—the Steel Alliance in the steel industry, the Automobile Industry Association in the car industry, and so forth. Generally their work involves gathering business information, formulating industrial standards, acting as the channel through which enterprises in the industry petition the government, and engaging in activities that relate to a social cause (such as the campaign for the elimination of industrial pollution). Also some anti-competitive activities are carried out by trade associations. Consequently, the AML provides for the regulation of trade

[19] See, for details, Matsushita, *Keizaihō Gaisetsu* (*Introduction to Economic Law*) (Tokyo, 1986), 40–4.

[20] In re Nihon Kenchikuka Kyōkai Case, FTC Decision, 19 Sept. 1979, *Shinketsushū*, 265 (1980), 25 *et seq*.

associations. Article 8(1) provides that trade associations shall not engage in cartel-like activities and unfair business practices. They will be analysed in a later section. Here we will deal with the definition of trade associations.

Article 2(2) of the AML defines a trade association as: 'any combination or federation of combinations consisting of two or more enterprises and having as its principal purpose the furtherance of the common interest of its members . . .'. Organizations such as associations, foundations, and co-operatives are included within this category.

Sometimes an entity has the dual character of an enterprise and a trade association. For example, a farmers' co-operative is an entity composed of farmers for the purpose of furthering their common interest and so is a trade association. At the same time, the co-operative engages in selling and buying and, as long as it is engaged in market activities in such a way, it is regarded as an enterprise.

C. PARTICULAR FIELDS OF TRADE

In General

In order to determine whether a private monopoly or an unreasonable restraint of trade occurs, or a merger or acquisition of stocks by a company of another company tends substantially to restrain competition, it is necessary to decide the scope of the market in which such conduct occurs. In other words, a market must be determined in which anti-competitive conduct takes place. For example, a merger between companies which together occupy 80 per cent of the market would probably restrain competition. The question, however, is what is the market of which the two companies hold an 80 per cent market share. Even if those two companies occupy 80 per cent of the market when only a single product is taken into consideration, there may be other competing products, and if all those are taken into consideration the market share of the two companies may be only 10 per cent or less.

Therefore, it is necessary to determine the market in question and, in the AML, a market in this sense is referred to as 'a particular field of trade'. Although it is impossible to define it with mathematical exactitude, we can discuss some general criteria which are useful.

Product Markets

One criterion is the product market. One test is to determine whether a commodity or service is a substitute for another commodity or service. Theoretically, if there is 'cross-elasticity of demand' or 'reasonable interchangeability' between two or more products, they can all be substituted for each other and together they constitute a particular field of trade.[21] In the *Chūōseni-Teikokuseima* case,[22] there was a merger between two companies which occupied more than 70 per cent of the market for hemp yarn rope. However, if rope made of hemp yarn and that made of chemical fibre were put together, the market share of these two companies was less than 10 per cent. The FTC regarded rope made of hemp yarn and that made of chemical fibre as interchangeable and decided not to challenge the merger.

If a product is highly differentiated by brand name, grade, and prestige, there may be several sub-products within a product. For example, a cosmetic product of a high grade is differentiated from a product of lower grade since they have different customers.[23] In such a case, a sub-product constitutes a particular field of trade.

Geographical Markets

Even if two enterprises are engaged in the same business, there is no competition if the locations of their business are so far away from each other that competition is impossible. A geographical market is the geographical area in which competition takes place. There is no standard which can be applied uniformly to every case. However, generally, a geographical market in retail business is narrow and that in manufacturing and wholesale is wide.[24] When the FTC announced the guidelines on mergers and acquisitions in the retail industry, the FTC stated that the administrative boundaries of a city would be regarded as a particular field of trade in retail business except for the six large cities for the purpose of reviewing mergers and acquisitions.

D. SUBSTANTIAL RESTRAINT OF COMPETITION

Competition

There is a definition of competition in Article 2(4) of the AML which states that competition is:

> a situation in which two or more enterprises do or may, within the normal scope of their business activities and without undertaking any significant change in their business facilities or kinds of business activities, engage in any one of the following acts, (i) supplying the same or similar goods or services to the same consumers

[21] *United States* v. *E.I. du Pont de Nemours & Co.*, 351 US 377 (1956).

[22] See Kōseitorihiki Iinkai (The Fair Trade Commission), n. 5, above, pp. 199–202.

[23] *United States* v. *Guerlain, Inc.*, 153 F. Supp. 77 (SDNY 1957).

[24] In 1981, the Fair Trade Commission announced a set of guidelines titled 'On Mergers and Acquisitions in Retail Business' in which the Commission states that a particular field of trade in retail business is the city as an administrative unit or an area which is slightly larger than that except for the cases of large cities.

or customers; (ii) obtaining supplies of the same or similar goods or services from the same supplier.

From the wording 'may . . . engage', we can infer that potential competition as well as actual competition is included. Also it is clear that competition in the AML includes not only that among sellers but also that among purchasers.

Substantial Restraint of Competition

In several key provisions of the AML, the words 'substantial restraint of competition' appears. For example, in Articles 2(5) and 2(6), which define private monopolization and unreasonable restraint of trade, and Articles 10 and 15, which control acquisition of stocks and a merger respectively, these words are used. There must be a *substantial* restraint of competition (rather than a mere restraint of competition) when these provisions are applied.

According to a decision of the Supreme Court,[25] competition is substantially restrained if an enterprise or a group of enterprises can determine prices and other terms of business independent of market forces. This means that there exists a situation in which an enterprise or a group of enterprises have dominant power in a market and the price and other terms of business can, at least up to a degree, be manipulated by them.

Whether this situation exists or not must be decided on the basis of the specific set of facts involved in each case. Therefore, it is difficult to present the tests which can be applied uniformly to all cases. The FTC announced the guidelines concerning the regulation of mergers and acquisitions.[26] In those guidelines, the FTC states that the following tests are used. If there are these situations when a merger or acquisition is consummated, the merger or acquisition will be closely scrutinized: (1) if the market share of one or both of the parties to the merger is above 25 per cent, (2) if the ranking of the company in terms of market share after the merger is at the top and the market share is above 15 per cent, (3) if the ranking in terms of market share of the company after the merger is at the top and the difference in terms of market share between that company and other companies is great.

The above quantitative tests are only general guidelines by which the

[25] The Tōhō-Shintōhō case, Decision of the Supreme Court, 25 May 1954, *Minshū*, 8/5 (1954), 950 *et seq*.

[26] The merger guidelines by the Fair Trade Commission are entitled 'Administrative Procedure Standards for Examining Mergers, etc. by Companies (1980)' and included in Nakagawa, n. 3, above, pp. 79 *et seq*. and the guidelines on stockholdings are entitled 'Standards for Examination of Stockholding by Companies (1981)' and included ibid. 89 *et seq*.

FTC proceeds in investigating cases of mergers and acquisitions. They are by no means the conclusive criteria by which to judge that competition in a market is substantially restrained. Also there may be a need to use somewhat different methods when judging whether a cartel restrains competition substantially or a merger restrains competition substantially. However, the above figures may give a good starting-point even if they do not provide the conclusive tests when considering whether a merger, the creation of a monopoly or a cartel, or the activity of a trade association restrains competition substantially.

E. THE PUBLIC INTEREST

In General

The words 'contrary to the public interest' appear in two provisions in the AML: Article 2(5) (private monopolization) and Article 2(6) (unreasonable restraint of trade). There is an acute difference of views with regard to the meaning of this term with respect to Article 2(6). Although the words are used in Article 2(5), their meaning has never been the subject of debate. The reason is that whether or not the creation of a private monopoly is held illegal depends on the conditions of the relevant market, the powers of the accused party compared with those of competitors, the ease or difficulty of new entry, the possibility of imports and other forms of international competition, as well as many other economic factors, and the issue of whether a monopolization is contrary to the public interest can be adequately considered in connection with these factors.

However, when the FTC or courts have to decide whether an unreasonable restraint of trade (a cartel) is illegal or not, they must consider whether a cartel agreement is contrary to the public interest. To put it simply, the question is: can you hold a cartel agreement as illegal when it substantially restrains competition or should you prove that the cartel is contrary to the public interest *in addition to the fact that it restrains competition substantially*?

The Views of the Fair Trade Commission and the Majority of Commentators

The FTC and the majority of commentators[27] assert that 'contrary to the public interest' provided in Article 2(6) is the same as 'substantial restraint of competition' in the same article. In their view, the term 'contrary to the public interest' has no independent meaning apart from 'substantial restraint of competition'. The reason is that the basic philosophy of the

[27] See Matsushita, n. 19, above, pp. 57–67.

AML is the maintenance of competition and, therefore, public interest in the AML should be regarded as competition as such. Therefore, if competition is substantially restrained by a cartel, the public interest is injured by that very fact. This view also maintains that, if 'contrary to the public interest' is something other than 'substantial restraint of competition', in order to prohibit a cartel the FTC or the courts would have to prove that (1) the cartel restrains competition substantially *and* (2) the cartel is contrary to the public interest in other ways. This would make the prohibition of cartels very difficult. This view has been strongly influenced by the *per se* illegality doctrine developed in United States antitrust laws with regard to cartels.[28]

The View of the Business Community

There is a different view expressed by the Keidanren (the Federation of Economic Organizations) which represents the opinion of at least part of the business community.[29] Although the MITI has not officially expressed its view as to how the meaning of 'contrary to the public interest' should be interpreted, some of the private writings by MITI officials take the same point of view.[30] This view, in short, holds that the public interest in the AML includes not only competition but also other economic and social goals such as the measures to deal with pollution, depression, and preservation of morals as well as the protection of consumers and other social values. Once an agreement among enterprises to increase international competitiveness was regarded as one of such goals but not any more.

The holders of this view argue that a cartel or an agreement among enterprises to eliminate competition among themselves should not be held as a violation of the AML simply because it restrains competition substantially. There may be situations in which competition is substantially restrained but agreement to do so may serve a useful social purpose. For example, an agreement among enterprises jointly to cut back production in a depression serves the useful purpose of avoiding bankruptcy and preserving enterprises in the market even if competition among them is substantially restrained.

The View of the Supreme Court

The Supreme Court expressed its view of the meaning of 'contrary to the public interest' in the *Oil Cartel Price Fixing* case.[31] The Supreme Court took a middle-of-the-road approach and synthesized the above two

[28] *United States* v. *Socony-Vacuum Oil Co.*, 310 US 150 (1940).
[29] See Matsushita, n. 19, above, p. 60.
[30] See n. 29, above.
[31] Decision of the Supreme Court, 24, Feb. 1984, *Keishū*, 38/4(1984) 1287 *et seq.*

approaches. According to its view, the public interest in the AML is in principle the maintenance of competition, but there are exceptions. It states that 'contrary to the public interest' means in principle a situation in which competition is substantially restrained but there can be an exceptional situation in which an agreement among enterprises restrains competition substantially but has sufficient redeeming virtue to hold it lawful. In this situation, the FTC and courts should weigh the advantage of maintaining competition against what would be accomplished by such an agreement, and, if the advantages which accrue from the agreement are greater than those which would be accomplished through maintaining competition, the agreement should be held as not contrary to the public interest even though it restrains competition substantially.

The Supreme Court did not specifically show what those redeeming virtues should be. One can speculate, however, that the Supreme Court had in mind factors such as avoidance of pollution, preservation of good morals, and elimination of danger to public safety. Therefore, for example, if an agreement among enterprises is aimed at abolishing a substance which causes environmental pollution or a food additive which may be injurious to the human body, or is aimed at prohibiting publication of obscene literature, it may be regarded as having a sufficient redeeming virtue even if the agreement restrains competition among the participants substantially in the particular field of trade concerned.

Commentary

It seems that the view taken by the Supreme Court is the most balanced and appropriate one. The view taken by the FTC and the majority of commentators is pure and faithful to the philosophy of competition. However, if this interpretation is applied uniformly and without any exception at all, the result may not be a desirable one. For example, there could be a situation in which manufacturers of insecticide conclude an agreement whereby they jointly decide not to use an additive which may be a hazard to the environment and to public health. If the use of this substance is totally eliminated by this agreement, competition in purchasing the substance is abolished. At the same time, competition in selling the insecticide which contains this substance is eliminated. However, one can hardly say that this agreement should be prohibited by the AML. If one were to apply the prohibition to any agreement among enterprises which restrains competition without exception, this would be too stiff and inflexible.

On the other hand, the view held by the Keidanren seems to be too vague. In its view, there is no limitation to the scope within which the public interest in Article 2(6) of the AML should be interpreted. This will create instability in interpretation and, since a violation of Article 2(6) and Article 3 of the AML can be a criminal offence, an undefined scope for the interpretation of the public interest in Article 2(6) is highly undesirable. Also, if this view were to be adopted, it would indeed be difficult to prohibit cartels and collusive agreements since there are always some reasons for these as the proponents of the view of the FTC and the majority of commentators fear.

Compared with the two interpretational doctrines above, the view of the Supreme Court seems to be more balanced. It is based on the premiss that competition is the basic value in the AML and, therefore, this view is faithful to the philosophy of competition. It is also flexible in the sense that it allows some exceptions to the rule of competition if it is absolutely necessary for the purpose of accomplishing something of social or economic value. It should be emphasized that, in this doctrine, the prohibition of cartels and similar collusive activities is the principle and exceptions are allowed only in those situations where the valid reason for an agreement which restrains competition is sufficiently vindicated, and that therefore this doctrine is closer to the view of the FTC and the majority of commentators than to that of the Keidanren.

However, as mentioned before, the scope of exceptions to the rule of competition is not clear from a reading of this decision yet. This decision merely declares the general principle and a general direction to which the FTC and courts should look to reach a right and stable interpretational doctrine. Therefore, it is probably correct to say that the question of what should be the right kind of interpretation of the public interest in Article 2(6) is not settled yet.

2.5 The Enforcement Agency and the Procedure of the Anti-monopoly Law

A. THE FAIR TRADE COMMISSION AND ITS ORGANIZATION

In General

The enforcement of the AML is entrusted to the FTC and the courts. In brief, the FTC has the power to investigate suspected violations, hold an administrative hearing about the case, and determine whether there is a violation or not. A decision of the FTC is reviewable by the Tokyo High Court and the Supreme Court.

There are three types of legal consequence to a violation of the AML. First, the FTC proceeds against the violation and issues a cease-and-desist order. The FTC issues an order to impose an administrative surcharge on a party which is held to have engaged in a price cartel or any other cartel affecting price. This is an administrative process.

The second is an action by a private party to seek the recovery of damages sustained by the party on account of a violation of the AML. A private damage action can be brought under either Articles 25 and 26 of the AML or Article 709 of the Civil Code as a tort claim. Third, some violations of the AML are punishable as crimes. Among the above three, the administrative process by the FTC is most frequently used.

The Organization of the Fair Trade Commission

The FTC is an independent administrative commission and the agency created for the purpose of the enforcement of the FTC. Officially, the FTC is part of the Prime Minister's Office (see Fig. 2.1). However, no agency, including that of the Prime Minister, can exercise control over the decision-making of the FTC and, therefore, its independence with regard to the determination of violations, the choice of measures to be applied, and other forms of exercise of the enforcement power is guaranteed. The FTC is composed of one Chairman and four commissioners. Candidates for the Chairman and commissioners must be persons aged 35 or above and possess knowledge of law and economics. They are appointed by the Prime Minister with the consent of the House of Representatives and the House of Councillors, and the appointment of the Chairman must be certified by the Emperor. The term of office for the Chairman and the commissioners is five years. There is a secretariat attached to the Commission which has various sections and divisions.

As stated above, the appointment of the Chairman and commissioners is made by the Prime Minister with the consent of both Houses of the National Diet, and the budget of the FTC is, of course, decided by the National Diet. In this way, the appointment of the Chairman and commissioners can be influenced by political forces. The FTC must report its activities to the National Diet annually. However, once the appointments have been made and the budget has been decided, the FTC is independent from other administrative powers and political influences except for the fact that its decisions are reviewable by the courts.

The Powers of the Fair Trade Commission

The powers of the FTC can be classified into three categories: (1) administrative power, (2) quasi-legislative power, and (3) quasi-judicial power. The quasi-judicial power is that of enforcing provisions of the FTC by holding particular conduct as a violation of the AML and issuing an order which would impose on the violating party the obligation to refrain from the conduct. This is probably the core of the powers of the FTC. We will examine it in a later section. In this section, we will examine the administrative power and the quasi-legislative power.

The administrative power includes a variety of powers such as the

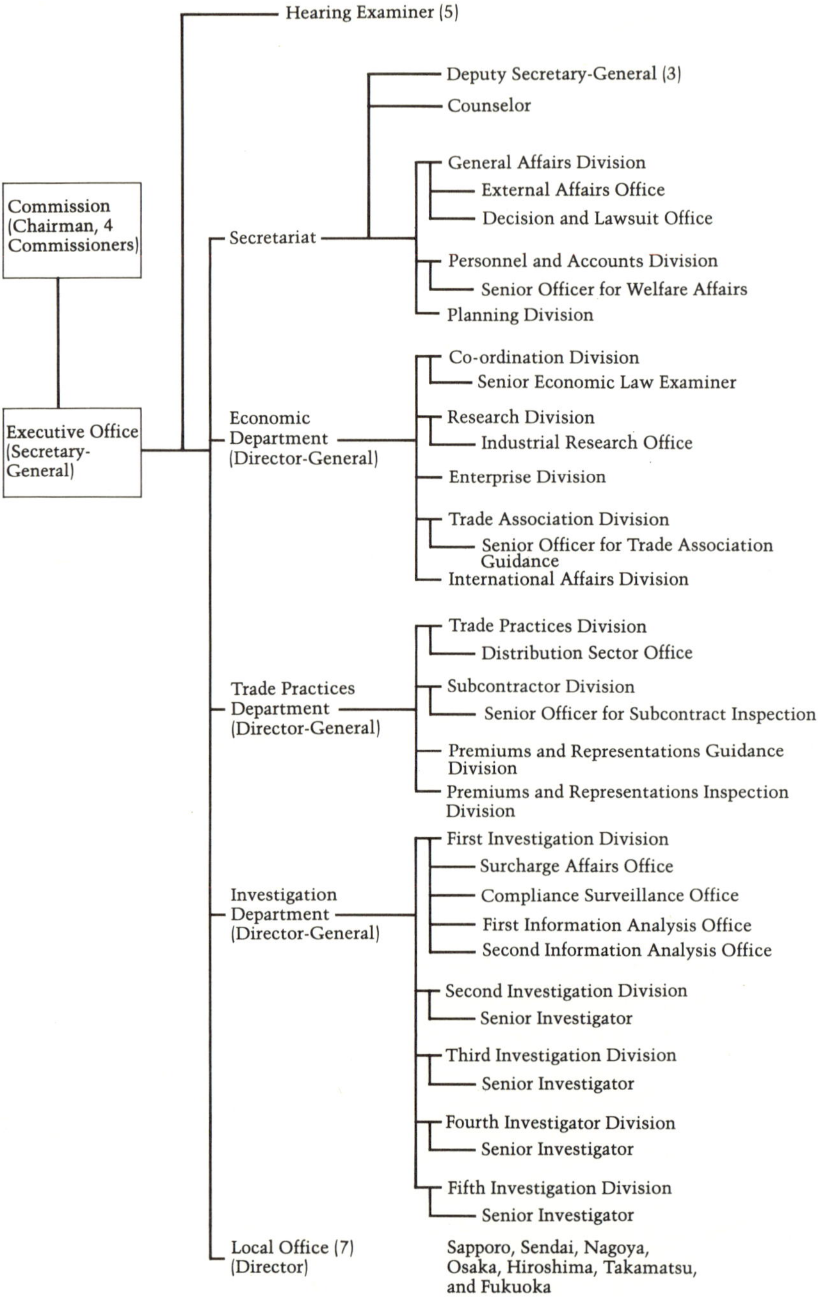

FIG. 2.1 Organization of the Fair Trade Commission (31 August 1991)

licensing of some agreements, consulting with other agencies, and requesting some dispositions from other agencies, and related matters. Among those, however, the power to license depression cartels, rationalization cartels, and fair competition codes are the most important.

Article 24.3 provides that the FTC can license an agreement among enterprises to deal with a depression (a depression cartel). When a depression comes, enterprises can agree on the terms of competition in order to deal with it such as cutting back production, and file the draft of such an agreement with the FTC. The FTC can license the agreement if it judges that the requirement for a depression cartel is satisfied. If an agreement is licensed under Article 24.3, it is exempted from the application of the AML.

Likewise Article 24.4 provides that the FTC can license an agreement among enterprises to rationalize their operations including an agreement to standardize the form of a product, the methods of testing a product, and related matters. When an agreement is licensed by the FTC, the agreement is exempted from the application of the AML.

Under the Law to Prevent Unreasonable Premiums, Representation, and Related Matters, enterprises are allowed to draw up a 'fair competition code', in which they agree on the terms of competition with regard to the maximum value of the premium and the ways in which they use representation including advertising of their commodities. When enterprises agree on a draft code, they are required to submit it to the FTC. The FTC examines the content and, if it judges that the draft satisfies the requirement for granting a licence, it gives a licence to the code. Once given a licence, the use of the code of competition is exempted from the application of the AML.

Some provisions of the AML require reporting or filing by enterprises of specific information with the FTC. They include: Article 8(2), which requires that, when enterprises organize a trade association, the details of the association must be reported; Article 6(2), which requires that when an enterprise concludes specific kinds of international contracts, as designated by the FTC, these must be reported to the FTC; and Article 15(2), which requires that when companies intend to merge, details must be reported to the FTC. In these situations the FTC receives reports filed by enterprises, and if there are any problems it takes appropriate measures.

Another important aspect of the FTC's administrative power is to consult other government agencies and to put requests to them. There are several laws which authorize agreements and cartels for a variety of purposes and some of them are enforced by other agencies. There are usually provisions in such laws which require that the enforcement agency must consult the FTC when it licenses an agreement or cartel. For example, under Article 34(1)–(5) of the Export and Import Transactions Law, the MITI is required to consult the FTC when it licenses an agreement (a cartel) between enterprises to restrict competition with regard to exports. The MITI is not bound by the result of such a consultation. However, the FTC is given the chance to express its view on the agreement from the standpoint of competition policy. Also, under the Small Business Organizations Law,[32] the MITI is required to obtain the consent of the FTC when it licenses an agreement between small enterprises to fix prices.

In some situations, the FTC is authorized to request other agencies to withdraw a licence to an agreement which restricts competition among enterprises. For example, under Article 34(9) of the Export and Import Transactions Law,[33] the FTC can request that the MITI withdraw a licence given to an export cartel or an import cartel on the grounds that the conditions which necessitated the licence no longer exist.

Recently the FTC has engaged in so-called 'preventive administration'. This means that the FTC issues a series of guidelines, announcements, and memos explaining the details of the enforcement policy of the FTC with regard to the matters concerned. Enterprises can study such guidelines and announcements and take the necessary steps to avoid violations. Sometimes these guidelines provide a consultation system in which enterprises discuss with the FTC the legality of their proposed conduct. If the FTC advises that the conduct in question does not contravene any provision of the AML, the enterprises are safe to engage in the conduct concerned. The idea of this system is to provide a way of preventing possible violations of the AML by enterprises.

One such example is 'the Anti-monopoly Law Guidelines Concerning Activities of Trade Associations', announced by the FTC in 1979. These guidelines classify conduct which trade associations may engage in into three categories, namely: (1) that which is regarded as unlawful in principle (such as price-fixing), (2) that which may be held as unlawful under some circumstances, and (3) that which is held lawful in principle. A trade association which intends to engage in a programme can submit the facts and data with regard to the programme and request the FTC's opinion concerning it. When the FTC, after reviewing the facts and data, expresses the view that the proposed programme is not a violation of the AML, the FTC is bound not be take any legal measure against it unless the facts and data submitted are false or the facts have changed, in which situation the FTC is required to withdraw its already expressed view before it takes any legal measure. This system is somewhat similar to the

[32] Chūshōkigyō Dantai Hō, Law 185, 1957.
[33] Yushutsunyū Torihiki Hō, Law 299, 1952.

negative clearance system used in the EC authority in enforcing Articles 85 and 86 of the Treaty of Rome.[34]

Our next enquiry turns to the quasi-legislative power of the FTC. This power of the FTC is the rule-making power. Full legislative power is, of course, vested only with the National Diet. However, under the AML, a wide scope of power is delegated to the FTC to make rules in some areas, and in those areas this power is practically equivalent to making law. Some examples are given.

Article 2(9) of the AML states that the FTC shall designate unfair business practices within the six categories provided for in the article. This means that the provisions in Article 2(9) are not directly applied to the conduct of enterprises. Unless the FTC designates a particular conduct, it is not subject to the prohibition as an unfair business practice. Formally this power of the FTC is nothing but an administrative act based on the delegation by law. However, in substance, the exercise of this power is not so dissimilar from the exercise of legislative power in the sense that the enforcement of the law entirely depends on the decision of the FTC.

Under Article 24.2 of the AML, the FTC is authorized to designate commodities regarding which resale price maintenance is exempted from the application of the AML. Resale price maintenance is generally held to be a violation of the AML except in the area of books and printed matter or commodities exempted by the FTC under this provision. Whether resale price maintenance is prohibited or not depends on the decision of the FTC. This is another example of the exercise of quasi-legislative power.

Beside the above, the FTC is empowered to make rules with regard to the adjudication procedure, the filing of reports concerning mergers and acquisitions, the establishment of trade associations, and the conclusion of international contracts. The way in which those rules are formulated affects the actual enforcement of the AML, and, in this sense, such powers may be classified as quasi-legislative.

B. THE ADMINISTRATIVE PROCEDURE BY THE FAIR TRADE COMMISSION (QUASI-JUDICIAL POWER)

In General

As above stated, the FTC is given quasi-judicial power which is probably the most important power of the FTC. Judicial power is, of course, vested with the Supreme Court and lower courts. However, under the AML, the

[34] See Korah, *An Introductory Guide to EEC Competition Law and Practice* (Oxford, 1990), 90.

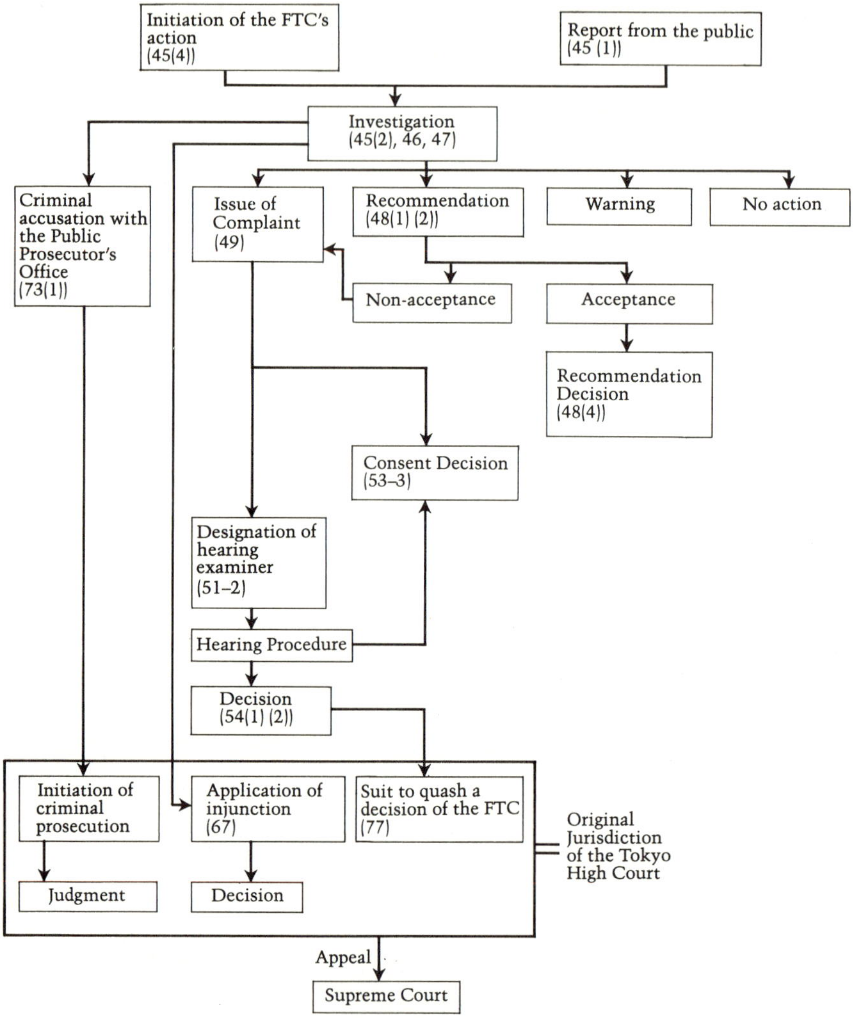

FIG. 2.2 Flow Chart of the Fair Trade Commission Procedures

Note: Figures in parentheses indicate the section number of the relevant provisions of the Antimonopoly Act.

FTC is given a wide scope of power to investigate, hold hearings, and decide whether a conduct is a violation of the AML. The FTC can issue an administrative order commanding a party in violation of the AML to cease and desist from the conduct of which they are accused. This entire process is carried out through an open tribunal and an adversarial proceeding is provided for.

Investigation

There are four ways in which an investigation by the FTC is initiated: (1) through information provided by a private citizen, (2) by notification of the Prosecutor General, (3) by notification of the Small Business Administration of the MITI, and (4) by an *ex-officio* decision of the FTC.

Under Article 45 of the AML, a person who thinks that there is a violation of the AML can inform the FTC of it and request appropriate action. However, the FTC is not obliged to initiate legal proceedings. In the *Newspaper Price Raising* case,[35] a consumer organization informed the FTC that there had been a price-fixing agreement behind the simultaneous price raising by the newspaper companies and requested a legal measure. The FTC did not initiate any legal proceedings and the consumer organization sued the FTC. The Supreme Court held that to inform the FTC under Article 45 was no more than a mere information-giving by a person and did not confer on the person the right to request the FTC to take any legal action.

However, in 1977, Article 45 was amended to incorporate a provision which states that, if a person notifies the FTC of a violation in writing with some evidence, the FTC must in turn notify the person of any action taken or the reason why no action has been taken, if that is the case.

The Prosecutor General is required to notify the FTC of a violation if he comes across a violation in the process of any criminal investigation.[36] This provision has never been invoked yet.

The Small Business Administration of the MITI is an agency in charge of protecting small businesses and is authorized to notify the FTC of a violation when it finds it in the process of its administrative activities.[37]

The FTC is continuously engaged in investigation to see whether there is a violation by its own staff members and, in the course of such investigations, some violations may be found.

When the FTC deems that there is enough evidence to initiate a formal investigation, it names investigatory attorneys from among the staff members of the Secretariat who will be in charge of the case concerned.

[35] Decision of the Tokyo High Court, 26 Apr. 1961, *Gyōsai Reishū*, 12/4 (1961), 933 *et seq*.

[36] Art. 74 of the AML.

[37] Art. 31 of the Law Establishing the Medium and Small Business Administration.

In the process of investigation, the FTC is authorized to use its compulsory power to examine any books and documents of the suspected enterprise, and other related matters. When the investigation is finished, a report will be submitted by the investigating attorneys to the Commission. If evidence is insufficient to initiate a formal proceeding, the FTC decides not to go any further.

Recommendation and Hearing

If there is sufficient evidence to initiate a proceeding, the FTC can either issue a recommendation or initiate a formal hearing. Article 48 of the AML stipulates that whenever there is a violation of the AML the FTC can issue a recommendation to the party engaged in conduct which violates the AML to refrain from the conduct in question and to take the necessary steps to eliminate the effect of the violation. A recommendation must specify the facts which are in violation and must be served on the party to whom it is addressed.

If the party accepts the recommendation, the FTC can issue a decision without the process of hearing along the same lines as the recommendation. This decision is called a 'recommendation decision'.[38]

When the FTC deems that there is a violation and that to open a hearing proceeding serves the public interest, it can initiate a hearing. A hearing can be conducted either by the Commission or by an examiner named by the Commission and this is the usual practice. When the FTC initiates the hearing procedure, it must prepare a formal complaint and serve it on the respondent.[39]

The hearing procedure is basically an adversarial process in which investigative attorneys named by the Commission act as the prosecuting party and are responsible for maintaining the accusations and allegations in the complaint. The respondent, usually represented by defence attorneys, is the defendant. He argues that the allegations and accusations in the complaint are not based on correct facts and the proper interpretation of the provisions of the AML.

When the hearing process is concluded, the examiner at the hearing prepares the draft decision and sends it to the Commission with records of the case and also to the respondent. The respondent can file with the Commission an objection to the draft. According to Article 53.2(2) of the AML, which was added by the 1977 amendment, the respondent can file with the Commission an objection even when the hearing being conducted by the examiner still continues.

[38] Art. 48 of the AML. In Japanese, it is 'kankoku shinketsu'.

[39] Art. 48 of the AML states that the Commission can delegate the authority to conduct hearings to hearing examiners. However, hearing examiners are explicitly excluded from rendering a decision.

The Commission decides the case on the basis of the draft decision, the records of the case, and the objection by the respondent, if any. A decision issued in this way may be called a formal decision.[40]

There is no requirement that the FTC must issue a recommendation before it initiates a hearing process. However, with rare exceptions,[41] it is the usual practice of the FTC to issue a recommendation first and, when the recommentation is rejected, to initiate a formal hearing process.

During the process of hearing, the respondent can state to the Commission that it admits the facts and accusations as written in the complaint and propose a measure which it will take to eliminate the effect of the illegal conduct in question. If the Commission regards this measure as appropriate, it terminates the proceedings at this point and issues a decision in line with the proposal. This decision is called a consent decision.[42]

A hearing procedure may take a long time before it comes to its conclusion. There may be a situation in which it is difficult to restore the original conditions which existed before the violation occurred or irreparable damage is caused if the conduct in question is allowed to continue until the FTC issues a decision. Therefore, if the FTC judges that such a situation exists, it can apply to the Tokyo High Court for a temporary injunction which would temporarily restrain the respondent from engaging in the conduct in question. For example, if a merger between two companies is at issue in a hearing, it would be extremely difficult to do away with the effect of the merger some years after it was consummated. Therefore, the Commission applies to the Tokyo High Court for a temporary injunction to stop the merger for a while. In the *Yawata–Fuji Steel Companies Merger* case,[43] the FTC applied for a temporary injunction to the Tokyo High Court which issued an injunction restraining the companies from consummating the proposed merger until the decision of the FTC was handed down. When the hearing is concluded, the Commission issues a decision and orders the repondent to refrain from the conduct which is held as a violation of the AML.

C. ADMINISTRATIVE REMEDIES

Cease-and-Desist Orders

When a decision is handed down, whether it is a formal decision, a recommendation decision, or a consent decision, the FTC usually issues

[40] In Japanese, it is 'seishiki shinketsu'.

[41] In the Komatsu-Bucyrus case (Decision of the FTC, 26 Oct. 1981, *Shinketsushū*, 26 (1980), 79 *et seq.*), the Fair Trade Commission initiated a hearing without issuing any recommendation.

[42] Art. 53.3 of the AML.

[43] Decision of the FTC, 30 Oct. 1970, *Shinketsushū*, 16 (1970), 50 *et seq.*

a cease-and-desist order to the respondent. A cease-and-desist order requires the party to whom it is addressed to refrain from engaging in the conduct which is held to be a violation and to take related measures such as, for example, to make publicly known the fact that the price cartel (for instance) has been cancelled. If the conduct has already ceased to exist by the time the decision is handed down, the FTC may issue a decision stating that the conduct was a violation.

The enforceability of a FTC decision is backed up by the criminal penalty. For non-compliance with a FTC decision and order, a non-penal fine is imposed before the decision becomes final,[44] and, after it has become final, a criminal fine is imposed.[45]

Administrative Surcharge

The administrative surcharge was introduced by the 1977 amendment. Before this amendment, the only available remedy to price-raising cartels was a cease-and-desist order. There was a criminal penalty but it was rarely invoked. A cease-and-desist order could only stop an unlawful cartel but no more. Therefore, when enterprises were held as having engaged in a price-raising cartel, the FTC only ordered the enterprises to cancel the cartel. Under this circumstance, enterprises could cancel the cartel and engage in another one later. Extra profit which they earned through the cartel remained untouched. This created the belief among the business community that cartels could be profitable.

To deal with this situation, the 1977 amendment introduced the provision for an administrative surcharge by which the FTC must impose a surcharge on enterprises which engage in a price-raising cartel or a cartel which affects price computed by a certain formula. This is provided for in Article 7.2 of the AML.

The purpose of the administrative surcharge is to take away the extra profit that enterprises which participated in a cartel must have earned by the cartel. Since it is difficult in practice to calculate the actual amount of extra profit earned in this way, a standard formula is used to calculate the extra profit, and this the amount is levied as the administrative surcharge.

An administrative surcharge is imposed on enterprises which were engaged in a price-raising cartel or a cartel which affected prices by an agreement among them to reduce the amount of production. It is computed on the basis of a certain percentage of the total sales of the enterprises which participated in the cartel activity during the period in which the cartel was effectively in force. In enterprises other than small enterprises, it is 6 per cent of the total sales of the enterprise during the period in which the cartel was effectively in force in areas other than

[44] Art. 97 of the AML.
[45] Ibid. Art. 90.

wholesale and retail (generally manufacturing areas). It is 1 per cent in the wholesale business and 2 per cent in the retail business. This percentage is based on the estimated average profit rate of enterprise in those areas of business. In small enterprises, the percentage is reduced to about half a per cent.

There is a statutory limitation to an administrative surcharge with regard to retroactivity. An administrative surcharge can retroactively be imposed on cartel activity up to three years prior to the order to pay an administrative fine being issued, but not before this time.

There is no discretion on the part of the FTC to decide whether to impose an administrative fine or not. It is mandatory on the FTC to impose an administrative fine whenever it deems that there is a price-raising cartel or a cartel which affects prices. However, if the amount of administrative surcharge is less than 500,000 yen, the FTC cannot impose it. Often the FTC imposes an administrative surcharge when a decision determines that there is a cartel. However, in cases where a cartel has ceased to exist, the FTC can impose on the parties which engaged in the cartel an administrative surcharge without such a decision.

Price-Reporting System

If enterprises raise their prices simultaneously by a cartel agreement, the FTC can order a cancellation of the agreement and prohibit the continuation of it. However, if prices are raised simultaneously by enterprises without any proof of a cartel agreement, the FTC cannot prohibit such parallel price rises since the existence of the cartel is not proved. Yet often prices of a product are simultaneously raised without any proof of a cartel. In an oligopolistic market, this often occurs. It may be that there was no cartel but prices went up simultaneously due to an oligopolistic interdependence of enterprises in the market. Or it may be that there was a cartel but it was carried out so skilfully that it was impossible to detect it.

The price-reporting system was introduced by the 1977 amendment to deal with this situation. Through this system, the FTC can order large enterprises to report the reasons for price rises when the prices they charge are raised simultaneously. Article 18.2 of the AML provides that the FTC can determine that there is a simultaneous price-raising and order the major enterprises in the market in which it takes place to report to it the reasons for such price-raising, if, in a market in which total sales of the product concerned are above 30 billion yen or more and the market share of the top three enterprises is 70 per cent or above, more than two major enterprises including the top-ranking enterprise raise their prices to the same or similar level, or by the same or similar percentage, within a three-month period. When the FTC has collected data concerning simultaneous price-raising under this provision, it must report to the National Diet a summary of such data.

Under this system, the FTC is authorized only to order a reporting of the reasons of price-raising but not to order the reduction of price. In this sense, therefore, it has nothing but a reporting duty. Even if the report filed by a major enterprise states that it merely followed the price leadership of the top-ranking enterprise, it is sufficient, since only a reporting is required.

However, this provision has worked rather effectively since the FTC is given a wide scope of authority to order filling of data, including sensitive data such as the cost of production and related matters, although enterprises are generally reluctant to submit such data to the FTC even if confidentiality is strictly kept. Consequently, enterprises tend to refrain from simultaneous price-raising which may induce the FTC to invoke this authority. In this sense, it may be said that this provision has worked as an informal deterrent to simultaneous price-raising.

D. JUDICIAL REVIEW

The Exclusive Jurisdiction of the Tokyo High Court

From a decision of the FTC, an appeal can be taken to the Tokyo High Court.[46] In this suit, the plaintiff is usually the party to whom the FTC decision and order is directed and the defendant is always the FTC. The Tokyo High Court has the exclusive jurisdiction as the court of first instance on legal actions for cancellation of FTC decisions. After the Tokyo High Court, the party can bring a petition to the Supreme Court, which is the final court. Therefore, as far as judicial review of FTC decisions is concerned, there is a two-step structure, namely, the Tokyo High Court and the Supreme Court. This means that the FTC proceeding is regarded as something similar to a judicial process and it is a substitute for the court of first instance.

The substantial evidence rule is recognized whereby the Tokyo High Court is bound by the facts as determined by the FTC in its examination of an appeal from a FTC decision when the facts found by the FTC are backed up by substantial evidence.[47] Therefore, the Tokyo High Court is empowered to examine only the 'matter of law' as opposed to the matter of fact. This means that it can in principle only examine whether the interpretation of law adopted by the FTC was correct or not. The Tokyo High Court is not authorized to engage in fact-finding if there is substantial evidence with regard to the case. However, whether or not there is substantial evidence is determined by the Tokyo High Court. In this

[46] Art. 77 of the AML. [47] Ibid. Art. 80.

sense, the Tokyo High Court has a considerable degree of discretion even as regards the matter of facts.

Standing to Sue

The question is: 'Who can bring an action in the Tokyo High Court for cancellation of a FTC decision?' The AML merely states that any person who is 'dissatisfied with the decision' can bring an action. There is, of course, a limit to the scope of persons who are entitled to bring an action against a FTC decision. In the jurisprudence of administrative law, it is recognized that a person whose legal interest is adversely affected by a disposition of the administrative agency can bring an action against it. This principle applies here also.

It is clear that a person to whom a decision of the FTC has been handed down holding a conduct in which the person was engaged as unlawful, and an order has been issued prohibiting the person from continuing this conduct, has the standing to challenge the FTC order since his legal interest is adversely affected. In a case in which a person is ordered to refrain from a certain conduct by a recommendation decision and order of the FTC, there is doubt whether or not the person possesses the standing to challenge it. We shall touch on this later.

The scope of standing to sue has been narrowly interpreted by courts and it is unlikely that any person other than the one to whom a FTC decision has been issued is held to have the standing to challenge it. We have already touched on the *Novo* case and the *Juice Representation* case.[48] In both cases, the issue is whether or not a person other than the one to whom a FTC decision is addressed can bring a legal action against the decision and seek for cancellation of it. As we noted, courts including the Supreme Court denied the standing of such a person to bring an action against the FTC decision for the reason that the interest which had been adversely affected by the FTC decision was merely a 'factual' interest or a 'reflective' interest. Judged from the decisions of both the Supreme Court and lower courts, it is safe to expect that the standing to challenge a decision of the FTC of a person other than the respondent in the FTC proceeding or the party to whom the decision is addressed will not be recognized.

Commentators criticize this attitude of the courts for the reason that it is sometimes extremely difficult to draw a line between 'the legal interest' and 'the factual interest' and that, as a general proposition, opportunities for citizens to challenge decisions of the administrative agencies should be

[48] The Novo case (Decision of the Supreme Court, 28 Nov. 1975, *Minshū*, 29/10 (1975), 1592 *et seq.*); The Juice case (Decision of the Supreme Court, 14 Mar. 1978, ibid. 32/2 (1978), 211 *et seq.*).

widely open.[49] It is true that so-called factual interests which are adversely affected by a decision of the administrative agency may be extremely important to the party concerned. It should be emphasized that to dismiss it altogether as factual as opposed to legal interest is too formalistic a viewpoint.

As noted already, another question is whether or not a person to whom a recommendation decision by the FTC has been issued can challenge it in the Tokyo High Court. We have already seen that the FTC issues a recommendation and, when the party to whom it is addressed accepts it, the FTC issues a recommendation decision. Therefore, although the person to whom a recommendation decision is directed is affected by it, the person has chosen to accept it, and this circumstance may affect the standing to bring a challenge to it in the Tokyo High Court.

This issue was discussed in the *Oil Cartel Recommendation Decision* case.[50] In this case, the respondent accepted a recommendation of the FTC that the respondent discontinue a cartel and the FTC handed down a recommendation decision holding the cartel unlawful and ordering the respondent to discontinue it. The respondent, however, brought an action in the Tokyo High Court and alleged that the recommendation decision should be revoked since the acceptance by the respondent of the recommendation was based on the previous practice of the FTC that there would be no criminal accusation against it if the respondent accepted the recommendation, but in fact the FTC did bring an accusation after the respondent had accepted the recommendation.

The Tokyo High Court dismissed the claim of the plaintiff (the respondent in the FTC proceeding) on the ground that the plaintiff could not bring a claim since the plaintiff was estopped from doing so by the fact that he had accepted the recommendation of the FTC and the action of the plaintiff would be contrary to his previous position as expressed in the acceptance with regard to the recommendation. This decision by the Tokyo High Court is based on the doctrine of estoppel which prohibits a person from claiming something which is contrary to what the person has already claimed. The case was taken on appeal to the Supreme Court which also held that the plaintiff had no standing to challenge the FTC recommendation decision.

E. CRIMINAL PENALTY

There are some provisions in the AML which provide for criminal penalty for violation. Article 98 stipulates that a private monopolization, an

[49] See Matsushita, n. 19, above, pp. 203–5.

[50] Decision of the Supreme Court, 4 Apr. 1978, *Minshū*, 32/3 (1978), 515 *et seq*.

unreasonable restraint of trade, and the conduct of a trade association which substantially restrains competition are punishable. Also, Article 90 provides a criminal penalty for violations of Article 6 (international contract) and of Article 8(1) (iii) and (iv) (restrictive activities of a trade association). Violations of the filing requirements are generally punishable under various provisions of the AML. However, there is no criminal provision for unfair business practices. The reason is that such practices are regarded as less serious offences of the AML as compared with a private monopolization and an unreasonable restraint of trade.

The FTC is obliged to bring a criminal accusation to the Prosecutor General when it deems that there is a breach of the AML which violates a criminal provision of the AML. However, it is interpreted that it belongs to the discretion of the FTC to decide whether or not to bring a criminal accusation, and, in fact, the FTC rarely does so.

An accusation by the FTC is the prerequisite for a criminal action by the Prosecutor General and unless there is an accusation by the FTC, the Prosecutor General cannot bring an indictment against the defendant. There have been few criminal actions brought against defendants. However, in the *Oil Cartel* case[51] (close examination of which will be made in a later section), a criminal indictment was made and some defendants were held guilty.

In the SII, the Japanese government promised that it would increase the criminal enforcement of the AML, and in 1991 the FTC brought a criminal accusation against a number of companies and individuals in the wrapping materials industry which were engaged in price cartel activities. Also a bill was introduced in the National Diet which would raise the maximum fine on corporations to 100 million yen. This bill passed both Houses of the National Diet in 1992 and is enforced since 1993.

F. RECOVERY OF DAMAGE

If damage to a property is caused by conduct which is in violation of the AML, the person whose property has been damaged can seek for recovery of it either on the basis of Articles 25 and 26 of the AML or Article 709 of the Civil Code, which provides for the right of recovery in tort cases.

Action to Recover Damage under Articles 25 and 26 of the Anti-monopoly Law

A person whose property has been damaged by conduct which amounts to private monopolization, unreasonable restraint of trade, or an unfair

[51] See Chap. 2, 2.7, below.

business practice can bring an action for recovery of the sustained damage to the enterprise which was engaged in the conduct.

Article 25(1) states that an enterprise involved in a private monopoly, unreasonable restraint of trade, or an unfair business practice and has caused damage to the property of a person shall be responsible for indemnification of the damage. It seems clear from this wording that, under Article 25(1) of the AML, only an 'enterprise' is responsible, but not other entities such as trade associations. Also only a conduct which has caused damage and which amounts to a private monopoly, an unreasonable restraint of trade, or an unfair business practice is actionable. With regard to other conduct which violates the AML, such as an illegal merger or acquisition, a person who suffers damage by such conduct must seek a recovery under Article 709 of the Civil Code.

Article 25(2) of the AML states that the defendant in a case in which Article 25(1) is invoked cannot escape from liability by proving that the defendant had no malicious intent or no fault. This means that liability under this article is a no-fault liability and the plaintiff need not prove an intention or fault on the part of the defendant.

Article 26 states that to bring an action on the basis of Article 25 of the AML, a decision of the FTC which holds the conduct in question unlawful under the AML must have been handed down and become finalized. It can be a formal decision, a consent decision, or a recommendation decision. However, there must be some kind of FTC decision before the plaintiff can invoke Article 25.

The Tokyo High Court has exclusive jurisdiction over cases in which an action under Articles 25 and 26 of the AML is involved. After the Tokyo High Court decision, of course, an appeal can be taken to the Supreme Court.

Tort Claims under Article 709 of the Civil Code

There have been controversies as to whether or not a person whose property has been damaged by an act which is a violation of the AML can bring a tort claim under Article 709 of the Civil Code, which generally provides for recovery of damage caused by tortious conduct. There are both positive and negative schools of thought on this issue. Recently, however, the predominant view maintains that a person whose property has been damaged by an act which amounts to a violation of the AML can recover the damage under Article 709 of the Civil Code. Also court decisions including Supreme Court decisions note that an action can be brought under Article 709 of the Civil Code.[52]

Therefore, a person who intends to bring an action for recovery of

[52] See Matsushita, n. 19, above, pp. 205–11.

damage caused by conduct of an enterprise which is a violation of the AML can choose either to bring it under Articles 25 and 26, if a FTC decision on the conduct has been handed down, or to bring it under Article 709 of the Civil Code as a tort claim.

Both have advantages and disadvantages. If the plaintiff chooses to utilize Articles 25 and 26 of the AML, he need not prove an intention or fault on the part of the defendant as long as a FTC decision holding it unlawful has been handed down. On the other hand, he can bring this action only in the Tokyo High Court. Also the scope of action is limited to private monopolization, unreasonble restraint of trade, or an unfair business practice.

If he chooses to bring an action under Article 709 of the Civil Code, there is no requirement for a FTC decision holding the conduct a violation of the AML before a damage action can be brought. Also the court which has jurisdiction is determined by the rules in the Civil Procedure Code. (Usually the district court which has the jurisdiction in the area in which the defendant resides is empowered to handle the case.) There is no limitation to the scope of conduct covered. Therefore, conduct other than private monopolization, unreasonable restraint of trade, and an unfair business practice can be challenged under Article 709. On the other hand, if the plaintiff chooses to bring an action under Article 709 of the Civil Code, he must prove an intention or fault of the defendant.

Linkage between Unlawful Conduct and Damage

When a plaintiff brings an action for the recovery of damage caused by conduct which is a violation of the AML, he must prove that there is a linkage (a cause and result relationship) between the unlawful conduct and the damage which he sustained. This applies regardless of whether an action is brought under Articles 25 and 26 of the AML or Article 709 of the Civil Code.

There are several court decisions, including those of the Supreme Court, with regard to the proof of this linkage. Generally speaking, however, a stringent rule has been adopted by courts with regard to this proof and, as a result, it is difficult for the plaintiff to prove this linkage. A case in point is the *Oil Cartel Price Fixing* case.[53]

In this case, petroleum refineries and wholesalers concluded an agreement among themselves to raise the price of petroleum products. The products were sold from the refineries–wholesalers to jobbers and then to retailers. The plaintiffs who brought a claim for recovery of damage under Article 709 of the Civil Code maintained that price-fixing at the

[53] Decision of the Supreme Court, 2 July 1987, *Minshū*, 41/5 (1987), 785 *et seq.*; Decision of the Supreme Court, 8 Dec. 1989, ibid. 43/11 (1988), 259 *et seq.*

level of refineries–wholesalers pushed up the jobbers' price and then the retail prices at which the plaintiffs purchased the products.

The Supreme Court held that to recover the damage caused by the conduct in question, the plaintiffs must show that the agreement among the refineries–wholesalers pushed up the prices charged to jobbers, that the retail prices went up, and also that the subsequent economic events which occurred between the time the price was raised by the agreement and the time at which the plaintiffs purchased the products did not affect the price at retail level. The Supreme Court held that the plaintiffs did not prove this last requirement and, therefore, recovery was denied. It would be quite difficult to prove that the subsequent economic events did not affect the retail price and, as long as this rule of proof prevails, plaintiffs will have little chance for recovery of damage. There is no case so far in which the plaintiff has succeeded in gaining the recovery of damage caused by an action which is in violation of the AML.

A suggestion has been made that the FTC as the administrative agency with expertise on such matters should provide assistance to a plaintiff who brings an action for the recovery of damage caused by a violation of the AML by way of filing its view in the court in which such a cause is pending and by providing economic data concerning the case.

In 1991, the FTC announced a detailed programme for providing private plaintiffs with documents and materials for the proof of damage when plaintiffs and/or courts request them.

2.6 Monopolies, Mergers, and Monopolistic Situations

A. IN GENERAL

The control of private monopolization is one of the 'three main pillars' of the AML together with the prohibition of unreasonable restraint of trade and unfair business practices. A private monopolization signifies that a powerful enterprise accomplishes a monopoly by excluding or controlling the business activities of other enterprises and stifles competition in a market. As touched upon later, a private monopolization is defined in Article 2(5) and is prohibited by the former part of Article 3. It is basically the control of the 'conduct' of an enterprise as opposed to the control of the 'structure' of an industry.

There are two other related rules in the AML. One is the control of mergers and acquisitions as provided for in chapter 4 of the AML. That is the control of concentration of business power by mergers and acquisitions. In relation to the prohibition of private monopolization, it is a preventive measure, since a private monopolization is possible only if the party who monopolizes possesses sufficient economic power, so by controlling mergers and acquisitions and thereby arresting the tendency towards a concentration of economic powers, it is possible indirectly to prevent a private monopolization.

The other is the control of monopolistic situations. Since the prohibition of a private monopolization is prohibition of conduct directed towards monopolizing a market, this cannot be invoked, even if an industry is highly monopolistic or oligopolistic, as long as the oligopoly is the result of natural growth, innovative management, or a major development of technology by one enterprise. In such a situation, there is no 'wrongful conduct' which is responsible for the monopoly or oligopoly. Yet there is no competition in the market any more and undesirable economic results may be brought about. The control of monopolistic situations is designed to deal with a situation in which there is a monopoly or oligopoly with undesirable economic consequences and yet there is no evidence that the party in the monopolistic situation has engaged in a 'monopolization' by excluding or controlling thc activities of other enterprises.

B. PRIVATE MONOPOLIZATION

Definition

Article 2(5) of the AML defines private monopolization as: 'such business activity by which any enterprise, individually, or by combination or conspiracy with other enterprises, or in any other manner, excludes or controls the business activities of other enterprises, thereby causing, contrary to the public interest, a substantial restraint of competition in any particular field of trade.' The former part of Article 3 prohibits a private monopolization.

The above definition suggests that a private monopolization can be conduct by an enterprise or that of several enterprises in concert, that it involves either 'exclusion' or 'control' by an enterprise of the business activities of other enterprises and that competition in the relevant market is substantially stifled. One question is whether or not it is necessary that the enterprise which is engaged in a private monopolization has a certain degree of economic power in terms of the market share and the size of assets. There is no wording in the AML which clarifies this question. However, by the very nature of private monopolization, it is impossible for a small and weak enterprise to exclude or control the business activity of other enterprises and eliminate competition in a market. Therefore, naturally, it is a large enterprise in terms of market share or otherwise which is capable of committing a private monopolization.

Exclusion

'Exclusion' is not defined in Article 2(5) of the AML. Generally, an exclusion can be either an activity of one powerful enterprise, such as predatory pricing wherein the enterprise sets its price at a very low level (below the cost of production) and eliminates the business activities of competing enterprises, or activities in which several enterprises act in concert, such as an exclusive dealing arrangement agreed upon between a manufacturer and dealers which prevents enterprises competing with the manufacturer from using the dealers and denies access to the dealers' network.

However, since there is no definition or limitation in Article 2(5) of the AML as regards the forms of exclusion, any type of conduct, either engaged in by a single enterprise or a number of enterprises, can be an exclusion in the sense of Article 2(5).

Even though there are only a handful of cases in which private monopolization has been challenged, they serve as valuable precedents. We will examine only one of those decisions: the *Yukijirushi* case.[54]

In the *Yukijirushi* case, the Yukijirushi Milk Products Company ('Snow Brand', hereafter referred to as 'Yukijirushi') and the Hokkaidō Butter Company (hereafter referred to as 'Hokkaidō') jointly attempted the exclusion of competing manufacturers of milk products in Hokkaidō Island. Originally these two companies were one entity, the Hokkaidō Rakunō Company, which held a predominant position in Hokkaidō Island until the end of the Second World War. It was split into Yukijirushi and Hokkaidō as a result of the deconcentration measure after the War. Enterprises producing milk products purchased milk from farmers and those two companies held the market share of about 70 per cent of total milk collection.

It was quite important for the farmers to raise finance to purchase cows, and, at that time, there was only one financial institution available—the Nōrin Chūo Kinko (a semi-public entity; hereafter referred to as 'Nōrin'). The farmers organized themselves into the Federation of Farmers Co-operative in Hokkaidō Island (hereafter referred to as the 'Federation'). Yukijirushi and Hokkaidō on the one hand and Nōrin and the Federation on the other were linked together through stock-holdings and interlocking directorates. Those four parties jointly agreed to the following. (1) Nōrin would issue loans to farmers on the condition that they would not sell any milk to enterprises competing with Yukijirushi and Hokkaidō, and the Federation would guarantee repayment on the same condition. (2) Nōrin would provide higher loans in areas where competitors of Yukijirushi and Hokkaidō were strong compared to those

[54] FTC Decision, 28 July 1956, *Shinketsushū*, 8 (1957), 12 *et seq.*

areas where their competitors were weak. (3) Directors of Yukijirushi and the Federation would solicit farmers to take loans from Nōrin and, in doing so, they would indicate to farmers that the loans were made conditional on the exclusive sale of milk to Yukijirushi and Hokkaidō, and that if the farmers sold milk to competing companies, there would be other disadvantages to the farmers.

The plan was ruthlessly executed. Nōrin introduced 1 billion yen in loans (a very large amount of money at that time) for a period of three years in Hokkaidō Island on the above conditions, and competing companies were deprived of a source of supply of milk and had great difficulty in pursuing their business operations.

The FTC initiated proceedings against the above practice and held, in a consent decision, that the conduct of Yukijirushi and Hokkaidō amounted to a private monopoly in the sense of excluding the business activities of competing enterprises in purchasing milk. As to the conduct of Nōrin and the Federation, the FTC held that this amounted to unfair business practices. All the respondents were ordered to discontinue the practices.

In the above case, although Yukijirushi and Hokkaidō were held to have committed a private monopolization, the FTC held that Nōrin and the Federation were engaged in unfair business practices. Commentators point out[55] that this aspect of the decision raises a problem, since, in the above situation, all four parties participated in a private monopoly as 'equal partners' and should be given the same legal treatment. Unfair business practices are regarded as offences somewhat lighter than a private monopolization and, in fact, no criminal penalty is attached to unfair business practices. Therefore, commentators say that to treat Nōrin and the Federation as having commmitted offences somewhat less serious than that committed by the other two parties (Yukijirushi and Hokkaidō) is unjustifiable. Without analysing the details of these arguments, it should be noted that these criticisms are well-grounded.

Control

The other type of private monopolization is 'control' by one enterprise of the business activities of other enterprises. Here again, there is no definition of control in Article 2(5) of the AML and this indicates that there is no limit to it as far as forms of conduct are concerned. As explained below, however, in the previous court and FTC decisions, there are two types of conduct which constitute a control under Article 2(5) of the AML. One is a direct control and the other is an indirect control. It is good to explain both by citing cases decided by the courts and the FTC.

[55] See Matsushita, n. 19, above, p. 74.

In the *Tōyō Seikan* case,[56] the issue was direct control. The Tōyō Seikan, K.K. (a large tin can manufacturing company hereafter referred to as 'Tōyō') had a market share of 54 per cent of the tin can manufacturing market in Japan. It acquired stocks of four competing companies, that is: (1) Hokkai Seikan, K.K. (hereafter referred to as 'Hokkai'), (2) Shikoku Seikan, K.K., (3) Honshū Seikan, K.K., and (4) Mikuni Kinzoku, K.K. Tōyō controlled the four companies through holding stocks and through interlocking directorates. Tōyō and the four companies together (the Tōyō Group) held a market share of 74 per cent of the Japanese tin can manufacturing market. The company which ranked second after the Tōyō Group was the Daiwa Seikan, K.K. (hereafter referred to as 'Daiwa'), which had a market share of 23 per cent. This meant that the Japanese tin can manufacturing market was dominated by one group (the Tōyō Group) and Daiwa.

The acquisition of stock by Tōyō was carried out over a period of several decades. The acquisition by Tōyō of the Hokkai stock was of the greatest importance and so we will examine this aspect closely. Hokkai was originally part of Tōyō before the end of the Second World War. A deconcentration measure was applied to Tōyō and one part of the company was separated out and Hokkai was created.

However, Tōyō attempted to control the business activities of Hokkai right from the beginning and acquired Hokkai stock through a second party. It established a vocational school (which later became a junior college) and the school acquired Hokkai stock. Tōyō controlled the activities of Hokkai indirectly by controlling the management of the school. In this way, Tōyō held 29 per cent of the outstanding stocks of Hokkai in 1972, the year in which a FTC decision was issued.

Tōyō attempted to annex Hokkai by way of a merger. For this purpose, it was important to prevent competition between the two companies from occurring and to keep the business activities of Hokkai within a certain limit, both in terms of geography and also of product lines. The policy of Tōyō was to limit the business area of Hokkai to Hokkaidō Island. When Hokkai proposed building a factory in the Saitama Prefecture near Tokyo, Tōyō accepted the plan on condition that the President of Tōyō became the President of Hokkai and that the types of cans which Hokkai was allowed to sell were restricted.

Tōyō held stocks of the other three companies and directors and high-ranking officials of Tōyō were also directors of the three companies. The three companies were also used by Tōyō as subcontractors to supply various types of can to Tōyō.

The FTC deemed these stock-holdings and interlocking directorates,

[56] FTC Decision, 18 Sep. 1972, *Shinketsushū*, 19 (1973), 87 *et seq.*

together with the conditions which Tōyō attached to Hokkai concerning its manufacturing and sales activities, amounted to the control of the business activities of other enterprises and a private monopolization, and issued a recommendation. Tōyō accepted the recommendation and a recommendation decision was issued. By this recommendation decision, Tōyō was ordered to divest itself of more than 1.2 million Hokkai stocks and to withdraw the restrictive conditions which it had attached to the building of the factory and the sale of products.

Some of the customers of Tōyō (food companies which used cans) initiated programmes for in-house tin can manufacturing by introducing technology from steel companies. Tōyō regarded in-house manufacturing as basically undesirable and the Tōyō Group refused to supply cans to those customers which also engaged in in-house tin can manufacturing. Daiwa, the second-ranking company, followed suit and likewise refused to supply cans to those customers. In this way, in-house tin can manufacturing by food companies was eliminated. The FTC regarded this as an exclusion of the tin can manufacturing activities of other enterprises and ordered Tōyō to refrain from refusing to supply cans to customers which also engaged in in-house tin can manufacturing.

The above case can be regarded as one of direct control. Tōyō held the control of the four enterprises through stock-holdings and interlocking directorates. What is not so clear is the reason why the FTC did not order Tōyō to divest itself of stocks of the three companies other than Hokkai. It may be that the FTC judged that the core of this monopolistic structure was the link between Tōyō and Hokkai and, as long as this linkage was abolished, there would be room for competition in the tin can manufacturing market.

In the *Noda Soy Sauce* case,[57] the issue was of one indirect control. In this case, the Noda Soy Sauce Company (hereafter referred to as 'Noda'), which had the trade mark 'Kikkoman' (and whose trade name later changed to the Kikkoman Company), held a market share of 37 per cent in the Tokyo market in soy sauce. Although there were numerous producers of soy sauce in Japan, most of them sold soy sauce only in local markets. There were only four companies which sold soy sauce on a nation-wide scale. Those companies were Noda, Yamasa, Higeta, and Marukin.

There was a peculiar structure in the soy sauce industry. The market was highly oligopolistic and Noda was the leading company. Products were highly differentiated by product grade or rankings. There were three grades of soy sauce which were known as 'Supreme', 'Superior', and

[57] Decision of the Tokyo High Court, 15 Dec. 1957, *Kōsai Minshū*, 10/10 (1957), 743 *et seq*.

'Best' in descending order from high to low. The grades were reflected in price—there was a price difference between 'Supreme' products and 'Superior' products and the same was true with respect to 'Superior' products and 'Best' products. Originally the grades were determined by quality. However, there was no objective criterion for judging the quality of soy sauce, so price became the indicator of the grade.

Noda, Yamasa, Higeta, and Marukin were regarded as the producers which produced and sold soy sauce of 'Supreme' grade. Among those four companies, however, the position and prestige held by Noda was predominant. It was Noda which set prices and the other three followed. It could not be otherwise, since if any other company had set its price below that set by Noda, its products would be regarded as being of lower grade, such as 'Superior' or 'Best'. No company could set its price higher than that set by Noda, since, if it had, even though the product belonged to the same grade as that of Noda, it would lose sales. As a consequence, the prices of soy sauce set by those four companies were always the same. The normal pattern was that Noda set its price first and soon after that the other three set their prices at the same level.

In 1950, Noda issued a 'request' to wholesalers and retailers 'asking' them to raise their wholesale prices and retail prices to certain levels indicated by Noda. Even though this request was in the form of a recommendation or suggestion, there was a *de facto* pressure exerted on wholesalers and retailers to comply with Noda's sales policy. To those wholesalers and retailers unwilling to go along with Noda's request, a threat was made to cut off supply of the products. Therefore, they raised their prices in accordance with the request by Noda. In a few days, Yamasa, Higeta, and Marukin issued similar requests to wholesalers and retailers and their prices went up to the same level as that of Noda's products.

The FTC initiated an action against Noda, opened a hearing and held that the conduct of Noda amounted to a private monopolization. In its decision, the FTC stated that Noda controlled the decisions of Yamasa, Higeta, and Marukin to raise their wholesale and retail prices by raising the wholesale and retail prices of its own products. The FTC noted that, whereas normally 'control' in the sense of Article 2(5) of the AML meant a direct control by an enterprise of the business activities of other enterprises, 'indirect' control could be included within this scope since there was no statutory limitation to its scope.

The gist of the decision was that, given the peculiar market structure in the soy sauce industry with its high degree of oligopoly and firmly established grading of products, Noda could effectively cause Yamasa, Higeta, and Marukin to raise their wholesale and retail prices by raising its own prices, and that this amounted to an indirect control by Noda of the business activities of Yamasa, Higeta, and Marukin.

An appeal was taken by Noda to the Tokyo High Court and then to the Supreme Court. The Tokyo High Court supported the decision of the FTC on the ground that control in Article 2(5) was not circumscribed by any definition and could be interpreted liberally, and that it could include indirect control. The Supreme Court did not rule on this issue.

The decisions in the *Noda Soy Sauce* case are regarded as confirming the interpretation that the term 'control' in Article 2(5) can include a wide range of control. In the *Noda Soy Sauce* case, Noda did not have any direct contact with Yamasa, Higeta, and Marukin. All it did was to set the prices of its own products. However, under the oligopolistic structure and a high degree of product differentiation in terms of product grading, the action of Noda touched off parallel actions by the other three companies and this was held as an indirect control.

There is a view that this concept of control is too wide, since the term control should only mean that an enterprise issues a directive to other enterprises or otherwise exerts direct pressure over them to make them conform to its policy. According to these views, the pressure exerted on wholesalers and retailers by Noda to raise their prices of Noda's products could be held as control of the business activities of other enterprises but no more. On the other hand, there are commentators who maintain that, as mentioned by the Tokyo High Court, the wording of Article 2(5) does not exclude the interpretation that 'control' encompasses conduct in which no direct contact with other enterprises is involved and yet which produces a strong impact on the decision-making of the other enterprises. They maintain that, so long as such an interpretation is not prohibited, it should be adopted in view of the fact that the measure to deal with oligopoly is an important issue in the enforcement of the AML.[58]

Conduct or Structure?

A question which arises when we review the decisions such as that in the *Noda Soy Sauce* case is whether the prohibition of private monopolization is the prohibition of conduct or structure. The language of Article 2(5) clearly requires that there be 'exclusion' or 'control' by an enterprise of the business activities of other enterprises and, in this sense, the prohibition of private monopolization is the prohibition of a particular conduct. However, the market structure in which the conduct at issue took place vitally affected the decision of the courts and the FTC when evaluating it in light of the AML and, in this connection, the structure of the relevant market is not entirely a separate issue. Conduct such as resale price maintenance (which was at issue in the *Noda Soy Sauce* case) may not constitute a control of other enterprises if it is regarded as a separate issue from the structure of the market. However, when it is exercised in

[58] On this issue, see Matsushita, n. 19, above, pp. 78–80.

the setting of the market characterized by oligopoly and a high degree of product differentiation, its effect may spread beyond the products of the party exercising it and vitally influence the decisions of enterprises competing with that party to adopt similar practices. In this sense, the structure of the relevant market is also an important factor to be considered.

C. MERGERS AND ACQUISITIONS

In General

Provisions in chapter 4 of the AML (Articles 9–18) are devoted to the control of mergers and acquisitions. On the whole, the role of provisions in this chapter is regarded as that of preventive measures in relation to the prohibition of private monopolization. It is usually a large enterprise with some market powers which is capable of engaging in a private monopolization and often a large enterprise with a high concentration of economic power comes into being as a result of a merger and acquisition. Therefore, it is important to prevent an excessive concentration of economic power in the hands of one enterprise in order to prevent a private monopolization. Articles 9, 9.2, and 11 provide for the control of a general concentration of economic power, and the other articles are devoted to the control of a specific concentration of economic power.

Prohibition of Holding Companies

Article 9 of the AML prohibits holding companies. A holding company is defined in Article 9(2) of the AML as a company whose major business is to hold stocks of other companies and to control them. Therefore, companies which engage in business and own subsidiaries do not come under the purview of Article 9, since, in those cases, they carry out their own business as well as owning subsidiaries. Companies owning subsidiaries and yet doing business of their own may be called 'operating holding companies' in contrast to a 'pure holding company', which is defined in Article 9(2) of the AML.

The peculiarity of Article 9(1) is that it prohibits the establishment of a holding company regardless of whether the holding company in question causes an anti-competitive impact in a market, and, in this sense, the prohibition is applicable as long as the form of a holding company is used. The reason for this formalistic prohibition, as we have seen, can be traced back to legislative history and the experience of the period before and during the Second World War. Before and during the War, there were 'zeibatsu' combinations in Japan which controlled the major sectors of the economy and wielded the dominant power over the economy. Those *zeibatsu* combinations were characterized by the holding company system in which a holding company controlled stocks of various companies which belonged to the same group. For example, in the Mitsui Zeibatsu, the Mitsui Headquarter Company (which was a holding company) held stocks of major companies which belonged to the Mitsui Group.[59]

When they were dissolved and the AML was enacted, the legislative policy was adopted that the prohibition of forms of business which could be used as a tool for controlling industries should encompass as wide an area as possible. Therefore, it was thought that the prohibition of holding companies would be useful to prevent the resurgence of *zaibatsu* combinations.

At present, the prohibition of holding companies under Article 9(1) is regarded as a preliminary preventive measure in relation to the prohibition of private monopolization. As touched upon earlier, the provisions in chapter 4 of the AML, of which Article 9(1) is part, are devoted to the prevention of private monopolization. Commentators explain that, among those provisions, the prohibition of holding companies is designed to arrest the growth of a monopoly at a very preliminary stage and, in this sense, it can be classified as a preliminary preventive measure.[60]

However, a holding company may not produce an anti-competitive effect. It may be a useful tool for achieving some business purposes. Therefore, the prohibition of holding companies has been criticized by business groups as an outmoded remnant of the period immediately after the Second World War.[61] Indeed, it would be desirable to amend Article 9(1) so that only a holding company which produces or tends to produce an anti-competitive effect would be prohibited.

Quantitative Limitation of Stock-Holding

Article 9.2, which was introduced into the AML as part of the 1977 amendment, prohibits a large company engaged in business other than financial services from holding stocks of another company above the value of its own capital, or its net worth, whichever is greater. A large company is defined as a company whose capital is 10 billion yen or more or whose net worth is 30 billion yen or more. There are some exceptions to this prohibition in designated business areas in which a large amount of capital is required and there is a high degree of business risk, such as the development of nuclear energy, space research, and ocean development.

[59] On *zaibatsu* combinations, see Bisson, *Dissolution of Zaibatsu in Japan* (Berkeley, Calif., 1954).

[60] Matsushita, n. 19, above, pp. 82–3.

[61] Keidanren (The Federation of Economic Organizations), *Keidanrenno Dokkinhōkankei Ikenshū* (*A Collection of Views of Keidanren on Anti-monopoly Law Issues*) (Tokyo, 1982), 16.

When this provision was introduced in 1977, the legislative purpose was explained as preventing trading companies from holding an excessive amount of stock of other companies. It was felt that, if trading companies held excessively large number of stocks of other enterprises, it would contribute to an increase in the general concentration of business power even if it might not produce immediate anti-competitive effects in a given market. Therefore, the framers of this provision thought that an upper limit should be established to the holding of stocks by large companies. Companies in financial services are excluded from the scope of Article 9.2 because their stock-holding is restricted by Article 11.

Article 11 prohibits, with some exceptions, financial companies, which include those engaged in banking, securities exchange, and insurance, from holding stocks of other companies above 5 per cent (with regard to insurance companies, 10 per cent) of the outstanding stocks of the acquired company. Here again the legislative intent is to prevent banks and other financial entities from exercising excessive influence over other companies or an industrial sector.

Acquisition and Holding of Stocks

Article 10(1) of the AML states that if, as the result of acquisition of stocks by one company of another company, competition in a market tends to be substantially restrained, the acquisition of stocks is unlawful. It also states that an acquisition of stocks by a company through means which amount to an unfair business practice is prohibited. Article 10(2) stipulates criteria for the filing requirements with regard to an acquisition of stocks. Article 13 prohibits the interlocking directorates and Article 14 prohibits an acquisition of stocks by a person other than a company if this tends to restrain competition substantially in a market.

Under Article 10(1) of the AML, an acquisition of stocks by one company of another company is prohibited if, as the result of such acquisition, competition in a market tends to be substantially restrained. The requirement that competition must tend to be substantially restrained, provided for in Article 10(1), is common with that in Article 15(1), which provides for the merger control. There are two sets of guidelines which contain the details of the control for Article 10(1) and also Article 15(1).[62] We will discuss them in connection with the merger control later.

Article 10(1) deals with the situation in which a company acquires stocks of another company and controls the acquired company through the ownership of stocks, and yet each company stays a separate company. Here the question is how much stock acquisition and holding by one company of another company is necessary to constitute control by the acquiring company of the acquired company. The FTC issued guidelines

[62] See n. 26, above.

on acquisitions and holdings of stocks by one company of another company in 1981 which set out the details as follows.

There is control if: (1) stocks of another company make up more than 50 per cent of a company's outstanding stocks, or (2) if the acquired company amounts to a 'related company' as defined in the rules on financial statements issued by the Minister of Finance.[63]

Beside the above, there is control if: (3) the acquiring company holds more than 25 per cent of the outstanding stocks of the acquired company, (4) if the acquiring company holds more than 10 per cent but less than 25 per cent of the outstanding stocks of the acquired company and is the first-ranking stockholder, or the acquiring company and the acquired company are in a competitive relationship, or (5) companies jointly hold stocks of another company in the form of a joint venture and the holding companies are in a competitive relationship. In the above situations (3)–(5), there are some additional conditions such as the distribution of stocks among stockholders and the difference in terms of ratio of stockholding and related matters.

If, as the result of control through stock-holding by a company of another company, competition in a market tends to be substantially restrained, then the acquisition of stocks is held unlawful.

There is paucity of cases in which a violation of Article 10(1) has been at issue. One of few such cases is the *Yamaha Gakki* case[64] in which Yamaha, the leading manufacturer of musical instruments, indirectly acquired 24.5 per cent of voting stocks of Kawai, a competing manufacturer. Yamaha's market share in piano-manufacturing was 54 per cent, in organs 64 per cent, and in harmonicas 28 per cent of total production in Japan. Kawai held a market share of 16 per cent in pianos, 13 per cent in organs, and 7 per cent in harmonicas. If this acquisition had been allowed to proceed, Yamaha's market share after the acquisition would have been 70 per cent in pianos, 77 per cent in organs and 35 per cent in harmonicas. The FTC deemed this acquisition unlawful and a divestiture was ordered.

Mergers

Article 15(1) of the AML provides that a company shall not consummate a merger with another company if, as the result of the merger, competition in a market tends to be substantially restrained or if the merger is carried out through an unfair business practice. Article 15(2) of the AML requires the filing of a report with the FTC when companies intend to

[63] Generally a 'related company' in financial statements of the Ministry of Finance is defined as a corporate entity whose outstanding stocks are owned by another corporate entity by 20% or more.

[64] FTC Decision, 30 Jan. 1957, *Shinketsushū*, 8 (1957), 51 *et seq*.

merge, and that they shall not effect the merger until thirty days after filing.

The term 'merger' means typically a merger of the absorption type or that of the creation type. In the former, a company is absorbed into another company and thereby loses its corporate identity, and in the latter, two merging companies merge into a third company and both of them lose their corporate identity.

Article 15(1) states that a merger shall not be consummated if, as a result of the merger, competition in a market tends to be substantially restrained. The question here is the meaning of 'tends to'. It is generally interpreted that the term 'tends to' indicates a 'probability' and not necessarily a certainty. Therefore, a merger can be prohibited under Article 15(1) as long as there is a probability that competition in a market is likely to be substantially restrained by the merger. This means that Article 15(1) is applicable even if competition in a market is not restrained but there is a likelihood that competition will be restrained. In this sense, Article 15(1) can be regarded as a measure to arrest the concentration of business power in its incipiency.

The FTC announced the guidelines for the merger regulation in 1980 in which it laid out the detailed tests that it would use when judging whether to proceed against a merger or not. In these guidelines, some general tests are announced and mergers are classified into horizontal mergers, vertical mergers, and conglomerate mergers. Criteria to be used are enumerated with regard to these three types of mergers. We do not need too much detail of these tests. Therefore, we will look at some of the general rules in the guidelines.

If the value of the total assets of each of the companies intending to effect a merger is 5 billion yen or less, in principle, there is no examination as to the substance of the merger. This means that the merger is examined only from the viewpoint of whether it satisfies formal requirements such as providing the necessary information and filing the appropriate documents and related matters. This enforcement policy is intended to exclude from the scrutiny of the FTC mergers consummated between small enterprises.

On the other hand, a merger is closely examined if: (1) the market share of one of the companies intending to effect a merger or the aggregate of the market shares of both companies together is 25 per cent or above, (2) one or both of the companies is the first in ranking and occupies a 15 per cent market share, or (3) one or both of the companies ranks first in market share and the difference between the top ranking and lower ranking companies in terms of market share is great. A merger is also closely examined if: (1) the ranking in market share of one or both of the merging companies is within the top three and the aggregate of the market shares of these three amounts to 50 per cent or above, (2) the number of competitors in the market in which one of the merging companies belongs is small, or (3) the total assets of one of the merging companies is above 10 billion yen and those of the other company is 1 billion yen or more.

The above criteria are generally quantitative tests. When the FTC examines the validity of a merger, other economic or qualitative factors are taken into consideration, such as the conditions of competition in the relevant and related markets in horizontal mergers and the degree of foreclosure of the market in vertical mergers.

Article 15(1) also prohibits a merger carried out through an unfair business practice. Examples include a merger forced upon a company by another company after intensive dumping practices by the latter company which has caused the former company to give up business and succumb to the demand of the latter company to absorb it.

As touched upon earlier, Article 15(2) provides for the filing requirement with regard to mergers, and the companies intending to effect a merger must file a prior report with the FTC and they cannot effect the merger until thirty days have elasped after the filing. During this period, the FTC examines whether the merger is in violation of Article 15(1) or not. If the FTC judges that there is sufficient reason to suspect that the merger in question violates Article 15(1) of the AML, the FTC either issues a recommendation to the parties intending to merge to discontinue the plan or initiates the formal hearing procedure. It should be noted, however, that, if the FTC takes no action during this time period, it cannot in principle take any further action with regard to the merger. The reason is that to allow the FTC to proceed against a merger long after it has been consummated would be too disruptive of activities with regard to mergers and acquisitions.

The Yawata-Fuji *Merger case*

There are only a handful of cases with regard to merger control, and, in none of these cases, was a merger prohibited under Article 15(1). In this regard, it may be admitted that merger control in Japan has not been very effectively enforced. It may be that, in many cases, the FTC intervenes informally when it suspects that a merger would be contrary to Article 15(1) and causes the parties to cancel or modify their plans to merge.

Cases in which mergers were at issue include the *Yukijirushi-Clover* case,[65] the *Mitsubishi Heavy Industries, Ltd.* case,[66] and the *Teikokuseima-Chūoseni* case.[67] However, in none of these cases, did the FTC take any

[65] Koseitorihiki Iinkai, n. 5, above, pp. 194–9.
[66] Ibid. 199–202.
[67] Ibid.

formal action. In all these cases, after contemplating whether the merger in question was contrary to Article 15(1) of the AML, the FTC decided not to initiate any legal action. In this sense, therefore, the *Yawata–Fuji* case[68] is the only major case in which the FTC decided to take a formal action. It involved a merger plan between the Yawata Steel Company and the Fuji Steel Company. Both companies were one entity before the end of the Second World War—the Japan Steel Corporation, which was divided into Yawata and Fuji as part of the deconcentration measures after the War. In 1969, Yawata and Fuji planned to merge, entered into a contract, and filed a report with the FTC. The FTC decided that this merger would be a violation of Article 15(1) of the AML. If these companies had merged, the market share of the company after the merger would have been 100 per cent in rail production, 98.3 per cent in sheet pile, 61.2 per cent in tin plate, and 56.3 per cent in iron ingots. The FTC deemed that in those particular fields of trade, competition would be substantially restrained.

The FTC issued a recommendation requesting the companies to withdraw the plan. But this proposal was rejected by the companies, and the FTC initiated an administrative hearing procedure. At the same time, the FTC applied for a temporary injunction to stop the merger in the Tokyo High Court, which was granted. The hearing went on for a while and the respondent companies proposed to the FTC that they would take the necessary measures to restore competition in those areas. They would sell parts of their assets to competing companies and also give them technical assistance so that they would be more viable competitors in steel production. For example, in rail production, they would give technical assistance to a steel company and this company would make a new entry into the market and there would be no monopoly.

The FTC, deeming these measures appropriate, issued a consent decision requiring the respondent companies to carry them out. The merger was approved on this condition, and the Japan Steel Corporation came back into being. Since the case was resolved by a consent judgment, legal questions surrounding the case were not closely analysed and answered by the FTC. However, a number of interesting legal questions were discussed. We will briefly touch upon them below.

The respondent companies raised the issue of the relevant market. As explained above, the FTC asserted that competition would be substantially restrained in the four areas, namely, the production of rails, sheet piles, tin plate, and iron ingots in Japan. The respondent companies argued that, since they competed vigorously in foreign markets such as the United States and Europe, the relevant market should include foreign

[68] FTC Decision, 30 Oct. 1970, *Shinketsushū*, 16 (1970), 50 *et seq.*

markets as well as the domestic market. While it is true that exports and imports should be taken into consideration when deciding the relevant market, the issue in this case was whether or not there would be a substantial restraint of competition in the production and sale of the four items listed above and, therefore, there was a limit to the extent to which the FTC could take exports and imports into consideration.

The respondent companies maintained that the proposed merger would bring tremendous advantages in improved management, technology, investment, and other related business activities. In short, their assertion was that the merger would enhance the efficiency of the enterprises in question. The FTC's investigative attornyes stressed that the FTC would consider only whether the proposed merger would substantially restrain competition or not. In their view, the efficiency question was not relevant to the issues involved in the case. The efficiency question is probably not relevant when the merger of the two largest companies is at issue although this may be a factor to be considered when lesser companies are concerned.

A group of economists objected to the proposed merger on the grounds that it would create a huge concentration of economic power in the hands of the new company which would bring about a market structure in which collusion rather than competition would be the predominant feature. This may be true. However, the theory cannot be accepted as an interpretation of Article 15(1) since Article 15(1) only requires that competition in a particular field of trade must tend to be substantially restrained. The prediction of a general decline of competition in the oligopolistic market structure alone does not justify the application of Article 15(1) to the proposed merger. This economic theory, however, was adopted as part of the control of a monopolistic situation, introduced by the 1977 amendment, which will be touched upon below.

D. CONTROL OF A MONOPOLISTIC SITUATION

In General

The control of a monopolistic situation provided for in Articles 2(7) and 8.4 is designed to cope with the situation in which competition has declined due to a monopolistic or oligopolistic market structure when that structure was not created through conduct which would constitute a private monopoly. Under these articles, the FTC is authorized to apply measures to break up a large enterprise because of its size as long as there is some proof that the economic performance of the enterprise is undesirable. These measures are not designed to prohibit the specific conduct of an enterprise but to control the structure of an enterprise and the market and, in this sense, may be termed 'structure control' in contrast to 'conduct control'.

The causes of a monopolistic or oligopolistic market structure are many and not all of them can be attributed to conduct which would be prohibited by the AML. There may be a situation where an enterprise has attained a dominant position in the market through skill and ingenuity in management or through technological innovation and breakthrough. Even in those situations, however, competition in a market may decline.

Whether or not one should take measures to deal with this situation is a policy decision. Various countries have dealt with this question in different ways depending on the political and economic situation of the country and the antitrust philosophy adopted.

One way to handle the situation is 'to do nothing'. This approach is based on the consideration that a monopoly created through skill and ingenuity is a natural reward for distinguished accomplishment and that to intervene would be a disincentive to innovation. This school of thought would also maintain that, if monopoly power is abused by raising prices, it would undermine the very existence of the monopoly by attracting new entries into the market through high prices as long as the entry barrier is low. In the long run, the monopoly would collapse.

Another school of thought would maintain that, even if a monopoly power is abused by raising prices, new entries may not occur. There may be the need for large amounts of finance, hugh capital investment, a high degree of product differentiation, a highly integrated distribution network, and related matters which may not always be easy to overcome. In this school of thought, there is a need for legal measures to deal with a monopolistic situation.

The AML has adopted the second approach and incorporated the control of a monopolistic situation by the 1977 amendment.

Definition of a Monopolistic Situation

There are several elements in the definition of a monopolistic situation, as provided for in Article 2(7). First, the issue can be raised only with regard to a market in which the total value of supply in the past year has been 50 billion yen or more. This is to exclude a small market in which a relatively small enterprise may hold a large portion of the market. In a market in which the value of supply is 50 billion yen or more, there is a monopolistic situation if there are the following conditions. (1) An enterprise has a market share of 50 per cent or more, or two enterprises have a market share of 75 per cent or more. (2) New entry into the market is difficult. (3) The price in the market is rigid (that is, it is likely to go up but unlikely to come down regardless of demand and supply conditions) and the enterprise's profit is in excess of the standard profit rate prevailing in that business, or the enterprise spends an excessive amount on general expenses.

In short, a monopolistic situation is that in which an enterprise or enterprises hold a large market share, new entry is difficult, the price structure is rigid (a high-level price), and the profits or general expenses are excessively high. The requirement listed in (1) above may be termed the 'structure' requirement and that in (2) the 'performance' requirement. If both these requirements are satisfied, the enterprise is held to be in a monopolistic situation.

Measures to Restore Competition

When the FTC decides that the structure and performance requirements exist and an enterprise is in a monopolistic situation, it can apply measures to restore competition. A measure to break up or split the enterprise is included in such measures and, for this reason, the control of a monopolistic situation can be said to be a deconcentration measure.

Since a deconcentration measure is the ultimate measure which should not be easily invoked, there are some precautionary requirements. First, when the FTC issues an order to an enterprise in a monopolistic situation to restore competition, it must take account of the smooth operation of the business activities of that enterprise and related enterprises, the stability of life for employees, and related matters. The FTC must first apply measures other than the one to break up the enterprise if that is sufficient to restore competition. Also, even if there is a monopolistic situation, the FTC cannot apply a measure to restore competition if, by applying the measure, the optimum size for operation is lost, the finance of the enterprise becomes unstable, and the maintenance of international competitiveness becomes difficult.

There are some procedural hurdles. When the FTC deems that a monopolistic situation exists, it must inform the minister in charge of the industry and the minister can express his view on this matter. Secondly, when the FTC initiates an administrative proceeding to decide if there is a monopolistic situation, it must hold a public hearing. Thirdly, the FTC cannot issue a recommendation to an enterprise in a monopolistic situation. Fourthly, a FTC decision concerning a monopolistic situation must be made by the vote of more than 2:3 including the Chairman and commissioners. Fifthly, the decision cannot be enforced unless it has become finalized. Lastly, an appeal to cancel the FTC order can be brought within three months after it was issued.

Under Article 245 of the Commercial Code, when a company sells an important part of its business, it must hold a stockholders' meeting and obtain a special resolution. If the FTC has ordered a divestiture of an important part of the business of an enterprise in a monopolistic situation, the enterprise must hold a stockholders' meeting and request a special resolution to part with that business. What happens if the stockholders' meeting refuses to pass the special resolution? Will a criminal penalty be imposed on the directors of the company for not complying with the FTC order? Possible legal consequences are not clear.

When the FTC has issued an order for divestiture, the directors of the company are obligated to convene a stockholders' meeting and propose the divestiture. It is clear that this much is an obligation of the directors, non-performance of which incurs a criminal liability. However, if the stockholders' meeting refuses to pass the special resolution, there is little that the directors can do and they are probably immune from criminal liability. This is a defect in the law and it may make it impossible to execute the FTC order completely.

Role of the Control of Monopolistic Situations

Since the control of monopolistic situations was introduced in 1977, there has been no instance in which a deconcentration measure has been applied. Will it be enforced in the future and what is the role of this control?

It is highly unlikely that the control of a monopolistic situation will ever be actually applied. The reasons are that, since it is a drastic measure, it can be applied only in extreme situations, that a large enterprise will refrain from raising prices when its market share is above 50 per cent or approaches 50 per cent so as to avoid fulfilling the performance requirement, and that the minister in charge of the industry will take some measures to reduce the market share or otherwise direct the enterprise in question to avoid price-raising.

An enterprise with a large market share is not challenged by the FTC unless it satisfies both the structure and performance requirements. Also, it must satisfy all the elements in the performance requirement, one of which is that the price in the relevant market stays at a high level, goes up easily, but is not likely to come down in response to changes in the supply and demand relationship. An enterprise will refrain from raising its prices first and avoid the fulfilment of this requirement. In this way, a large enterprise with a big market share can escape a challenge by the FTC.

It does not mean, however, that the control of monopolistic situations has no use. At least it has the effect of causing the leading company with a large market share to refrain from raising its prices first and acting as the price leader. In this sense, therefore, it will work as an informal price control to prevent undue price rises when the price structure in an oligopolistic market is rigid and the prices easily go up.

On the other hand, the control of a monopolistic situation may work in a paradoxical way. As explained above, an enterprise with a large market share is pressed to refrain from raising its prices. If the largest enterprise refrains from raising its prices and lesser enterprises in the market raise their prices, the likely consequence will be that the market share of the large enterprise will go up even further, which makes it more difficult for the enterprise to raise its price. In this situation, the large enterprise will be caught in the dilemma of having to refrain from raising to prices and having to avoid a further increase in market share.

As touched upon earlier, whether to control a monopoly even though it has come into being without violating the AML in the traditional sense or to leave it alone is a difficult policy decision. Even if a decision has been made to control a monopoly, there is no perfect system to control it without any problems. It seems that, in the imperfect world in which we live, we have no choice but to be satisfied with a system which is less than perfect.

The control of monopolistic situations is regarded as a supplementary measure to the prohibition of private monopolization. As explained above, the control of monopolistic situations is basically a control of market structure rather than that of the specific conduct of an enterprise. The prohibition of private monopolization has the serious limit of not being able to handle a monopoly, if the monopoly has not been created as a result of an intentional action, and yet there are some situations in which there is a monopoly, and competition is declining, without any specific conduct by the enterprise.

2.7 Cartels and Trade Associations

A. AN OVERVIEW OF THE REGULATION OF CARTELS AND TRADE ASSOCIATIONS

Laws on Cartels

One of the basic objectives of the AML is to prohibit cartels. Cartels are agreements among enterprises to stop competition among themselves and are therefore anti-competitive in nature. Since the very purpose of such agreements is to restrict competition, it runs counter to the basic principle of competition which underlies the AML. Therefore, the AML prohibits cartels or unreasonable restraints of trade, in principle.

However, due to policy considerations other than the competition policy, exemptions are allowed in Japan, and some cartels are authorized. When we study laws on cartels in Japan, we need to examine both the legal rules prohibiting cartels and those which exempt them from the application of the AML. Since, however, we will deal with some exempted cartels in a later chapter, we will look at the rules for prohibiting cartels in the present chapter.

In the AML, a cartel is termed as an 'unreasonable restraint of trade'. The prohibition of an unreasonable restraint of trade or a cartel is one of the three major categories of the AML. A cartel or an unreasonable restraint of trade is an agreement among enterprises to restrict competition among themselves. Examples include agreements to fix or raise prices, restrict production, and to allocate territories.

Closely related to the prohibition of cartels is the regulation of the activities of trade associations. Anti-competitive collusions are often planned and executed through trade associations, and therefore to control the anti-competitive activities of trade associations is also an important policy objective of the AML.

Definition of a Cartel

Article 2(6) of the AML defines unreasonable restraint of trade as: 'such business activity, by which enterprises by contract, agreement, or any other concerted activity mutually restrict or conduct their business activities in such a manner as to fix, maintain, or increase prices, to limit production, technology, products, facilities, customers, or suppliers, thereby causing, contrary to the public interest, a substantial restraint of competition in any particular field of trade.' The latter part of Article 3 prohibits enterprises from engaging in an unreasonable restraint of trade or a cartel as above defined.

According to this definition, an unreasonable restraint of trade is: (1) concerted activity among enterprises by means of a contract, agreement, or understanding, which (2) mutually restricts their business activities, (3) fixes prices, limits production and other terms of business, and (4) which causes, contrary to the public interest, a substantial restraint of trade in any particular field of trade. The aspect (4) of the above provisions has been already discussed in previous sections.

There are two other provisions in the AML which are relevant to the prohibition of a cartel. One is Article 8(1)(i)–(iii), which prohibits anti-competitive activities of trade associations, and the other is Article 6(1) which prohibits enterprises from entering into an agreement which contains provisions amounting to an unreasonable restraint of trade or a cartel.

B. VERTICAL AGREEMENTS

What is a Vertical Agreement?

A vertical agreement is often contrasted to a horizontal agreement which is entered into between enterprises in a competitive relationship and which restricts competition among them, such as a price-fixing agreement. A vertical agreement is an agreement between enterprises which are not in a competitive relationship but in a transactional relationship or in different stages of transactions, such as one in an upstream stage of distribution and the other in a downstream stage. Examples include a resale price maintenance agreement between the manufacturer of a product and distributors of it whereby the distributors agree to fix their prices at the level directed by the manufacturer, and a territorial arrangement whereby the manufacturer allocates an exclusive territory to each distributor and excludes the others from that territory.

There is no doubt that a horizontal agreement is included within the scope of Article 2(6) of the AML. However, there are some questions as to whether or not a vertical agreement is subsumed under this article.

The Newspaper Distribution *case*

The decision of the Tokyo High Court in 1953 in the *Newspaper Distribution* case[69] is the leading case today. In this case, newspaper companies (Asahi, Yomiuri, Mainichi, Nikkei, and Tokyo) entered into a tacit agreement among themselves and, on the basis of this agreement, each company entered into distribution agreements with retailers by which each retailer was assigned an exclusive territory within which it could engage in sales activities. These agreements were vertical agreements since the newspaper companies were engaged in producing and publishing newspapers and the distributors were engaged in the retail business of selling newspapers.

The FTC proceeded against the newspaper companies, holding that the agreements between the newspaper companies and the distributors amounted to an unreasonable restraint of trade in the sense of Article 2(6) of the AML, and ordered the newspaper companies to cancel the agreements. On appeal by the newspaper companies, the Tokyo High Court took up the case and reversed the decision of the FTC.

The ground of the reversal was that the language of Article 2(6) required that there be a 'mutual restriction' in an unreasonable restraint of trade, meaning that the parties to an agreement imposed the same kind of restriction. It held that, whereas, in the *Newspaper Distribution* case, newspaper companies had imposed on them the restriction that they could not do business outside the territories which were assigned to them, the newspaper companies did not have a similar restriction imposed on them and, therefore, these agreements lacked the mutuality in restriction which was a necessary element to constitute an unreasonable restraint of trade in the sense of Article 2(6).

[69] Decision of the Tokyo High Court, 9 Mar. 1953, *Kōsai Minshū*, 6/9 (1953), 435 *et seq.*

Views of Commentators and the Fair Trade Commission

The view of commentators on this issue are divided.[70] On the one hand, there are some who argue that the position taken by the Tokyo high Court is basically correct for the reason that a strict reading of the wording of Article 2(6) requires mutual restriction in order for an agreement to be held an unreasonable restraint of trade. On the other hand, there are some commentators who argue that the term 'mutual restriction' does not have to be limited to the situation in which both parties of an agreement are under the same kind of obligation and that an agreement can be included within the coverage in which both parties obligations have imposed on them but the obligations imposed on one party are different from those imposed on the other party. They maintain that, as long as the wording of Article 2(6) does not explicitly prohibit this interpretation, this should be adopted.

According to this school of thought, to take the view adopted by the Tokyo High Court in the *Newspaper Distribution* case would cause practical problems. For example, let us envisage the following situation. In a resale price maintenance contract, a manufacturer imposes an obligation on distributors to sell the products at a certain price level directed by the manufacturer and thereby avoid price competition among them. Although the obligation to maintain the price at a certain level is formally imposed on the distributors by the manufacturer, it is often the desire of the distributors to effectuate the resale price maintenance since it is they who engage in price competition with regard to the manufacturer's product, and who wish to avoid that competition. Therefore, the distributors or their trade association often put pressure on the manufacturer to enforce resale price maintenance. The manufacturer decides to impose resale price maintenance on the distributors as a result of such pressure.

Under the doctrine enunciated by the Tokyo High Court in the *Newspaper Distribution* case, this agreement does not amount to an unreasonable restraint of trade since there is no mutuality in obligations imposed on the distributors and those imposed on the manufacturer. The distributors are obligated to maintain the level of price directed by the manufacturer. However, the manufacturer is not subject to similar obligations.

The only way to make a resale price maintenance unlawful under this doctrine is to treat it as an unfair business practice. There will be an extensive explanation of unfair business practices in a later section. It is sufficient here to state that, in an unfair business practice, the malefactor is regarded as imposing an unreasonable condition on the other party in a transaction. In the context of the above case, the manufacturer is held to

[70] See Matsushita, n. 19, above, pp. 99–102.

have imposed an unreasonable term on the distributors and, therefore, is the malefactor, and the distributors are regarded as victims. This would mean that the distributors are immunized from the application of the AML even though they participated in, and, in fact, demanded the resale price maintenance, and, therefore, should be held as malefactors also.

For the above reasons, this school of thought objects to the interpretation of Article 2(6) as regards a vertical agreement adopted by the Tokyo High Court for the reason that this would catch only part of the co-conspirators and let others get away. Since this decision, the FTC has adhered to this interpretation and has not challenged vertical restraints, including resale price maintenance agreements, through Article 2(6). However, recently there seems to be a slight shift in thinking in the FTC as regards this point.

A task force organized by the FTC to study antitrust problems in distribution published a report in 1990.[71] This report stated that if a manufacturer and distributors jointly agreed that the distributors would refuse to supply a product to specific retailers (such as discounters), or a manufacturer and retailers jointly agreed that the retailers would not handle imported products which competed with those of the manufacturer, that agreement might be held as an unreasonable restraint of trade. This agreement is entered into between the manufacturer on the one hand and the distributors/retailers on the other, and, therefore, it is a vertical agreement in nature. The position taken by this report seems to be that a vertical agreement can be included within the scope of Article 2(6) of the AML.

In 1991, the FTC announced a set of guidelines on distribution and business practices (hereafter 'the 1991 FTCJ Guidelines')[72] in which it stated that, in the following situations, an agreement may be held to constitute an unreasonable restraint of trade: (1) if a manufacturer and distributors agree that the distributors will not sell imported products which compete with that of the manufacturer, (2) if a manufacturer and distributors agree that the manufacturer will not sell the product to a newly entering distributor in order to block the new entry, and the distributors will refuse to purchase from a manufacturer which supplies the product to the newly entering distributor, or (3) if manufacturers of raw materials and a manufacturer of the finished product agree that the manufacturer of the finished product will not purchase imported raw materials, and the distributors refuse to purchase from a manufacturer of

[71] The Advisory Group to the Fair Trade Commission on Distribution Systems, Business Practices, and Competition Policy, *Distribution Systems, Business Practices and Perspective of Competition* (1990).

[72] Executive office of the Fair Trade Commission, *The Anti-monopoly Act Guidelines Concerning Distribution Systems and Business Practices*, 1991.

the finished product which purchased imported raw materials, in order to block the new entry of imported raw materials.

The view of the FTC as regards the question as to whether or not a vertical agreement as such constitutes an unreasonable restraint of trade is unclear. The position of the 1991 FTCJ Guidelines is vaguer than that expressed in the report. On the whole, it seems that the FTC is attempting to move away from the interpretation adopted by the Tokyo High Court in the *Newspaper Distribution* case. In light of the above, the view that Article 2(6) encompasses vertical agreements as well as horizontal agreements as long as they restrain competition substantially may be a prevailing one in the future.

C. WHEN IS A CARTEL ILLEGAL?

Article 2(6) of the AML states that the requirements for an unreasonable restraint of trade are satisfied when there is an agreement which contains a provision mutually to restrict competition among the participants and when competition in a particular field of trade is substantially restrained. A question arises whether, for example, an agreement to fix prices is unlawful as soon as it is entered into or when it is put into practice and competition in a particular field of trade is thereby substantially restrained.

The importance of this question is that it is related to a subsequent question of when is the FTC allowed to proceed against an agreement? Can the FTC proceed against an agreement as soon as it is entered into or should it wait until it is put into practice and competition in a market is substantially restrained? Since the language of Article 2(6) expressly states that there has to be a substantial restraint of competition by an agreement, it may be interpreted that the FTC can proceed against it only when it is put into practice and competition is actually restrained. On the other hand, it may be foolish to maintain that the FTC has to wait until a cartel agreement is actually put into practice even though the existence of that agreement is already known.

There are two schools of thought with regard to this interpretational question.[73] Commentators who belong to one school maintain that an agreement whereby the participants agree mutually to restrict competition is unlawful as soon as it is entered into. They maintain that, when enterprises in a competitive relationship agree to stop competition among themselves, a common consciousness is created among them that they will refrain from competition and this affects their competitive behaviour. They argue that, under this circumstance, competition among them

[73] Matsushita, n. 19, above, pp. 102–8

cannot be expected any more. Therefore, according to this school of thought, as soon as a cartel agreement is made, there is little room for competition and the requirement in Article 2(6) that there be a substantial restraint of competition is satisfied.

This school of thought maintains that, if a cartel agreement became unlawful only after the agreement had been put into practice, the FTC would not be able to take a measure until it had been put into practice and this would be contrary to the principle that unlawful conduct should be stopped at as early a stage as possible.

The Supreme Court stated in the *Oil Cartel Price Fixing* case [74] that an agreement which contains a mutual restriction of competition among the participants is deemed to be unlawful as long as it is recognized that competition is substantially restrained even though the time of its execution has not come or the agreement has not yet been put into practice. The meaning of this statement of the Supreme Court is not entirely clear. However, the position of the Supreme Court seems basically similar to that of the school of thought mentioned above.

Commentators who belong to the other school of thought maintain that an agreement among enterprises to refrain from competition is unlawful only when it is put into practice since the wording of Article 2(6) clearly requires that competition be substantially restrained by the agreement and, until and unless the agreement is put into practice, competition is not automatically restrained. Article 4 of the AML, which prohibited cartels, and which was deleted by the 1953 amendment, did not require a substantial restraint of competition. Under this defunct provision, a cartel agreement was illegal as soon as it was entered into regardless of whether it had been put into practice or not. They argue that the deletion of Article 4 by the 1953 amendment suggests the legislative intent that there must be a substantial restraint of competition in order to hold an agreement as an unreasonable restraint of trade in the sense of Article 2(6).

The FTC has never announced its position officially on this matter. However, there are some cases in which the FTC intervened when the participants of a restrictive agreement took preliminary steps to implement the agreement.

It seems that the position taken by the FTC in those cases is probably the most correct interpretation of Article 2(6) with regard to this question. The reason is that, since the language of Article 2(6) explicitly requires a substantial restraint of competition in a particular field of trade, it is hard to ignore this requirement altogether. Yet it is desirable to construct an interpretation to speed up a legal measure to be taken by the FTC *vis-a-vis* a cartel agreement. A compromise would be to con-

[74] Decision of the Supreme Court, 24 Feb. 1984, *Keishū,* 38/4 (1984), 1287 *et seq.*

struct a theory which would hold that an agreement among enterprises to restrict mutual competition is unlawful as soon as the participants take the first step to implement it. By taking the first step to implement it, at least a part of the agreement is already being enforced and this would inevitably lead to a substantial restraint of competition if it were not prohibited.

To take an example, a price-fixing cartel agreement is unlawful as soon as the participants to the agreement begin the first step to implement the agreement. If, in a price-fixing agreement, the participants begin such activities as making new price tags on which the new prices are written down and drafting new notifications to distributors that the price should be raised, the first steps to implement the agreement are put into practice. The correct interpretation seems to be that, at this stage, the FTC is authorized to proceed against the participants of the agreement.

D. PROOF OF CARTEL

In General

Proof of a cartel is probably the most important problem in its prohibition. The question is what kinds of evidence are required to prove that there is a cartel agreement. Since a cartel agreement is regarded as unlawful unless authorized by an exempting law, the participants seldom enter into an explicit agreement. Often such an agreement is made under some subterfuges or camoumflaged under some kind of guise. In this sense, therefore, cartels are often concluded and executed in secret.

Also when a market becomes more and more oligopolistic and the number of participating enterprises in the market becomes fewer, the 'transparency' of the market increases. In an oligopolistic market in which only a handful of enterprises participate, each enterprise is well aware of the market conduct of another enterprise. It happens often that the leading firm in the market takes an initiative in, for example, raising prices and others follow suit. This may happen even without any explicit agreement among them. Enterprises wait until the leading firm decides and announces its price and they engage in parallel conduct such as simultaneous price-raising. In such a market, economically their actions are mutually dependent on each other.

In an oligopolistic market, in order for the participating enterprises to take parallel or uniform actions in a collusive way, they may not need an explicit agreement. Only a slight sign or signalling by an enterprise to other enterprises in the market indicating the conduct that it will take, will suffice to induce others to engage in similar conduct.

For the above reasons, it is often difficult to prove the existence of a cartel agreement by a concrete piece of evidence. Often the FTC, the plaintiffs who challenge a cartel, and courts must rely on indirect or circumstantial evidence to prove a cartel. The question is then: how much indirect or circumstantial evidence is sufficient to prove a cartel? Is it sufficient if the conduct of enterprises is the same? Or is it necessary to prove that there was a discussion among the participants as to the terms of business?

Generally speaking, commentators agree that there must be a piece of evidence indicating that there was a 'communication' of intentions among the participating enterprises and uniform or parallel conduct among them. A mere indication that their conduct is the same would be insufficient to make their conduct a cartel, since the uniform conduct may have been caused by independent judgments by the enterprises without any communication of intentions. On the other hand, mere evidence of communication of intentions is not sufficient if that communication is not followed by uniform conduct. In such a case, it is clear that the cartel agreement, even if it existed, was not put into practice, and no harm had been caused. Therefore, the correct formula should be: communication of intentions plus uniformity of conduct.

Cases Dealing with Proof of Cartel

There are some cases in which the issue was the kind of evidence that was sufficient to hold that a cartel agreement existed. Let us examine two such cases and see how the above formula operates in practice.

The *Plywood Bid-Rigging* case[75] was decided by the FTC in 1949. This is an old case, but considered as one of the leading cases on this question. In the case, the Special Procurement Agency (an agency in charge of procurement of supplies for the Occupation Forces) announced that it would purchase 940,000 sheets of plywood by way of open bidding. The announced method of purchase was that the Agency would request each supplier to submit an estimate and the Agency would allocate contracts to those suppliers which submitted the lowest prices. It would start allocating contracts to the lowest price and move up to higher prices up to a certain price level.

The Agency came up with the provisional price for the product, which it constructed on the basis of the estimated cost of production, general overhead costs, and profit. This price was kept confidential within the Agency and would be used to serve as the maximum price. If the lowest bidder's price was above this price, then no party would win the contract and there would be another round of bidding. This process would be

[75] FTC Decision, 30 Aug. 1949, *Shinketsushū*, 1 (1950), 62 *et seq.*

repeated until the lowest bidder's price came down to the provisional price.

Information on this provisional price leaked out and became known among suppliers. They gathered twice in restaurants and engaged in 'conversations' among themselves. Their intention was to decide which bidders would win the contract and, for this purpose, some suppliers were designated as the winning bidders. The winning bidders would bid at the provisional price and other bidders would bid at prices above the provisional price. Then the winning bidders would get the contract. In subsequent bids, a similar process would be repeated and other suppliers would be designated as winning bidders.

In their meetings, the representative of one supplier indicated a certain level or price (which was above the provisional price) and said: 'This is a good price', and others also said: 'Indeed this is a good price.' The meaning of these statements was that the 'good price' was a price above the provisional price and those suppliers other than those designated as the winning suppliers should bid at prices around this price.

The bid was held and the prices offered by those suppliers other than the designated bidders were around the level of 'good price'. The FTC proceeded against those bidders, initiated an administrative hearing process, and held that the records of meetings in restaurants were sufficient evidence to indicate that the bidding was rigged. The FTC reasoned that, although there was a series of exchanges of information among the participating enterprises, the information exchanged in those meetings was closely related to a specific level of prices and specific transactions and that, through such exchanges of information, they were able to co-ordinate their activities in the bid. The fact that the bids of those suppliers other than the winning bidders were at similar levels indicated that there was a uniformity in conduct and this uniformity of conduct reinforced the conviction of the FTC that the bidding was rigged.

The FTC decided that there was bid rigging and, therefore, an unreasonable restraint of trade. The Special Procurement Agency revoked the bid on discovering that it had been rigged.

In the *Barber Shops Association* case,[76] a trade association composed of barber shops in the Akita Prefecture conducted a survey of the opinions of barber shop operators who were members of the association. It sent out questionnaires to the members and requested them to answer two questions: 'Do you wish to raise your price and if you do, what is the appropriate price level?'

The association collated the questionnaires, analysed the contents, and announced that, according to this survey, most of the members of the

[76] FTC Decision, 11 Aug. 1965, ibid. 13 (1966), 55 *et seq.*

association wanted to raise their prices, and that the price level which most of the members thought to be appropriate was 300 yen. The association then formulated the 'standard price' at 300 yen and requested that each member should decide its price 'independently' but 'taking into consideration this standard price'. All of them set their prices at 300 yen.

The FTC proceeded against these activities of the association and held that they amounted to a violation of Article 8(1)(i) of the AML, which prohibited trade associations from engaging in activities which substantially restrain competition in a particular field of trade.

In this instance, there is no direct evidence that the trade association imposed the standard price on the members. However, the association exerted pressure on the members to set their prices at 300 yen by announcing the result of the survey. This activity of the association could be evaluated as a piece of circumstantial evidence for price-fixing. By this anouncement, the members were informed that the majority of them thought that the price should be set at 300 yen. This would make it more difficult for the members to act in a different way as far as price-setting was concerned.

E. CARTELS AND ADMINISTRATIVE GUIDANCE

The Nature of the Problem

Sometimes the government uses private associations and agreements as a tool for accomplishing government policy. For example, to achieve industrial policy goals, the MITI has utilized agreements in areas such as the protection of small enterprises and of depressed industries and the promotion of basic research and development. In some cases, there are laws which exempt private agreements entered into for the purpose of accomplishing government objectives from the application of the AML. However, this is not always true. There are situations where the government advises enterprises to form a group or enter into an agreement to accomplish goals such as overcoming depressions and promoting basic research and development activities, and yet there is no law which would exempt such activities from the application of the AML.

In such situations, agreements may be challenged under the AML even if they have been made under administrative guidance and for the purpose of implementing government policies. The reason why such a conflict occurred between an administrative guidance and the AML was the fact that there were conflicts between the competition policy as embodied in the AML and industrial policies exercised by the MITI. This meant that government policies were split in different directions.

Today such a conflict occurs rarely since the policy of the MITI in exercising industrial policies is to refrain from using cartels. However, even today, it is worth while to investigate the legal relationship between the AML and an administrative guidance. The legal question is whether or not an agreement among enterprises is immune from the application of the AML for the sole reason that it is made under an administrative guidance and for the purpose of achieving a government policy.

Court and FTC Decisions

There are several cases in which the FTC held that a cartel was unlawful even if it was entered into among enterprises under the directive or guidance of a governmental agency when it satisfied the requirements of Article 2(6) or Article 8(1)(i) of the AML, and as long as it was not exempted from the application of the AML by another law.

One such cases is the *Noda Soy Sauce Company* case[77] in which the Price Control Administration advised a trade association of soy sauce producers to fix the maximum price of soy sauce for the purpose of combating a sharp price increase. The association formulated a programme to enforce it and the member companies complied. The FTC challenged the setting of a maximum price by the association on the ground that it amounted to a substantial restraint of competition contrary to the AML. In issuing a decree, the FTC stated that the administrative guidance given by the Price Administration could not be used as an excuse since to admit it as an exonerating factor would mean that a government agency which had no authority on the enforcement of the AML would be able to exempt an activity simply by issuing a guidance.

Another important case is the *Chemical Fibre Association* case (1953)[78] in which the issue was a programme for production cut-back formulated by a trade association in the chemical fibre industry under an administrative guidance of the MITI. The industry was facing a severe depression after the Korean War and, in order to deal with the depression, the MITI advised the Chemical Fibre Association to cut back annual production and indicated a range of the amount to be produced (but without specifying the exact amount). The Association complied with this advice, formulated a production cut-back programme, and allocated quotas to each member company. The FTC proceeded against this programme and held it as unlawful.

With regard to the role of administrative guidance, the FTC stated that, although it would have been very difficult for the directors of the Chemical Fibre Association to refuse to comply with the MITI's advice, it was not a sufficient reason to exonerate them from the illegality, since to

[77] FTC Decision 4 Apr. 1952, ibid. 4 (1953), 1 *et seq*.
[78] FTC Decision, 6 Aug. 1953, ibid. 5 (1954), 17 *et seq*.

hold otherwise would mean that exceptions to the AML would be easily created by giving advice contrary to the principle incorporated in the AML.

In the *Oil Cartel Production Cutback* case,[79] the Tokyo High Court dealt with this problem. The issue involved was a production cut-back programme exercised by the Petroleum Association under an administrative guidance by the MITI. Details are explained elsewhere. The court stated that the programme was originally contemplated by the association, later taken up by the MITI, and, therefore, was not the product of administrative guidance. The court stated, in *dicta*, that an agreement to restrain competition could be justified, even without exempting laws, if it was based on a directive or entrustment of the government or it was an instrument for carrying out the petroleum policy whose execution was vested in the MITI. The Supreme Court expressed basically the same view in the *Oil Cartel Price Fixing* case.[80]

Comparing decisions of courts and those of the FTC, there is a difference in emphasis. The FTC decisions emphatically stress that there is no exception to the prohibition of cartels even though a cartel is based on an administrative guidance. On the other hand, court decisions allow, at least as an abstract principle, that there are some situations in which a cartel may he held to be justified due to an administrative guidance exercised by a government agency.

2.8 Unfair Business Practices

A. AN OVERVIEW

The prohibition of unfair business practices is one of the 'three main pillars' of the AML. Let us look at the relevant provisions first and then the role of the prohibition of unfair business practices.

The Relevant Provisions

Unfair business practices are defined in Article 2(9) of the AML as: 'any act coming under any one of the following paragraphs, which tends to impede fair competition and which is designated by the Fair Trade Commission.' The provision lists: (1) unreasonable discrimination, (2) unreasonable price, (3) unreasonable inducement or coercion of customers, (4) unreasonable restriction imposed on the other party to a transaction, (5) unreasonable use of bargaining position, and (5) unreasonable interference in the affairs of a competitor.

[79] Decision of the Tokyo High Court, 26 Sep. 1980, *Hanrei Hihō*, 983 (1980), 22 *et seq.*

[80] See n. 74, above.

Article 19 prohibits enterprises from engaging in unfair business practices. Article 6(1) prohibits enterprises from entering into an international contract, which contains such items as constitute unfair business practices. Also, Article 8(1)(v) prohibits trade associations from causing an enterprise to engage in unfair business practices. There are two pieces of legislation which supplement the above provisions. They are: (1) the Law Prohibiting Unreasonable Premiums and Representations and Related Matters[81] and (2) the Law Prohibiting Unreasonable Delay in Payment to Sub-Contractors and Related Matters.[82]

The FTC Designations

Article 2(9) states that the FTC shall designate unfair business practices within the categories of conduct listed in Article 2(9). The FTC has announced two designations of unfair business practices, namely, the general designation of unfair business practices and the specific designation of unfair business practices. The general designation which was announced in 1982,[83] and applies to conduct of enterprises generally, includes sixteen articles, the details of which will be touched upon below.

There are six specific designations announced by the FTC. They apply to conduct of enterprises which belong to specified industries, except for the designation on advertisements, in which premiums by lottery are included. The specific designations are those on (1) department stores, (2) textbooks, (3) ocean freight, (4) canned and bottled foods, (5) newspapers, and (6) advertisements in which premiums by lottery are included. Owing to the limited scope of application, an account of the specific designations is omitted.

Tendency to Impede Fair Competition

Article 2(9) requires that the FTC designate conduct which tends to impede fair competition. 'Tends to impede' is interpreted to mean the possibility that conduct may impede fair competition. It is not necessary, therefore, for particular conduct actually to impede competition for it to fall within the category of unfair business practices. As long as it has the tendency to impede fair cometition, it can be challenged as an unfair business practice. It is generally explained that, if unfair business practices are freely exercised without control, they would cause concentration of economic power in the hands of those enterprises which exercise them and that such a concentration of economic power would be the seed-bed on private monopolization. In this sense, therefore, the prohibition of

[81] Futōkeihinrui Oyobi Futōhyōji Bōshi Hō, Law 134, 1962.
[82] Shitaukedaikin Shiharai Chientō Bōshi Hō, Law 120, 1956.
[83] FTC Notification 15, 1982.

unfair business practices is designed to be a preventive measure in relation to the prohibition of private monopolization.

B. UNREASONABLE DISCRIMINATION

The Provisions

Article 2(9)(i) of the AML states that unreasonable discrimination exercised by an enterprise is an unfair business practice. On the basis of this provision, the FTC designated five categories of conduct, which are: (1) collective refusal to deal (boycott), (2) other refusal to deal, (3) price discrimination, (4) discriminatory dealing, and (5) discrimination in a trade association. We will discuss only the first three of these designations.

Collective Refusal to Deal (Boycott)

General Designation No. 1 states that a collective refusal to deal by agreement among competing enterprises is unlawful in principle. This includes an agreement for a primary boycott as well as that for a secondary boycott. An example of such a boycott is the *Market Stabilization Council* case,[84] in which manufacturers of household television sets jointly determined through a decision of a trade association (the Market Stabilization Council) that they would impose resale price maintenance of TV sets on wholesalers and retailers and, if a retailer cut the price below the resale price level designated by manufacturers, all the manufacturers would direct wholesalers to stop supplying the products to the retailer.

Boycott is regarded as unlawful in principle since it is a collective use of the economic power of the participants to put down competition. However, there are some exceptions to the prohibition even though they are rare. One example of such an exception is a collective refusal to deal for the purpose of self-defence. On one occasion a trade association of soy sauce brewers requested the FTC's opinion regarding the legality of an association decision to the effect that members would not submit to pressures employed by large supermarkets demanding them to contribute money to the supermarkets and purchase certain commodities from them. The FTC informally stated that it would not challenge such a decision.[85] Such a decision can be justified as a self-defence measure *vis-à-vis* an abuse of buying powers wielded by the supermarkets.

In the *Clearing House* case,[86] the issue was the legality of a rule established by an association of banks to the effect that a person who

[84] FTC Decision, 17 Oct. 1957, *Shinketsushū*, 9 (1958), 11 *et seq*.

[85] Tanaka (ed.), *Fukōseina Torihiki Hōhō (Unfair Business Practices)* (Tokyo, 1982), 42.

[86] Decision of the Tokyo High Court, 17 Nov. 1983, *Kinyū-Shōji Hanrei*, 690 (1983), 4 *et seq*.

issued a bad cheque twice or more in a period of six months would be subject to refusal to deal by all the banks that were members of the association. The Tokyo High Court upheld this rule on the ground that it was intended to preserve the credibility of the cheque and banking systems.

As touched upon earlier, in the 1991 FTCJ Guidelines on distribution and business practices, the FTC states that boycott agreements may include those entered into among manufacturers and distributors whereby either manufacturers or distributors are obligated to refuse to deal with a party. This means that a boycott can be an agreement which is not strictly horizontal. For example, if manufacturers and distributors agree that the distributors should refrain from handling imported products which compete with those produced by the manufacturers, this is held as an agreement to boycott.

Other Refusals to Deal

Another refusal to deal is a refusal to deal exercised by one enterprise. This may be termed an individual refusal to deal. This category of conduct is dealt with by General Designation No. 2. Since there is freedom of contract recognized in Civil Law, an enterprise cannot be forced to transact with another party if it does not wish to do so. Therefore, an individual refusal to deal is regarded as basically lawful unless there is a specific reason for unreasonableness. An individual refusal to deal is regarded as unlawful when it is exercised to support other illegal conduct. For example, if a manufacturer imposes resale price maintenance on wholesalers and retailers and, when a wholesaler or a retailer does not comply with this mandate, the manufacturer refuses to supply the product, it is held as unlawful since, in this example, the refusal to deal is used to support a resale price maintenance which is unlawful in itself.

When a refusal to deal is exercised by a powerful enterprise, it may be held unlawful since the party to whom the refusal is applied may have no chance to deal with another enterprise and it may be so detrimental to its business that it may have to withdraw from the market. The question is, what is 'powerful'? There is no definite answer to this question. Although the 1991 FTCJ Guidelines state that, if an enterprise's market share is 10 per cent or less, or its ranking in the market share is not within the top three, the enterprise is not held to possess a powerful position, any enterprise above this threshold is certainly not automatically held to possess a powerful position. The FTC once ruled that a refusal to deal exercised by a business entity with the market share of 80 per cent amounted to an unreasonable refusal to deal.[87] It seems that a high

[87] The Osaka Burashi Kogyo Kumiai case, FTC Decision, 20 Sept. 1955, *Shinketsushū*, 7 (1956), 20 *et seq*.

degree of market share is required in order to hold that an individual refusal to deal is unlawful.

Price Discrimination

Under General Designation No. 3, an unreasonable price discrimination is an unfair business practice. This provision covers both offering of a commodity or service at different prices to different customers or territories and also accepting it at such terms. However, a mere difference in price is not unlawful as such. The question is, when is a price discrimination unlawful? Generally, an offering of a commodity or service or accepting it at a discriminatory price is unlawful if it is detrimental to competition, a situation which arises when there is a tendency for competition to be impeded and an anti-competitive impact to be felt by the majority of enterprises in the relevant market.

There are only a few cases in this area. One is the *Hokkoku Shinbun* case,[88] in which a newspaper company which had a predominant market share in one locality sold the same newspaper at a much lower price in another locality in which it had no such dominant position for the purpose of driving out competitors. The FTC held this price discrimination to be unlawful. Another is the *Tōyō Linoleum* case[89] in which the leading manufacturer of floor materials agreed with its competitors to fix the manufacturers' price and, in order to enforce this price-fixing effectively, solicited purchasers (construction companies) to form a co-operative. The manufacturer sold the product at a lower price to construction companies which joined the co-operative than the price at which it sold the product to construction companies that were not members of the co-operative. The FTC held that this price discrimination was unlawful. It should be observed, however, that the core of this case was price-fixing and the price discrimination only played a supplemental role to make the price-fixing effective.

C. UNREASONABLE PRICE

Article 2(9)(ii) states that unreasonable pricing is an unfair business practice and the FTC designated General Designations Nos. 6 and 7. The former deals with sale below cost and the latter unreasonably high price. However, the former is far more important in practice than the latter, and we will discuss only the former.

In General Designation No. 6, a sale below cost of production or purchase, as the case may be, is unlawful if the price is substantially

[88] Decision of the Tokyo High Court, 18 Mar. 1957, *Gyōsai Reishū*, 18/3 (1967), 443 *et seq*.

[89] FTC Decision, 7 Feb. 1980, *Shinketsushū*, 26 (1980), 85 *et seq*.

below the cost and carried out continually. 'Cost', in this context, is the sum of the cost of production or purchase plus general overhead expenses. In the *Chūbu Yomiuri Shinbun* case,[90] the Tokyo High Court dealt with the concept of cost. In this case, a newspaper company (Chūbu Yomiuri Newspaper Company) sold its newspaper at the price of 500 yen per year. The Association of Newspaper Companies complained to the FTC that this price was below the cost of producing newspapers and was unlawful. The company presented evidence which proved that the cost of production was 500 yen.

However, the company was heavily subsidized by the Yomiuri Company through the supply of news and other resources necessary to produce newspapers. The Tokyo High Court held that the cost of production in this case was not the cost which had been actually incurred but the constructed cost which would have been incurred if the company had not received any such assistance. The Tokyo High Court stated that, if computed in this way, the cost was above 500 yen.

In the *Maruetsu-Harōmāto* cases,[91] two supermarkets were engaged in a price war in selling milk. As the result, a carton of milk was sold at 100 yen by the supermarkets for several months even though the wholesale purchase price was 160 yen. The FTC held that this pricing was an unfair business practice. More recently the Supreme Court dealt with a case in which a sale below cost was the issue. This is the *Tokyo Slaughterhouse* case,[92] in which a slaughterhouse owned and operated by the Tokyo government processed animals at a price which was way below cost. The price of slaughtering animals must be licensed but, in this case, the licensed price was below the cost. The loss incurred by the slaughterhouse was paid by a subsidy given by the Tokyo government. Another slaughterhouse operated by a private enterprise initiated a tort action against the Tokyo government alleging that the price charged by the slaughterhouse operated by the Tokyo government was below the cost of operation and was unlawful and a predatory pricing and sought the recovery of damages caused by this below-cost selling.

The Supreme Court reasoned that to raise the price of slaughtering animals would cause customers to turn away from slaughterhouses in the Tokyo area to those in other regions and result in a decrease of meat handled in the slaughterhouse operated by the Tokyo government and in an increase of the price of meat in the Tokyo area. The Supreme Court also observed that the price which was below cost was set for the

[90] Decision of the Osaka High Court, 30 Apr. 1975, *Kōsai Minshū*, 28/2 (1975), 174 *et seq*.

[91] FTC Decision, 6 Mar. 1982, *Shinketsushū*, 29 (1983), 13 *et seq*.; FTC Decision, May 28 1982, ibid. 29, 18 *et seq*.

[92] Decision of the Supreme Court, 14 Dec. 1989, *Minshū*, 43/12 (1989), 316 *et seq*.

purpose of stabilizing meat prices. It stated that, although the fact that the price was set at this level to achieve the above policy objective did not necessarily justify below-cost selling, the price in this case could be justified by taking into consideration the geographical extent of the competition and the fact that the plaintiff was processing animals at a price below the licensed price.

The wording employed in this decision is vague and it is not at all clear whether or not a sale below cost can be justified by the fact that the purpose of this low price is to implement a governmental policy for the public good. As far as the language of the decision is concerned, the Supreme Court seems to deny it. However, if one reads this case in the context of the factual situations, such an interpretation may be possible.

D. UNREASONABLE INDUCEMENT OR COERCION OF CUSTOMERS

Unreasonable Inducement

Article 2(9)(iii) provides that unreasonable inducement or coercion of customers is an unfair business practice, and the FTC's general designation Nos. 8 and 9 respectively provide that deceptive inducement and inducement of customers with excessive economic advantage are unfair business practices. Designation No. 8 envisages false advertising and misrepresentation, and No. 9 aims at sales with excessive premiums.

Although there are a few cases with regard to these provisions, in actuality, the regulation under the Law Prohibiting Unreasonable Premiums and Representations and Other Matters (for the sake of brevity, we will call this law 'the Premium Law') is far more important. Therefore, we will review the major provisions of this law.

The Premium Law provides that an excessive premium offered by the seller of a commodity is prohibited. 'Premium' is a commodity, service, or any kind of economic advantage which is offered in connection with the sale of a product (or services) in the form of a prize, competition, or an offer to every purchaser. The FTC is authorized to issue regulations which set up a maximum premium. There are many regulations issued by the FTC which provide for the maximum value of a premium.

The Premium Law also provides that false and misleading advertisement or representation is prohibited. There are some principles in the enforcement of the prohibition of false and misleading advertisement or representation. As examples, two of them will be touched upon. First, if an expression can be interpreted in several ways and if one of these interpretations is contrary to the truth, it is a misleading representation. Secondly, when judging whether or not an expression is false or misleading, the judgement of ordinary people is used. In judging whether or not an expression with regard to the quality of, for example, a machine is false or misleading, the judgement of ordinary people is used instead of that of an expert. Therefore, even if an expert can easily detect the falsehood or misleading nature of the expression, that does not count.

The Premium Law provides for a fair competition code. Enterprises can enter into an agreement whereby they set up standards to be observed with regard to the offering of a premium and the ways in which they advertise or represent their products. They can file the draft of such an agreement for FTC approval. If the FTC approves it, the agreement is exempted from the application of the AML and the enterprises can enforce it lawfully. This is called the fair competition code. The system of fair competition code may be regarded as the private enforcement of the regulation against excessive premiums or false and misleading advertisements.

Unreasonable Coercion

General Designation No. 10 states that an unreasonable obligation imposed by the seller of a commodity on a purchaser, in that he or she must purchase another commodity from the seller or another party designated by the seller, is an unfair business practice. This is a 'tie-in' or 'tying' contract. A tie-in contract is regarded as unlawful when the seller of a commodity who imposes such a condition has sufficient economic power with regard to the tying commodity (as opposed to the tied commodity) to do this.

The *Textbook* case[93] is relevant here. In this case, a wholesaler of textbooks—the only textbook wholesaler in Nagano Prefecture—had a dominant position and forced textbook sellers who also sold ordinary books to purchase ordinary books to the value of at least two-thirds of the value of the textbooks they bought, however, the total value of the ordinary books had to be at least 3 million yen annually. This imposition was held to be an unfair business practice.

In the *Farmers' Co-operative* case, [94] a farmers' co-operative which was authorized to issue the agricultural modernization loan (a governmental subsidy loan at an interest rate lower than the market rate) and had a strong bargaining position in relation to farmers who were members of it and who were borrowers of the loan, made the loan conditional on the purchase of agricultural machines which it sold. The FTC held that it was an unfair business practice.

As shown in the above two cases, a tie-in contract is held unlawful if it is used by the seller of a commodity with sufficient economic power with

[93] FTC Decision, 11 Feb. 1964, *Shinketsushū,* 12 (1965), 100 *et seq.*

[94] FTC Decision, 12 Dec. 1963, ibid. 39 *et seq.*

regard to the tying commodity. However, if it is necessary to combine the sale of a tying commodity with that of tied commodity for quality control or the promotion of efficiency, it may be justified.

E. EXCLUSIVE DEALING ARRANGEMENT

In an exclusive dealing arrangement, one party in a transaction has imposed on him the condition that he refrains from dealing with competitors of the other party. Typical examples include an arrangement whereby a manufacturer imposes on dealers the prohibition that the latter cannot deal with commodities of manufacturers who compete with the former, or whereby a trading company imposes on manufacturers the condition that they cannot sell their products to its competitors. An exclusive dealing arrangement is one of the conducts covered in Article 2(9)(iv), which states that an unreasonable arrangement whereby one of the parties to a transaction has imposed upon him the condition that he refrain from certain activities or that he perform them is unlawful.

General Designation No. 11 also provides for an exclusive dealing arrangement. Under this provision, an exclusive dealing arrangement is unlawful in two situations. If a manufacturer imposes on dealers the condition that they must stop dealing with commodities which they were previously handling (or it can be the condition imposed on manufacturers by a trading company that the former must stop selling to its competitors), such a condition is unlawful. The rationale behind this rule is that the oppressiveness of unilaterally demanding from other parties to a transaction that they stop dealing with other enterprises with which they previously have been dealing is the basis of the unlawfulness. Although there are some critical comments that this alone is insufficient to prove the anti-competitive nature of the conduct, this is a rule incorporated in previous FTC decisions.[95]

In the other situation, an enterprise with strong market power imposes the condition on other parties in a transaction that the latter cannot deal with its competitors. If the powerful enterprise imposes such a condition, its competitors are deprived of access to the market. If, for example, a large car manufacturer imposes the condition on car dealers that they cannot sell cars produced by its competitors, the competitors may be deprived of market access if the dealers' network under the control of the manufacturer is large, and to construct a separate distribution network would be difficult. In this situation, the core of the issue is that of market foreclosure.

The test here is to judge whether the party imposing such a condition is

[95] See Matsushita, n. 19, above, p. 166.

a powerful enterprise. There is no single answer to this question. However, the 1991 FTCJ Guidelines give some hints.

The 1991 FTCJ Guidelines state that if a powerful enterprise imposes a non-price restriction (such as an exclusive dealing arrangement) and the impact on the market is great, it is likely to be challenged as an unfair business practice. It states that to judge whether an enterprise is 'powerful' or not the FTC will use the threshold based on the market share or the ranking of the enterprise in question. If an enterprise has a market share of 10 per cent or above or the ranking in terms of market share is within the top three, then it will be subject to examination.

The Guidelines also state that the mere fact that an enterprise has surpassed this numerical test does not make it a 'powerful' enterprise automatically but that factors such as the following will be taken into consideration: (1) the structure of the relevant market (such as the concentration ratio, the peculiarities of the commodity involved, the degree of product differentiation, the distribution channels, and the ease or difficulty of new entry), (2) the position of the enterprise which imposes a non-price restriction (such as the market share, the ranking, the prestige of a brand name or trade name), (3) the number of distributors which have the restriction imposed upon them and their positions in the market, (4) the effect of the restriction in question on the activities of distributors, and (5) the effect of the restriction on competition among manufacturers, and among distributors, and new entry.

The criteria stated in the Guidelines are vague and it is hard to pinpoint the exact factors which will be used in a concrete case. However, it can be interpreted that the Guidelines set up a safe harbour for the enterprise whose market share is 10 per cent or below or its ranking in terms of market share is lower than the top three. Even if an enterprise has a market share of 10 per cent or more or its ranking is within the top three, this does not make the enterprise a 'powerful' enterprise automatically. The FTC considers the factors enumerated from (1) to (3) above as well as the market share or the ranking and decides whether the enterprise is a powerful enterprise or not on a case-by-case basis.

There are a number of cases in which the FTC held exclusive dealing arrangements unlawful. Without going into the details of the cases, it should be mentioned that, in those cases, the market share possessed by the manufacturer in question was quite high. For example, in the *Muto Kōgyō* case,[96] the manufacturer of drafting instruments with a market share of 70 per cent imposed on distributors the condition that they could not sell competing products. The FTC held that this restriction was an unfair business practice.

[96] FTC Decision, 22 Nov. 1974, *Shinketsushū*, 21 (1975), 148 *et seq.*

F. RESALE PRICE MAINTENANCE

In resale price maintenance, a manufacturer of a commodity directs wholesalers and retailers to maintain the level of wholesale or retail price. This has the effect of eliminating price competition among wholesalers and retailers as regards the commodity supplied by the manufacturer (elimination of intra-brand price competition). General Designation No. 12 provides that supplying, without a justfiable reason, a commodity to purchasers with the following conditions amounts to an unfair business practice: (1) to fix the price of the commodity at which the purchaser must sell it, or otherwise restrict the freedom of the purchaser to set the sales price, or (2) to fix the price of the commodity at which an enterprise which purchases the commodity from the purchaser must sell it and cause the purchaser to control that price or otherwise cause the purchaser to restrict the freedom of the enterprise to set its sales price.

It is recognized in Supreme Court decisions and FTC decisions that a resale price maintenance is unlawful in principle unless exempted from the application of the AML by Article 24.2 of the AML.[97] The reason for this illegality is that resale price maintenance can be effectively enforced only if the manufacturer which imposes it on distributors has a strong influence in the market and, therefore, it is anti-competitive in its nature.

Resale price maintenance is unlawful if it is binding on wholesalers and retailers. The question here is the meaning of 'binding'. The Guidelines give the following illustrations of arrangements that are binding on wholesalers and retailers. (1) If there is an agreement, whether it is a written or an oral agreement, between a manufacturer and distributors that the latter will resell the commodity supplied by the manufacturer at the price directed by the manufacturer, it is binding. (2) If the manufacturer utilizes a coersive method to cause distributors to comply with the price directed by the manufacturer, by imposing economic disadvantages or suggesting that they would be imposed if they did not comply with it, such a direction is regarded as binding. Such economic disadvantages include, for example, withholding supply of the commodity and cutting rebate to distributors in the event of non-compliance.

Article 24.2 of the AML provides that resale price maintenance with regard to books and other matters which are objects of copyright is exempted. Likewise two kinds of commodity designated by the FTC are exempted from the application of the AML: cosmetics and pharmaceuticals.

[97] As a representative case, see the Wakōdō case (Decision of the Supreme Court, 11 July 1975, *Minshū* 29/6, 888 *et seq*.

G. VERTICAL TERRITORIAL AND CUSTOMER RESTRICTIONS

Generally, in a vertical territorial restriction, a manufacturer allocates territory to each dealer within which he can engage in business, and, in a vertical customer restriction, a manufacturer restricts the customers with whom a dealer can engage in transactions. For example, a manufacturer designates retailers to whom a wholesaler can sell the manufacturer's product and not to any others.

The Guidelines list three major types of vertical territorial arrangements. (1) The area of primary responsibility, (2) the restriction of location of establishment, (3) the strict territorial allocation. In the area of primary responsibility, a manufacturer assigns to each dealer a geographical area as 'the area of primary responsibility'. Each dealer is not allocated the exclusive territory but an area in which he has the primary responsibility. Therefore, a dealer is not absolutely prohibited from engaging in business in other areas. In a restriction of location, a manufacturer designates the location at which a dealer can set up his business establishment. In a strict territorial allocation, each dealer is given a territory and is prohibited from engaging in business in other areas.

The 1991 FTCJ Guidelines state that if a powerful enterprise imposes a strict territorial restriction on dealers and if it has the effect of maintaining the price of the commodity supplied by the manufacturer, it is unlawful. They state also that if an enterprise not only restricts the sales territory of a dealer but also prohibits them from selling to any customer who is located outside the territory allocated, and if, as the result, the price of the commodity supplied by the manufacturer is maintained, it is unlawful.

The Guidelines provide that a customer restriction imposed by a manufacturer on dealers is unlawful if it is used as a means of maintaining the price of the commodity supplied by the manufacturer.

In the above situations, the important requirement is that the enterprise which imposes restrictions be a 'powerful' enterprise. The meaning of a 'powerful' enterprise as used in the 1991 FTCJ Guidelines has been already explained.

There are a few cases in which the FTC proceeded against vertical restraints imposed by manufacturers on dealers. One such cases is the *Fuji X-Ray* case[98] in which a manufacturer of X-ray film with a 70 per cent market share imposed vertical territorial restrictions on each dealer and eliminated competition among the dealers. In the *Morinaga* case,[99] a manufacturer of powdered milk with a large market share imposed the restriction on dealers that they could sell the product supplied by the

[98] FTC Decision, 11 May 1981, *Shinketsushū*, 28 (1982), 10 *et seq*.

[99] FTC Decision, 28 Nov. 1977, ibid. 24 (1978), 106 *et seq*.

manufacturer only to those retailers which had been designated by the manufacturer. The FTC held that it was unlawful.

H. ABUSE OF DOMINANT POSITION

Article 2(9)(v) of the AML states that 'dealing with another party by unwarranted use of one's bargaining position' is an unfair business practice. The FTC announced Designation No. 14 which specifies the following conduct as amounting to unfair business practices: (1) requiring the party to a continuous transaction to purchase goods or services other than those which are the subject of the transaction; (2) requiring the party to a continuous transaction to offer money, services, or other kind of economic benefit to oneself; (3) setting or changing business terms which are unduly disadvantageous to the other party to a transaction; (4) unduly disadvantaging the other party to a transaction with regard to the terms and enforcement of the transaction other than the above three items; and (5) requiring the other party to a transaction to follow a directive or to obtain prior approval concerning the selection of such other party's directors.

The above provisions require that the malefactor is in a dominant position in relation to the other party to a transaction. Even though 'dominant position' is nowhere defined, in the *Miyakawa* case,[100] the Supreme Court held that a dominant position means a dominance in a transaction and not necessarily a dominance in a market. Therefore, even if a small enterprise is engaged in a transaction, it can be in a dominant position if the other party to the transaction is even smaller. In the *Miyakawa* case, a financial co-operative, which was not a large enterprise, imposed on a borrower of money the condition that the latter had to deposit a large amount of money in return for a loan which it received. Since the borrower was a very small enterprise, the Supreme Court held that this condition amounted to an abuse of dominant position.

The next question is the meaning of abuse of dominant position. Here again there is no definition of abuse. In transactions, there is often a difference between the parties in terms of their economic power and the weaker party must sometimes suffer a disadvantage. To hold that any disadvantage incurred by the weaker party to a transaction is an abuse of dominant position by the stronger party would be an excessive intervention in the freedom of contract. However, if unduly harsh conditions imposed by the stronger party are left uncontrolled, fairness in transactions will be seriously damaged.

Whether a condition imposed by the stronger party to a transaction on the weaker party amounts to an abuse or not depends on the particular

[100] Decision of the Supreme Court, 20 June 1977, *Minshū*, 31/4 (1988), 449 *et seq.*

factors involved in each case and needs a case-by-case analysis. However, to hold a condition imposed by the stronger party to a transaction imposed on the weaker party an abuse of dominant position, it is necessary that some oppressive measures such as threat or intimidation are used.

A famous case in this area is the *Mitsukoshi* case.[101] Mitsukoshi was the largest and probably the most prestigious department store and, due to the prestige it enjoyed, it was a great benefit to suppliers of commodities to be able to supply them to Mitsukoshi. Mitsukoshi took advantage of this position, demanded that suppliers purchase certain luxury items such as paintings and jewels, contribute money for festivals sponsored by Mitsukoshi to promote its business, and bear the costs of repairing and renovating Mitsukoshi retail stores, without guaranteeing that products supplied by suppliers contributing such funds would be exhibited there. The FTC claimed that if a powerful purchaser such as Mitsukoshi made a request, suppliers had no choice but to comply, and, therefore, the mere fact that Mitsukoshi made such proposals constituted an abuse of dominant position.

This case was resolved by a consent decision and, therefore, legal issues involved in the case were not analysed to a full extent. However, this case is an illustration of types of conduct which are likely to be challenged as abuse of dominant position.

The Law to Prevent Unreasonable Delay in Payment to Subcontractors (the Subcontractors Law) is aimed at protecting small subcontractors who supply parts and components to large manufacturers and prohibits large manufacturers from abusing their bargaining position by, for example, unreasonably delaying payment to subcontractors, refusing to accept previously ordered products from subcontractors, and unreasonably forcing subcontractors to reduce prices. The Subcontractors Law is a piece of legislation which supplements the AML. The law requires large enterprises to file detailed reports with the FTC concerning their transactions with subcontractors. Conduct prohibited by this law is typical of examples of abuse of dominant position by a large manufacturer.

2.9 Regulation of International Contracts

A. AN OVERVIEW

Article 6 of the AML specifically provides for the regulation of international contracts. Article 6(1) of the AML states: 'No enterprise shall

[101] FTC Decision, 17 June 1982, *Shinketsushū*, 29 (1982), 31 *et seq*.

enter into an international agreement or an international contract containing provisions which constitute an unreasonable restraint of trade or unfair business practice.' An international contract containing provisions which constitute an unreasonable restraint of trade is a so-called international cartel agreement. An international contract containing provisions which constitute an unfair business practice is generally a contract which contains provisions which unilaterally restrict business activities of one of the parties to the agreement, such as a contract between a Japanese importer and a foreign exporter whereby the Japanese importer is imposed on him the condition that he must maintain the price in Japan of the imported commodity as directed by the exporter.

Article 6(2) of the AML authorizes the FTC to designate kinds of international contract subject to notification to the FTC. Under this article, the FTC has designated several types of international contract coming under this filing requirement.[102]

Article 8(1)(i) prohibits trade associations from entering into an international agreement containing provisions which constitute an unreasonable restraint of trade or an unfair business practice. For example, a trade association composed of manufacturers of commodity X enters into an agreement with foreign competitors whereby the members of the association limit the amount exported to the country to which the foreign competitors belong.

There will be a more detailed discussion in a later chapter of the guidelines announced by the FTC with regard to items such as patent/know-how licensing agreements and the sole import distributorships. In this section, we will touch only on general aspects of the control of international contracts under Article 6(1).

[102] FTC Regulation 1, 1971 as amended. The latest amendment took place on 30 March 1992. Under the current regulation, international contracts which fall under one of the following categories must be notified to the FTC: (1) those in which licensing of patent, utility model and other technology (including computer programs protected by the Coypright Law) is involved and whose term is one year or more (i) if the domestic party to the contract occupies 10 per cent or more in the total supply in Japan of the products similar to those which are the object of the technology in question and the ranking in terms of market share of the party is within the third from the top or (ii) if provisions with regard to sales price or resale price in Japan of such products are incorporated in the contract; (2) those in which the exclusive right to sell a commodity in the designated area is involved and whose term is one year or more (i) if the domestic party to the contract occupies 10 per cent or more in the total supply in Japan of products similar to those which are the object of the contract and the ranking in terms of market share of the party is within the third from the top or (ii) if provisions with regard to sales price or resale price in Japan of such products are incorporated in the contract; (3) those in which the domestic and foreign parties jointly operate a business by acquiring stocks or shares of a company and those term is more than one year.

B. WHAT IS AN INTERNATIONAL CONTRACT?

In order to come under the control of Article 6(1), a contract must be an international contract. The AML gives no definition of an international contract. However, it is generally understood by commentators that there are some necessary requirements for an international contract. In a contract between individuals, whether the contract is international or not is determined by whether it is entered into between two or more persons who belong to different countries. Therefore, a contract between a Japanese national and a British subject is an international contract. In corporate entities such as corporations, the internationality of a contract is based on the fact that the parties are established by the laws of different countries. Therefore, a contract between a company established by the Japanese Commercial Code and a company established by the Delaware Corporation law in the United States is an international contract.

A contract entered into between a Japanese company and a Japanese branch of a foreign company is an international contract since the branch is part of the foreign company. Likewise a contract entered into between a foreign branch of a Japanese company and a foreign company is an international contract. However, a contract between a Japanese company and a Japanese subsidiary of a foreign company is generally regarded as a domestic contract since the Japanese subsidiary of a foreign company is an entity established under the Commercial Code of Japan. A contract entered into between a foreign subsidiary of a Japanese company and a foreign company is not an international contract since the foreign subsidiary of the Japanese company is established under the local law.

To adhere to this principle strictly may sometimes be unrealistic since there may be no substantial difference between a subsidiary of a company and a branch of it. It may, therefore, be necessary to pierce through the corporate veil and treat a subsidiary and the parent as one entity. However, such treatment should be limited to those cases in which the sameness of a subsidiary and the parent is obvious.

C. THE PROHIBITION OF CONCLUDING OR ENTERING INTO AN INTERNATIONAL CONTRACT

A unique feature of Article 6(1) is that it prohibits enterprises from 'concluding' or 'entering into' an international contract which contains such provisions as those constituting an unreasonable restraint of trade or an unfair business practice rather than committing an unreasonable restraint of trade or an unfair business practice.

This provision poses some interpretational problems especially with reference to the prohibition of international cartels. As discussed before,

Articles 2(6) and 3 prohibit an unreasonable restraint of trade or a cartel. Therefore, if an international agreement contains provisions which constitute an unreasonable restraint of trade, it would come under those provisions. Then why do we need Article 6(1) to prohibit an international contract that contains provisions which constitute an unreasonable restraint of trade?

There is no satisfactory doctrine propounded by commentators which explains the necessity or *raison d'être* of Article 6(1) in this regard. There are, however, two theories proposed.[103] One of them maintains that although Articles 2(6) and 3 are applicable to an international agreement that contains items which constitute an unreasonable restraint of trade, it is not clear by reading the language of Articles 2(6) and 3 that they are so applicable, and so Article 6(1) confirms that Articles 2(6) and 3 apply to an international agreement that contains provisions which constitute an unreasonable restraint of trade. This theory has a fatal flaw in that there is a difference between the penalty for a violation of Article 3 and that for a violation of Article 6(1). If Article 6(1) is nothing but a confirmation that Articles 2(6) and 3 are applicable to an international agreement that contains items which constitute an unreasonable restraint, why is there this difference?

The second theory maintains that whereas Article 2(6) and Article 3 are applicable when an international agreement containing items which constitute an unreasonable restraint of trade is put into practice, Article 6(1) is applicable to such an international agreement as soon as it is concluded or entered into since Article 6(1) prohibits the conclusion or entering into of such a contract and whether or not such a contract has been put into practice is irrelevant. This theory states that, for this reason, Article 6(1) is a preventive measure in relation to Articles 2(6) and 3 as far as the prohibition of international cartels is concerned. We may call this theory 'a prevention theory'.

This theory is not without problems. There is no similar preventive measure for a domestic contract. Why is there a preventive measure only for an international contract? There is no satisfactory answer to this question. However, as compared with the confirmation theory, the flaw of this preventive theory is less fatal. Therefore, we should probably adopt the preventive theory.

With regard to the prohibition of an international agreement which contains provisions which constitute an unfair business practice, Article 6(1) has a distinct role different from that of Article 19, which prohibits enterprises from engaging in unfair business practices. For example, if an international contract contains a provision that the Japanese party (the

[103] Matsushita, n. 19, above, pp. 180–5.

purchaser) of the commodity supplied by the foreign party (the exporter) must keep up the resale price of this commodity in Japan, it amounts to an international contract which contains such items as constitute an unfair business practice. However, if the foreign party has no establishment in Japan, Article 19 is not immediately applicable to this contract since Article 19 prohibits an enterprise from 'engaging' in an unfair business practice and, in this case, the malefactor who is engaged in an unfair business practice is the foreign party to which the jurisdiction of the FTC does not extend. However, since Article 6(1) prohibits an enterprise from concluding or entering into an international agreement, the Japanese party who has entered into this international contract is in violation of Article 6(1). In this situation, the FTC can issue an order to the Japanese party requiring it to cancel the provision of the international contract which provides for resale price maintenance.[104]

It may be observed that, as applied in this way, Article 6(1) prohibits the 'victim' instead of the malefactor in an international contract from complying with the unfair term. In substance, Article 6(1) is intended to be applied to the Japanese party to an international contract which contains such provisions as constitute an unfair business practice in the situation where the FTC cannot catch the foreign malefactor. Therefore, some commentators say that Article 6(1) is the provision for 'indirect extraterritorial application' of the AML.[105]

D. REPORTING DUTY OF INTERNATIONAL CONTRACTS

Article 6(2) authorizes the FTC to designate the types of international contract which are subject to the reporting duty. The FTC designated five types of international contract as being subject to the reporting duty. They are: (1) a contract with regard to technology transfer, (2) a long-term contract for sale of purchase whose term extends for more than one year, (3) a contract for a joint venture whose term extends for more than one year, (4) a contract for assigning a trade mark or copyright or for licensing it, whose terms extend for more than one year, and (5) a sales purchase contract whereby Japanese enterprises which are in a competitive relationship jointly enter into a contract with a foreign enterprise for more than one year, or a contract between a Japanese enterprise and a foreign enterprise in competitive relationship with regard to a continuous transaction and whose term extends for more than one year.

An enterprise which enters into an international contract which belongs

[104] An example is the Novo case (Decision of the Supreme Court, 20 June 1976, *Minshū*, 29 (1976)), 1592 *et seq*.

[105] Yazawa, 'Interim Report of the Committee on the Extraterritorial Effects of Trade Regulation', *Japanese Annual of International Law*, 9 (1965), 174–7

to any of the above categories is required to file the contract with the FTC within thirty days after the contract is concluded.

E. CASES UNDER ARTICLE 6(1)

Most of the issues under Article 6(1) are resolved by way of informal administrative guidance and the contents of those cases are not fully disclosed. Usualy the parties intending to enter into an international agreement consult with the FTC before the agreement is executed and the FTC advises the parties to delete or modify a provision in it which may cause a problem under Article 6(1) of the AML. When such a provision is deleted or modified, the FTC does not proceed any further. The number of cases resolved in this way is reported in the annual report of the FTC which it submits to the National Diet.[106]

There are, however, a handful of cases in which the FTC took a formal action. In some of them, the issue was that of an unreasonable restraint of trade or an international cartel, and, in some others, the issue was that of an unfair business practice. Some of the important ones are touched upon below.

The *Chemical Fibre* cases decided in 1972 are important in terms of the control of international cartels under Article 6(1). The *Chemical Fibre* cases consist of five cases in which international cartel arrangements between Japanese and foreign enterprises were challenged. Since the content of the five cases is basically the same, we will touch upon only one of them. This case is the *Asahi Chemical Company* case[107] in which European manufacturers of chemical fibre and Japanese manufacturers of the same product divided the European and the Japanese markets by agreement. After the United States–Japan Textile Agreement, the Japanese manufacturers were restricted in exporting chemical fibre to the American market. The European manufacturers, fearing that the Japanese manufacturers of chemical fibre would shift the export to the European market, negotiated with the Japanese manufacturers and an agreement was reached between the Japanese and European manufacturers to the effect that the Japanese manufacturers would respect the 'traditional market' of the European manufacturers and the European manufacturers would respect the traditional market of the Japanese manufacturers. In fact, this meant that each side would refrain from exporting the product to the other's traditional market. In order to

[106] In 1990, for example, the Fair Trade Commission advised private parties to modify their international contracts in 232 cases. See The Fair Trade Commission, *Kōseithiki Iinkai Nenji Hōkoku (Annual Report of the Fair Trade Commission)* (1991), 111.

[107] FTC Decision, 27 Dec. 1972, *Shinketsushū*, 19 (1973), 124 *et seq*.

implement this agreement, the Japanese manufacturers entered into an export cartel agreement and restricted exports to the European market.

The German Cartel Authority detected the existence of this agreement, proceeded against the German parties to the agreement and imposed a heavy fine on them.[108] Thereafter the German Cartel Authority notified the FTC of the existence of this agreement and the FTC issued a recommendation to the Japanese parties. The Japanese parties accepted the recommendation and a recommendation decision was handed down by the FTC requiring them to cancel the agreement.

This case is significant not only from the viewpoint of applying Article 6(1) to an international cartel agreement but also from that of co-operative effort between the enforcement agencies in controlling international cartels.

The *Komatsu/Bucyrus* case[109] is an important case in which the issue was that of unfair business practice. In this case, the FTC terminated the proceeding for the reason that the parties to the dispute settled the matter and no decision was handed down. Nevertheless a number of interesting legal questions are involved in this case.

Komatsu was a Japanese company manufacturing power shovels and Bucyrus was a US company producing the same product. Komatsu intended to introduce from Bucyrus technology to produce power shovels. After negotiation between the two companies, they decided to enter into the followng arrangement.

Komatsu and Bucyrus (and a trading company) would establish a joint subsidiary in Japan whose name was Komatsu/Bucyrus. Bucyrus would license technology to Komatsu/Bucyrus. Komatsu/Bucyrus would pay royalties to Bucyrus and use Komatsu as a subcontractor to produce power shovels. Komatsu/Bucyrus would sell power shovels to Komatsu, and Komatsu would sell them to third parties. The arrangement between Bucyrus and Komatsu/Bucyrus was subject to cancellation by a prior notice of either party.

The above was a formal agreement. However, Komatsu/Bucyrus was nothing but a paper company without any substance. It had one office, several employees, and nothing else. Therefore, in fact, Komatsu acquired the technology from Bucyrus thorugh Komatsu/Bucyrus and paid royalties. On the board of directors of Komatsu/Bucyrus, directors from both Komatsu and Bucyrus were present and decisions had to be made by unanimous vote.

The above arrangement meant that, while Bucyrus could cancel the agreement whenever it wished to do so, Komatsu could not cancel it and

[108] Decision of the German Federal Cartel Office, 1972, *Wirtschaft und Wettbewerb* (WuW), 525–48, BKart A 1393, 1407, 1411 and 1915.

[109] FTC Decision, 26 Oct. 1981, *Shinketsushū*, 28 (1982), 79 *et seq.*

had to keep paying royalties unless the director of Komatsu/Bucyrus representing Bucyrus agreed to it. This agreement was validated under the Foreign Investment Law. This agreement was filed with the FTC and the FTC did not object to it.

After more than ten years, Komatsu became dissatisfied with this agreement and complained to the FTC that inequality in terms of cancellation of the agreement amounted to an unfair business practice and that the agreement which contained this cancellation clause was contrary to Article 6(1) of the AML.

The FTC initiated proceedings against both Komatsu and Bucyrus. Since, however, Komatsu and Bucyrus came to a settlement, the FTC terminated the proceedings.

The above is an outline of the case. Since the FTC terminated the proceedings, there is no formal decision by the FTC. However, we can note several interesting legal problems. First of all, the FTC did not disclose on whom the complaint was served. Under the AML, the FTC must serve the complaint on the party to whom it is addressed.[110] Bucyrus had no branch in Japan and the question is on whom it could have been served. Komatsu/Bucyrus was a joint subsidiary of Komatsu and Bucyrus. However, the complaint to Bucyrus of the FTC could not have been served on Komatsu/Bucyrus since the FTC claimed in the complaint that Komatsu/Bucyrus had no substance and to serve the complaint to Bucyrus on Komatsu/Bucyrus on the theory that Komatsu/Bucyrus was a substantial establishment of Bucyrus in Japan would be inconsistent with this claim.

Secondly, this agreement was validated under the Foreign Investment Law. Since there was a provision in the Foreign Investment Law which stated that the validation under this law did not prevent the FTC from stepping in whenever it deemed that a provision was contrary to the AML, the initiation by the FTC of administrative proceedings was lawful. However, the validation under the Foreign Investment Law would create the appearance of lawfulness of the arrangement which was validated, and a later intervention by the FTC would cause a legal insecurity and, as a matter of enforcement policy, it was probably unwise. Now that the Foreign Investment Law has been abolished, this problem is moot.

Similarly, the agreement had been filed with the FTC and no objection was made by the FTC when it was filed. The FTC proceeded against the agreement after more than ten years. The fact that the FTC did not object to the agreement when it was filed did not give any immunity to the agreement from the application of Article 6(1) of the AML. Indeed

[110] Art. 50(1) and (2) of the AML state respectively that the Fair Trade Commission shall initiate a hearing by a written complaint and that the hearing process is effectively initiated when the complaint is served on the respondent.

the claim of the FTC was that it had no objection to the formal contents of the agreement but it questioned the actual operations of the agreement. Here again, however, this treatment by the FTC is likely to create legal instability.

In this case, both Komatsu and Bucyrus were made the respondents. Since Komatsu and Bucyrus were the parties to this agreement, it was formally correct for the FTC to proceed against both parties on the ground that they had entered into an international agreement which contained a provision amounting to an unfair business practice. However, Komatsu suffered the adverse effect of this agreement and it had all the reasons to have it treated as unlawful while the position of Bucyrus was the opposite. Therefore, even though both parties were made the respondents, their interests were diametrically opposed to each other. The FTC should have proceeded against Bucyrus only and should have left Komatsu out.

2.10 Exemptions

There are some exemptions from the application of the AML. They can be classified as those which are based on provisions in the AML and those which are based on provisions in other laws. Only brief comments will be made on them. Since this topic will be dealt with in later chapters, we will briefly describe the basic provisions here.

Articles 21–24.4 of the AML provide for exemptions. Article 21 states that conduct inherent to natural monopolies such as the railway, gas, and electric power businesses is exempt from the AML. It is important to bear in mind that what is inherent varies from time to time depending on technological developments. For instance, the telecommunications business was once regarded as a natural monopoly. However, nowadays it has been liberalized and several companies are competing in the long-distance telephone business.

Article 22 provides for an exemption from the AML for activities based on laws which license and regulate business. Article 23 states that the exercise of intangible property rights is exempted. Intangible property rights include those based on the Patent Law,[111] the Utility Model Law,[112] the Trademark Law,[113] the Design Law, [114] and the Copyright Law.[115] Typically infringement suits under those laws are regarded as the

[111] Tokyo Hō, Law 121, 1959.
[112] Jitsuyō Shinan Hō, Law 123, 1959.
[113] Shohyō Hō, Law 127, 1959.
[114] Ishō Hō, Law 125, 1959.
[115] Chosakuken Hō, Law 48, 1970.

exercise of the right. There will be some discussion of the exemption based on intangible property rights with regard to licensing agreements in a later chapter. Article 24 states that activities of co-operatives are exempted from the application of the AML. This aspect will be touched upon in a later chapter.

Article 24.2 provides for an exemption from the AML of resale price maintenance under some conditions. This exemption has been discussed already. Article 24.3 and Article 24.4 respectively provide for an exemption from the AML of depression cartels and rationalization cartels. They will be treated in a later chapter.

There are a number of laws which exempt some activities from the application of the AML. Such exemptions are given in the areas such as the export–import trade, small business activities, marine transportation, and insurance. Most of them exempt some types of agreements (or cartels) from the application of the AML. They will be discussed later in connection with foreign trade and industrial policy.

3
Foreign Trade and Investment Laws

3.1 The Major Foreign Trade and Investment Laws

A. MAJOR LAWS AND REGULATIONS

Overview of Laws

The laws regulating international trade and investment are numerous. If we take a broad definition of laws and regulations which affect international trade and investment, the major parts of the Civil Code which deal with contracts and properties and those of the Commercial Code dealing with corporations and commercial transactions are relevant. However, laws dealing with private transactions such as contract laws and corporation laws will be treated in other volumes in this series. In this book, our focus is on the public regulation of international trade and investment.

Even in this more limited definition, the scope of laws which affect international trade and investment is great. What should be included within the category of laws which regulate trade and investment depends on the definition of foreign trade and investment. For example, laws such as the Large-Scale Retail Stores Law which restricts new entry of supermarkets into local markets is a domestic law but has a restrictive effect on foreign supermarkets which intend to make an entry into the Japanese market. Likewise many laws which provide the licensing requirements for new entrants into the business areas which are subject to them (such as the laws regulating transportation) are designed to regulate primarily domestic enterprises and yet they may have some impact on foreign enterprises which plan to enter into those areas. For practical purposes, it is impossible to include every law and regulation which has some bearing on foreign trade and investment. We must be satisfied with the list of laws and regulations which have a direct impact on them.

The major laws include at least: the Foreign Exchange and Foreign Trade Control Law ('the Control Law'), the Export and Import Transactions Law ('the Transactions law'), the Customs and Tariff Law, the Tariff Law, the Anti-monopoly Law and the laws on intellectual property rights. Beside those major laws, there are some specific laws which regulate trade in particular areas such as agriculture. For example, the Foodstuffs Control Law prohibits the importation of rice. Some laws which deal with product standards, testing methods, and product representations have become a major trade issue. It has been claimed also that there are some non-legal barriers which constitute impediments to trade such as restrictive business practices exercised by private enterprises, business customers, and corporate structures. We will take up some of the important laws and regulations and examine them in detail later in this chapter. However, before we do it, it is perhaps useful to provide a brief summary of those laws and also the major enforcement agencies.

The Foreign Exchange and Foreign Trade Control Law

The Control Law is one of the basic laws which regulate external economic relationships. Broadly classified, this law controls both foreign exchange and investment and foreign trade. The law covers the areas of: (1) foreign exchange control, (2) the control of capital transactions, which include direct and indirect investment into Japan and foreign countries, (3) the control of exports, (4) the control of imports, and (5) the control of transfer of services in which transfer of technology is included. The MOF is in charge of (1) and (2) and the MITI has jurisdiction over (3), (4), and (5).

The Export and Import Transactions Law

The Transactions Law permits private enterprises to agree on the terms of export and import business. The law allows enterprises to enter into an 'export cartel' and an 'import cartel'. This law permits private enterprises to conclude an agreement amounting to an export or import agreement and exempts it from the application of the Anti-monopoly Law. In substance, however, the government (the MITI) takes an initiative and, by way of administrative guidance, directs enterprises to conclude an agreement. This is often done in the area of exports for the purpose of 'voluntary export restrain'.

The Customs and Tariff Law

This law provides for the basics of tariffs such as customs valuation, tariff quotas, anti-dumping and countervailing duties, emergency tariff, and retaliatory tariff.

The Tariff Law

The Tariff Law is a separate law from the Customs and Tariff Law and provides for matters such as the procedures for collecting customs duties and for entries of foreign ships and aircraft into Japan, bonded areas, export and import permits, and the procedure for the seizure of contraband commodities. While the Customs and Tariff Law is a substantive law providing for the basic principles for the tariff system, the Tariff Law is basically a procedural law which lays out the details of the procedure for the enforcement of the tariff system in Japan.

The Anti-monopoly Law

A detailed account of this law was given in Chapter 2. As touched upon there, the law is not designed to deal with international trade as such. Its primary objective is to regulate private enterprises' activities in the domestic market by prohibiting private monopolies, unreasonable restraint of trade, and unfair business practices. However, this law touches on some aspects of international trade and investment. Agreements of enterprises under the Transactions Law which go beyond the exemption are scrutinized by the FTC, and the MITI, in granting permission for export and import cartels must notity the FTC, consult with it, or obtain an agreement from it as the case may be. Also in areas such as a sole import distributorship, as explained later, the FTC has announced a set of guidelines which are used to regulate the conduct of sole import distributors.

The Intellectual Property Law

The Intellectual Property Law includes a variety of laws such as the Patent Law,[1] the Utility Model Law,[2] the Trade Mark Law,[3] the Design Right Law,[4] the Copyright Law,[5] and the Maskwork Law.[6] All of them provide for the exclusive rights on technology, marks, designs, expressions, and related matters. Generally, products which infringe any of the above laws are prevented from being imported into Japan. Therefore, one aspect of all of the above laws is that of international trade law. Beside the above, the Unfair Competition Law provides for the protection of trade secrets.

The Export Insurance Law

Unlike the laws described above, the Export Insurance Law[7] is not a regulatory law which controls the activities of business enterprises in international trade and investment. The role of this law is that of the promotion of foreign investment by extending insurance coverage to

[1] Tokkyo Hō, Law 121, 1959.
[2] Jitsuyō Shin-an Hō, Law 123, 1959.
[3] Shōhyō Hō, Law 127, 1959.
[4] Ishō Hō, Law 125, 1959.
[5] Chosakuken Hō, Law 48, 1970.
[6] Handōtai Shūsekikairono Kairohaichi Nikansuru Hōritsu, Law 43, 1987.
[7] Yushutsu Hoken Hō, Law 67, 1950.

private enterprises which invest in a foreign country and which may incur business losses due to 'country risk'.

Miscellaneous Laws

Beside the major laws which are touched upon above, there are a multitude of miscellaneous laws which have impacts on some aspects of trade. One of the important categories of law is that of laws on technical standards. There are many laws which establish, among other things, product safety standards, testing procedures of products, and the requirements for representation of the quality of products. The difference between the standards existing in Japan and those in other countries in those areas cause difficulties to foreign exporters who intend to export products to Japan.

There are some specific laws (mostly in agriculture) which prohibit or restrict importation of specified agricultural products. The prime example is the prohibition of the importation of rice under the Foodstuffs Control Law,[8] and there are several laws of a similar nature.

Non-Legal Barriers to Trade

It has been pointed out that non-legal barriers constitute impediments to trade and investment into Japan by foreign enterprises. Items which have been claimed as *de facto* barriers are many and cannot be fully explained here. We will briefly mention some of the important ones. Distribution networks in Japan are claimed to be too complicated, exclusive, and lengthy. Some restrictive business practices engaged in by private enterprises such as an exclusive 'keiretsu' (closely associated links between enterprises through stock-ownerships, interlocking directorships, long-standing business relationships, and related matters), business customs such as 'dango' (bid-rigging by enterprises in public procurements) are claimed to operate as factual barriers to entry into the Japanese market. Although they are not legal measures, they may be barriers and need to be addressed also.

B. ADMINISTRATIVE ORDERS

The major laws as above touched upon often provide only the general framework, and details are delegated to the enforcement agency in charge of the law in question. Therefore, it is vitally important to examine the regulations issued by the relevant enforcement agency. Usually, under the law, there is a Cabinet order or decree which provides some specifics of the regulation and also there are ministerial regulations which lay out the details of regulation.

[8] Shokuryō Kanri Hō, Law 40, 1942.

For example, the Control Law regulates foreign trade and investment. In the regulation of export trade, under the law, there is the Export Control Order (a Cabinet decree)[9] and ministerial orders issued by the MITI. The situations are similar with other laws also.

C. ENFORCEMENT AGENCIES

Each law is enforced by a ministry and a brief description will follow. As touched upon earlier, the Control Law provides for the regulation of foreign exchange, capital transactions including foreign investments, transfer of services including technology, and export–import trade. The MOF is in charge of the regulation of foreign exchange and capital transactions (foreign investment) and the MITI administers those parts of the law which relate to the control of transfer of services including technology and the export–import trade.

The Transactions Law authorizes private enterprises to enter into export–import agreements whereby they jointly decide the terms of business such as price, quantity, areas of business, and related matters. It is the practice of the MITI to issue an administrative guidance (the MITI calls it a 'directive') to private enterprises to enter into an agreement under this Law. Moreover, this law anthorizes the MITI to intervene if agreements entered into among private enterprises are not sufficient to achieve the policy objectives of the law. Therefore, in actual operations, we can say that the enforcement agency of this law is the MITI.

The enforcement authority of the Customs and Tariff Law is vested in the MOF. Items such as the customs valuation, the tariff quotas, the emergency tariff, and the retaliatory tariffs are enforced by the MOF. However, in anti-dumping and countervailing duties, the MOF, the MITI, and the ministry in charge of the product in question are jointly responsible for investigating, to determine whether or not there is dumping, and whether or not an anti-dumping duty should be imposed.

The Tariff Law is exclusively enforced by the MOF. This law provides for the procedure of collecting duties and the powers of collecting them are vested in the Customs House which is part of the MOF.

A detailed explanation has already been made of the enforcement angency of the AML, which is the FTC or FTCJ.

Laws which protect intellectual property rights (except for the copyright law) are generally enforced by the Patent Administration, which is part of the MITI, and the Copyright Law is enforced by the Culture Administration, which is part of the Ministry of Education. However, courts play an important role in the enforcement of the rights under those

[9] Yushutsu Bōeki Kanri Rei, Decree 378, 1949.

laws. Whereas the administrative agencies such as the Patent Administration are authorized to handle the granting of rights and the invalidation of them, courts are authorized to determine whether an act is in infringement of the right under a law such as the Patent Law, issue an injunction to order the defendant to stop the infringement, and award damages to the successful plaintiff. There are criminal provisions incorporated in those laws. Criminal penalty can be imposed only by a decision of a court.

With regard to the prohibition of importation of a product from abroad which infringes the rights under any one of the intellectual property rights, the MOF has jurisdiction under Article 21 of the Customs and Tariff Law. Under this provision, the MOF can direct the custom houses to stop at the border products which infringe the right under any of those laws.

There are many laws which regulate the technical standards. With regard to laws relating to technical standards, there are several ministries in charge of enforcing them. We will mention the major ones. They are the Ministry of Health and Welfare (in pharmaceuticals and cosmetics), the MITI (in industrial products), the MOF (in such matters as customs procedures), the Ministry of Agriculture, Forestry, and Fishery (the MAFF) (in agricultural and food products), the Ministry of Construction (in products which relate to the construction industry), and others.

Laws relating to agriculture are generally enforced by the MAFF. For example, the Foodstuffs Control Law is enforced by the MAFF.

Judicial review is available with regard to any administrative decision made by a ministry in the enforcement of the law in its charge. As touched upon earlier, an appeal can be taken from a decision of an administrative agency under the Administrative Cases Litigation Law[10] or the Administrative Claims Examination Law[11] to courts in jurisdiction or to a higher branch of the administration. If the damage has been caused by the wrongful act of an official in the course of his or her duty, the plaintiff can bring a suit against the government under the State Redress Law[12] to recover the damages sustained.

There is a specialized agency which is entrusted with the settlement of trade disputes with the government in foreign trade and investment. This is the Office of Trade and Investment Ombudsman (the OTO).[13] The OTO is attached to the Administration of General Affairs of the Cabinet. It is composed of officials of various ministries and assisted by two

[10] Gyōsei Jiken Sosho Hō, Law 139, 1962.

[11] Gyōsei Fufuku Shinsa Hō, Law 160, 1962.

[12] Kokka Baishō Hō, Law 125, 1947.

[13] See Matsushita and Schoenbaum, Japanese International Trade and Investment Law (Tokyo, 1989), 44–5.

advisory councils. When a foreign exporter or investor, the government of a foreign country, or an importer has a claim against the Japanese government with regard to the ways in which laws affecting foreign trade and investment adversely affect the interest of a foreign exporter, investor, or importer, they can bring a claim to the OTO. The OTO has no power to change laws. However, it is entrusted with the task of recommending suitable solutions of disputes to the relevant ministry.

3.2 Regulation of Imports

A. TARIFFS, CLASSIFICATION, VALUATION, AND RELATED MATTERS

Under Article 84 of the Constitution, any tax must be imposed under a law. This applies to tariffs since they are part of the tax system in Japan. Article 3 of the Tariff Law states that tariffs are imposed on imported commodities on the basis of this law or other laws which provide for tariffs. It also states that, when there is a provision in a treaty to which Japan is a contracting party, tariffs may be based on it. Since Japan is a contracting party to the GATT, Japan is bound to observe the basic tariff rates agreed upon in the multilateral trade negotiations in the framework of the GATT. Japan has accepted the Multilateral Trade Negotation agreements concluded in the Tokyo Rounds including the code on tariff reduction. Therefore, the basic rates of tariffs are those contained in the Tokyo Round agreement.

Japan is a member of the Customs Co-operation Council (CCC) which is the major international organization established for the purpose of harmonizing tariff nomenclature and, as the result, Japanese tariffs are classified according to the Harmonized Commodity Description and Coding System established by the CCC convention for the classification of Goods in Customs Tariffs.

Customs valuations are the process through which the *ad valorem* tariff on a commodity is computed. In order to apply the tariff rate to a commodity, the value of the commodity must be determined first. If, for example, the tariff is 5 per cent of the value of the commodity, the value of it must be decided by one of the following methods.

Customs valuations are provided for in Article 4 of the Customs and Tariff Law under which the valuation must be based on the 'transaction value' of the imported commodity. The transaction value is the actual price of the commodity paid or payable by the importer of the commodity plus the cost of transport and certain other costs to the extent that they are not included in the price actually paid for the commodity. If the transaction value of the commodity is not known, the valuation is based on the transaction value of a similar or the same commodity exported on the same day as the commodity in question was exported or some day close in time. If none of those methods is possible, customs valuation is based on a price arrived at by calculating backward from the domestic sales price or a price arrived at by adding manufacturing cost and other costs. If all the methods above described are impossible, the valuation is based on the methods determined by the Cabinet.

The above valuation system is in accord with the system provided for in the Customs Valuation Code agreed upon in the Tokyo Round Negotiation. Before the Tokyo Round, the valuation was based on a constructed value which was the price which would prevail if the purchaser and the seller were independent from each other and if there were perfect competition in the market in which they were operating. Since the criteria were so general and abstract, there was room for manipulation on the part of the customs appraisers and there were some complaints that 'customs uplifts' occurred.[14] The Customs and Tariff Law was amended as the result of the Tokyo Round Negotiations and the present valuation system was established.

Article 9(3) of the Customs and Tariff Law provides for tariff quotas. The tariff quota is a system in which a lower tariff (the primary rate) is applied to an imported commodity up to a certain quantity level of imports and a higher tariff (the secondary rate) is applied to an imported commodity which is imported in excess of this level. This is a device to satisfy the demand for the commodity and, at the same time, protect the domestic industry producing the same or a similar commodity. For example, if the domestic demand for a commodity is 100 units, the domestic producers produce 50 units, and another 50 units are imported, the lower tariff rate is applied to the imported commodity up to the quantity of 50 units and the higher tariff rate is applied to the imports in excess of this quantity.

The tariff quota system has been utilized often by the Japanese government to protect domestic industries and, at the same time, secure imports of a commodity from abroad. For this purpose, there are a number of commodities which are subject to the tariff quota system. The tariff quota system can be invoked also as a safeguard measure which is touched upon in the following section.

[14] United States–Japan Trade Study Group, *A Special Progress Report* (Tokyo, 1980), 17.

B. IMPORT RESTRICTIONS

The GATT Obligation

Article 11 of the GATT generally prohibits contracting parties from imposing import restrictions other than tariffs such as import quotas. Although Japan is a contracting party to the GATT and, therefore, is obligated, under Article 11 of the GATT, to refrain from imposing import restrictions other than tariffs, there are a few laws which authorize import quotas and emergency tariffs. The GATT allows a few exceptions to the general prohibition on import restrictions other than tariffs. To cite two examples, one of them is Article 19 of the GATT which states that a contracting party can impose a safeguard measure in the form of a tariff or quantity restriction if, as the result of increased imports, the domestic industry producing the same or similar commodity suffers a serious injury or there is a threat thereof. The other is Article 11(2)(c) of the GATT which permits a quantity restriction on the import of agricultural products under certain conditions.

Whether or not the quantity restrictions on imports exercised by the Japanese government by law are justified under those provisions must be decided by a-case-by-case analysis.

Import Quotas

The import quota system is established by Article 52 of the Control Law and Articles 4 and 9 of the Import Control Order. Article 52 states that, in order to promote the development of foreign trade and the national economy, a person who intends to import a commodity may have the duty imposed to obtain an import approval. Under this article, the MITI can designate commodities which are subject to the import quota system. If a commodity is designated as subject to the import quota system, any person who intends to import the commodity must obtain an import quota and then an import approval. In granting an import approval, the MITI can attach conditions to it including the maximum quantity to be imported, the import price, the import channels, and related matters. The MITI can also decide to prohibit the import of a commodity.

There are several ways in which import quotas are allocated to importers. One is the 'first come, first served' system in which any importer who applies first gets the quota. In a sense, this system is a fair one since no conditions or qualifications are attached. However, this system may cause a confusion by the fact that potential importers may rush to apply for the quotas. Another is the allocation of quotas according to previous achievement. In this system, allocation of quotas is based on the previous import achievement. While this system has the advantage of stability, it has a defect in that the quotas are fixed by the previous achievement and entrepreneurship or innovative marketing is not taken into account. Still another way is to allocate quotas equally to all the applicants. Even though the equality may be a merit, this system would make the quota system too rigid.

No matter which system one adopts, there is a problem, and, in actuality, the quota system is used on the basis of any of the above systems depending on the peculiar situations of the case concerned. Probably the best way to handle the situation is to hold an auction in which the high bidders will get the quotas.

There is no provision which authorizes a private party to petition the government to invoke the import quota system. Therefore, any private party who desires to request the government to invoke the import quota system with regard to the import of an item must take a 'political' approach and pressurize the government or politicians who are influential with the policy-makers.

At present, quotas are imposed on certain agricultural items. With regard to those, there have been trade conflicts between Japan and other countries, especially the United States.

The import quota system under Article 52 of the Control Law can hardly be justified by Article 19 of the GATT since, in Article 52 and provisions of the Import Control Order, there is no requirement that an import has increased and that the increased import has caused a serious injury to a domestic industry. There is also no procedure to determine a domestic industry and a serious injury. Whether or not the import quota system is justified by Article 11(2)(c) of the GATT depends on specific measures which are taken by the Japanese government with regard to the agricultural items which are subjected to import quotas, as will be touched upon later in connection with the *Twelve Agricultural Items* case.

Beside the quota system under the Control Law, the import of a commodity may be prohibited by a specific law. The prime example is the prohibition of rice imports. The Foodstuff Control Law authorizes the government to exercise control over rice. Under this law, the government has the power to purchase rice from producers and to sell it to consumers. The purchase price and sales price are determined by the government.

Article 1(1) of the law provides that the import and export of rice shall not be made unless government approval is given thereto and that the person who has imported rice under approval shall sell it to the government. In this sense, the law does not necessarily require an absolute prohibition of rice imports. However, the Japanese government has maintained the policy of not allowing any import of rice from abroad for political reasons and the market share of foreign rice in the total consumption of rice in Japan is below 1 per cent.

This prohibition of rice imports has been one of the basic policies of the government and also the Liberal Democratic Party (the LDP), which has controlled the government due to the fact that farmers are an important constituency for the LDP. The reasons given for this absolute prohibition of rice imports are: (1) that rice is the only agricultural item in which Japan can achieve self-sufficiency and (2) to maintain rice fields with water is necessary for the conservation of the natural environment. The compatibility of this enforcement policy with the principle of the GATT is dubious since Article 11(2)(c) requires a minimum access in order for an import restriction be qualified for an exception.

The Twelve Agricultural Items *Case*

There were (and still are) several important international disputes with regard to the import quotas imposed by the Japanese government on the import of agricultural products. The primary one is rice which has been touched upon already. Another one is the Beef and Orange Agreement entered into between the Japanese government and the United States government whereby the Japanese government agreed to lift the import quotas. Since the beef and orange problem was to be solved by the agreement, the United States government did not petition to the GATT on this issue.

Still another important case is the *Twelve Agricultural Items* case.[15] In this case, the United States government took Japan to the GATT under Article 23 and claimed the import quotas imposed on twelve agricultural items enforced by the Japanese government under the Control Law were contrary to the prohibition of import quotas provided in Article 11 of the GATT. The GATT held that the Japanese import quotas on ten agricultural items were contrary to Article 11(a) of the GATT. A brief account of this case follows.

Import quotas had been effective on the twelve agricultural items under the Control Law. They were: (1) prepared and preserved milk and cream, (2) processed cheese, (3) lactose, (4) dairy food preparations, (5) dried leguminous vegetables, (6) starch and insulin, (7) glucose and other sugars, sugar food preparations, (8) groundnuts, (9) prepared and preserved beef, (10) fruit purée and paste, fruit pulp, certain fruit juices, (11) prepared and preserved pineapple, and (12) tomato juice, tomato sauce, and ketchup.

Upon the petition of the United States government, the GATT organized a panel and it reported in 1987 that the quotas on ten items were contrary to Article 11(a) and, in 1988, the GATT formally adopted a decision that they were contrary to Article 11(1). The Japanese govern-

[15] See Porges, 'Introductory Note on General Agreement on Tariffs and Trade: Dispute Settlement Panel Report on Japanese Agricultural Import Quotas ("GATT 2") and Japanese–US Exchange of Letters on Beef and Citrus' (1988) XXI ILM 1539 *et seq*.

ment accepted this decision with some reservations and decided to eliminate the import quotas on eight items.

The main points of this GATT decision are as follows. First, although Article 11(2)(c) permits exemptions of agricultural products from the quantitative prohibition of import, they apply only in those situations where a minimum access to the market is secured. The import was totally prohibited with regard to four items including dairy and fruit products, and, for this reason, this exemption did not apply to those four items.

Secondly, Article 11(2)(c) permits import restriction only under circumstances where the government restricting import is engaged in a programme for reducing domestic production of the item in question. No such reduction of production was put into effect in starch and beef, and, therefore, a requirement for exemption was lacking. However, the Japanese government took measures to reduce production of leguminous vegetables by a directive issued by the Ministry of Agriculture to the Governor of Hokkaido and also for groudnuts by means of administrative guidance. Therefore, the import quotas on those two items were not contrary to Article 11(1) if it could be proved that minimum access was guaranteed.

Thirdly, the exemption under Article 11(2)(c) covers agricultural products in their early stage of production. Prepared and preserved milk and cream, processed cheese, starch, and pinapple products could not be regarded as agricultural products in their early stage of production. In tomato products, the importation of the ingredient (tomato purée) had been liberalized, and, therefore, it could not be said that the domestic production cut-back programme of tomatoes would be hindered by the importation of tomato ketchup.

Fourthly, whereas prepared and preserved milk and cream were state-trading items, import quotas applied to them were also subject to the prohibition of import quotas under Article 11(1).

Fifthly, whereas items covered by the exemption should not exceed the necessary minimum, some of the import quotas in question were enforced even in those years in which there was no doemstic production of similar products. This was excessive and contrary to Article 11(1).

In accordance with this GATT decision, the Japanese government decided to: (1) liberalize eight items by 1990, (2) liberalize partly and renegotiate the issue in 1990 with regard to two items (dried leguminous vegetables and groundnuts), (3) with regard to starch in which no liberalization would made, to improve the market access of corn (raw material for starch) by reducing progressively the secondary tariff rate in the tariff quota applied to this item, and (4) with regard to prepared and preserved milk and cream in which no liberalization would be achieved, to enlarge import quotas and allocate quotas to new entrants.

This GATT decision is significant in that it recognized that the GATT disciplines apply to activities of state trading agencies and that it elaborated on the meaning of the minimum market access with regard to agricultural items.

Emergency Tariffs

An emergency tariff is provided for in Article 9.2 of the Customs and Tariff Law. Under this article, when the import of a commodity increases due to a sudden drop in its price abroad or to an unexpected change in circumstances and a domestic industry producing the same or a similar commodity suffers a serious injury or there is a threat thereof, an emergency tariff may be imposed on the import of this commodity whose amount is equal to the difference between the wholesale value of the same or a similar commodity in Japan and the price of the import minus the amount of the regular tariff.

In this article, there are requirements that an import be increased and that there be a serious injury to a domestic industry and the wording of this article is almost identical to that of Article 19 of the GATT, and, therefore, as far as its compatibility with Article 19 is concerned, there is no problem. However, there is no provision for the procedure through which the requirements for the above are tested and determined. Since the authority to enforce this article is vested in the MOF, the MOF should enact ministerial rules which would lay out the details of the procedure.

No Procedure for Private Initiative

What is striking about the above provisions of laws which provide for import restrictions is the lack of procedure through which a private party petitions the government to request a measure to restrict import and the affected parties (such as importers or exporters of the commodity in question) present their view before the enforcement agency (the MITI or the MOF) makes any decision. Whether or not to invoke a measure under any of those laws belongs to the discretion of the agency. To increase a transparency of the governmental process, however, it is desirable that a new set of procedures which would govern the process be enacted.

C. IMPORT AGREEMENTS

Import agreements permitted under Article 7(2) of the Transactions Law may be used to restrict imports, and, when used in this way, they may operate in a similar way to the import quotas. In an import agreement, importers enter into an agreement whereby they fix the price of the commodity to be imported, the quantity to be imported, the channels of import, and other related matters. Although import agreements are agreements entered into among private enterprises, the government can direct them to conclude agreements to implement government purposes. Therefore, in a broader sense, Article 7(2) of the Transactions Law is a trade law and a government measure.

However, the scope of Article 2(7) of the Transactions Law includes not only a utilization of a private agreement as a substitute for an import restriction by the government but other things as well. Therefore, it is appropriate to treat it as a separate subject.

The Requirements for Import Agreements

Import agreements under Article 7(2) are not permitted unconditionally but are subject to some 'positive' requirements, namely, the conditions which must be proved to exist before an import agreement is authorized. In this respect, import agreements are different from export agreements (which will be touched upon in a later section) in which there are no such positive requirements.

One of the following three conditions must be met before an import agreement is permitted. First, export competition in the country where the export comes from must be substantially restrained or import competition in Japan must be excessive. Typical situations envisaged here are those in which importers in Japan import a commodity from a state-trading agency in a non-market economy country or from exporters in a country where they form an export cartel. In those situations, if Japanese importers of the commodity negotiate individually with the state-trading agency which has a monopoly over the supply from that country or exporters who are organized in an export cartel and have a dominant position with regard to the export from that country, they may be forced to make an undue concession and this may result in an excessively high price.

There are state-trading agencies in non-market economy countries as well as in market economy countries. It is also true that export cartels are permitted in the majority of countries in which competition laws are enforced such as the United States, the EC, Japan, and others.[16] One of the purposes of Article 7(2) is to address the disparity of bargaining power between foreign exporters and Japanese importers, and, in this sense, it may be said that an import cartel formed for this purpose is that of a countervailing cartel. It may be true that such a countervailing

[16] In the United States, export associations are exempted from the application of US antitrust laws under the Webb–Pomerene Act (15 USC ss. 61–6 (1982) and the Export Trading Act of 1982 (15 USC ss. 4001–21 (1982)) under certain conditions.

import cartel will have little impact unless the importers who are members of this cartel have an influential position as buyers in the world market since, if otherwise, exporters would simply shift the direction of supply to other buyers to avoid the lower price which would be forced on them by the import cartel. Often, however, the amount of Japanese imports is big enough to make import cartels effective as buyers.

Secondly, import agreements are allowed for the purpose of implementing a trade agreement between the Japanese government and the government of a foreign country. Importers are allowed to form an import agreement when, under an international agreement between Japan and the government of a foreign country, Japan is obligated to import an amount of a commodity and yet the price of the commodity in that country is higher than that of third countries. This is also a variation of a counter-vailing cartel, since it is a device to offset the disadvantages of the price difference by increasing the bargaining power of Japanese importers of the commodity in question *vis-à-vis* exporters of that country whether they are a state trading agency or private exporters supported by their government.

The third type of import agreement is quite different from the above two. In the third type, private enterprises are permitted to enter into an import agreement if it is necessary to promote the exploitation of natural resources overseas. A situation which qualifies for this requirement would be the following hypothetical case.

Japan imports a large quantity of coal from Australia. The Australian coal-mining industry heavily depends on the import of coal by Japanese importers. Since the exploitation and development of a coal-mine require a large amount of capital and financial resources, it is impossible to do so unless there is a reasonable assurance that Japanese importers will purchase the coal which is produced when the mine has been developed.

Japanese importers of coal are largely electric power companies and steel companies. Although the demand and requirement for coal of each company are limited, the total amount of demand would be very great if that of all the companies is pooled together by an agreement among users of coal.

Under this circumstance, Japanese users of coal (electric power companies and steel companies) can enter into an import agreement whereby the demand of each user is pooled together in a big package. They then negotiate with foreign enterprises engaged in the exploitation and development of coal-mines and assure them that this aggregated demand will be a guarantee that a large amount will be purchased regardless of ups and downs in the economy and failures of some users of coal and that there will always be a stable market for them. In an import agreement of this type, importers may agree to purchase a certain amount of the commodity from a country each year and allocate quotas among themselves.

As we have seen, the last type of import agreement is quite different from the ones previously explained. While import agreements which belong to the first and second type are essentially a defensive measure *vis-à-vis* a foreign monopoly, the third type of agreement is designed to promote the development of natural resources abroad. Since Japan is a highly industrialized and yet resource-poor country, it is essential to make sure that the import of natural resources is guaranteed and, from this standpoint, this device is potentially an important one.

The draft of an import agreement must be filed with the MITI and it must be approved by the MITI before it is put into effect. The MITI can invoke 'an outsider regulation' under Article 30 of the Transactions Law. When, after an import agreement has been approved and put into practice, it is proved that the import agreement cannot achieve its objective, the MITI can invoke an import order whereby the MITI fixes the terms of import such as price, quantity, and channels of import.

When this order is issued, all the importers of the commodity, whether they are insiders or outsiders of the import agreement, are bound by this order, and a violation of it incurs a criminal liability.

This order is called 'an outsider regulation' since its primary objective is to deal with the situation where the effect of an import agreement is impeded by activities of 'outsiders' who are not bound by the terms of the agreement and, therefore, free, for example, to buy the commodity at a higher price than the price fixed by the agreement or a greater quantity of it than that fixed by the agreement. Strictly speaking, however, the term 'outsider regulation' is a misnomer since not only outsiders but also insiders are bound by the order. In order for the MITI to invoke an import order, there must be a pre-existing import agreement and proof that it has failed to be effective.

The existence of an import order indicates that an import agreement is not merely a private agreement although it was entered into by private enterprises. Since the MITI is authorized to back up the effectiveness of an import agreement if it is rendered ineffective due to the operations of outsiders or by other causes, it is designed to be an instrument to implement governmental purposes.

An import agreement can be put into effect by way of organizing an import association. An import association is an entity composed of importers of a commodity to accomplish the object of controlling the import activities of members. An import association can fix the terms of import to be observed by the member importers such as the price, the maximum quantity, and related matters. An import association may be more stable and effective than a mere import agreement concluded among enterprises since an import association has often some organizational facilities such as headquarters with some staff members.

Legally speaking, when importers intend to agree on some terms of import for a commodity, they must do so under the authority of the Transactions Law, and an agreement which is not so authorized is contrary to that law. However, there have been some *de facto* import agreements entered into among importers without the authority of the Transactions Law when they have relatively little impact on the market.

An import agreement entered into under the authority of the Transactions Law that has been approved by the MITI is exempted from the application of the Anti-monopoly Law.[17]

Cases of Import Agreements

As compared with export agreements which will be touched upon later, there are few instances in which an import agreement or import cartel has been utilized. Setting aside some minor cases, there are two important cases and a description of these two cases follows.

One is the *Scrap Iron* case of 1974.[18] In this case, the United States government invoked the Export Administration Act and imposed an embargo on the export of scrap iron. There was a shortage of scrap iron in the United States and, as a result, there was a sharp price increase in it. This shortage and drainage of supply of scrap iron were attributed to excessive purchases by Japanese trading companies.

When the embargo by the United States government was imposed on the export of scrap iron, the Japanese government invoked the import quota system under the Control Law and banned the import of this product from the United States. This measure was taken in order to co-operate with the export ban imposed by the United States government. Shortly after, however, the ban imposed by the United States government on the export of scrap iron was lifted, and accordingly the MITI withdrew the import ban under the Control Law. However, the MITI issued a directive to importers to the effect that they should form an import agreement and refrain from excessive purchases of scrap iron from the United States. According to this directive, Japanese importers agreed on an import agreement and stabilized the import of scrap iron from the United States. This measure was taken by the MITI and Japanese importers to avoid the situation that the import from the United States of scrap iron might suddenly increase and another embargo on the export of it from the United States be touched off again.

[17] Art. 33 of the Transactions Law.

[18] *Nihon Keizai Shinbun* (*Japan Economic Newspaper*), 8 Jan. 1975.

Another case is the *Chinese Silk* case.[19] This case was closely related to the facts described in the *Kyoto Necktie* case of which a detailed explanation was made in Chapter 1. Since the import into Japan of raw silk was restricted by the amendment of the Silk Price Stabilization Law, exporters of silk in Korea and China slightly processed raw silk and made it into a semi-processed product which was outside the jurisdiction of the Silk Business Agency which had the exclusive authority to import raw silk into Japan and sell it. Due to this circumstance, the import of this semi-processed silk product suddenly increased. Although this product was a processed silk, it was quite easy to convert it back to raw silk by a simple operation, and this product flooded the Japanese market. This was contrived by exporters in the exporting countries to circumvent the import restriction imposed by the Japanese government.

There was a series of negotiations between the Japanese government and the government of Korea, and the government of Korea agreed to put into effect a voluntary export restraint of the product to Japan. However, the government of China declined to go along with this voluntary export restraint. Therefore, the Japanese government and the Chinese trading agency informally agreed that the Japanese government would take an informal import measure.

Since this increase of raw silk could not be coped with by the Silk Price Stabilization Law and the import of the processed silk product (a type of textile) was under the jurisdiction of the MITI, the MITI decided to issue a directive to importers to the effect that they should conclude an import agreement whereby they would impose import quotas on each member importer. This directive was made effective by importers and an import agreement was concluded whereby the maximum import quantity was fixed and a quota was imposed on each member importer. The MITI decided to invoke an outsider regulation and put the import of this product under its control.

The above two examples are important as far as the economic effects were concerned. However, it should be mentioned that, in each of those two cases, an import agreement or an import cartel was not used for the purposes for which an import agreement is designed to serve. In the *Scrap Iron* case, the purpose was an 'orderly import' whereby the Japanese government wished to control the import of scrap iron for the purpose of co-operating with the export policy of the United States. In the *Chinese Silk* case, the purpose of an import agreement was to

[19] Task Force on Government Regulation and the Competition Policy, *Dokusen Kinshi Hō Tekiyojōgaiseidono Minaoshi* (*Review of the Exemptions from the Application of the Anti-monopoly Law*) (Tokyo, 1991), 41.

deal with the circumventing activities of exporters. Whether or not the requirements under the Transactions Law were satisfied in those two cases is somewhat dubious.

D. IMPORT RESTRICTION BY ADMINISTRATIVE GUIDANCE

There have been some instances in which the import of a commodity from abroad has been restricted by administrative guidance, a non-legal means. A detailed account of administrative guidance as applied in the domestic regulation has already been made in Chapter 1. In this section, we will give a brief explanation of two cases in which import was restricted by administrative guidance.

One is the *Naptha Import* case[20] and the other is the *Lions Oil* case.[21] It is necessary to explain the petroleum policy exercised by the MITI since the import restriction was enforced as part of this broader policy. As touched upon earlier, the MITI had held the policy that the refining of crude oil into petroleum products such as gasoline and kerosene must be done in Japan. To achieve this purpose, the MITI constructed the programme in which Japanese petroleum enterprises imported crude oil from abroad and refined it into petroleum products such as gasoline and kerosene. To promote domestic refining of petroleum products, the import of petroleum products was prohibited in principle. The policy described above is said to be based on the national economic security of the country. However, in prohibiting the import of petroleum products, the MITI did not use a law but relied upon an informal way, that is, administrative guidance.

The Petroleum Business Law[22] provided that any person who intended to import petroleum product should report to the MITI. Therefore, as far as the wording of this law was concerned, there was no legal prohibition of imports of petroleum products and importers could import them by reporting to the MITI that petroleum products would be imported. However, in actuality, the MITI 'advised' importers not to report to the MITI and, in this way, import was restricted.

In the *Naptha* case, there was a conflict between the policy of the MITI and the interests of the petrochemical industry. With regard to the import of naptha, the policy of the MITI was to allow the import of it only to petroleum refining enterprises, and, therefore, petrochemical enterprises were restrained from 'reporting' to the MITI their desire to import

[20] Okumiya, 'The Role of the Administrative Branch in Trade: Government Order and Administrative Guidance Concerning Trade Problems', in Schoenbaum, Matsushita, and Dallmeyer (eds.), *Dynamics of Japanese–United States Trade Relations* (Athens, Ga, 1986), 112–14.

[21] See n. 20, above, pp. 116–18.

[22] Sekiyugyō Hō, Law 128, 1962.

naptha. This policy was adopted as part of the broader policy of securing the production of petroleum products in Japan and promoting domestic refineries. Enterprises producing petrochemical products had to purchase naptha which was imported by those enterprises which produced and imported naptha. This meant that the purchase price of naptha was higher than it would have been if petrochemical enterprises had been allowed to import it directly.

The petrochemical industry grew dissatisfied with the high price caused by this scheme and decided to make a 'forced report'. After negotiations among the MITI, the refining industry, and the petrochemical industry, a compromise was reached between the MITI and the petrochemical industry whereby the latter would establish a joint purchasing company which would buy naptha from petroleum refining enterprises but petroleum refining enterprises would sell naptha at the price requested by this joint purchasing company.

While, according to the settlement, the petrochemical industry was not allowed to import naptha from abroad, the industry accomplished its objective of securing naptha at a cheaper price by the above scheme.

In the *Lions Oil* case, the situation was different. In this case, a small company called the Lions Oil Company decided to import gasoline from Singapore. Despite the objection of the MITI, Lions Oil reported to the MITI the import of gasoline from Singapore and it was shipped from Singapore to a Japanese port. At this point, it is reported that the MITI negotiated with financial institutions and persuaded them to cut off finance to Lions Oil. The president of Lions Oil stated that it was deprived of the financial means of import and gave it up. It is also reported that the MITI stepped in and persuaded a domestic refinery to purchase the imported gasoline. The imported gasoline was purchased by the petroleum refining enterprises as 'naptha'. In this way, formally there was no import of gasoline!

In the *Lions Oil* case, news travelled abroad quickly and there were critical comments by foreign officials on this case that the import restrictions were contrary to the principle of free trade. Thereupon the MITI changed its position and prepared a bill which would establish that import of petroleum products would be allowed if some requirements were met. In 1985, the Law concerning the Temporary Special Measures on Import of Specific Petroleum Products[23] was passed. Under this law, a person who intends to import petroleum products must register himself with the MITI and the MITI is required to grant a registration as long as the person owns production and storage facilities as specified by the MITI's regulation.

[23] Tokutei Sekiyu Seihin Yunyū Zanteisochi Hō, Law 95, 1985.

The enactment of this law signifies that the MITI's control, as far as the regulation of import of petroleum products is concerned, has shifted from control by administrative guidance to that by law. However, due to the existence of the requirements with regard to production and storage facilities, small importers are effectively eliminated from importing petroleum products.

The *Lions Oil* case signified that there was a basic contradiction in the policy of the MITI concerning the import of petroleum products. While the import was legally allowed under the Petroleum Business Law as long as a report was filed with the MITI, it was *de facto* blocked by administrative guidance. The importer in the *Lions Oil* case challenged this contradiction and pushed it through by making a 'forced report'. This way of controlling imports may be held to be incompatible with Article 11 of the GATT which prohibits government measures other than tariffs to restrict imports. This is especially true now that the GATT has decided, as we will examine in the next section, that an export control by means of administrative guidance amounts to a government measure which is prohibited under Article 11 of the GATT.[24] There should be an analogy with regard to an import control under Article 11.

E. TECHNICAL BARRIERS TO TRADE

An Overview

In Japan, as well as in many other countries, there are laws and regulations which govern product safety standards, testing procedures, and the representation of products (hereafter referred to as 'standards'). They are enacted to secure the safety of the lives of people. Recently, however, the differences in terms of standards among nations have been regarded as trade barriers since a product produced under the standards of one country may be denied entry into another country due to a difference of standard in that country. The number of laws and regulations on standards in recent decades has increased tremendously as modern life becomes more and more complex, and, as international trade increases, the differences in standards become a serious impediment to trade.

The framers of the GATT were apparently aware of this problem and Article 10(1) of the GATT states that contracting parties shall publish laws and regulations which affect the sale, distribution, testing, processing, and mixing of products and related matters as well as providing in Article 3 the principle for national treatment.

[24] BNA, *International Trade Reporter*, 5 (30 Mar. 1988); Dallmeyer, 'The United States–Japan Semiconductor Accord of 1986: The Shortcomings of High Tech Protectionism', *Maryland Journal of International Law and Trade*, 13/2 (1989), 179 *et seq.*

However, the provisions in Articles 3 and 10(1) of the GATT are too general and, to cope with specific problems, more detailed rules are necessary. In light of this situation, an international code was signed in the Tokyo Round Negotiations called the Agreement on the Technical Barriers to Trade (which will be referred to as 'the Standards Code') in which some principles are declared.

In the Standards Code, there are provisions for standards, the approval system, information, the developing countries, and the dispute settlement procedure. An account of the provisions for standards and the approval system follows.

In the Code, standards are divided into the mandatory standards (those which must be observed) and the optional standards (those whose adoption is optional). Article 2 of the Standards Code states the basic principles to be observed by the contracting parties as follows. (1) Contracting parties shall not establish and apply standards in such a way as to cause impediments to international trade. (2) There shall be no discrimination against products produced abroad with respect to the application of standards. (3) Domestic standards must comply with international standards if there is an international standard (or it is close to completion). (4) Standards must be formulated in accordance with the nature of the products concerned. (5) When a contracting party formulates a standard in the absence of any international standard or, if there is an international standard, which is at variance with the existing standard and which would affect international trade, it must announce its plan in advance, notify other contracting parties through the GATT, and give the opportunity to other contracting parties for an expression of views. (6) A standard which has been established must be published sufficiently in advance so that exporting countries can make necessary adjustments to it.

Articles 5–9 of the Standards Code provide for the approval system including the testing system. With regard to the testing system, it provides that there shall be no discrimination between domestic and foreign products, that the result of testing must be published so that the interested parties can take corrective measures, that information obtained through testing a foreign product must be kept confidential, and that the results of testing conducted in a foreign country must be accepted as much as possible.

On the approval system, it provides that there shall be no discrimination, that, in formulating a new approval system, it must be published in advance to give other contracting parties the opportunity to express their views and their views must be respected and that the formulated approval systems must all be published.

Japan accepted the Standards Code as a treaty in 1980 and, therefore, is obligated to observe its terms. Accordingly, amendments were made to domestic laws on the subjects covered by the Standard Code.[25]

The Japanese Standards Laws

There are many laws which are concerned with standards. It is not necessary to refer to the details of each piece of legislation. We must be satisfied with a general account of the legal system with respect to standards.

A book published by the Japanese government on this subject[26] lists twenty-five laws. They are: (1) Consumer Product Safety Law, (2) High Pressure Gas Control Law, (3) Law Concerning the Securing of Safety and the Optimization of Transactions of Liquified Petroleum Gas, (4) Law Concerning the Examination and Regulation of Manufacture of Chemical Substances and Related Matters, (5) Measurement Law, (6) Electrical Applicances and Material Control Law, (7) Gas Utility Industry Law, (8) Industrial Standardization Law, (9) Fertilizer Control Law, (10) Agricultural Mechanization Promotion Law, (11) Agricultural Chemicals Regulation Law, (12) Law Concerning Safety Assurance and Quality Improvement of Feed, (13) Law Concerning Standardization and Proper Labelling of Agricultural and Forestry Products, (14) Domestic Animal Infectious Diseases Control Law, (15) Plant Protection Law, (16) Law for Improvement and Increased Production of Livestock, (17) Nutrition Improvement Law, (18) Pharmaceutical Affairs Law, (19) Food Sanitation Law, (20) Road Vehicles Law, (21) Ship Safety Law, (21) Industrial Safety and Health Law, (23) Radio Law, (24) Public Telecommunications Law, and (25) Fire Service Law.

The above list is not exhaustive but illustrative. Moreover, there are many regulations issued by the enforcement agencies which are vested with the powers to enforce laws. Consequently, this area seems like a huge maze.

However, from their titles one can recognize the subject-matters which are covered by these laws. They can be classfied into: (1) laws which establish the standards for safety and quality of a product, (2) laws which establish the standard for testing products and regulate the procedures for examination, and (3) laws which set up the standard for representing products. Among the first category is included, for example, the Consumer Product Safety Law which establishes the safety standards for consumer products. The Food Sanitation Law provides both for the

[25] Jackson, Louis, and Matsushita, *Implementing the Tokyo Round: National Constitutions and International Economic Rules* (Ann Arbor, Mich., 1984), 107–15.

[26] Intra-Governmental Council on Standards and Certification Systems, *Standards and Certification Systems in Japan* (Tokyo, 1984).

safety standards of food products and the testing process. The Industrial Standardization Law establishes the 'JIS' system which authorizes the manufacturer of a product produced in a duly approved factory to use the representation 'JIS' which means 'Japanese Industrial Standard'.

Some of the domestic laws and regulations which incorporate standards have been regarded as a trade barrier. One of the reasons is that generally standards in Japan are more stringent and products which are approved by standards of other countries are often not approved under the corresponding laws in Japan.[27] The second reason is that product approval in Japan is conducted under the leadership of the government whereas, especially in the United States, product approval is often based on the self-certification system.[28] A good example is the approving of a new motor car. Whereas, in the United States, the approval for a new car is based on the results of testing conducted by the manufacturer and submitted to the government authority, the Japanese government conducts the whole process of testing the model without relying on data submitted by the manufacturer. In the process taken by the Japanese government, the testing requires much more time than in the system where the government agency uses the results submitted by private enterprises.

Thirdly, it has been claimed by foreign exporters and governments that, in Japan, the approval process of standards is not made open to the public and foreign enterprises find it difficult to know the new developments in the formulation of standards.

According to the reports of the OTO (Office of Trade and Investment Ombudsman), complaints about standards can be classified according to the ministries which enforce them as follows: The Ministry of Health and Welfare ranks top, the MITI comes second, the MOF comes third, and the Ministry of Agriculture, Forestry and Fishery comes fourth. Many of the complaints directed against the Ministry of Health and Welfare are concerned with the difficulty in obtaining approval with regard to the import of pharmaceuticals, cosmetics, foods, and the like. Those directed to the MITI are in the area of industrial products such as high pressure gas equipment, and those directed to the MOF are largely complaints with regard to customs procedures.

The Japanese government has not been unaware of the problem and there have been a series of steps taken by the government to ease the difficulties. The Japanese government undertook 'the Action Programme'

[27] Nihonbōekikai-Bōekikenkyūjo (Japan Foreign Trade Council–The Institute of Foreign Trade), *Kijun Ninshō Seidono Nichibei Hikaku* (*A Comparison of the Japanese and US Standards and Certification Systems*) (Tokyo, 1988).

[28] Office of Trade and Investment Ombudsman (OTO), *Annual Report* (May 1990), 9.

which began in 1986 and ended in 1988.[29] This programme was aimed at the reduction of the number of items which would come under the approval system. As part of this programme, the shift from the government approval system to the self-certification system was adopted in some areas such as fertilizer (a change in the enforcement of the Fertilizer Law) and microwave ovens (a change in the enforcement of the Radio Law).

Secondly, there was an attempt in the Action Programme to increase the acceptance of the results of foreign testings. It was decided that test results achieved in foreign countries would be accepted in areas such as products covered by the Pharmaceutical Affairs Law (enforced by the Ministry of Health and Welfare) and the Electric Appliances Control Law (enforced by the MITI).

Thirdly, it was decided to take measures to increase transparency by providing the opportunity to interested parties including foreign enterprises to present their views when a new standard was being formulated. In areas such as foods, food-wrapping materials, and electrical applicances, it was decided that the Japanese standards would be made to conform to the international standards. Then there was a change in the enforcement of laws in general to expedite and simplify the testing process.

Fourthly, in 1983, a law was passed which amended seventeen laws on standards to make it easier for foreign manufacturers to acquire approval from the Japanese government. This law amended, among others, the Consumer Product Safety Law, the High Pressure Gas Law, the Electrical Appliances Control Law, the Pharmaceutical Affairs Law, and the Road Transportation Vehicles Law. Whereas, before this amendment, foreign manufacturers had had to apply through their Japanese importers for approval of their products which were exported to Japan and every time the importer changed, a new registration had to be made, this amendment made it possible for foreign manufacturers to register themselves in the ministry in charge and acquire approval from the ministry for new models without the relying on their Japanese importers.

Lastly, the Industrial Standardization Law was amended[30] to permit foreign manufacturers to affix a JIS mark on goods manufacturered in a foreign country on the condition that Japanese officials inspect the factory in a foreign country which produces the product and certify that the factory meets the necessary requirements for producing products.

[29] On the Action Programme, see Naikakukanbō Tokumeijikō Tantoshitsu/ Keizaikikakuchō Chōseikyoku (Office of Specific Tasks of the Cabinet Secretariat/Bureau of Adjustment of the Economic Planning Agency), *Action Programme* (1985).

[30] Jackson, Louis, and Matsushita, n. 25, above, pp. 111–13.

F. GOVERNMENT PROCUREMENT

An Overview

Government procurement refers to purchases by government agencies. It includes not only purchases by government agencies of goods but also construction projects conducted on government budgets. In any developed country, the total amount of government procurement is very large since the scope of government activities is so large. Therefore, whether or not government procurement is open to foreign suppliers affects the flow of international trade, and, in this sense, government procurement is a trade issue.

Article 3 of the GATT provides for the principle of national treatment under which contracting parties are obligated to accord treatment to imported commodities which is not less favourable than domestically produced commodities. This principle applies to government procurement also. However, Article 3(8)(a) of the GATT states that the national treatment principle does not apply to laws and regulations which provide for purchases by government agencies of products for government purposes.

However, Article 3 of the GATT is general and lacks the specificity which would guide the contracting parties in enacting domestic legislation dealing with government procurement. In light of this situation, in the Tokyo Round of GATT trade negotiations which was concluded in 1979, an international agreement entitled 'The Agreement on Government Procurement' (hereafter referred to as 'the Procurement Code') was signed. As a contracting party to the Procurement Code, Japan is obligated to observe the terms contained in it.

The Procurement Code consists of the preamble, nine articles, and two commentaries. There are also four attachments. In the preamble, the basic principles are declared. They are: (1) the principles of national treatment and non-discrimination, (2) the transparency and openness of laws, procedures, and practices with regard to government procurement, and (3) special treatments for less developed countries.

Some of the highlights of the Procurement Code are touched upon below. Article 1 defines the scope of application of the Code. Under this article, provisions in the Code apply to any procurement by a government agency as listed in Attachment 1 and whose value is above 150,000 SDR. Article 2 declares the principles of national treatment and non-discrimination. Article 3 is concerned with less developed countries and provides that the contracting parties enforce laws and regulations with regard to procurement in such a way as to promote imports from less developed countries, that less developed countries are partly exempted from the obligation of national treatment on the condition that an *ex post facto* examination takes place, that the developed countries provide technical assistance to a less developed country when requested, and that the developed countries establish information centres in order to provide the necessary information with regard to government procurement to less developed countries.

Article 4 provides for specifications. According to this article, specifications used by the government of a contracting party should not affect adversely the international trade and, if there is an international standard, the government of a contracting party should conform to it.

Article 5 states that, in government procurement, the open tendering system or the selective tendering system should be the principle, and the single tendering system (which means procurement by an individually negotiated contract) should be used only when the above two systems cannot be used or it is the only possible way of procurement in the given situation.

The Japanese Government Procurement System

Since the Japanese government ratified the Procurement Code as a treaty, the government was obligated to amend the domestic laws and regulations to make them conform to the contents of the Procurement Code. A series of amendments took place after the conclusion of the Tokyo Round Negotiation in 1979. An outline of the Japanese government procurement system is as follows.

The basic law which controls government procurement in Japan is the Account Law and there are several regulations thereunder.[31] Under this law and other regulations, a government procurement must be based on the open tendering system, and if the use of the open tendering system is difficult for some reason, the selective tendering system. If the use of the above two systems is not feasible, then the single tendering system may be used.

Essentials of a government procurement can be summarized as follows:[32]

1. Notice of Proposed Purchase and Tender Documentation. The notice of proposed purchase by means of open or selective tendering procedures must be published in the Official Gazette (*Kampo*) at least thirty days prior to the day for submitting tenders.

2. Open and Selective Tendering Processes. Open and selective tendering procedures are adopted in accordance with the provisions of the Procurement Code. Where selective tendering procedures are adopted, the invitation for participation in the tendering shall be issued on the same date as the publication of notice for the tendering.

[31] Jackson, Louis, and Matsushita 119.

[32] Ibid.

3. Use of Single-Tendering Procedures. Use of single-tendering procedures is limited to those cases permitted under the Procurement Code (Article 29.3 of the Accounts law, Articles 10 and 11 of the Special Cabinet Order).

4. The Lowest Bidder. Purchasing agencies award a contract to the supplier submitting the tender that offers the lowest price within the limits of the provisional value of the contract. Agencies may, because of the nature or objective of a contract, award a contract to the supplier submitting the most advantageous tender in terms of price and other factors.

5. National Treatment and Non-discrimination. The principle of equal treatment for domestic and foreign suppliers is one of the bases for the new procedures for procurement in Japan, and the principle has been confirmed by the MOF Minister's directive entitiled 'With regard to the implementation of the Cabinet Order stipulating special procedures for government procurement of goods', issued on 27 December 1980.

6. Local Government. On 23 January 1981, the Ministry of Foreign Affairs and the Ministry of Home Affairs sent to all prefectural governments, municipal or local governments, and some city authorities a joint letter describing the contents of the Procurement Code and urging them to comply with the provisions it contained.

However, in practice, the open tendering system is seldom used in government procurement in Japan. The most frequently used system is the selective tendering system and this is especially true with public construction work. The following is an outline of the way in which a contract for a public construction is usually given.

When a public construction is needed, the government agency (the purchasing agency) designates the enterprises which are qualified to participate in the bid, and only those enterprises designated by the purchasing agency can participate in the bid offered by the agency. The designation is based on the judgement on the part of the purchasing agency with regard to the qualifications of enterprises in terms of technological, managerial, and financial capabilities. Often the qualification is judged on the basis of previous achievements. This may give some disadvantages to foreign enterprises which engage in a bid for the first time since there is no achievement record of that foreign party.

There are proposals that achievement in foreign countries should be taken into consideration and it is hoped that there will be more opportunities for foreign enterprises to participate in bids for public construction work in Japan. However, the system by which the purchasing agency is authorized to judge the qualifications of bidders tends to create exclusivity. It should be stressed that ideally there should be a system in which an examination board independent of the purchasing agency would be given the authority to decide the qualification of bidders.

Dango

There is another problem in the Japanese public procurement especially with regard to public construction. This problem is that of bid rigging or 'dango' in Japanese. It occurs in the following way.

Officials in charge of the project in the government agency which is carrying out the construction project compute the estimated cost of the construction, add 3 per cent profit margin, and come up with the provisional value which is used as the maximum value for the project. The designated parties participate in the bid and each offers an estimated price for the construction. The government agency must give a contract to undertake the construction to the party which offers the lowest price. However, if the lowest price offered is higher than the provisional value, no contract is given and there is another bid, and bidding is repeated until the lowest bid price goes down to the level of the provisional value or below.

It is reported that enterprises often engage in bid-rigging before a bid takes place and decide which party will win the contract. The provisional value of a construction project is regarded as confidential but often it leaks out somehow. The enterprises designated by the purchasing agency to submit bids agree that a named party among them will win the contract and, in order to effectuate it, further agree that the named party shall bid at the provisional value and all the other parties will bid at prices higher than the provisional price. In this way, the named party wins the contract. When another bid is held, the same process takes place again and another enterprise is nominated as the candidate to win contract. In this way, each enterprise gets its share sooner or later.

The above practice is contrary to the relevant provisions of the Anti-monopoply Law and also, under some conditions, the Criminal Code.[33] However, this practice takes place frequently. One reason why it takes place is that the purchasing agency has the predominant bargaining power over the private enterprises which participate in a bid. The provisional value is quite inflexible and there is no chance that a contract is given unless the lowest bid is at or below the provisional value. The purchasing agency has the power to eliminate any party from the designation. Small enterprises depend on public construction and they are in a situation in which somehow they have to live with this system. In this situation, enterprises engage in bid-rigging in order to offset their deficiency in bargaining power in relation to the purchasing agency.

[33] Art. 96.3 of the Criminal Code provides that bid-rigging which adversely affects the formation of fair price is punishable by imprisonment of not more than 2 years and a fine of not more than 2.5 million yen.

Recently, however, this system has come increasingly under fire. The government of the United States has claimed that one of the reasons why US engineering enterprises cannot participate in bids in Japan is due to the existence of bid-rigging practice. The FTC (the enforcement agency of the Anti-monopoly Law) has tightened up the enforcement *vis-à-vis* bid-rigging engaged in by construction companies and trade associations. In the *Yokosuka Naval Base* case,[34] the FTC issued an order to members of a trade association which was instrumental in requiring them to pay an administrative surcharge according to the relevant provisions of the Anti-monopoly Law with regard to bid-rigging for construction work at the US Naval Base in Yokosuka. Thereafter, the United States government threatened the Japanese construction companies which participated in the bid-rigging to bring an action under United States antitrust laws to collect treble damages. The Japanese companies settled the matter with the United States government and paid a large amount of settlement money.

The purpose of bid-rigging (a type of cartel) is not necessarily an exclusion of foreign enterprises from a bid. Its primary purpose is to eliminate competition among the participants in a bid. It seems, however, that bid-rigging practice raises a problem with foreign participation as well as a legal problem in relation to the Anti-monopoly law and the Criminal Code. First, since bid-rigging is unlawful, it is carried out secretly. It is decided by a secret discussion among the participating parties. It makes the process of procurement intransparent to outside parties and the public in general. This non-transparency or opacity is itself a barrier for foreign participants wishing to enter into bids in Japan. Secondly, if bid-rigging is repeatedly held, there is a tendency among the participants to form an informal but strongly coherent group. There will be frequent exchanges of information with regard to technology and business matters among the participants. This will create the structure of an industry which excludes outside parties.

Even though this is not the place to propose changes in this regard, it should be stressed that the reform of this system requires not only stringent law enforcement against bid-rigging practices but also changes in the governmental practice such as the provisional value system.

G. STRUCTURAL TRADE IMPEDIMENTS

An Overview

An important trade issue raised in connection with the market access in Japan is that of structural trade impediments. It has been claimed that there are some structural barriers which prevent the market access of

[34] The Beigun Kōji Anzengijutsu Kenkyūkai *et al.* Case, FTC Decision, 8 Dec. 1988, *Shinketsushū*, 35 (1988), 57 *et seq.*

foreign products and enterprises in Japan. The major items of such structural barriers include such things as (1) the distribution system which is said to be too complex, lengthy, and exclusive, (2) business customs which are different from those of other countries and which create *de facto* difficulties to foreign enterprises, (3) restrictive business practices in which enterprises engage in practices, such as an exclusive dealing arrangement, tie-in arrangements, and others, and (4) 'keiretsu', which denotes a closely inter-related business relationship among enterprises through stock-holdings, contracts, or long-standing personal connections among business persons in which transactions are made among the participants thereby excluding outside parties.

Structural trade impediments are an important subject-matter when one discusses trade issues in the context of the openness of the Japanese market. A large proportion of the problems is non-legal and factual in nature, and an analysis of such problems requires the disciplines of economics and sociology rather than law. For this reason, a close analysis of structural trade impediments is outside the scope of this book. However, due to its importance in the context of trade, some explanations are useful.

The Structural Impediments Initiative

The Structural Impediments Initiative (hereafter referred to as the SII) is an agreement between the United States government and the Japanese government in which the Japanese government promised to take steps to reduce or eliminate alleged structural impediments in the Japanese market after extensive discussions between the officials of both governments. The SII was initiated in 1990 and the United States government and the Japanese government agreed that both governments would implement the contents of the SII over the years to come. The report published as the result of the SII is a comprehensive account of structural problems in the Japanese market. Therefore, we will examine the highlights of the SII as an illustration of structural impediments in Japan.

It is useful to give a brief description of the background of the SII. The United States Congress enacted the Omnibus Trade and Competitiveness Act of 1988[35] in which Super Section 301 was included. According to this provision, the United States Trade Representative was directed to submit to the Congress in 1989 and 1990 a report entitled 'the National Trade Estimate' in which governmental practices of various countries which were trading with the United States that constituted impediments to international trade were named. The United States Trade Representative

[35] On this law, see US Congress, House of Representatives, Report 100.576, *Omnibus Trade and Competitiveness Act of 1988*, Conference Report to Accompany HR. 3 (20 Apr. 1988).

had to designate 'priority items' from among those items listed in the report. Priority items were those which would promote United States exports if removed or improved and, under Super Section 301, the United States Trade Representative had to initiate a Section 301 investigation with regard to those items.

In 1989, the United States Trade Representative named three practices of the Japanese government as 'priority items' and initiated an investigation with regard to those items. They were: the purchase of super computers, the purchase of equipment for satellites, and standards with regard to wood products. After the initiation of an investigation, the United States government and the Japanese government agreed to settle the matter by international agreements.

Those three items were relatively minor items. Major trade problems with regard to international trade between the United States and Japan were structural problems such as the distribution system, business customs, and restrictive business practices. The United States Trade Representative decided not to make those major items the target of Super Section 301 since it would create a major confrontation between the United States government and the Japanese government. With regard to those major structural problems, the United States government and the Japanese government agreed to hold a series of informal discussions and to seek remedial steps.

Therefore, an informal negotiation took place between the two governments. This is the SII and, in this sense, the SII was initiated in lieu of Super Section 301.

In the report, the Japanese government agreed to take steps in six areas. They are: (1) the pattern of savings and investment, (2) the use of land, (3) the distribution system, (4) exclusive business practices, (5) 'keirestsu' relationships, and (6) the price mechanism. Among the above, (3), (4), and (5) are important for our purposes. They are inter-related issues since these represent three different dimensions of Japanese business structure and customs. The structural impediment question is an enormously complex one. It may be true that there are exclusionary practices exercised by Japanese enterprises which hinder the market entry of foreign enteprises. It may be that business customs and the behaviour of Japanese consumers are different from those of foreign countries. It may be true also that competition in Japan is very keen. Probably all of them are true to a certain extent.

In 1990, the Fair Trade Commission (FTC) conducted a survey of complaints by foreign enterprises operating in Japan concerning the difficulties which they have encountered.[36] Questionnaires were sent to

[36] Shinjō, 'Gaishikeikigyō Karamita Nihonshijōno Jittai' ('The Reality of the Japanese Market Viewed by Foreign Enterprises'), *NBL* 452 (July 1990), 12 *et seq*.

more than 1,000 companies, answers were collected and analysed. The FTC published a report of the survey and, according to the report, there are two items which foreign enterprises operating in Japan feel are the most important difficulties. One is continuous business relationships among Japanese enterprises. This aspect will be touched upon in the following sections. The other is price-cutting by Japanese enterprises. Many foreign companies stated in their answers that whenever a foreign enterprise offers a low price to a customer, there is always a Japanese enterprise which cuts the price even more and gets the business. This means that there is intensive price competition in the Japanese market.

A well-known case is that of a Japanese computer company which participated in a bid organized by a local government in Japan. This company is reported to have offered the price of 1 yen and got the contract.[37] Another example is that of the purchase of super computers by national institutions. This problem was raised by the United States Trade Representative under Super Section 301 of the Omnibus Trade and Competitiveness Act of 1988. As noted already, the United States government named the purchase of super computers as one of the priority items and initiated an investigation. The issue involved is that Japanese computer companies usually offer 60 or 70 per cent discount from the listed price to customers when selling computers to national institutions such as ministries and national universities. The complaint is that this unduly low price hinders the sales activities of United States companies in selling computers.

Therefore, when we think about the nature of the Japanese market, we should not forget that intensive price competition is one of the major characteristics of it. However, we will not touch on this issue here.

The Distribution System

In the distribution system, problems raised by the United States government included items such as an inadequate infrastructure with regard to airports, seaports, roads, and other overhead social capital, and inefficient procedures for the inspection and approval of imports in the customs houses.[38] The United States government also claimed that the regulation of entry of large-scale retail stores under the Large-Scale Retail Stores Law, the restriction imposed on the offering of a premium in selling commodities by the Premium Law, and the policy of the MOF

[37] On this case, see Miwa, *Nihon No Torihiki Kanko* (*Business Practices in Japan*) (Tokyo, 1991), 132–49.

[38] Texts of the Final Report on Structural Impediments Initiative Negotiation are published in: Tsūshōsangyō Chōsakai (Institute of International Trade and Industry), *Nichibei Kōzōmondai Kyōgi Saishū Hōkokusho* (*Final Report on Structural Impediments Initiative Negotiation*) (Tokyo, 1990).

to limit liquor licences, are barriers for foreign commodities to enter the Japanese market and constituted barriers to entry of foreign enterprises.

It was also pointed out that business customs in Japan such as the rebate paid by manufacturers to distributors, the returning of unsold commodities to manufacturers, and suggested prices announced by manufacturers to distributors tended to create exclusive and inefficient distribution networks.

The Japanese government promised to relax the control under the Large-Scale Retail Stores Law and the Liquor Licence Law as well as to take steps to improve customs procedures. It was also promised that the FTC would issue guidelines which would provide rules to regulate restrictive practices in the distribution system. This aspect has been discussed in Chapter 2 of this book. The MITI issued its guidelines on business customs (hereafter referred to as 'The MITI Guidelines'). These guidelines contain some directives to private enterprises. They are not legal mandates but informal guidance which private enterprises are urged to observe voluntarily in their business conduct.

The MITI Guidelines state that it is necessary to improve transparency in business customs in Japan. Although some business customs may not be exclusive in nature, the intransparency of business customs creates practical difficulties for foreign enterprises intending to enter the Japanese market. For example, the terms of transaction are often not made clear among the parties. The MITI Guidelines recommend that the terms of transactions be made clear by, for example, writing them out in the form of a contract.

One of the issues raised is that of the rebate paid by manufacturers. In Japan, different kinds of rebate are paid by manufacturers to distributors. They are paid sometimes as incentives and are used as an instrument to control the conduct of distributors. The MITI Guidelines recommend that manufacturers should establish clear standards for paying rebates and maintain transparency with regard to payment of them.

Return of goods is a business custom which has existed in Japan for a long time. When a retailer purchases goods from a manufacturer or a wholesaler but cannot sell them out, the retailer returns the goods to the manufacturer or wholesaler. This practice is especially prevalent in department stores and supermarkets. It has been claimed that this commercial custom tends to exclude foreign goods from the Japanese market. The reason is that, since retailers cannot return foreign goods even if they cannot sell them, as they can if they purchase domestically produced goods, they tend not to purchase foreign goods for resale at their retail stores.

With regard to this aspect, the MITI Guidelines state that the terms of transactions in purchasing goods should be made clear. For example, it is desirable to make clear whether a retailer is acquiring goods from a manufacturer by purchase or by consignment. If it is a purchase, a return of goods should not be allowed in principle. It should be allowed only when there is a justifiable reason such as when goods are defective, a different kind of goods from the ones ordered were supplied, or the delivery is too late. If it is a consignment, the retailer is justified in returning unsold goods.

The MITI Guidelines also recommend, among other things, that when a manufacturer announces the suggested wholesale or retail price to distributors, it should make clear that the suggested price is not binding in nature and that a suggested price should be set at the level which is close to the market price.

Exclusionary Business Practices and 'Keiretsu' Relationships

In this category are included a variety of business practices. Major ones, among others, are practices such as an exclusive dealing arrangement between a manufacturer and distributors in which the manufacturer imposes the condition on the distributors that they cannot deal with products of competitors of the manufacturer, a group boycott whereby enterprises agree among themselves to exclude an outside party from a transaction, a reciprocal dealing arrangement whereby enterprises agree to engage in selling and buying among themselves and thereby exclude outside parties from transactions, a vertical territorial arrangement whereby a manufacturer assigns an exclusive sales territory to each distributor and prohibits him from doing business in the territory assigned to other distributors, and customer restrictions in which a manufacturer restricts the sales of distributors to designated retailers.

'Keiretsu' is a vague expression and it is hard to give a precise definition. However, it generally means a group of enterprises closely connected with each other through stock-ownerships, interlocking directorates, contractual relationships, or any other means. It can be a vertical combination; namely, a business relationship among parties at different transactional stages (such as a combination between a manufacturer and distributors). It can be a horizontal combination in which enterprises on the same level of transaction are combined together (such as an agreement among manufacturers of the same product).

It can be a combination of both horizontal and vertical agreements in which, for example, a manufacturer producing parts and components as well as the finished product is engaged in purchasing parts and components from suppliers.

Due to its complexity, it is difficult to state generally whether a *keiretsu* is exclusive and anti-competitive in its inherent nature. There are some commentators who maintain that it is not necessarily exclusive.[39] Even though enterprises may be linked together through stock-holding or otherwise, it does not necessarily mean that transactions are conducted only among themselves. If there are good outside sources, enterprises which belong to a *keiretsu* will procure products from outsiders.

On the other hand, there is a group of commentators who argue that a group of enterprises bound together in the form of a *keiretsu* tend to deal with each other and exclude outsiders.[40] They maintain that, through reciprocal dealings among themselves, those enterprises acquire acquaintance and knowledge of each other and this leads to a tight link among them.

It seems that the question of whether a *keiretsu* is exclusive and anti-competitive or not depends on the nature of each *keiretsu* and requires a case-by-case analysis. However, in the SII, the United States government insisted that the existence of *keiretsu* relationships among Japanese enterprises is an important cause for the exclusivity of the Japanese market.

In order to deal with this problem, the Japanese government agreed to strengthen the enforcement of the Anti-monopoly Law. Since a detailed account has already been made of unfair business practices under the Anti-monopoly Law, we will only briefly touch upon the recent developments.

In order to implement the contents of the SII, the FTC (the enforcement agency of the Anti-monopoly Law) drafted the guidelines on business practices and distribution (the 1991 FTCJ Guidelines). The major contents of the Guidelines are as follows.

Part I deals with restrictive business practices with regard to continuous and exclusive business relationships. It has been claimed by foreign enterprises entering into the Japanese market that the Japanese market is characterized by continuous business relationships among enterprises which tend to exclude any outside parties including foreign enterprises. Often Japanese enterprises prefer to stick to business partners with whom they have been doing business regardless of whether this is the most efficient way of business rather than changing and choosing partners on a spot basis. This business custom creates 'in-groups' in which transactions are carried on among members of the group.

Such in-group relationships are sometimes created by stock-holdings, are sometimes a long-standing *de facto* relationship, and again are sometimes a contractual relationship. Undoubtedly some of them are based on a sound business judgement. However, there may be a situation

[39] Yoshitomi, 'Keiretsu: A Legitimate Viable Capitalist Approach', *International Economy* (May/June 1991), 69–75.

[40] Laurence, 'Keiretsu and Japan's Rigged Distribution System', ibid. 64–7.

in which this relationship is unduly and excessively restrictive to outsider parties and, in such situations, it may be barrier to foreign enterprises at least at the initial stage of market entry.

From the above viewpoint, Part I of the Guidelines enumerates the following items: (1) a restriction of competition in acquiring new customers, (2) a group boycott, (3) a refusal to deal by a single enterprise, (4) an exclusive dealing arrangement, (5) an unreasonable reciprocal dealing, (6) other anti-competitive conduct based on continuous business relationships. and (7) anti-competitive conduct executed by means of the acquisition or holding of stocks of an enterprise which is the other party to a transaction.

The above items are nothing but traditional items which are regulated by the Anti-monopoly Law and, as far as the legal rules are concerned, the Guidelines are merely a confirmation of the previous rules and doctrines already enunciated by previous cases and interpretational theories.

However, the announcement of the Guidelines indicates the FTC's determination to crack down on exclusionary business conduct, and this will improve the situation, if not provide a total cure of the problem.

Part II of the Guidelines deal with exclusionary practices with regard to distribution. In this part, there are two issues. One of them is a variety of exclusionary practices exercised by a manufacturer in which the manufacturer imposes restrictive conditions on distributors and the other is an abuse of purchasing power by a powerful buyer such as a supermarket or a department store.

With respect to exclusionary practices exercised by a manufacturer, the Guidelines enumerate (1) resale price maintenance, (2) an exclusive dealing arrangement whereby a manufacturer prohibits distributors from handling products produced by competitors of the manufacturer, (3) a territorial arrangement by which each distributor is allocated an exclusive sales territory, (4) customer restriction by which distributors can deal with only certain designated customers, (5) restriction on the methods of sale by distributors by which distributors are obligated to use a designated sales method (such as requiring them to establish a corner in their shops in which only the products of the manufacturer are sold), (6) an unreasonable rebate which means a rebate used arbitrarily or excessively for the purpose of forcing distributors to comply with the policy of the manufacturer, and (7) an unreasonable interference into the managerial affairs of distributors. In the above, generally the conduct is unlawful if exercised by a powerful enterprise and has a big anti-competitive impact on the market in question.

With regard to an abuse of purchasing power by a supermarket or a department store, the Guidelines enumerate (1) a return of unsold goods,

(2) a request for dispatch of sales persons to shops, (3) a coercion to purchase, and (4) a coercive collection of contributions from suppliers. A return of unsold goods has been discussed in connection with the MITI Guidelines already. The FTC Guidelines state that this practice may be unlawful under the Anti-monopoly Law if used in oppressive ways. A request for dispatch of sales persons to shops is sometimes made by a department store to suppliers of commodities. Sales persons dispatched by a supplier act as sales personnel at the department store. Although there is nothing inherently wrong with this practice, if it is done with the *de facto* coercion that the department store will refuse to accept goods produced by a supplier which declines to dispatch sales personnel, it may have an anti-competitive effect.

A coercion to purchase means that a department store forces suppliers of commodities to purchase some commodities (usually expensive luxury items such as high-priced cosmetics, pictures, pearls, and so forth) and if a supplier declines to purchase, the department store will terminate the relationship with that supplier. In coercive collection of contributions from suppliers, a department stores forces suppliers to contribute an amount of money for events such as festivals sponsored by the department store.

The above is an outline of the rules contained in the 1991 FTCJ Guidelines. As stated earlier, the rules incorporated in them are a confirmation of the existing doctrines already expressed in cases and interpretational theories. However, it is significant that these rules are placed in the setting of trade issues by the 1991 FTCJ Guidelines.

H. ANTI-DUMPING AND COUNTERVAILING DUTIES

An Overview

'Dumping' is the export of a commodity at a price lower than the price of the same or a similar commodity in the domestic market of the country of export. When an export at such a price causes a material injury to a domestic industry of the importing country, the dumping is regarded as an unfair export practice.'[41] 'Export subsidy' is a grant by the government to an export. If a subsidized export causes a material injury to a domestic industry of the country of import, the subsidy of the import is regarded as an unfair export practice. Although the economic theory behind these propositions is vague and not necessarily persuasive, the GATT and subsequent agreements regard them as unfair.

Under Article VI of the GATT, contracting parties are authorized to

[41] On anti-dumping regulations of the major countries, see Jackson and Vermulst (eds.), *Antidumping Law and Practice* (Ann Arbor, Mich., 1989).

enforce anti-dumping laws against an import at an export price lower than that in the domestic market of the country of export as long as there is a material injury to a domestic industry. This article also allows contracting parties to enforce countervailing duty laws against an import which is subsidized by the government of the exporting country. To implement this article, there are two international agreements, i.e. the International Anti-dumping Code and the International Subsidy and Countervailing Duty Code.

Japan is a member of both these international codes as well as the GATT. To implement these international agreements, there are several laws and regulations in Japan. Article 9 of the Customs and Tariff Law[42] provides for the imposition of an anti-dumping duty, and Article 8 provides for the imposition of a countervailing duty. The Cabinet Decree on Anti-dumping Duties (hereafter referred to as 'the AD Decree') and the Cabinet Decree on Countervailing Duties provide detailed rules.[43] There are also 'Guidelines on the Procedure of the Anti-dumping and Countervailing Duties and Related Matters' (hereafter referred to as 'the AD Guidelines') (1986).[44] Since the anti-dumping law is more important than the countervailing duty, the following comments will primarily focus on the anti-dumping law.

Dumping is defined in Article 9 of the Customs and Tariff Law as 'the selling for export of an article at a price which is lower than the price of the same or a similar article for domestic consumption in the market of the country of export'. The price of the commodity for the domestic market (the market of the country of export) is 'normal value'. Dumping occurs when an export of a commodity to Japan is made at a price which is lower than the normal value of the same or a similar product.

When a domestic industry sustains a material injury by reason of such dumping, the Japanese government is authorized to impose, in addition to the regular duty on the product in question, an anti-dumping duty whose maximum amount is the difference between the export price and the normal value of the commodity (dumping margin).

Investigation

The International Anti-dumping Code states that an investigation should be initiated when there is a petition by an interested party in principle and a self-initiation by the government is an exception. Accordingly, in compliance with the GATT rules, the Japanese anti-dumping law and

[42] Gaikokukawase Oyobi Gaikokubōeki Kanri Hō, Law 228, 1949.

[43] Both of those decrees have been translated and published in: The Fair Trade Center, *Antidumping Law in Japan* (Tokyo, 1990), 37–44.

[44] The guidelines have been translated and published ibid. 45–62.

regulations state that an anti-dumping investigation is started in principle by the petition of an interested party, although a self-initiation by the government is possible as an exception.

An interested party can file a complaint with the Customs and Tariff Section of the MOF when he deems that a product from a country is imported at a price lower than its domestic price and that a Japanese domestic industry suffers a material injury by reason of such dumping. The complaint should state the article in question, the manufacturer, the brand, the model, the features of the commodity, the exporter, and the country of export, and outline the facts of the dumping, the material injury, and other relevant data. The petitioner must produce evidence that is 'reasonably available'.

The interested party can be an individual, corporation, or trade association. However, it is often a trade association which represents the industry affected by dumping. Such a trade association must show that its constitution states that it is authorized to act on behalf of its members or otherwise prove that it is authorized to do so.

The enforcement agency of the anti-dumping regulation consists of the following three ministries; (1) the MOF, (2) the MITI, and (3) the minister in charge of the product in question. An investigatory group composed of officials of the MOF, the MIT, and the ministry in charge of the product under investigation carries out the investigation. For the sake of brevity, the enforcement agency will be referred to as 'the AD Authority' hereafter.

The AD Authority may initiate a formal investigation if the petition filed by a private party is supported by sufficient evidence. The AD Authority has to decide within two months after the petition was filed whether to initiate a formal investigation or not. Even though self-initiation is exceptional, the AD Authority can initiate an investigation when there is evidence of dumping and of material injury to a domestic industry.

Interested parties are guaranteed the opportunity to produce evidence and the AD Authority can request private parties to submit evidence. If the party submitting information requests it, the information is kept confidential. However, the AD Authority can request the party to provide a non-confidential summary of the information.

The AD Authority can request foreign exporters and producers to submit information with regard to price and other relevant matters. Submission of information is voluntary for the foreign exporters and producers. However, if the foreign party so requested does not co-operate without a good reason, the AD Authority can base its judgement on the 'best information available'.

If requested by the parties involved in a case, the AD Authority holds a confrontation meeting in which both parties present their views and a cross-examination of witnesses is permitted.

Domestic Industry

The term 'domestic industry' is a key concept in the AD regulation. The AD Decree defines a domestic industry as manufacturers who produce a considerable portion of the commodity which is in competition with the dumped product. Under the AD Guidelines, a 'considerable portion' is defined as at least a 50 per cent share in the production. Also, under the AD Guidelines, those domestic manufacturers who import the commodity under investigation or who are related to foreign exporters must be excluded from the scope of domestic industry. The reason is a 'clean hand' principle. If a domestic manufacturer benefits from an affiliation with a foreign exporter or a domestic importer of a dumped product, there is no reason for the anti-dumping law to protect that domestic manufacturer.

However, there is some flexibility with regard to this issue. If a domestic enterprise ceased importing the commodity under investigation six months prior to the filing of a complaint, it is included within the scope of domestic industry.

Provisional Measures and Final Measures

A provisional measure can be taken under critical circumstances. If it is determined that there has been dumping of a commodity and an injury to a domestic industry is likely to occur, the MOF can invoke a provisional measure in the form of a provisional duty or a bond or security for an amount equal to the provisional duty. The maximum period of a provisonal measure is four months, although this period can be extended to six months upon the request of the interested party. A provisional measure is taken when there is a circumstance that a domestic industry would be injured by a surge of dumped products unless a preventive measure were promptly taken.

After the facts of dumping and injury have been established, an anti-dumping duty is imposed on the import in question. The maximum amount of anti-dumping duty is the difference between the export price and the normal value (the dumping margin).

Price Undertaking

Since an anti-dumping investigation is quite lengthy and burdensome on the foreign exporter, the importer, and the government which enforces the anti-dumping law, there is a way of settling the matter through a price undertaking. A foreign exporter can propose to the AD Authority that he will stop exporting the dumped product or increase the export price so as to eliminate the dumping margin. The AD Authority can suspend the anti-dumping investigation if it judges that the proposal is appropriate to resolve the issue. It should be noted that this is an agreement between the Japanese government and the foreign exporter but not an agreement between the foreign exporter and the domestic petitioner. An agreement between the foreign exporter and the domestic industry by which the domestic industry will withdraw the complaint if the foreign exporter raises its export price is likely to be held as unlawful under the Anti-monopoly Law.

Normal Value and Export Price

'Dumping' is the export of a commodity at an export price lower than the normal value of the same or a similar commodity sold in the market of the exporting country. Therefore, to determine whether there is dumping of a commodity or not, the export price of the commodity and the normal value of it must be compared in order to determine if there is a difference between them.

'Normal value' is, in general terms, the domestic price of the commodity in question, that is, the price of the commodity in the home market of the country of export. It is the price charged by the manufacturer/exporter of the commodity in the home market of the country of export to an independent purchaser. If the manufacturer/exporter of a commodity sells the commodity to a wholesaler who is independent of the manufacturer/exporter in the home market of the country of export, that price is the normal value. If the manufacturer/exporter of the commodity sells it to a wholesaler who is related to it through a stock-holding, an interlocking directorship, or otherwise, then the transaction between the related parties is disregarded. In such a case, the normal value is computed on the basis of the price charged by the wholesaler to the first independent purchaser. Therefore, if the manufacturer and the wholesaler are related parties, the normal value is based on the price which the wholesaler charges to an independent retailer. If the manufacturer, the wholesaler, and the retailer are all vertically integrated and there is an insufficient number of sales to independent purchasers, then the normal value is computed by using the constructed value.

Also, the sale by the manufacturer/exporter in the home market at a price below the production cost of the commodity may be disregarded by the enforcement agency, in which case a constructed value is used to compute the normal value. 'Constructed value' is the price which is obtained by adding the estimated cost of producing the commodity, the estimated general expenses, and a reasonable profit. The reason for disregarding a domestic price which is below the cost of production is that a price below the cost of production is not a normal price formed in the normal business process and, therefore, is not appropriate to be used as the basis of normal value.

The International Anti-dumping Code permits that if there is no domestic price of the commodity, either a third-country export price or the constructed value may be used as the normal value. A third-country export price is the price at which the commodity is exported to a third country. The Code makes no preference as to whether a third-country export price or the normal value should be used first and so either price can be adopted.

'Export price' is generally the price at which the manufacturer/exporter sells the commodity for the purpose of export. If, therefore, the commodity is sold by the foreign manufacturer/exporter to a Japanese importer, the price paid by the importer is the export price of that commodity. If the foreign manufacturer sells the commodity to an independent trading company in the foreign country and then the trading company exports the commodity to a Japanese importer, the export price may be computed on the basis of the price paid by the trading company.

If the foreign manufacturer/exporter exports the commodity to an importer in Japan who is related to the manufacturer/exporter, the transaction between those related parties may be disregarded since the price paid in this context may not reflect the market price. In this situation, the export price may be computed on the basis of the price charged by the importer in Japan to an independent third party. For example, if a foreign manufacturer owns a subsidiary in Japan, the manufacturer exports a commodity to the subsidiary and then the subsidiary sells it to third parties in Japan, the export price of the commodity is usually the price at which the Japanese subsidiary sells the commodity to the third parties.

The International Anti-dumping Code requires that both export price and normal value must be computed at the same level of trade and, if possible, at the ex-factory level. Therefore, in order to arrive at the export price, it is necessary to start from the price paid by the importer to the exporter (a case in which an independent importer imports the commodity) and deduct expenses incurred by the exporter. This involves the deduction from the original price of such items as transportation costs, tariffs, expenses for packaging if special expenses are required, and other incidental expenses. Likewise, in arriving at the normal value, it is necessary to go through a similar process of back-calculation.

Also, adjustments of the difference between prices due to special circumstances are necessary. For example, if a foreign manufacturer gives technical assistance to domestic wholesalers in the country of export with regard to the commodity it sells, while no such technical assistance is given to Japanese importers and distributors, the foreign manufacturer incurs more expenses in the sale of the commodity in the home market and the normal value must be adjusted accordingly. It must be reduced by the amount by which such assistance is given. Likewise, if there is a difference in the methods of payment which results in a difference of interest, such a difference must be taken into consideration. If, for example, a foreign wholesaler pays the foreign manufacturer for the commodity he buys in the home market of the country of export by a promissory note whose term is, say, four months, while Japanese importers pay the foreign manufacturer of the commodity by means of a letter of credit payable on sight, then the interest for the period of those four months should be taken into consideration, and the normal value should be reduced by the amount of such interest.

If a rebate is given by the manufacturer/exporter to distributors in the home market, the amount equal to the rebate may be reduced as long as it is proved that the rebate is directly related to the sale of the commodity in the home market.

Another important item for adjustment is a quantity discount. If the commodity in question is sold in the home market at a discount price for sufficient quantity, the discount price may be adopted as the normal value.

The above are but a few examples of items which should be taken into consideration when making adjustments with regard to an export price and a normal value. In practice, the process of calculating an export price and a normal value may be enormously complex. Since precedents are so scarce, it is yet to be seen how the practice will grow in this regard in the future.

Material Injury

If there is dumping of a commodity as explained above and, by reason of such dumping, a domestic industry is materially injured and there is a causation between the dumping and the injury, then the requirements for imposing an anti-dumping duty are all satisfied. There is no precise definition of material injury in the law and regulations. However, it is generally understood that a material injury is an injury lighter than a 'serious injury' as the term is used in the safeguard measure.[45] Various economic indicators are considered when deciding whether or not there has been a material injury by dumping. First, an increase in imports of the commodity under investigation is considered. If the rate of increase is quite rapid or the quantity of imports is great, this is an important indicator for determining the existence of an injury. Secondly, the pricing of the commodity in question is taken into consideration. If the domestic

[45] On safeguard measures, see Bronckers, *Selective Safeguard Measures in Multilateral Trade Relations* (Deventer, 1985).

price has been depressed or a rise in the price is stopped by the influx of the dumped goods, this is regarded as contributing to an injury.

Thirdly, the effect of dumping on the domestic industry is considered. This involves a close examination of economic factors such as a decrease in the rate of profits, a decline in the utilization of production facilities, and an increase in unemployment. In order to determine an injury, all those factors (and others if any) must be considered and weighed as a whole.

Another important problem is that of causation or linkage between a dumping and an injury. The International Anti-dumping Code requires that an injury caused by factors other than dumped imports should not be attributed to the dumping. Although this language is somewhat vague, it indicates that a dumping must be an important cause of an injury instead of a negligible one. If, therefore, there are several other important factors contributing to an injury, and dumping is a small cause, it should not lead to any finding of injury to a domestic industry.

Countervailing Duty

A countervailing duty is imposed when a foreign government provides an export subsidy for the export of a commodity, thereby causing an injury to a domestic industry in the importing country. The International Subsidy and Countervailing Duty Code provides requirements which contracting parties must observe when enforcing their domestic countervailing duty laws. Since Japan is a contracting party to the Code, Japan is obligated to observe these terms. The Code lists as export subsidies a number of practices including rebates given to exporters in proportion to the amount of exports, tax exemptions, preferential financing by the government or by government-related agencies at a rate of interest more favourable than the prevailing market rate, and government aid afforded to the manufacturer of products to be exported.

'Indirect subsidies' can be the subject of a countervailing duty. For example, if a foreign government subsidizes the production of parts to be incorporated into a finished product for export to Japan, such a subsidy may be regarded as an 'indirect subsidy'. If such a subsidy is given exclusively for the production of parts used in exported products, it may be regarded as an indirect export subsidy. If a foreign government issues financial aid to producers of parts and components of a product at a more favourable rate than the market rate, the product is exported and there is no domestic market for that product in the country of export, then such financial assistance may be regarded as an indirect subsidy.

The procedure of investigation to impose a countervailing duty is similar to that for an anti-dumping duty. A person who represents a domestic industry and who believes that the domestic industry has been injured by an increase of imports aided by subsidies granted by a foreign government can file a complaint with the government. In addition, a self-initiation of investigation by the government is possible, although it is exceptional as in the case of the anti-dumping regulation. The investigation must be completed within one year. If the facts of subsidy, injury, and the linkage between the two are established, a countervailing duty may be imposed on the imports of the product in question, whose maximum amount is equal to the amount of the net subsidy in addition to the regular duty.

The tests used to determine an injury to a domestic industry and the linkage between the subsidized import and a material injury are similar to those used in an anti-dumping investigation.

As in an anti-dumping investigation, the issue may be settled by an undertaking on the part of the foreign government after an investigation has been started with regard to a possible subsidy given to an export. If the foreign government promises to eliminate the subsidy or otherwise take a measure which would eliminate the injurious effect of the subsidy, the investigation can be suspended.

Cases of Anti-dumping and Countervailing Duties

There have been few cases in which a petition has been filed by a Japanese domestic industry on the basis of the anti-dumping and countervailing duty regulations. The reasons, among others, are that until the late 1960s there were a number of quantitative restrictions on imports and there was little need for an anti-dumping or countervailing duty, that since that time Japanese industries have generally enjoyed a high degree of international competitiveness, and that the government has been heavily engaged in protecting and promoting small enterprises by means other than the regulation of imports. However, some traditional industries may lose comparative advantage *vis-à-vis* competing industries of other countries (especially those in NIEs), while industries in those countries are making a rapid progress. In such a situation, there may be a need for an anti-dumping or countervailing duty. Therefore, in the future, there may be an increase of petitions under the anti-dumping and/or countervailing duty regulations.

There have been five cases in which domestic industries petitioned the government for relief under the anti-dumping and countervailing duty laws. In 1982, the Japanese Cotton Spinners' Association brought a petition to the Authority claiming that Korean products had been dumped on the market and had caused material injury to the textile industry. It also claimed that the Pakistani government gave an export subsidy in the form of export financing at a preferential interest raate and a rebate to exporters at the rate of 7.5 per cent of the income derived from export. It was claimed that because of an increase of imports aided by the government, there had been a material injury to the Japanese domestic industry.

With regard to the Korean dumping issue, there was a negotiation in Korea between the representatives of the Japanese and Korean industries, and the Korean industry agreed to put into effect a voluntary export restraint. The Japanese industry accepted this settlement and withdrew its petition.

On the Pakistani subsidy issue, there was a conference between the Japanese and Pakistani governments, and the Pakistani government promised to abolish the preferential financing and the rebate. The Japanese government considered that the tax reduction would produce only a *de minimus* effect and decided to terminate the investigation.

The third case is the ferro-silicon case. The ferro-alloy industry had been designated by the MITI as a depressed industry under the Law to Promote Improvement of Industrial Structure in Specific Industries[46] and was in the process of an industrial reorganization. In 1980 and 1981, there was a sharp increase in imports of this product, and foreign imports occupied 62 per cent of the market. The Ferro-Alloy Association in Japan claimed that the products had been dumped on to the market by French and Norwegian producers and that a subsidy had been given by the Brazilian government to export the product to Japan. However, before an investigation was initiated with regard to the dumping and subsidy question, conferences were held between the Japanese government and the governments of the countries in question. The foreign governments promised that they would ensure that there would be no dumping or export subsidy. Meanwhile the market condition in Japan improved remarkably. The Ferro-Alloy Association decided to drop its petition after considering all these factors.

The fourth case is that of knit textile products in 1987, the import of knit textile products surpassed the export of these products from Japan for the first time in history. The major foreign sources of supply were Korea and China. The Japan Knitting Industry Association filed a petition with the government in 1988 under the anti-dumping regulation claiming that exports to Japan from Korea had been dumped. In early 1989, the Korean exporters announced that they would restrain the export of the products voluntarily, and the Japanese association decided to withdraw its petition.

In the fifth case, the Ferro-Alloy Association filed a petition with the government alleging that ferro-silicon manganese imported from China, Norway, and South Africa was dumped into the Japanese market. It

[46] Tokutei Sangyōkōzō Kaizen Rinjisochi Hō, Law 44, 1983.

claimed, among other things, that due to dumping, the market share of the domestic industry dropped from 49 per cent in 1989 to 34.4 per cent in 1991. An investigation was initiated in November 1991. It is the first case in which the Japanese government formally initiated an anti-dumping investigation. At the time of writing, the case is pending.

As seen above, there are five cases in which an anti-dumping and countervailing duty issue was raised. Although there has been no case so far in which an anti-dumping or countervailing duty was imposed, we can expect that there will be petitions filed by Japanese domestic industries and that these laws will be employed more frequently.

I. RETALIATION FOR UNFAIR TRADE PRACTICES

Article 7 of the Customs and Tariff Law provides that the government can impose a special tariff on any product coming from a country which discriminates against Japanese goods, shipping, or airlines. This provision has not been invoked yet. This may be similar to Section 301 of the Trade Act of 1974 in the United States[47] and the New Commercial Policy Instrument of the European Communities.[48] However, there are some important differences.

Whereas in Section 301 of the Trade Act of 1974 and the New Commercial Policy Instrument, the scope of retaliatory measures is wide and includes tariffs, quantitative restrictions, and others, Article 7 of the Customs and Tariff Law provides for an imposition of special tariffs only. Secondly, Article 7 of the Customs and Tariff Law can be invoked only when there is a discrimination against Japanese goods, shipping, or airlines and its scope does not include such items as impediments with regard to investment opportunities and technology licensing, whereas those seem to be included in the scope of Section 301 of the Trade Act of 1974 and the New Commercial Policy Instrument.

The Japanese government has announced that it will utilize the dispute settlement procedure as incorporated in Article 23 of the GATT to settle disputes with foreign countries. Under Article 23, a contracting party can bring a case with the GATT when there is a violation by another contracting party of a GATT provision or other practice of the country which nullifies the benefit which the GATT bestows on contracting parties. When the GATT permits a retaliation, then the contracting party which has brought a claim can take a measure within the permitted scope. If the GATT permits Japan to take a measure against a contracting party,

[47] See Vakerics *et al.*, *Antidumping, Countervailing Duty and Other Trade Actions* (New York, 1988), 415–86.

[48] Van Bael and Bellis, *Anti-Dumping and Other Trade Protection Laws of the EEC* (Bicester, 1990), pt iv, 331 *et seq.*

what legal instruments are there to implement it? Although it is not clear what laws should be utilized for this purpose, Article 7 of the Customs and Tariff Law is a candidate. However, the scope of measures permitted under this law seems to be too narrow.

As discussed earlier, a comprehensive law which authorizes the government to take trade measures is the Control Law. The import quota system provided for in Article 52 of the Control may be invoked. Also, there are provisions in the Control Law which authorize the MOF to take restrictive measures with regard to foreign exchanges and capital transactions. However, as we have seen already, the decision of the Tokyo District Court in the *COCOM* case held that an export restriction is permitted only within the scope of the legislative purpose of the law.[49] Although this decision was concerned with only an export control, the same rationale seems to apply to an import control, an exchange control, and control of a capital transaction. There is no clear language in the Control Law which explicitly states that the law can be utilized for the purpose of retaliation against a foreign country. In this respect, there is no appropriate instrument and, when Japan utilizes the GATT dispute settlement procedure more in the future, there will be greater need for a more comprehensive legal instrument in this regard.

3.3 Regulation of Exports

A. AN OVERVIEW

The Purposes of Export Control

The regulation of exports is carried out for a variety of purposes. Among them, however, there are two most important objectives. One is the regulation of exports for the purpose of orderly marketing or orderly export. Often trade conflicts occur between Japan and her trade partners and it is necessary to restrain exports to a foreign country. Sometimes the government of a foreign country requests the Japanese government to take a measure to enforce a 'voluntary export restraint'. Sometimes the Japanese government takes a precautionary measure and puts into effect a measure to restrain exports in the anticipation that an increase of exports to foreign countries will cause trade problems in future.[50]

Once upon the time, export control was used by the Japanese government to prevent commodities of inferior quality from being exported.

[49] Decision of the Tokyo District Court, 8 July 1969, *Gyōsai Reishū*, 20/7 (1969), 842 *et seq*.

[50] On voluntary export restraint, see Chap. 3, 3.3, D, below.

Japanese commodities were once regarded as 'cheap and of inferior quality'. The government restricted export of commodities of inferior quality in order to maintain international confidence in the Japanese commodity. This has already become past history. At present, trade problems are often caused by the imbalance between the competitiveness of Japanese enterprises and that of competing enterprises in importing countries. In some areas of manufacturing, Japanese industries enjoy a high level of international competitiveness and there is an imbalance in international competitiveness between the Japanese industries and foreign industries which compete with those in Japan. Due to this imbalance, Japanese commodities sometimes occupy an ever-increasing market share in a foreign country and an apprehension is aroused in that country. Today, the regulation of exports in this regard plays a different role from that of the 1950s and 1960s.

The other is the regulation of exports for the purpose of implementing an international agreement such as the COCOM. As a member of the COCOM, the Japanese government is obligated to restrict or prohibit the export of certain items of commodities and technology to the designated countries.[51] The Japanese government undertakes an export ban on those items to the designated countries through her domestic export control mechanisms. An export ban may become necessary due to changes in international relations. For example, in the Gulf War of 1991, it was necessary to prohibit export of commodities and technology to Iraq as part of the co-operative scheme with the United States and other allies. Situations such as this may arise in the future.

The above two are probably the most important among the objectives for regulating export. However, there may be some additional reasons for the regulation of exports. It may be necessary to control export of a commodity in short supply. For example, some materials are simply rare and hard to obtain (e.g. tungsten). It may be necessary to maintain the control on exports of such an item in order to avoid depletion of it.

In order to maintain public order in international trade, it is necessary to prohibit the export of some items, such as: obscene literature, narcotics, weapons, and explosives. With regard to specific goods, there is legislation which prohibits the possession, sale, import, and export of the items concerned. For example, the Law to Control Guns[52] prohibits the possession, sale, import, and export of weapons such as guns.

Export of such items which are classified as 'national treasures' or other important cultural objects is controlled and this control may be regarded

[51] On the COCOM and related subjects, see articles in Oda (ed.), *Law and Politics of West-East Technology Transfer* (Dordrecht, 1991).

[52] Jūhōtōkenruitō Torishimari Hō, Law 6, 1958.

as for the protection of cultural identity. The regulation of the export of such items may be exercised through a general law such as the Control Law or through a specific piece of law. For example, there is a law entitled 'The Law to Protect National Treasures'[53] which prohibits the export of designated national treasures.

Some agricultural items are also subject to export control. For example, under the Foodstuffs Control Law,[54] export of rice as well as its import is subjected to a licensing requirement, although, as we have seen already, the major purpose of this law is to control the import of rice rather than its export.

An Outline of the Law and Regulations

There are two basic laws which regulate exports. One is the Control Law[55] and the other is the Transactions Law.[56] Under the Control Law, the MITI is authorized to control the export of commodities and also technology. The MITI can control exports directly by designating commodities or technology as controlled items and requiring exporters of such items to obtain export approval from the MITI when they wish to export them to the designated areas.

The Control Law delegates a wide scope of powers to the MITI to implement the contents of the law. A Cabinet decree entitled 'The Export Control Decree'[57] assigns the power to enforce this law and the MITI has issued ministerial orders to provide for details. To understand the actual operations of this law, it is important to be familiar with the details of not only the Control Law but also the Cabinet Decree and ministerial orders.

On the other hand, the Transactions Law merely authorizes private exporters to agree on the terms of export and enter into an export agreement (or an export cartel). In actuality, however, the MITI is deeply involved in the enforcement of this law. The MITI often issues an administrative guidance or a 'directive' to private exporters and causes them to enter into an agreement. In this way, those two pieces of legislation are used interchangeably by the MITI.

The Freedom of Export

Article 47 of the Control Law provides for the freedom of export and Article 48 establishes the export approval system. Article 47 states that:

[53] Bunkazai Hogo Hō, Law 214, 1950.
[54] Shokuryō Kanri Hō, Law 40, 1942.
[55] Gaikokukawase Oyobi Gaikokubōeki Kanri Hō, Law 228, 1949.
[56] Yushutsunyū Torihiki Hō, Law 299, 1952.
[57] Yushutsubōeki Kanri Rei, Decree 378, 1949.

'Export of goods is permitted with the minimum restrictions as long as such restrictions are in accord with the basic objectives of this law.' From this wording, it is clear that export is basically free and can only be restricted exceptionally.

We have already discussed the *COCOM* decision handed down by the Tokyo District Court in 1969 in which the court stated that the right of export belongs to the freedom of occupation (in which the freedom of trade is included), as guaranteed by Article 25 of the Constitution, that Article 1 of this law provided that the objective of the law was to maintain an equilibrium in the international balance of payment, to promote the healthy development of the national economy (that is, an economic objective), and that to invoke an export control under this law to achieve an objective other than ones of an economic nature would be unconstitutional. This unconstitutionality issue was partially remedied by the amendment of 1987 (as explained below), even though Article 1 of the Control Law has never been amended.

B. EXPORT CONTROL FOR POLITICAL PURPOSES

Export Control for the Purpose of Maintaining International Security

Article 48 of the Control Law provides for the export approval system. Article 48(1) states: 'A person who wishes to export a specific commodity to a specific area whose export has been designated by a Cabinet Decree *as threatening the maintenance of international peace and security* must obtain an export approval of the Minister of the MITI in accordance with the provisions of the Export Control Decree' (emphasis added). This provision was added to the Control Law by the amendment of 1987 to remedy the unconstitutionality declared in the *COCOM* case.

Under this provision, export approval is based on a political purpose rather than an economic purpose. An exporter of the designated commodity to the designated area must obtain approval from the MITI, and the MITI can achieve an export prohibition by denying an export approval when an application is made. In order to prevent a circumvention of this control, the MITI is authorized to apply the export approval requirement to exports of the commodity to areas other than the designated area. For example, the MITI can attach a condition that the commodity which is exported to an area other than the designated area shall not be re-exported from there to the designated area. Although this may be insufficient to prevent a circumvention, an export of the commodity to an area other than the designated area with the purpose or knowledge that it will be re-exported to the designated area constitutes a violation of the Control Law.

The Amendment of the Control Law in 1987

The amendment of 1987 was made in response to the *Toshiba Machinery Company* case.[58] In 1987, Toshiba Machinery, a subsidiary of Toshiba which had manufactured and sold machine tools, was accused of having exported a machine tool which the Soviet Navy could use to reduce the sound of screws of Russian submarines. Although personnel of the company involved in the export of the prohibited item and the company itself were indicated and a guilty judgment was handed down by the Tokyo District Court, it was not sufficient to calm down the animosity aroused by the incident in the United States Congress.

The United States Congress which was in the process of considering a bill which became the Omnibus Trade and Competitiveness Act of 1988 reacted by inserting in the bill a provision for imposing sanctions on Toshiba and Toshiba Machinery.[59] The provision would prohibit Toshiba Machinery from exporting products to the United States as well as excluding the company from public procurement in the United States and would prohibit Toshiba from selling products to the United States with certain exceptions. The bills became part of the law when the Omnibus Trade and Competitiveness Act of 1988 was enacted.[60]

In response to this move in the United States, the Japanese government introduced a bill in the National Diet which would increase the penalty for a violation of the Control Law and change Article 48(1) to make it clear that the provision could be used to control exports for the purpose of implementing international agreements designed to accomplish political or strategic purposes such as the *COCOM* agreement. The penalty for a violation of the export control provision of the Control Law was a fine not exceeding 1 million yen or imprisonment not exceeding three years or both. Under the amended provision, the penalty was increased to a fine not exceeding 2 million yen or imprisonment not exceeding five years.

As stated earlier, the constitutional problem posed by the *COCOM* Decision in 1969 was only partially remedied by inserting the wording in Article 48(2) that this provision was designed to exert export control for the purpose of maintaining international peace and security. However, the *COCOM* decision stated that the basic objective was determined by Article 1 of the Control Law which set forth the objective of the Law but Article 1 was not changed for political reasons. Viewed in this light, the

[58] On this case, see 'The State of Japan v. Toshiba Machine Co. *et al.*, Tokyo District Court, Judgment of 22 March 1988', *Japanese Annual of International Law,* 31 (1988), 206 *et seq*.

[59] See n. 35, above.

[60] Sect. 2444 of the Omnibus Trade and Competitiveness Act of 1988, 102 Stat. 1107 (1988).

amendment of 1987 was less than perfect in correcting the constitutional problem posed by the *COCOM* Decision. Since, however, Article 48(1) contains clear wording that the provision can be used for international political or strategic purposes, the present system would probably be held constitutional if challenged on the ground of a violation of Article 25 of the Constitution as it was in the *COCOM* Case.

By the amendment of 1987, Article 64.4 was introduced in which the Minister of Foreign Affairs can request a consultation with the Minister of MITI with regard to the enforcement of Article 48(1) of the Control Law. The purpose of this provision is that the Minister of Foreign Affairs who is in charge of international diplomacy can have a chance to have his/her voice heard by the MITI.

Penalty for Violation

A criminal penalty is provided for a violation of Article 48(1) (as well as Article 25(1) which will be explained below). According to Article 69.6(1) of the Control Law, a person who exports a prohibited good or technology to the designated area is subject to imprisonment not exceeding five years or a fine not exceeding 2 million yen. Both the penalties can be imposed at the same time. If five times the value of the object of the transaction which is in violation exceeds 2 million yen, the maximum fine is the amount which is five times as much as its value.

The above penalty is heavier than that imposed when a person violates the other portions of the Control Law (Article 48(2), which controls export for the purpose of orderly marketing or orderly export) and this shows that the legislative intent of this article is to regard a violation of Article 48(1) as a more serious offence than a violation of other provisions.

Administrative sanctions which are imposed by the MITI involve: (1) an injunction against a violation of Article 48(1) prohibiting the violating party from engaging in a transaction in which a specific item under control is involved for the maximum of a three-year period.

Control of Technology Transfer

Nowadays strategic technology is at least as important as goods which may be used for military purposes. Therefore, in order to achieve the purpose of export control for maintaining international peace and security, the Control Law provides for specific provisions. The relevant articles are Articles 25(1) and (2) of the Control Law. The wording used in Articles 25(1) and (2) is the control of 'services'. However, technology and the transfer of technology are interpreted as falling under transactions with regard to services. Article 25(1) provides for the general control and Article 25(2) deals with circumventions, and the MITI has the authority to implement this regulation.

Under Article 25(1), when a resident of Japan enters into a transaction with a non-resident in which the former transfers a 'specific technology' to the latter in a 'specified area' which is designated in a Cabinet Decree as the area to which an export of the technology would endanger the maintenance of international peace and security, he/she shall obtain approval from the MITI. The MITI can prohibit this transaction by refusing to grant an approval.

'Specific technology' is defined in a foreign exchange control order promulgated under the Control Law and includes: (1) 14 kinds of technology relating to weapons, (2) 16 kinds relating to nuclear substances, and (3) 160 kinds relating to the COCOM Agreement. As to 'specific areas', every area is designated with respect to (1) and (2). This means that the export of technology which falls under (1) or (2) is subject to approval regardless of the destination, and generally the export is prohibited.

With respect to (3), the COCOM areas are designated as specific areas'. Specific areas may, of course, change because of changes in international political situations.

Control of Circumvention

The prohibition of export of technology under the Control Law may be circumvented. A company may disguise a transaction in which a prohibited technology is to be transferred to an entity in a designated area by camoumflaging the transaction so that it appears to occur between the Japanese company and a company in an area which is not designated as a prohibited area. To prevent circumvention, it would be useful to engage in 'extra-territorial application' of the export control legislation as in cases of the Export Administration Act in the United States. However, an extra-territorial application would cause international conflicts as exemplified in the *Siberian Pipeline* Case.[61] Therefore, in principle, there is no extra-territorial application of the Control Law.

There are, however, some devices to prevent circumvention. Article 25(2) of the Control Law provides for measures to prevent circumventions. Under this article, the MITI can impose the obligation on a resident who intends to transfer a 'specific technology' to a non-resident in an area other than a 'specific area', when the MITI judges that such an imposition of obligation is necessary to ensure the effectiveness of Article 25(1) of the Control Law.

[61] On the case, see the International Law Association, *Report of the Sixty-Fourth Conference* (1990), 313 *et seq*.

Under Article 25(1) of the Control Law, as mentioned before, the export of a designated item to a designated area needs to be approved and any party which desires to transfer a specific technology which belongs to them must obtain an approval from the MITI before it performs the transaction. The MITI can prohibit the transfer of the technology in question by refusing to give an approval. However, an exporter of the prohibited technology may try to export the technology via a third party in an area which is not designated as a controlled area.

In effect, Article 25(2) is invoked in order to deal with the situation in which a domestic enterprise transfers a prohibited technology to a party in a non-designated area and then the technology is transferred again from there to a designated area and thereby circumvents the control. For example, if a Japanese company transfers a technology which belongs to the controlled items to a company in France (which is not included in the controlled areas) with the knowledge that the French company will transfer it to an entity in, for example, Vietnam, and if the Japanese company does not disclose this fact to the MITI when it obtains an approval, it is regarded as a prohibited transaction and the MITI can withhold approval. Another example would be a case in which a Japanese company enters into an agreement with a French company which it is known would transfer the technology to an entity in the designated area. To disguise the transaction, the Japanese company reports to the MITI that the transaction would occur between the Japanese company and another French company and obtain an approval from the MITI. In this example, the actual transaction takes place between the Japanese company and the former French company. In this situation, the MITI regards this transaction as not being reported and can subject the Japanese company to a penalty.

Although the above devices may be of relatively little effect to combat circumventions, there is naturally a limit to what a single nation can do to cope with this problem. If the Japanese government is to prevent circumventions without using extra-territorial enforcement, the above described devices would be the limit of what it can do. Prevention of circumventions must be carried out through an international co-operative scheme in which the member nations enforce their own export control laws vigorously.

International Agreements

There are several international agreements to which Japan is a contracting party and which authorize the restriction of exports for the reason of maintaining national security. The above described export control scheme may be authorized by the international obligations which the Japanese government is obligated to observe.

Article 21 of the GATT declares that exceptions from the obligation to liberalize trade are permitted within limits. Under this provision, a contracting party is authorized to refuse to disclose information whose disclosure would be adverse to the need for maintaining national security, to take measures relating to nuclear materials and to transactions involving weapons, ammunitions, and other strategic materials, to take measures in a state of emergency, such as wars and other similar situations. It also allows a contracting party to adopt a measure to comply with the obligations under the United Nations Charter.

Article 21 of the Treaty of Friendship, Commerce, and Navigation between the United States and Japan states that each contracting party is not prevented from taking a measure necessary to implement the obligations with regard to the maintenance of international peace and security or the restoration thereof or which is necessary to protect an important interest of national security. This wording is even more widely couched and it seems clear that measures for the control of exports taken by the Japanese government for the purpose of maintaining international peace and security is supported by this treaty.

The United Nations Charter provides for the collective security and economic sanctions which may be taken to safeguard the collective security. Articles 39 and 41 are the articles for this purpose. Article 39 states that the Security Council can adopt measures to maintain international peace and security and Article 41 states that the Security Council can adopt measures which do not involve the exercise of military forces and request the member nations to apply such measures. Such measures often involve economic sanctions such as the restriction of export of goods and technology.

The COCOM is an informal international co-operative scheme created by the initiative of the United States in the Cold War period which followed the end of the Second World War. Members include the member nations of NATO minus Iceland plus Japan. The major objective of this scheme is to decide items of goods and technology of which the member nations would prohibit export to areas and countries (such as Communist countries) in order to prevent the military build up in those countries or to slow down such a build up. As a member of the COCOM, the Japanese government is obligated to observe the terms decided by the COCOM.

Although the COCOM is not a treaty like the GATT, non-compliance with it would create political tension and might lead to a retaliation as exemplified in the Toshiba Clause in the Omnibus Trade and Competitiveness Act of 1988.

C. EXPORT CONTROL FOR ORDERLY MARKETING AND ORDERLY EXPORTING

An Overview of the Major Laws and Regulations

Export control is often utilized by the Japanese government to prevent trade conflicts with Japan's trading partners. Since the later 1960s, there have been trade conflicts between Japan and other trading nations. Although there was 'the one dollar blouse' problem in the 1950s,[62] there was little trade conflict between Japan and other nations until about 1968. As Japanese industries regained their international competitiveness, however, Japan's trading partners (especially the United States and the European Communities) began to utilize trade measures such as the quantitative restrictions of imports, anti-dumping laws, antitrust laws, and intellectual property laws to prevent (or at least slow down) the export of products from Japan to those countries. In the 1970s and 1980s, trade conflicts were more diversified in different products and generally came to include not only traditional items such as steel and cars but also high technology products such as semi-conductors and machine tools. In the 1990s, trade issues are still a serious problem of the trade policy in Japan.

In order to avoid trade conflicts, the Japanese government has utilized export control. Often the governments of other nations requested the Japanese government to effectuate export control, and in order to implement this request, the Japanese government has also utilized export control.

There are two basic laws in this area, the Control Law and the Transactions Law.[63] As we will see later, these two laws, although different in their ways of enforcement, work together.

Export Control by the Control Law

Article 48(3) declares:

> The Minister of the MITI may, in accordance with the provisions of the relevant Cabinet Decree, impose the obligation to obtain an export approval on a person who wishes to export goods of a specific kind, destined to a specific area, by a specific method of export or through a specific method of payment within the limit necessary *to maintain the international balance of payment and the healthy development of the international trade and the national economy*. (emphasis added)

[62] In the 1950s, a blouse made in Japan could be sold for one dollar in the United States. This aroused concern in the US textile industry that this would have an adverse effect on the domestic industry. On problems with regard to imports of Japanese textile products to the United States, see Lynch, *Toward An Orderly Market* (Tokyo, 1968).

[63] See nn. 55 and 56, above.

Here it is made clear that this control is designed to achieve economic objectives such as preventing trade conflicts with other nations. The wording in italic in the article above shows that this provision should be used to implement trade policy objectives.

This article authorizes the MITI to designate commodities which are subject to export approval. Once so designated, an exporter who wishes to export this item must first obtain an export approval from the MITI. The relevant Cabinet decree is the Export Control Decree. Article 1 of the Decree states that the MITI can impose the obligation on an exporter of a designated commodity to obtain an export approval and Article 2 provides: 'the Minister of the MITI can refuse to grant an export approval under Article 1 or attach conditions to such an export approval under Article 1 when he deems it necessary to maintain the equilibrium of the international balance of payment and the healthy development of the international trade and the national economy.'

In extreme cases, the MITI can take the policy of not permitting export of a designated commodity. However, usually the MITI attaches a condition to an export approval and thereby attempts to achieve trade policy objectives. Such conditions include things like the control of export price, the quantity of export, and other related measures. The control of export price is sometimes called 'check price' and involves the condition that an export approval is given on condition that the export price stays at or above the minimum level as indicated by the MITI. This is to avoid an export of this commodity at too law a price and a challenge to the export in a foreign country on account of dumping.

The control of quantity generally involves the determination by the MITI of the maximum quantity of the commodity to be exported and the export of this commodity is permitted within this maximum amount as set forth by the MITI. The question here is how to allocate export quotas among exporters. There are several ways including (1) the allocation to exporters of good performance, (2) the allocation based on previous achievement, and (3) the first come, first served method. Each has its advantages and disadvantages. The best way is probably the auction of export quotas in which all the existing and potential exporters can join. There can be a combination of some of the above such as a combination of the price control and the setting of the maximum quantity.

Beside the above, the export controls under the Control Law may involve items such as the product standards, export channels, designs of the exported commodity, and the method of payment. The regulation of product standards means that exporters must maintain a certain level of, for example, product safety when exporting the product. The control of the design of a commodity involves the prohibition of a product with a design which may infringe upon the intellectual property rights in a foreign country. The regulation of method of payment is utilized when it is necessary to prevent unduly disadvantageous terms of payment from being imposed on Japanese exporters. However, the above items were important in the 1950s and 1960s and have lost their importance today.

For a violation of Article 48(3) of the Control Law, the penalty is an imprisonement not exceeding three years or a fine not exceeding 1 million yen. If three times the value of the object of the violation is above 1 million yen, then the maximum fine is that amount. Compared with the penalty for a violation of Article 48(2) above explained, the penalty is lighter.

Export Control by the Transactions Law

The Transactions Law is another important legal instrument by which the MITI implement export control in order to prevent trade conflicts with other nations. As regards the control of exports, the Transactions Law consists of two parts. In the first part, it deals with the prevention of unfair export practices such as misleading or false representation with regard to a commodity to be exported or violation of an export–import contract. This part was important in the past but has lost its importance today. Therefore, an account of this part will be omitted.

The second part of the Transactions Law deals with the orderly marketing or orderly exporting by allowing exporters to enter into an export agreement or export cartel agreement. An export agreement is an agreement in which exporters agree among themselves and decide price, quantity, and other terms of business in export trade.

Unlike an import agreement discussed in a previous section, there are no 'positive requirements' with regard to export agreements under the Transactions Law. Therefore, exporters can agree on an export agreement under any circumstances. However, there are 'negative requirements' as follows: (1) an export agreement is not contrary to a treaty or other international agreements to which the Japanese government is a party, (2) it does not unduly harm the interest of importers in the country of destination and thereby injure the international credibility of Japanese exporters, (3) it does not otherwise hamper the sound development of the export trade, (4) it is not unduly discriminatory, (5) it does not restrict entry into it or withdrawal from it, and (6) it does not unduly cause disadvantage to the domestic entities engaged in agriculture, fishery and forestry, small enterprises, or the general consumers.

The Transactions Law permits enterprises to agree on three types of export agreement. Type 1 is an agreement among exporters with regard to terms of business in export trade. Article 5(1) of the Transactions Law allows exporters of a commodity to enter into an export agreement in which they fix price, quantity, quality, design, and other terms of a commodity in export transactions by filing a report with the MITI. For example, if exporters of X commodity agree to set the minimum export price when they export it to the United States, this would be an example.

Type 2 is an agreement among exporters with regard to terms of business in domestic trade of a commodity which will be exported later. Article 5.2 of the Transactions Law states that exporters of a commodity can agree, by filing a report with the MITI and obtaining an approval thereof, on the terms of transaction for a commodity in domestic trade when the commodity is exported later. An example would be an agreement among exporters of X commodity to the effect that they would fix the maximum amount of that commodity which they would buy from domestic producers of it and they would not buy beyond this maximum. This would guarantee that the limit in terms of quantity would be set as regard the export of this commodity since the amount of domestic purchase is thereby regulated already. The negative requirements are the same as above.

Type 3 is an agreement among producers of a commodity which will be exported later. This agreement is concerned with the domestic terms of transaction for the commodity such as the sales price or the maximum quantity to be sold. Producers can enter into such an agreement by filing a report with the MITI and obtaining approval of it. An example would include an agreement among producers of X commodity to the effect that they would set up the maximum quantity of this commodity to be sold to exporters and to be exported to the United States by the exporters. By establishing the maximum quantity of this commodity which is sold by producers to exporters, the producers can ensure that there will be an upper limit to the quantity of this commodity to be exported to the United States. The negative requirements are the same here also.

The above agreements can be put into effect through an export association rather than in the form of an agreement.[64] Exporters or producers can form an export association, the association determines the terms of transaction as above, and the members observe the terms of transaction as determined by the association. In fact, export associations are more frequently used than export agreements.

The Transactions Law provides measures to ensure that the effectiveness of an export agreement, duly filed or approved, will not be hampered by the activities of outsiders. When exporters of a commodity agree on terms of export trade such as the export price or the maximum quantity to be exported, there may be 'outsiders' who are not the members of the agreement and who are not bound by the terms of the

[64] Art. 8–19 of the Transactions Law (see n. 56, above).

agreement. An export agreement may be rendered ineffective due to the activities of such outsiders. For example, even if exporters of X commodity have agreed to maintain a certain level of export price when they export X commodity to the United States to avoid anti-dumping actions which may be brought by the competing industries in the United States, there may be outsiders who cut the export price even more. If the activities of such outsiders are left without being regulated, the effectiveness of an export agreement is undermined.

Article 28(1) of the Transactions Law provides that, when an export agreement has been entered into with regard to the export of a commodity to a certain destination, the export by the members of this agreement occupies a considerable part of the total export of the commodity to that destination, and the export agreement is not effective in maintaining order in the export of this commodity, the Minister of the MITI can invoke a ministerial order under the Cabinet Decree determining the export price, quantity, quality, design, or any other terms of transaction with regard to the commodity to be exported to the destination and this order binds all the exporters of the commodity regardless of whether they are insiders or outsiders of the agreement.

This means that the MITI takes a measure to support the effectiveness of an export agreement which has been duly reported or approved as the case may be by a ministerial order. This ministerial order is binding on all the exporters of the commodity destined for the designated area including both insiders and outsiders. A violation of this ministerial order is punishable by an imprisonement not exceeding 2 years or a fine not exceeding 300,000 yen or both.

Article 28(2) states that, when exporters of a commodity have agreed on terms of export of that commodity destined for a certain destination and the effectiveness of the agreement has been hampered for some reasons, the Minister of the MITI can issue a ministerial order designating a commodity subject to the export approval system. When this order has been issued, any exporter of the commodity to the designated area must obtain an export approval from the MITI. This system is quite similar to the export approval system established under the Control Law except for the fact that, whereas, in the Control Law, the MITI can unilaterally impose the export approval system on the export of a commodity, the MITI can invoke a ministerial order under Article 28(2) only after an export agreement has been entered into and the ineffectiveness of this agreement has been proved. This order cannot be invoked when the commodity in question has been covered by the export approval system under the Control Law.

Article 28(2) is provided since there are some situations in which the disclosure of export price, quantity, or some other terms of export may work adversely against the interest of exporters of the commodity from Japan to foreign countries. Whereas, under Article 28(1), the MITI must publish the content of the order (such as the export price, quantity, and other terms) in the Official Gazette, there is no comparable obligation on the MITI when it invokes Article 28(2) and, in this way, confidentiality of export price and quantity may be kept.

As we have seen above, an export agreement is a private agreement entered into among exporters even though it must be reported or be approved as the case may be. Viewed superficially, an export agreement may seem private in nature. Although this is not entirely untrue, it is not 100 per cent true either. As explained later, an export agreement is often formed as the result of administrative guidance or a 'directive' by the MITI. The MITI views it as a policy instrument rather than a purely private act. Also, as explained above, there are legal mechanisms in the form of an export order to ensure the effectiveness of a private export agreement by a ministerial order. This indicates that an export agreement entered into under the Transactions Law is not only a private agreement but also a governmental tool to achieve the objectives of trade policy.

An export agreement duly filed with the MITI or approved by the MITI enjoys an exemption from the application of the Anti-monopoly Law by Article 33 of the Transactions Law. However, no exemption is available when an unfair business practice is involved. In addition, according to a memo issued by the FTCJ, there is no exemption when an export agreement is used to implement an international cartel agreement between Japanese parties and foreign parties.[65]

Realities of Export Control: Interplay of the Control Law, Administrative Guidance, and the Transactions Law

We have examined the legal structures of the Control Law and the Transactions Law with regard to the control of exports. In reality, these two laws are used interchangeably by the MITI. The MITI regards them as two alternative methods of dealing with the export control issue. Generally, whenever there is a need to control exports for the purpose of avoiding trade frictions, the first step which the MITI takes is to advise or direct exporters to form an export agreement under the Transactions Law fixing the minimum price, the maximum quantity, and other terms of business with regard to the commodity to be exported. Administrative guidance plays a vital role at this stage. However, so far there is no government compulsion, and formally the role of the government is limited to advising private exporters to enter into an export agreement.

However, the policy of the MITI, revealed in past cases (an

[65] See Matsushita and Schoenbaum, n. 13, above, pp. 110–14.

explanation of some of those cases will be made in the following section), is to invoke the export approval system as regards the commodity in question when it becomes clear that an export agreement cannot be concluded because of internal discord among exporters or for other reasons. Usually when the MITI issues an administrative guidance directing exporters to form an export agreement, the MITI states that it will invoke the export approval system with regard to the commodity in question when the exporters fail to conclude one, or if the agreement is not effectively put into force.[66] In this way, the export approval system under the Control Law is used to support the effectiveness of the operations of the Transactions Law which allows an export agreement.

An important consideration in this connection is the antitrust laws of some of the important countries. Although an export agreement enjoys an exemption from the application of the Anti-monopoly Law in Japan, the antitrust law of an importing country may apply to the agreement. In countries such as the United States and the European Communities, antitrust laws are applied extraterritorially when conduct which occurs outside the country produces an 'effect' inside the country. An export agreement entered into among Japanese exporters with regard to a commodity exported to a country often produces the effect of raising the import price of the commodity in the importing country.

In this respect, there is a real risk that an export agreement entered into among Japanese exporters which is intended to avoid trade frictions with the competing industries in the importing country faces a challenge under the antitrust law of the importing country. Although this dilemma is created by a dichotomy between the competition law based on free competition and trade laws based on protectionism in the importing country,[67] this is a problem none the less.

The regulatory scheme constructed by the MITI through the use of an export agreement under the Transactions Law and the export approval system under the Control Law as explained above is a device at least in part to deal with antitrust problems in the importing country. The MITI claims that the export control system above described is subject to government compulsion and covered by the act of state doctrine or the foreign government compulsion doctrine.

This position of the MITI was made explicit in the position paper[68] submitted by the MITI to the United States Supreme Court in a United States antitrust case (*Zenith* v. *Matsushita Elec. Ind. Con., Ltd.*), in

[66] See Matsushita, 'Export Control and Export Cartels in Japan', *Harvard International Law Journal*, 20/1 (1979), 103 *et seq.*

[67] See Matsushita, 'A Japanese View of United States Trade Laws', *Northwestern Journal of International Law and Business*, 8/1 (1987), 30 *et seq.*

[68] See n. 66, above.

which Japanese TV manufacturers were accused by two TV manufacturers in the United States of engaging in a domestic cartel to raise the domestic price in Japan and in dumping TV sets in the United States through an export cartel. The MITI claimed that it had 'directed' Japanese exporters to enter into an export cartel agreement and it would have invoked the export approval system and put the whole export under tight government control if the export cartel agreement had failed to be effective. The position of the MITI is that although an export agreement is entered into among private exporters, it is based on a 'directive' of the MITI and non-compliance would incur the imposition by the MITI of an export approval system under the Control Law in which the entire export of the commodity to the United States is tightly regimented. The MITI argues that when one looks at this whole regime of export control, it is clear that it is an act of state or a foreign government compulsion.

The United States Supreme Court did not rule on this issue since the Supreme Court refused to accept the claims of the United States TV manufacturers against the Japanese manufacturers on another ground and the United States petitioners lost the case.[69]

The issue of whether this export scheme constitutes an act of state or a foreign government compulsion has been raised in other cases. Probably the most notable one is the *Automobile Voluntary Export Restraint* case[70] of which an account is made in the following section.

D. VOLUNTARY EXPORT RESTRAINT

Many of the important trade issues between Japan and her major trading partners have been resolved through 'voluntary export restraints'. In spite of criticisms raised against voluntary export restraint that it is a bilateralism and restrictive contrary to the GATT principles, it has played an important role in resolving trade conflicts. Prominent examples include the United States–Japan Textile Agreement, a series of agreements between Japan and the United States with regard to voluntary restraint of steel exports, the Automobile Voluntary Export Restraint, the TV Antitrust Litigation Case explained above, the 1977 Voluntary Export Restraint in TV Sets, the Semiconductor Agreement between the United States and Japan, and the Voluntary Export Restraint in Machine Tools. In this section, we will select a few of the important cases of voluntary

[69] *Matsushita Electric Industrial Co., Ltd.* v. *Zenith Radio Corp.*, 475 US 574 (1986).

[70] Matsushita and Repeta, 'Restricting the Supply of Japanese Automobiles: Sovereign Compulsion or Sovereign Collusion', *Case Western Reserve International Law Journal*, 14 (1982), 47 *et seq.*; Lockmann, 'The Japanese Voluntary Restraint Agreement in Automobile Exports: An Abandonment of the Free Trade Principles of the GATT and the Free Market Principles of the Antitrust Laws', *Harvard International Law Journal*, 27/1 (1986), 99 *et seq.*

export restraint between the United States and Japan and see how the Japanese regulatory scheme operates.

The 1977 Voluntary Export Restraint in TV Sets

In 1977, a petition was filed under Section 201 of the Trade Act of 1974 with the United States International Trade Commission by the United States domestic TV manufacturing industry alleging that the industry had been seriously injured by an increase in the import of foreign-produced TV sets to the United States. The Commission found that there was a serious injury to the domestic industry and recommended to President Carter that a 20 per cent *ad valorem* tariff be imposed in addition to the regular tariff.[71] President Carter, however, refused to accept the recommendation on the ground that: (1) since the major cause of injury was an increase of imports of Japanese TV sets, a non-discriminatory imposition of a high tariff on all imports from every country would be excessive, (2) a 20 per cent tariff would impose an excessive burden on United States consumers, (3) exporters could easily avoid the imposition of this additional tariff by slightly changing the specifications of TV sets and moving them to a different tariff classification. The President, therefore, negotiated with the Japanese government and requested that the Japanese government put into effect a voluntary export restraint on TV sets to be exported to the United States.

The MITI promised the United States government that it would set the maximum number of TV sets which could be exported to the United States from 1977 to 1980. In accordance with this international agreement, the MITI 'directed' Japanese TV manufacturers/exporters to form an export association and allocate export quotas among themselves under the Transactions Law. The MITI stated in its communication with the United States government that this measure was mandatory in nature. The MITI also encouraged Japanese TV manufacturers to promote direct investment in the United States.

The Automobile Voluntary Export Restraint

In 1980, the Ford Motor Company and the United Auto-Workers of America petitioned the United States International Trade Commission that the United States car industry had been seriously injured by an increase in imports of foreign-made cars and requested relief. After a careful study of the problem, the United States International Trade Commission came to the conclusion that, although the United States car

[71] US International Trade Commission, *Television Receivers, Color and Monochrome, Assembled or Not Assembled, Finished or Not Finished, and Subassemblies Thereof*, Report to the President on Investigation TA-201-9 under Sect. 201(b) of the Trade Act of 1974 (Mar. 1977).

industry was seriously injured, an increase in the import of foreign-made cars was not the substantial cause of such an injury.[72] According to the United States International Trade Commission, the major causes of that injury were that the United States industry could not adapt itself promptly to a new structure of demand in which smaller-sized cars were more emphasized, that high interest rates prevailing in the United States adversely affected consumer credit which consumers utilized when purchasing cars, and that the United States economy was in a recession.

Despite the negative determination by the United States International Trade Commission, however, it was necessary to take steps to alleviate the suffering of the United States industry since there were 200,000 unemployed in the industry and the car industry had a strong political influence in the United States. Therefore, the United States Trade Representative (Mr William Brock) negotiated with the MITI and the MITI promised to put into effect a voluntary export restraint on cars which would be exported from Japan to the United States.

The United States Trade Representative asked the United States Attorney General for his view on the negotiation between the United States and Japan with regard to voluntary export restraint of car exports to the United States. The Attorney General stated in his reply that if Japanese exporters of cars agreed in Japan on the maximum number of cars to be exported to the United States, it would be a violation of the Sherman Antitrust Law, that it would be advisable for the Trade Representative not to negotiate with the Japanese industry, and that the Trade Representative was advised not to suggest that the Japanese put into effect an export agreement.

To implement this agreement, the MITI constructed an elaborate export control scheme. The MITI indicated the maximum number of cars which each exporter could export to the United States and 'directed' each exporter not to exceed that maximum in exporting cars annually to the United States. It is noteworthy that in this case the MITI did not utilize the Transactions Law and did not direct exporters to enter into an export agreement.[73] Also the MITI invoked Article 25 of the Control Law which authorized the MITI to require exporters to report to the MITI the details of exports and orderd each exporter of cars to report to the MITI the number of cars that were exported to the United States. The MITI also issued a statement which said that the MITI would promptly invoke the export approval system under the Control Law and would place the export of cars to the United States under prohibition if the exporters failed to comply with the above directive.

[72] US International Trade Commission, *Certain Motor Vehicles and Certain Chassis and Bodies Thereof*, Investigation No. TA 10–44, USITC Publ. No. 1110.

[73] See Matsushita and Repeta, n. 70, above.

The Japanese Ambassador to the United States requested the view of the United States Attorney General with regard to the legality of this export control scheme, in light of United States antitrust laws. The Attorney General replied 'I believe' that this scheme would be immune from an antitrust challenge in the United States by the act of state doctrine or the foreign government compulsion doctrine.[74]

The above scheme was put into practice and it still continues today. No antitrust suit has ever been brought. Although the issue of antitrust liability is not entirely resolved, this export control scheme has become an established precedent.

The Semiconductor Agreement between the United States and Japan

The Semiconductor Agreement between the United States and Japan is different from any other international agreement to resolve trade conflicts between the United States and Japan.[75] Involved in the case were three actions in the United States. One was a petition filed with the United States government by the American Semiconductor Institute under Section 301 of the Trade Act of 1974[76], which alleged that the MITI had engaged in an industrial policy which promoted the Japanese semiconductor industry and artificially increased the international competitiveness of the Japanese industry. It also claimed that the MITI's industrial policy created an oligopolistic structure in Japan in which Japanese manufacturers and users of semiconductors were closely related to each other and which denied market access in Japan to outside parties including United States semiconductor manufacturers. The petition requested that an investigation be initiated under Section 301 of the Trade Act, an international negotiation be started, and appropriate measures be taken to remedy the situation.

There were two anti-dumping actions. One was self-initiated by the United States government (The *EPROM* case[77]) and the other was initiated by a petition filed by the United States industry (The *DRAM* case[78]).

In 1986, the United States and Japanese Semiconductor Agreement was entered into between the two governments to resolve all the above issues. This agreement involved suspension agreements between the Japanese manufacturers of semiconductor chips and the United States

[74] See ibid.

[75] For details of the agreement, see Dallmeyer, n. 24, above.

[76] Public Law 93.618, approved 3 Jan. 1975, 19 USC 2411.

[77] US International Trade Commission, *Erasable Programmable Read Only Memories from Japan*, Investigation No. 731-TA-288, USITC Publ. No. 1778 (1985).

[78] US International Trade Commission, *Dynamic Random Access Memory Semiconductors of 256 Kilkobytes and Above from Japan*, Investigation No. 731-TA-300, USITC Publ. No. 1803 (1986).

Department of Commerce, and promises made by the Japanese government to the United States government.

First, as regards the dumping issue, the Japanese semiconductor manufacturers entered into a series of suspension agreements with the United States government whereby the manufacturers promised to refrain from exporting at dumping prices to the United States. The manufacturers agreed to submit to the United States Commerce Department data with regard to the cost of production and related items and so that the Department could compute 'fair market value' on the basis of such data according to the anti-dumping law in the United States. The fair market value would recognize due changes in the cost of production and the Japanese manufacturers would make an adjustment to the export price so that it would not come below the fair market value.

Secondly, the Japanese government promised several things to the United States government. It agreed to monitor and supervise the export price of semiconductor chips made in Japan and exported to third countries in order to prevent circumvention of the prohibition of exporting semiconductor chips to the United States at dumped prices. Also the Japanese government agreed that it would take steps to promote sales of foreign-made semiconductor chips to Japanese customers. Lastly, the Japanese government agreed to take steps so that the production of semiconductor chips would not be excessive.

In 1987, however, the United States government invoked Section 301 and imposed 100 retaliatory tariffs on the import from Japan of small computers, electric tools, and colour television sets on the grounds that the Japanese government had violated the agreement in that it had not properly monitored and supervised the export price of semiconductor chips exported from Japan to third countries and that it had not kept the promise that it would promote the sale of foreign-made chips in Japan to Japanese customers. Although part of this retaliatory measure was lifted shortly thereafter, the other part remained effective until the new agreement was signed in 1991.

On the other hand, the European Communities took Japan to the GATT on the basis of Article 23 which sets forth the dispute settlement procedure on the grounds that the measures taken by the Japanese government with regard to the monitoring and supervision of the export price of the products to third countries and the cut back of domestic production amounted in fact to a quantitative restriction of exports prohibited under Article 11 of the GATT.

The GATT recognized this petition and decided that the Japanese measures were contrary to the GATT.[79] According to the finding of the

[79] See n. 24, above.

GATT, the Japanese government took measures to cut back production of semiconductor chips in Japan in order to prevent chips from flowing into 'grey markets' as well as monitoring and supervising the export price by means of 'administrative guidance' so that it would not fall below a certain level. The GATT decided that the combined measures amounted to a quantitative restriction of export which was prohibited under Article 11 of the GATT. An interesting point about this GATT decision is that measures taken by the Japanese government by way of administrative guidance were regarded as 'measures to restrict export', and held to be covered by Article 11 of the GATT.

The Semiconductor Agreement came to an end in 1991 and another negotiation was held. On 4 June 1991, the United States and Japan reached a new agreement. The new agreement, which is expected to last until 1996, contains provisions dealing with the efforts which the Japanese government will make in order to promote market access in Japan for foreign-made chips and dealing with the prevention of dumping. Some of the highlights of the agreement are as follows.

With regard to market access, the Japanese government recognizes that the semiconductor industry in the United States expects that the market share of foreign-made chips in Japan will be above 20 per cent by the end of 1992 and believes that it is possible to accomplish this market share. However, the Japanese government and the United States government agree that this is not an assurance of the market share or of the maximum or minimum figure thereof.

With regard to dumping, the agreement includes the following provisions. (1) When the United States government initiates an anti-dumping investigation with regard to semiconductor chips exported from Japan, the United States government and the Japanese government will engage in an emergency consultation. Japanese manufacturers will provide the United States government with business data promptly (within two weeks after the presentation of a questionnaire—fast track approach). (2) Suspension agreements are terminated for DRAMs and will continue for EPROMs with some modifications. (3) The United States government and the Japanese government recognize the importance of Article 12 of the Anti-dumping Code which provides that a contracting party can request the initiation of an anti-dumping investigation against another contracting party, that the Japanese government requests Japanese manufacturers of semiconductor chips to submit business data to the government of the third country when it initiates an investigation, and that the United States government will consult with the Japanese government in advance when the United States government requests the government of the third country to initiate such an investigation.

Comments on the above Cases

The 1977 TV Agreement between the United States and the Japanese governments is a typical voluntary export restraint agreement. There was a previous affirmative determination by the United States International Trade Commission and, therefore, there was no doubt that the President of the United States had the power to negotiate such an agreement with the Japanese government. In this respect, this is different from the *Consumers' Union* case[80] in which the power of the President to negotiate with the government of a foreign country and request it to effect a voluntary export restraint in the absence of an affirmative determination of the Tariff Commission was in dispute. On the Japanese side, there was little problem either legally or politically. In this respect, this case is different from the United States–Japanese Textile Agreement in which the Japanese textile industry challenged the power of the Japanese government to invoke the export approval system under the Control Law to implement the agreement.[81]

The Automobile Agreement is unique in that the Japanese government did not utilize an export agreement under the Transactions Law and resorted to a directive issued individually to each producer/exporter of cars. Avoidance of utilizing an export cartel under the Transactions Law in this case was due to the fact that, at that time, an important antitrust case (The Japanese TV Antitrust Litigation) was pending in the United States in which Japanese manufacturers of TV sets were accused of having engaged in an export cartel under the Transactions Law. It must have been a consideration of the MITI that to refrain from using a cartel would be advisable under the circumstances.

In the Automobile Agreement, the Japanese government requested the view of the United States Attorney General with regard to the legality of the export control sheme involved, to which the Attorney General replied in the affirmative. Although the Attorney General stated only that 'I believe' it is lawful, it is none the less an advice by an antitrust expert agency and carries some weight. The export control scheme used in the Automobile Agreement is probably the safest from an antitrust standpoint apart from the direct application of the export approval system under the Control Law.

The Semiconductor Agreement is quite unique and differs from other agreements in that it has four rather than one dimension. Involved in it are the suspension agreements between Japanese private exporters and the United States government, the monitoring and supervision by the Japanese government of the export price of chips to third countries, the

[80] *Consumers Union of U.S.* v. *Kissinger*, 506 F. 2d 136 (DC cir. 1974), cert. denied, 421 US 1004 (1975).

[81] On this case and source materials of it, see Matsushita, 'Export Control and Export Cartels in Japan', *Harvard International Law Journal*, 20/1 (1979), 102 *et seq*., 106 n. 17.

measure to increase access to the Japanese semiconductor market, and the measure to cut back domestic production. The above measures include not only those directly related to the trade relationship between the two countries but also those which are more directly related to the trade between one country and third countries. It also involves measures on domestic matters such as the cut back of domestic production.

Another interesting feature of the Semiconductor Agreement is that, in the United States, at least two sets of laws were involved. One was Section 301 of the Trade Act of 1974 and the other was the anti-dumping law. It is not clear, howeve, what was the legal basis for the United States government to enter into an agreement with the Japanese government with regard to the monitoring and supervision of the export price to third countries. Although Section 301 was probably considered as the basis, the legality of it is not entirely clear.

3.4 Regulation of Foreign Investment

A. AN OVERVIEW

Foreign investment can be classified into a direct investment and an indirect (or portfolio) investment. A direct investment involves transactions engaged in by an enterprise through which the enterprise establishes a branch, a subsidiary, or other forms of business establishment, acquires a company or assets, or engages in a joint venture with another company in a foreign country. An indirect investment means a purchase of stocks and other securities in a foreign country. Here the purpose is not to control a business entity in the country in which the investment occurs but to gain profit through dividends or sale of stocks.

A direct investment can be further classified into an inward investment and an outward investment. The former indicates a direct investment by a foreign enterprise in Japan and the latter means a direct investment by a Japanese enterprise overseas. Since an indirect investment and an outward direct investment involve few legal problems, we will omit them from this section except for a brief account of them in connection with the emergency control.

There are two sets of laws in Japan which regulate direct investment by a foreign enterprise in Japan. One category consists of laws which prohibit or restrict direct investment by a foreign entity in Japan in specified areas such as telecommunications and cabotage. The other category is the Control Law under which the MOF has the power to supervise a direct investment. The control under this law is different from that under laws which regulate foreign direct investment in specific areas in that it applies generally.

B. REGULATION OF DIRECT INVESTMENT IN SPECIFIC AREAS

There are several areas in which direct investment by a foreign entity in Japan is either prohibited or restricted. The most notable area is telecommunications. Article 11 of the Telecommunications Business Law,[82] which provides for first-class and second-class business licences, states that, as regards the first-class business licence, a licence will not be given to: (1) a person who does not have Japanese citizenship, (2) a foreign government or its representative, (3) a person or association established by foreign law. In the Broadcast Law,[83] there is a provision (Article 53.2) which states that a broadcasting station can refuse to register a foreign person or entity as a stock-holder.

In cabotage, the Ship Law[84] states that a ship which is not a Japanese ship cannot engage in transporting cargoes and passengers between Japanese ports. Under this law, a Japanese ship is a ship owned by the Japanese government, a Japanese citizen, a Japanese company, or a Japanese corporate entity. In natural resources, the Mining Law[85] states that a person cannot own the rights to minerals unless the person is a Japanese citizen.

Beside the above-mentioned laws, there may be a law which provides for things like the licensing of a business in which the person who initiates a business must obtain a licence from the government. Depending on the actual enforcement policies, those laws may have *de facto* regulatory effects on foreign enterprises' market entry into Japan.

C. THE FOREIGN EXCHANGE AND FOREIGN TRADE CONTROL LAW

An Overview

The Control Law is the basic legislation for the control of direct investment. The Control Law consists of the regulation of: (1) foreign exchange transactions, (2) capital transactions, and (3) both outward and inward foreign investments by domestic or foreign enterprises, as well as the regulation of exports and imports which is enforced by the MITI and which we have seen already in the previous section. With regard to those three items, the MOF is in charge of enforcement. There are several important Cabinet Decrees and many ministerial orders.

The Control Law, as originally enacted in 1949, adopted 'the prohibition principle' in which all transactions in foreign exchange were prohibited

[82] Denkitsūshin Jigyō Hō, Law 86, 1984.
[83] Hōso Hō, Law 132, 1950.
[84] Senpaku Hō, Law 46, 1899.
[85] Kōgyō Hō, Law 289, 1950.

unless permitted by Cabinet Decrees, ministerial orders, or other regulations. The purpose of this control was to effectuate a tight control on the flow of foreign exchange for the purpose of protecting foreign currency. At that time, the basic policy of the Japanese government was the promotion of exports and the tight control over the import trade as well as foreign exchange transactions. Any resident who obtained foreign currency was obligated to sell it to the government promptly and all foreign currencies were concentrated in the hands of the government.

With regard to foreign investments, the Foreign Investment Law (which was a supplementary law to the Control Law) provided for the selective introduction system whereby the government decided on a case-by-case basis whether to accept a direct investment from abroad after taking into consideration factors such as whether or not the investment in question would be beneficial to the development of the national economy. The control under this regime was gradually relaxed by numerous ministerial orders and regulations exempting transactions from the principle of prohibition.

In 1979, the Control Law was amended, the prohibition principle was abolished, and 'the permission principle' was introduced whereby foreign exchange and capital transactions in foreign currency were made basically free subject to regulation only under specific circumstances as stipulated by the Control Law. At the same time, the Foreign Investment Law was abolished and the Control Law assumed control over both foreign exchange and investment transactions. Article 1 of the Control Law, which declares the objective of the law, states that foreign exchange, foreign trade, and other external transactions are basically free and subject to minimum necessary regulations. Therefore, the principle under the existing Control Law is that foreign exchange transactions, current transactions, capital transactions, and direct foreign investment are basically free. They are subject to control in 'emergency situations' as provided for in the Control Law (which will be dealt with later).

Reporting Duty of Direct Investment

At present, there is no legal prohibition on direct investment in Japan by a foreign entity. However, a foreign investor is subject to reporting duty when he wishes to make a direct investment in Japan.

A 'foreign investor' is defined in Article 26(1) and (2) of the Control Law as follows: (1) a foreign person (an individual who is a non-resident of Japan), (2) a foreign corporation (a corporation established by the law of a foreign country), (3) a corporation wholly or partially owned by a foreign corporation, and (4) a corporation in which foreigners comprise more than half the members of the board of directors.

A 'foreign investment' includes transactions such as: (1) an acquisition by a foreign investor of stocks of a domestic corporation, (2) a transfer to a foreign investor of stocks of a domestic corporation from a non-resident who acquired the stocks before he became a non-resident, (3) an acquisition of stocks of a listed corporation above 10/100 of its outstanding stocks and above the proportion stipulated by Cabinet Decree, and (4) an important change of the purposes of a corporation.

When a foreign investor as above defined is engaged in a transaction which falls under one or more of the above enumerated investment transactions, the investor is making a direct investment in Japan. Until 1991, foreign investors, when making direct investment in Japan, were required to report to the MOF in advance. In the SII, however, the United States government claimed that this prior reporting system would have a chilling effect on a foreign investor who might wish to make a direct investment in Japan. The Control Law was amended in 1991 and the prior reporting system was abolished, and consequently the post reporting system was introduced.

Article 26 of the Control Law states that a foreign investor must report to the MOF the content of the direct foreign investment in Japan after it has been carried out except in two exceptional circumstances. Therefore, foreign investors can generally freely engage in the acquisition of stocks of domestic corporations and other activities as defined in the Control Law as foreign investment. Exceptions are that a foreign investor must report to the MOF in advance the contents of a direct investment in Japan which he intends to make if the investment in question: '(1) may injure the national security, may be detrimental to the maintenance of the public order or to the security of the people (in short, "the national security"), or (2) may have a negative impact on the smooth operation of the national economy.' Investments in which this prior reporting is necessary are provided for in a Cabinet Decree.

It can be seen from the above that the exceptions are based on political considerations as well as economic considerations. If a foreign direct investment is subject to the prior reporting duty, then the investor cannot make this investment until thirty days have elapsed after the date of his reporting. During this period, the MOF decides if this investment will have any detrimental effect on the national security or the smooth operation of the national economy.

Emergency Controls

Although, as mentioned above, a direct investment by a foreign investor in Japan is basically free, there are controls in emergencies. Article 27(1) of the Control Law provides that the Minister of the MOF and the minister in charge of the transaction in question can designate certain types of investment as those in which the prior reporting is necessary when it is judged that such designations are necessary in order to maintain the national security, and the ministers can determine that a foreign investor cannot consummate the reported investment transaction for a maximum period of four months after they receive the report. They examine the transaction during this period and, if they come to the conclusion that it is detrimental to the national security, then they are authorized to recommend a change in the investment plan or to cancel it altogether. If the recommendation is ignored, they can issue an order to the same effect.

The emergency control above described is based on Article 3 of the OECD Code of Liberalization of Capital Transactions[86] which states that a member country is authorized to take a measure necessary to maintain public order, health, morals, and security, to protect the national security, and to carry out the international obligations of the country.

The national security is a general and somewhat vague concept. A direct investment by a foreign investor in industries such as the nuclear industry, the space development industry, and the defence industry would be candidates for consideration under this heading. Generally, however, there is a domestic law which regulates such an industry and often new entry into the industry is regulated by that domestic law.

Control for the Protection of Domestic Industry

Article 27(1) of the Control Law states that a direct investment which may seriously affect a domestic industry can be subjected to the prior reporting system and the minister in charge can recommend or order the foreign investor to change the investment plan or to cancel it altogether. This is a control for the purpose of protecting a domestic industry. At present, the Japanese government invokes this provision and prohibits a direct investment by a foreign investor in agriculture, fisheries and forestry, mining, petroleum refining, and leather manufacturing. This control is based on Article 2(b) of the OECD Code of Liberalization of Capital Transactions which allows a member country to derogate from the obligation to liberalize foreign direct investments into the country for the purpose of protecting a domestic industry.

Control of Foreign Investment for Reciprocity

Article 27(1)(iii) states that a direct investment by a foreign investor can be restricted for the purpose of reciprocity. According to this provision, a direct investment by a foreign investor who belongs to a country with which there is no treaty or other international agreement can be controlled

[86] See OECD, Code of Liberalization of Capital Movements (Mar. 1982); Bertland, 'The Liberalisation of Capital Movements—An Insight', *The Three Bank Review*, 132 (1981), 3 *et seq*.

in order to equalize the treatment of this direct investment by a foreign investor with that which is accorded to a direct investment by a Japanese resident in that country by its government.

Article 8 of the OECD Code of Liberalization of Capital Transactions does not allow the application by a member country of the reciprocity principle to another member country even when that member country derogates from the obligation to liberalize and control investment. Therefore, the application of the reciprocity principle incorporated in Article 27(1)(iii) applies only with regard to a country which is not a member of the OECD Code of Liberalization of Capital Transactions.

D. AN EXAMPLE OF AN EMERGENCY CONTROL

As mentioned before, under the Control Law, activities of domestic and foreign enterprises in Japan with regard to foreign exchange, capital transactions, and direct or indirect investment are basically free and subject to control only in an emergency. The most recent example of emergency control are measures taken to cope with the Gulf War in 1991. A brief account of highlights of the measures will follow.

Shortly after the United Nations Security Council adopted a decision to impose economic sanctions on Iraq, on 9 August 1991, the MITI announced that all imports from Iraq and Kuwait were subject to the import approval system under the Control Law and that enterprises should refrain from engaging in trade with those countries. On 15 August the MITI issued an emergency control and stated that all exports directed to Iraq and Kuwait were subject to the export approval system. The above measures were taken under Articles 52 and 48 of the Control Law.

On 10 August 1991, the MOF invoked an emergency control under the Control Law. Article 16(2) states that the MOF can impose the obligation to obtain the approval of the Minister of MOF when a resident wishes to make a payment to a non-resident abroad when it is necessary to implement the obligations incorporated in a treaty or other international agreements. Under this article, the MOF (and the MITI with regard to some items) declared that all payments to Iraq and Kuwait were subject to approval.

Also, Article 21(2) and Article 24(1) of the Control Law state that the MOF can demand that a person who wishes to engage in capital transactions with a party outside Japan obtains an approval, if the capital transaction (i) makes it difficult to maintain the international balance of payment, (ii) causes abrupt and great fluctuations in the foreign exchange market, or (iii) affects adversely the financial market or the capital market in Japan by the movement of a large quantity of money. The MOF invoked this article and declared that all loans to those countries were subject to the prior reporting system and all outward investments directed to those countries were also subject to the prior reporting system.

3.5 Regulation of International Contracts

There are many public law regulations of international contracts in Japan and some of them, such as contracts in exports, imports, and direct investments, have been touched upon already. It is neither possible nor necessary to examine every item which may be included in this subject-matter. In the following pages, we will deal with some public law regulations of international contracts which are important in international business transactions.

A. PARALLEL IMPORTATION AND SOLE IMPORT AGENCY

What is Parallel Importation?

Parallel importation is generally understood to be imports of a foreign product by a plural number of importers. Typically a parallel importation occurs in a situation such as the following. Company A in Japan has been appointed as the sole import agency of Product X manufactured by Company B in the United States. Product X manufactured by Company B is regarded as a high quality good and the trade marks owned by Company B are well known all over the world. Company A registers the trade marks licensed by Company B in Japan as the exclusive licensee. Under the sole agency contract between Company A and Company B, Company A is obligated not to sell Product X to any other party in Japan.

Owing to the monopolistic position of Company A in Japan with respect to Product X, its price is high and Company C acquires Product X from third parties in the United States or countries other than Japan at a lower price than that which prevails in Japan with regard to Product X and imports it into Japan.

The above is one of the typical situations involved in parallel importation of a product. It often involves the importation of a prestigious product on which well-known trade marks or other marks are affixed. It is a parallel importation only if it is a genuine product. If it is the importation of a false product, of course, the sole import agency which has registered the trade marks can stop importation of it under the trademark laws. Such a high price of the imported product often occurs when the product involved is highly differentiated from other similar products and little competition exists between them.

A number of legal questions are raised with regard to parallel importation. There are, however, two most important questions. One is whether or not the parallel importation of a genuine good by an independent importer infringes the trade mark or the exclusive right of use owned by the sole import agency. The other is whether or not the blocking of a parallel importation by the sole import agency of a genuine product is a violation of the Anti-monopoly Law.

Those two questions are closed related to each other. If such a parallel importation infringes the trade-mark right, then the sole import agency of the product can bring a claim under the trade-mark law and cause the customs house to stop the importation at the border or cause a court to issue an injunction prohibiting the import and sale of the product by the parallel importer. In such a situation, a problem with regard to the AML can hardly occur since, under Article 23 of the AML, the exercise of the right with regard to intangible properties is exempted from the application of the AML.

On the other hand, if the blocking of a parallel importation of a genuine product by the sole import agency is not authorized by the trade-mark right in Japan, it may amount to an unfair business practice.

Parallel Importation and the Trade Mark Right

The case in point in this respect is the *Parker Fountain Pen* case[87] and our examination will start with this. Parker fountain pens are manufactured in the United States by the Parker Company (Parker) and sold all over the world. Parker owns the trade mark 'Parker', which is a mark known all over Japan and the world. Parker appointed the Shuriro Company (hereafter 'Company S') as the sole import agency of Parker fountain pens in Japan. Under the licence from Parker, Company S registered itself as the exclusive licensee to use the 'Parker' trade mark in Japan. Company S imported Parker fountain pens and sold them in Japan at a high price.

Another company in Japan whose trade name is 'The MNC Company' (hereafter 'MNC') intended to purchase Parker fountain pens in Hong Kong and other countries and to import and sell them in Japan at a lower price. MNC requested Company S for permission to import them from abroad, which was refused. Subsequently MNC initiated a suit in the Osaka District Court and sought for a declaratory judgment which would state that Company S did not have the right to block a parallel importation of Parker fountain pens by MNC.

The Osaka District Court handed down a decision in 1970 in which it stated that Company S did not have the right to block the parallel

[87] Decision of Osaka District Court, 27 Feb. 1970, *Mutaishū*, 2 (1970), 71 *et seq*.

importation of the products by MNC. The reasons given by the court were as follows.

The Court stated that there are two basic functions of a trade mark and, as long as these two functions are not impeded by a parallel importation of a commodity bearing the trade mark, there is no infringement of trade mark by the parallel importation. First, a trade mark identifies the origin of the commodity which bears it. As long as a parallel importer imports the genuine product which bears the same trade mark, this function of the trade mark is not impeded since the product is genuine even if it is imported by a party other than the sole import agency. In this case, MNC imported genuine Parker fountain pens and, therefore, there was no infringement of the trade mark 'Parker'.

Also the Court pointed out that a trade mark guarantees the quality of the commodity which bears it. Here again, this function is not hampered by a parallel importation of the genuine commodity since the product imported by a parallel importer was manufactured by the same manufacturer under the same specifications and has the same quality as those imported by the sole import agency. By importing genuine Parker pens, therefore, MNC did not infringe the trade mark 'Parker' in Japan.

As above stated, the gist of the decision in the *Parker* case is that a parallel importation of a genuine good does not constitute an infringement of a trade mark registered by the sole import agency and, therefore, the sole import agency has no right to restrain the parallel importer from engaging in the parallel importation.

Linguistically this decision may not be quite consistent with the wording of the Trade Mark Law in Japan since the Trade Mark Law states that an exclusive licensee has the right to use a registered mark exclusively and an importation is included in the 'use' of the mark.[88] This wording seems to suggest that an exclusive licensee of a trade mark in Japan has the right to block the use (including an importation) of the mark by any other party. The Osaka District Court approached the issue from a different angle and reached an opposite conclusion. The decision of the Court is based on a philosophical reflection on the basic functions of a trade mark rather than a literal interpretation of the wording employed in the Trade Mark Law.

Until this decision was handed down, the Customs Bureau of the MOF had blocked a parallel importation of a genuine good at the border under Article 21 of the Customs and Tariff Law which states that imported goods which infringe the intangible property rights in Japan should be restrained from being imported. When this decision came, however, the Customs Bureau changed the enforcement policy of this provision and

[88] Art. 2(3) of the Trademark Law (Shohyō Hō, Law 12:7, 1959).

began to allow the importation of genuine goods by parallel importers. The prices in Japan of some of the products imported from abroad (such as Scotch whisky, Swiss watches, and others) fell dramatically due to the activities of parallel importers.

Parallel Importation of a Patented Product

There exists a different situation with regard to patents. The holder of a patent in Japan can prevent the importation of a product which is the subject of the patent he holds. A case in point is the *Brunswick* case[89] and an explanation of this case follows.

The Brunswick Company (Brunswick), an American company and a manufacturer of bowling pins, held a patent in Japan which covered certain types of bowling pins. Brunswick also held the corresponding patents in the United States, Australia, and other countries. Brunswick licensed the patent in Australia to an enterprise, the enterprise manufactured bowling pins under this licence and sold them in Australia. Then those pins were exported to Hong Kong. A Japanese enterprise imported them from Hong Kong to Japan.

Brunswick brought a suit in Japan and claimed that this importation was an infringement of the patent. The Tokyo District Court handed down a decision which stated that the importation in question was an infringement of the right held by the plaintiff Brunswick under the Patent Law and granted an injunction restraining the defendant from importing and selling the products in Japan.

The rationale of the decision was based on the 'territorial principle'. According to this doctrine, even though a patent right is regarded as exhausted when the patented product is sold by the patentee to a third party, this exhaustion doctrine applies only within the territory of one country. Therefore, when the Australian licensee sold bowling pins to a third party in Australia, the patent right registered in Australia was exhausted but the effect of the exhaustion did not reach beyond the Australian boundary.

When the products are imported to Japan, they are treated as being covered by the corresponding Japanese patent and the imports constitute an infringement even though the patent is the same as that in Australia and owned by the same enterprise. This doctrine stands on the premiss that the patent law applies only within the territory of the country in which it is registered and the patent right under the patent law is independent from that under the corresponding right under the patent law of another country.

When we compare the treatment of a parallel importation of a genuine

[89] Decision of Osaka District Court, 9 June 1966, *Mutaishū*, 1 (1966), 160 *et seq*.

product, there is a marked difference between the Trade Mark Law and the Patent Law. This difference stems from the difference in purpose and function of these two laws. A trade mark is designed to protect the interest of consumers through the maintenance of the reputation of the good to which it is affixed as well as protecting the interest of the producer. In light of this objective of the law, the rationale expressed in the *Parker* Decision makes sense. However, the objective of a patent is to protect a technological invention and to promote inventions in the country. From this, it follows that the protection should be given against the import of a product covered by the domestic patent since to allow such an import would be a disincentive to inventors in the country.

B. SOLE IMPORT AGENCY

Functions of a Sole Import Agency and the Guidelines of the FTCJ

When a foreign enterprise intends to export goods to Japan, it often appoints a Japanese enterprise as the sole import agency of the goods which it wishes to export. Usually such a sole import agency is given the exclusive right to distribute the goods in Japan and the exclusive right to register the trade mark or to use any other marks that the foreign exporter owns.

A sole import agency contract is advantageous to foreign enterprises intending to export goods to Japan as well as to Japanese importers that are appointed as the sole import agencies. A foreign enterprise, when entering the Japanese market, can reduce business costs and risks by utilizing a sole import agency. Often a foreign enterprise is unfamiliar with the language, business, customs, and inclinations of consumers in Japan and one way to overcome such difficulties is to utilize a local enterprise which is familiar with these things. Also, a Japanese enterprise which is given the sole import agency contract enjoys the exclusive right to use prestigious marks and to distribute high quality products.

On the other hand, a sole import agency may have a monopolistic position with regard to the commodity which is supplied by the foreign exporter. When that commodity is highly differentiated from other similar products due to the fame of the producer or otherwise, the sole import agency is in the position in Japan to charge a monopoly price to consumers. Abusive conduct concomitant with a monopolistic position, such as a high price, a refusal to deal, and discriminatory treatment may occur.

Therefore, as a government policy, it is necessary to enforce a certain degree of regulation over the conduct of sole import agencies under the AML. In light of this, the FTCJ announced 'Guidelines on Unfair

Business Practices by Sole Import Agency Contracts and Related Matters (1972)' and 'A Memo on Unreasonable Impediments to Parallel Importations (1987)'. Since, however, these guidelines and memos were directed solely at international contracts whose contents were sole import distributorship and no corresponding guidelines were announced with regard to domestic contracts, there were criticisms raised by the United States government and others that they were discriminatory. When the FTCJ announced 'The 1991 Guidelines on Distribution Systems and Trade Practices' ('The 1991 FTCJ Guidelines'),[90] the FTCJ abolished the previous guidelines and memos and incorporated the major parts of them into this new set of guidelines.

Therefore, the 1991 FTCJ Guidelines are the rules which regulate sole import agency contracts today. It is to be noted, however, that the scope of these guidelines is not limited to international contracts which involve sole import agency, but includes domestic contracts in which one party appoints the other as the sole sales agency. It is, therefore, more appropriate to refer to this regulation as 'sole sales agency', which includes sole import agency.

Part 3 of the 1991 FTCJ Guidelines is devoted to provisions regulating sole sales agency contracts.

Sole Sales Agency Contracts between Competitors

Part 3, Section 1 of the 1991 FTCJ Guidelines sets out the basic enforcement policy of the FTCJ as regards sole sales agency contracts between competitors. According to provisions incorporated in this section, there are two situations in which a sole sales agency contract may raise a problem under the AML.

Cases where Market Share is 10–25 per cent

When a sole sales agency manufactures or sells a commodity which competes with the commodity which is the object of a sole sales agency contract (hereafter referred to as 'the commodity in question'), there may be an anti-competitive effect if the market share of the sole sales agency is 10 per cent or above or within three from the top in ranking in terms of market share. In such a situation, a review of the contract is made on a case-by-case basis and, if the contract is judged to have a tendency to impede fair competition, then it is held unlawful as an unfair business practice.

The FTCJ takes into account factors such as: (*a*) the market share of the sole sales agency, its ranking in terms of market share, the difference

[90] The guidelines have been translated into English and published by the Fair Trade Commission. See Executive Office, Fair Trade Commission, *The Anti-monopoly Act: Guidelines Concerning Distribution Systems and Business Practices* (1991).

in terms of market share between the sole sales agency and those of competitors, and the degree of changes in market share; (*b*) the total business power of the supplier of the commodity in terms of the total sales, the fame of brand, the position in the market, and related matters, (*c*) the market share of the commodity in question in the domestic market and its ranking, (*d*) the conditions surrounding competition in the market such as the number of competitors, changes in market share, and the ease or difficulty of new entry, (*e*) the unique quality of the commodity in question, the degree of competition between the commodity in question and the commodity which the sole sales agency produces or sells, the existence of substitute products and the sales price of the commodity in question, and (*f*) conditions surrounding distribution of the commodity in question.

Cases where Market Share is Above 25 per cent

When the market share of the sole sales agency is 25 per cent or above and the ranking in terms of market share is the top, a sole sales agency contract between the sole sales agency and its competitor is likely to produce an impediment to competition. Although a review in this situation is made on a case-by-case basis, the following factors are taken into consideration when judging whether it tends to impede fair competition: (*a*) whether or not the total business power of the supplier is great and (*b*) whether or not the commodity in question already occupies a considerable position in the domestic market.

Cases where Market Share is 10 per cent or Below

In the following two situations, there is generally no problem with regard to the AML: (*a*) when the commodity in question is sold in the domestic market for the first time, the contract term is relatively short (which means it is a 3–5-year period), the commodity in question is manufactured by the supplier on the basis of technological assistance given by the sole sales agency, or the supplier is a subcontractor for the sole sales agency, and (*b*) when the sole sales agency manufactures or sells a commodity which competes with the commodity in question but the market share of the sole sales agency is less than 10 per cent, or the ranking in terms of market share is the fourth or below.

Specific Provisions in a Sole Sales Agency Contract

Part 3, Section 2 of the 1991 FTCJ Guidelines incorporates provisions which relate to specific restrictions included in a sole sales agency contract as follows.

Resale Price Maintenance

If, in a sole sales agency contract, the supplier of the commodity directs the price at which the sole sales agency should sell the commodity in

Japan, or should cause purchasers of it to sell it at a certain price designated by the supplier, it is unlawful in principle.

Exclusive Dealing Arrangements

If, in a sole sales agency contract, the supplier prohibits the sole sales agency from handling competing products or otherwise restricts it, the contract is unlawful as long as the supplier is a 'powerful enterprise' (which occupies more than 10 per cent of the market in Japan or is within three from the top in terms of market share) and new entrants and existing competitors have difficulties in finding alternative distribution channels. Here the FTCJ refers to Part 2, Section 2, Item 2 of the 1991 FTCJ Guidelines.

If the supplier imposes a restriction on the sole sales agency that the latter cannot handle competing products after the sole sales agency contract has been terminated, that restriction is unlawful in principle unless it is necessary to avoid leakage of know-how or otherwise justifiable and limited to the necessary scope.

Sales Territory

If the supplier restricts the sales territory of the sole sales agency, such a restriction is unlawful as long as the supplier is a powerful enterprise, the restriction is absolute (that is, the sales agency is absolutely prohibited from selling the commodity outside the allocated territory), and the price of the commodity is thereby maintained. However, it is lawful for the supplier to impose a restriction on the sole sales agency that the sales agency should not engage in active sales activities outside the allocated territory.

Customer Restriction

If the supplier restricts the customers to whom the sole sales agency can sell the commodity supplied by the supplier, it is unlawful as long as such a restriction has the effect of maintaining the price of the commodity. It is unlawful if the customer restriction is used for the purpose of preventing the commodity from reaching a distributor or retailer who sells it at a low price. Also it is unlawful in principle for the supplier to prohibit the sole sales agency from selling the commodity to a retailer because the retailer sells the commodity at a low price, since this tends to have the effect of maintaining the price of the commodity.

Restriction on Sales Methods

Restrictions on sales methods involve practices such as directives issued by the supplier to the sole sales agency that the latter must make an explanation of the commodity in a certain way, make a direct delivery of the commodity to homes, observe some conditions for the purpose of maintaining the quality of the commodity, and establish a corner in the shop devoted exclusively to the display and sale of the commodity of the supplier. Imposition of such conditions is not unlawful as such. However, if the conditions are used to enforce other restrictions, such as resale price maintenance, they may be held unlawful.

Parallel Importation of Genuine Goods

As explained before, in the *Parker Fountain pen* case, the Osaka District Court stated that a sole import agency who registers a trade mark in Japan has no right to prevent a parallel importation by a third party of a genuine product. Therefore, if a sole import agency unduly blocks a parallel importation of a genuine good by a third party and thereby maintains its monopolistic position with regard to the commodity in question, it may be held unlawful under the AML. Part 3, Section 3 of the 1991 FTCJ Guidelines contains rules on this.

Prevention by the Sole Import Agency of The Acquisition of Genuine Goods by a Third Party Abroad

The sole sales agency of a commodity may engage in activities designed to block acquisition of the genuine commodity by a third party abroad and thereby maintain a high price of the commodity in Japan. Such activities may be held unlawful. The 1991 FTCJ Guidelines enumerate two examples of conduct which would be held unlawful: (*a*) that the sole sales agency exerts pressure on a purchaser of the genuine goods from the supplier in a foreign country (the foreign purchaser) to ensure that the foreign purchaser shall not sell the genuine goods to a party intending to import them into Japan (the parallel importer) when the parallel importer requests from the foreign purchaser the right to sell the commodity; and (*b*) that the sole sales agency detects the sources of supply of genuine goods abroad for a parallel importer in Japan by examining code numbers of the commodities and specifically requests the foreign distributors who have sold genuine commodities to a parallel importer in Japan not to sell them to the parallel importer by notifying them of the code numbers and related matters.

Restriction on Domestic Distributors

If the sole sales agency of an imported commodity sells the imported product to domestic distributors on the condition that they should not deal with genuine commodities imported by a parallel importer, it is held unlawful when it is used to maintain the price of the commodity in question.

Restriction on Domestic Wholesalers

If a sole sales agency imposes a condition on domestic wholesalers that they should not sell the commodity in question to retailers who sell the genuine commodities imported by a parallel importer, it is held unlawful when it is used to maintain the price of the commodity in question.

False Claim
If a sole sales agency claims that a commodity imported by a parallel importer infringes the trade mark which it has registered in Japan and requests the parallel importer and other parties to stop selling it even though the sole sales agency knows that it is a genuine commodity and does not infringe the trade mark, it is held unlawful as an unfair business practice.

Buying Up of a Commodity
A sole sales agency may dispatch personnel to the shops of retailers who sell genuine commodities imported by a parallel importer and buy them up in order to remove them from the market and maintain the price. Such a practice may be held unlawful as an unfair business practice.

Repair and Maintenance Services
A sole sales agency may refuse to provide a repair and maintenance service to persons who possess genuine commodities. Such a refusal is not unlawful as such as long as there are justifiable reasons such as that parts and components are in short supply. However, if the sole sales agency refuses repair and maintenance services or a supply of parts and components to persons who possess genuine commodities imported by a parallel importer in a situation in which the repair and maintenance or the supply of parts and components by other parties is difficult for the sole reason that the commodities were imported by a parallel importer, such a refusal may be unlawful as long as it is used as a method of maintaining the price of the commodity.

Advertisement of a Commodity
If a sole sales agency requests newspaper companies and advertisement agencies not to publish advertisements of genuine commodities imported by a parallel importer, it is held unlawful when it is used for the purpose of maintaining the price of the commodity.

C. PATENT AND KNOW-HOW LICENSING CONTRACTS

The 1989 FTCJ Guidelines

The FTCJ announced a set of guidelines on international patent and know-how licensing agreements in 1968. After two decades, however, many of the provisions incorporated in those guidelines became obsolete. In the light of changes, the FTCJ announced a new set of guidelines on patent and know-how licensing agreements in 1989, and those guidelines are in force today. Therefore, our review will focus on the provisions in this set of guidelines.

The Guidelines are entitled: 'Guidelines on the Regulation of Unfair Business Practices in Patent and Know-how Licensing Agreements' (hereafter referred to as 'The 1989 FTCJ Guidelines') and enumerate the major items in patent and know-how licensing agreements which the FTCJ considers as falling under unfair business practices as provided in the AML.[91] It is to be noted that the 1989 FTCJ Guidelines cover both international and domestic agreements which contain patent and know-how licensing and those in which the Japanese parties are the providers of technology as well as those in which they are the recipients, whereas the guidelines of 1968 covered only restrictions incorporated in patent and know-how licensing in international agreements or those in which the Japanese parties were the recipients of technology.

The 1989 FTCJ Guidelines provide a set of rules to be applied to restrictions in patent licensing agreements and another set of rules which apply to restrictions in know-how licensing agreements. In each part, the 1989 FTCJ Guidelines classify restrictions imposed by licensers of patent and know-how on licensees into three categories: (1) items which in principle are not held unlawful, (2) items which may be held unlawful, and (3) items which are likely to be held unlawful.

The 1989 FTCJ Guidelines enumerate major items in patent and know-how licensing agreements which may fall under the regulation of the AML. Therefore, they are not necessarily an exhaustive list of items which are held liable under the AML. However, it is safe to state that they cover almost all the major items which are regulated under the AML.

As we saw in the previous chapter, under Article 6(2) of the AML, international agreements as specified by the FTCJ are subject to the notification system. Since provisions in international agreements concerning patent and know-how licensing have been designated by the FTCJ as being subject to the notification duty, parties entering into these must notify the contents of the agreements within thirty days after they were executed. There is no corresponding duty with regard to domestic agreements which involve patent and know-how licensing.

Since the 1989 FTCJ Guidelines are quite lengthy and the provisions in the part dealing with know-how licence agreements are not so different from those in the part which deal with patent licence agreements, our discussion will focus on the provisions on patent licensing agreements. We will touch on know-how licensing agreements only slightly.

[91] The Guidelines have been translated into English and published by the Fair Trade Commission. See *FTC/Japan Views*, 6 (Apr. 1989), 16 *et seq*.

Patent Licensing Agreements

The 1989 FTCJ Guidelines state that the following are the major action's which in principle are not held unlawful.

(*a*) To grant the licence of a patent simply for manufacture, use, or sales.

(*b*) To grant the licence only for a certain period of time within which the patent is valid.

(*c*) To grant the licence only for a limited territory within the area in which the patent is valid.

(*d*) To grant the licence only in a certain technological area.

(*e*) To set the minimum quantity for manufacture or sale of the patented product or minimum frequency for the use of a patented process.

(*f*) To impose on the licensee the obligation to inform the licenser about any knowledge and experiences which the licensee has acquired with respect to the licensed technology or impose the obligation to grant to the licenser a non-exclusive licence for the improved inventions or applied inventions, provided that the rights and obligations of the parties are balanced.

(*g*) To require, within the necessary limits, the licensee to maintain a certain level of quality of the patented products, raw materials, or components in order to guarantee the usefulness of the licensed patent (that is, when the licenser has guaranteed the licensee a certain degree of usefulness of the licensed patent) or the good will of the trade mark or other representations (on the condition that the licenser has granted a licence to use the market to the licensee).

(*h*) To impose the obligation on the licensee to purchase raw materials, parts, and related items from the licenser or the party designated by the licenser when it is difficult to maintain the good will of the trade mark or other representations or the use of the licensed technology because of restrictions on the quality of raw materials, components, or related items.

(*i*) To restrict the export by the licensee of the patented products to one of the following areas: the area in which the licenser has registered the patent which covers the patented product, the area in which the licenser is actively engaged in the sales of the patented product, or the area in which the licenser has granted the exclusive right of sales of the patented product to a third party.

(*j*) To impose on the licensee a restriction on export price or quantity or the obligation to export through the licenser or the party designated by the licenser when the export area falls within one of the three areas specified in (*i*), provided that the restriction and obligation are reasonable.

(*k*) To use, for the sake of convenience in computation, the quantity of manufacture or sale of the finished product or the value thereof as the basis for computing royalties when the licensed patent relates to a part of the manufacturing process or to components; or to use, again for the sake of covenience in computation, the amount or frequency of use of raw materials or components necessary to manufacture the patented product as the basis for computing royalties.

(*l*) To require the licensee to accept a licence for a plural number of patents *en bloc* to the extent necessary to guarantee the usefulness of the licensed patent.

(*m*) To stipulate that the obligation of the licensee to pay royalties shall continue after the expiration of the patent to the extent that such payment is recognized as an instalment payment or deferred payment of royalties on the patent.

(*n*) To provide that the licence agreement can be cancelled if the licensee contests the validity of the licensed patent.

(*o*) To obligate the licensee to exert his best efforts in utilizing the licensed technology.

Actions which may be held unlawful:

(*a*) To prohibit, during the term of the licence agreement, the licensee from handling competing products or adopting competing technology. This item is held unlawful when the business opportunity from competing enterprises or the freedom of the licensee to choose products and technology is unduly restricted and thereby competition is lessened.

(*b*) To impose on the licensee the condition that the licensee sell the patented product through the licenser or the party designated by the licenser, or not to sell to a party designated by the licenser. This item is held unlawful when it unduly deprives the licensee of the freedom to choose sales outlets and thereby reduces competition in the market of the patented product.

(*c*) To impose on the licensee the obligation to inform the licenser about the knowledge or experiences which the licensee has acquired with respect to the licensed technology or to grant to the licenser a non-exclusive licence for the improved inventions or applied inventions which the licensee has accomplished, except for those cases in which the licenser's obligations are similar in kind and the obligations of both parties are balanced. This item is held unlawful if the licenser has not assumed similar obligations to those imposed on the licensee or the contents are unbalanced and thereby unduly disadvantageous conditions are imposed on the licensee.

(*d*) To impose on the licensee the obligation to use the trade mark or other representations designated by the licenser on the patented product. This item is held unlawful when the freedom of the licensee to choose the trade mark or other representations is unduly restricted. Also, by this item, the licensee may have to keep on using the trade mark designated by the licenser after the patent has expired, and this may be regarded as an unreasonable condition attached to the licence agreement.

(*e*) To set the standard for quality of raw materials, components, or the patented product, except for those cases in which such a restriction is necessary to maintain the good will of the trade mark or the usefulness of the licensed technology. This restriction is held unlawful when competition in the market of raw materials and components or that of the patented product is unduly restrained.

(*f*) To impose on the licensee the obligation to purchase raw materials or parts from the licenser or the party designated by the licenser except for those cases in which the maintenance of the good will of the trade mark or the effective use of the licensed technology is made difficult because of the restriction on the quality of raw materials or components or other similar restrictions. This restriction is held unlawful when the freedom of the licensee to choose raw materials or components is unduly restricted or competition in the market for raw materials or components is unduly restricted.

(*g*) To restrict the areas to which the licensee can export, except for those cases in which the restricted areas are: the area where the licenser has registered the patent, the area where the licenser is continuously engaged in sales activities of the patented product, or the area in which the licenser has granted to a third party the exclusive right to sell.

(*h*) To set the export price or quantity for the licensee or to obligate the licensee to export through the licenser or the party designated by the licenser, except for the cases in which the export area falls under the three listed in (*g*), and in which the restriction or obligation is reasonable.

(*i*) To require the licensee to pay royalties on products other than the patented product, except for those cases in which the quantity of manufacture or sale of the finished product or the value of manufacture or sale thereof is used as the basis for computing royalties for the sake of convenience in computation when the licensed patent relates to a part of the manufacturing process or to components; or in which the quantity or frequency of use of raw materials or components necessary to manufacture the patented product is used as the basis for computing royalties for the sake of convenience in computation.

(*j*) To require the licensee to accept a licence on a plural number of patents *en bloc*, except for the cases in which such a restriction is imposed to the extent necessary to guarantee the usefulness of the licensed patent.

(*k*) To impose on the licensee a unilateral disadvantage when cancelling a licence agreement, such as to stipulate that the agreement is subject to immediate and unilateral cancellation, without providing for an adequate grace period, for reasons other than the inability to fulfil the agreement on the part of the licensee due to insolvency or other justifiable causes.

(*l*) To impose on the licensee not to contest the validity of the patent. This item is held unlawful when the patent is preserved on a technology which is not patentable, the use of the technology by others is excluded thereby, and competition is unduly restricted. It is also held unlawful if the licensee has to keep paying royalties on the technology which is in the public domain and which the licensee is entitled to use without paying royalties.

Actions which are likely to be held unlawful:

(*a*) To set the resale price of the patented product in the domestic market. This restriction suppresses competition at the level of wholesalers and retailers of the patented product in the market and has no redeeming virtues. For this reason, this restriction is held to be unlawful in principle.

(*b*) To set the sales price of the patented product in the domestic market. This item restricts the competitive ability of the licensee, and price competition in the patented product is suppressed. It is not absolutely necessary for the purpose of securing royalty payment. For the above reasons, this item is held unlawful in principle.

(*c*) To prohibit the licensee from handling competing products or adopting competing technology after the term of the licence agreement has expired. A restriction after the expiration of the licence agreement cannot be justified for the reason that it is necessary to secure royalty payment and no other redeeming virtue is found.

(*d*) To prohibit the licensee from utilizing the technology incorporated in a patent or restrict the use thereof after the patent has expired or to impose the obligation on the licensee to pay royalties for use of technology incorporated in a patent after the patent has expired.

(*e*) To prohibit or restrict the licensee from engaging in research and development either alone or jointly with others with regard to the licensed patent or competing technology.

(*f*) To require the licensee to assign the improved inventions and applied inventions which have been achieved by the licensee to the licenser or to grant the licenser an exclusive licence thereof. This restriction tends to promote or maintain the market power of the licenser unduly and to limit the freedom of the licensee to use knowledge, experience, or improvements which have been developed by the licensee and to license them to third parties. This restriction is a disincentive to the licensee to engage in research and development and to promote the development of new technology. Also, if similar obligations were not imposed on the licenser, the licenser is deemed to be imposing unreasonable business conditions on the licensee.

Know-How Licensing Agreements

The 1989 FTCJ Guidelines provide rules with regard to restrictive clauses incorporated in know-how licensing agreements. As in the part dealing with patent licensing agreements, the rules are divided into three parts, namely, the items which are in principle lawful, those which may be held unlawful, and those which are likely to be held unlawful. We will examine only those rules which relate to items which are likely to be held unlawful.

The following items included in know-how licensing agreements are likely be held as unlawful.

(i) To set the resale price of the licensed product in the domestic market.

(ii) To set the sales price for the licensee of the licensed product in the domestic market. By this item, the competitive position of the licensee is considerably weakened, and competition in the market for the licensed product is likely to be adversely affected.

(iii) To prohibit the licensee from handling competing products or adopting competing technology after the licence agreement has expired, except for the cases in which such a restriction is necessary to prevent the licensed know-how from leaking out and the term of the restriction is limited to a short period of time.

(iv) To prohibit or restrict the licensee from using the technology incorporated in the licensed know-how when the licensed know-how has come into general circulation without the licensee being responsible or to require the licensee to pay royalties for the use of the technology after the licensed know-how has come into general circulation, except for the cases in which the obligation to pay royalties was imposed on the use of technology during the term of the agreement for a short period of time after the know-how had become generally circulated.

(v) To prohibit or restrict the licensee from engaging alone or jointly with others in research and development of the licensed know-how or a competing technology.

(vi) To require the licensee to assign to the licenser the rights to improved technology or applied technology which the licensee has developed or to grant an exclusive licence thereof. This item tends unduly to enhance the market power of the licenser, deprives the licensee of the freedom to use his knowledge, experiences, or improvements or to license them to third parties and thereby acts as a disincentive to the licensee to engage in research and development. Such a restriction tends to hinder research and development in new technology and to reduce competition in the product market and the technology market. Also, if the licenser does not bear a similar burden to that borne by the licensee and the contents of the burden borne by both parties are unbalanced, this amounts to imposing an unreasonable condition on the licence.

Comments on the 1989 FTCJ Guidelines

Although the 1989 FTCJ Guidelines apply both to international agreements and domestic agreements which involve patent and know-how licensing, the provisions incorporated in the Guidelines are more likely to be applied to restrictions involved in international patent and know-how licensing agreements. The reason is that under Article 6(2) of the AML, international agreements which incorporate patent and know-how licensing must be notified to the FTCJ whereas no corresponding obligation exists with regard to domestic agreements which incorporate patent and know-how licensing.[92] Therefore, problematical restrictions involved in international agreements are more likely to be spotted than those involved in domestic agreements.

When one examines the items both in the part of the Guidelines dealing with patent licensing and in the part dealing with know-how licensing, items which are likely to be held unlawful are those which would not come under the jurisdiction of the FTCJ if imposed by Japanese parties on foreign parties.[93] For example, take the case of resale price maintenance. If a Japanese party (the licenser of a patent) imposes the obligation on the foreign party (the licensee) to cause its distributors abroad to maintain the resale price of the commodity produced by the licensee under the licence given by the licenser, such conduct has no effect in the Japanese market and, therefore, would be outside the reach of the AML.

On the other hand, if a foreign licenser imposes a similar obligation on the Japanese licensee whereby the Japanese licensee is obligated to cause its distributors in Japan to maintain the resale price of the products produced by the licensee under the licence given by the licenser, the prohibition of the Guidelines will certainly be applied on the conduct. There is a similar situation with regard to other items involved in patent and know-how licensing agreements which are likely to be held unlawful.

A set of guidelines announced by the FTCJ in 1968 were heavily inclined towards protecting domestic enterprises from having restrictive conditions imposed by foreign licensers. The 1989 FTCJ Guidelines are an attempt to move away from this protective attitude and to apply

[92] Matsushita, 'Protection of Technology and the Liberal Trade Order: A Japanese View', in Yamamura (ed.), *Japan's Economic Structure; Should It Change?* (Seattle, 1990), 271 *et seq*.

[93] For a critical review of the guidelines by a foreign observer, see Davidow, 'The New Japanese Guidelines on Unfair Practices in Patent and Know-how Licenses: An American View', *World Competition*, 12/4 (1989), 5 *et seq*.

regulations equally to domestic and international agreements. This is certainly the right direction. However, in the structure and actual operations, even the 1989 FTCJ Guidelines are not enirely free from a remnant of the 'protectionism' which was so prevalent two or three decades ago, although this was probably not the intention of the framers of these guidelines.

As a whole, the 1991 FTCJ Guidelines still emphasize the protection of licensees or recipients of technology rather than that of the right of licensers. One of the notions which underlies the Guidelines is the equality or balance of interests of the licenser and the licensee in a patent or know-how licensing agreement. For example, in the part dealing with patent licensing agreements, the Guidelines state that the imposition by the licenser of the obligation on the licensee that the latter must notify the former about technological knowledge which has been acquired in the process of utilizing the licensed technology (an improved technology) may be held unlawful 'except for the cases in which the licenser's obligations are similar in kind and the obligations of both of the parties are balanced'.

This notion of equality of interests or balancing of interests between the licenser and the licensee reflects the enforcement policy at the time when Japanese enterprises were by and large recipients and licensees of technology from abroad. The situation has dramatically changed. However, the enforcement policy of two decades ago still lingers here. This is in sharp contrast to the Guidelines on International Operations announced by the United States Justice Department in 1988[94] in which the interests of licensers are so much emphasized and there seems to be hardly any case in which restrictions involved in patent and know-how licensing agreements are held unlawful.

D. ENFORCEABILITY OF UNLAWFUL INTERNATIONAL CONTRACTS

An Overview

In practice, in a dispute over an international contract, one of the parties claims that the contract in question is contrary to a public law and cannot be enforced. Let us suppose an example such as follows: Company A in Japan enters into a contract with Company B in the United States in which Company A promises to export a certain amount of Commodity X to Company B. Suppose that the export of Commodity X in Japan is prohibited by the Control Law.

[94] US Dept. of Justice, International Operations, Antitrust Enforcement Policy (Final Version), *CCH Trade Regulation Report* (extra edn.), 241 (1988).

When Company A exported a portion of the quantity of Commodity X stipulated in the contract, the MITI detected this violation, the export was stopped and, with regard to the rest of the quantity, the completion of the contract was frustrated. Company B brings a suit for damages in a Japanese court for non-performance of the contract and Company A brings a defence that the contract is contrary to the Control Law and null and void. Can Company B recover damages?

Similar claims may be made not only as litigation but also during the process of negotiating contracts. For example, when an American company and a Japanese company are negotiating a contract whereby the American company would license a technology to the Japanese company, the American party may insist that there be a clause in the contract which states that the Japanese company will purchase all raw materials, parts, and components from the American company or the party designated by the company. The Japanese company may claim that such a clause would be a violation of the AML and cannot be enforced in Japan.

The above problems are, in short, the enforceability of a contract which is contrary to a public law regulation in Japan. This is an enormously complex question. Article 90 of the Civil Code states that 'a juristic act which is contrary to the public order and good morals is null and void'. Of course, not all conduct which is contrary to public law regulations amounts to a violation of public order or good morals as provided for in the Civil Code. Conduct which constitutes grave offence of provisions in the Criminal Code such as murder, fraud, and embezzlement would fall under the category of conduct which is contrary to public order and good morals. However, the seriousness of the offence may not be so great for conduct which is a violation of an economic regulation. Also it may be contrary to the sense of fairness if a court allowed the party to a contract to reap benefit from the contract but deny its obligation by using a public law regulation.

The effect of a contract which is in violation of a public law in Japan may depend on the applicable law. If the applicable law is Japanese law and the contract is performed in Japan, courts in Japan have an easier time to find such a contract unenforceable. However, if the applicable law is the law of a foreign country and the contract is performed abroad, courts in Japan would be hesitant to declare that the contract was void due to its illegality under the Japanese law.

Whether or not a contract which is contrary to a public regulation in Japan is given private law enforceability depends on the nature of the law involved, the circumstances under which the claim for unenforceability is brought up, which party brings up such a claim, and many other factors. In deciding this issue, courts must consider whether there is wording in the law in question which states explicitly that a contract which contravenes the mandate of this law is void (such as that in the Anti-Usury Law touched upon in the *Miyakawa* case below), whether it is absolutely necessary to hold a contract which is in violation of this law void in order to achieve the objective of the law, and whether the contract in question falls in the category of conduct which is contrary to public order and good morals. These questions have to be examined on a case-by-case basis.

We cannot engage in a full-scale investigation of these questions here. Instead we will attempt to illustrate examples and see how courts attempted to solve them. We will select two areas of law, that is, foreign exchange control under the Control Law and the AML.

The Enforceability of Contract Contrary to the Control Law

The Enforceability of a Contract which Violates the Foreign Exchange Control under the Control Law

The case in point is the *Tomita* case[95] in which a Supreme Court decision was handed down in 1965. At the time the decision was handed down, there was tight control of foreign exchange transactions engaged in by residents of Japan. Any act which would create an obligation on the part of a resident of Japan to pay money to a non-resident of Japan had to be reported to the MOF and had to be approved by the Minister of the MOF. Any payment by a resident to a non-resident had to be approved by the MOF also.

In short, what was involved in this case was as follows: a Japanese resident (Y) borrowed money from an American person (A) (a non-resident of Japan) while the Japanese was travelling in the United States. When the American came to Japan, he assigned this money claim to another Japanese (X). X brought a suit against Y in a court in Japan and claimed that Y should pay money to X. Y brought a defence that the contract which created this obligation on the part of Y was contrary to the Control Law since this contract was executed without approval of the MOF and also that no permission for payment was obtained.

The Supreme Court ruled that this contract was enforceable as a matter of private law although it was contrary to the Control law and the penalty provided in the Control Law might be imposed on the party. The Supreme Court stated:

> [The Control Law] is a regulatory law of a temporary nature which controls external transactions for the purpose of the rehabilitation and development of the national economy. When we adopt the interpretation of Article 30 of the Control Law and Article 13 of the Foreign Exchange Control Decree as a regulatory law[96]

[95] Decision of the Supreme Court, 23 Dec. 1965, *Minshū*, 19/9 (1965), 2306 *et seq*.

[96] The Supreme Court used the expression 'regulatory law' (torishimari hōki).

and rule, we must say that an act which is contrary to them is criminally illegal but the illegality does not affect the private law effect of the contract. The loan and assignment involved in this case are not acts which are inherently impermissible. They require a governmental approval only for the sake of the necessity of regulation at this time. Therefore, to escape from the contractual obligation for the reason that such law and regulation exists is contrary to the principle of good faith and trustworthiness. . . . [The conduct in question] has not been approved [by the MOF] yet and is, therefore, illegal. However, it is not necessarily null and void and an approval can be obtained afterwards.

This decision established a precedent that a contract which is in violation of the foreign exchange control is not necessarily deprived of its private law effect for the sole reason that it is contrary to the foreign exchange control. As we have seen already, foreign exchange control has been much relaxed since this decision was handed down and a case of this sort would not occur today. However, the principle established by the Supreme Court that a contract is not necessarily held null and void only because it is contrary to a public law regulation of an economic nature which does not touch on the basic morality of the society still holds true today. There are some prohibitions of private conduct exercised by the ministries on the basis of regulatory laws which do not touch on the basic morality of the society any more than the foreign exchange control in force when this case was decided. In such cases, this decision would be used as a precedent.

Enforceability of Contract in Violation of Export Control

In the *Transistor Radio* case,[97] the issue was the enforceability of an international contract between a Japanese company and an American company wherein the Japanese company promised to export to the American company a certain number of transistor radio sets. At this time, the export approval system was applied on the export of transistor radio sets by the MITI and the MITI maintained the policy of setting up the export quotas on products and allocated quotas to enterprises which had had a prior export performance. When an exporter who had been allocated a quota applied for an export approval, the MITI attached the condition on this approval that the export price of transistor radio sets exported to the United States be kept above a certain level as determined by the MITI (the so-called 'check price' system).

A Japanese company, the defendant in this case, wished to export transistor radio sets to the United States at a lower price. It had no prior

'Regulatory law' is a law which restricts conduct and a violation of which is met with a criminal penalty or administrative sanction, while the illegality under the law does not affect the private law effect of the conduct.

[97] Decision of the Tokyo High Court, 28 Aug. 1965, *Kakyū Minshū*, 16/8 (1965), 1342 *et seq*.

export performance in the product. Anticipating that the MITI would not approve the export if the defendant applied for an approval for the export of transistor radio sets, it made a false statement to the MITI that it exported 'electric massage instruments' on which there was no export approval system but exported transistor radio sets. The defendant entered into an international contract with an American company (the plaintiff in this case), promised to export a certain number of transistor radio sets, and exported part of the number of transistor radio sets as agreed upon between the parties.

However, the export of transistor radio sets by making a false declaration was detected by the MITI, the MITI issued an order to prohibit the exportation, and the defendant could not export the rest of the transistor radio sets. The plaintiff initiated a suit in the Tokyo District Court for a breach of contract and sought for the recovery of damages. The defendant raised the defence that the export in question was in violation of the Control Law and, therefore, the contract between the parties was null and void.

The Tokyo District Court rejected this defence and held that the defendant was liable to pay damages. The Court stated:

> Since the sales contract in the present case is intended to be performed in a way which would impede the enforcement of the export policy of the MITI, it is, for this reason, highly undesirable. However, it does not necessarily follow that this contract is contrary to public order and good morals and null and void. Taking into consideration that many transistor radio sets were exported at prices lower than the check price, that the seller . . . would escape from the obligation if we held that this contract was null and void and that the plaintiff which is a foreign company would suffer damages due to the Japanese trade policy, it is appropriate to hold this sales contract to be enforceable. . . . The frustration of the performance of this contract was caused by the fact that the defendant did not have an export quota, made a false claim to the government that the exported item was an 'electric massage instrument' and was detected by the government. Therefore, the frustration is attributable to the defendant's responsibility.

Comments on the above Cases

There are two premisses in the above court decisions. One is that the export approval system is not a rule which protects the fundamental order of society. Therefore, its violation should be dealt with by a criminal penalty or by an administrative sanction. However, the private law effect of the contract should be recognized. Another is an implied 'clean hand' principle that courts should not render aid to a person whose hands are not clean. Also it seems to take into consideration the principle that a person who enters into a contract intentionally should not be allowed to use the illegality of it to escape from the responsibility created by the contract.

There is no decision so far which has held that a contract in violation of the Control Law was null and void. Together with the *Tomta* case, this precedent established the case law doctrine that international contracts are generally enforceable even if they are in violation of the Control Law.

The Enforceability of Contract in Violation of the Anti-monopoly Law

In cases in which the issue is the enforceability of a contract which is in violation of the AML, the situation is more complex. Cases and views of commentators are divided on this issue. In some cases, a contract which violated the AML was held as enforceable in spite of its illegality, although there is another set of cases in which courts reached the contrary result. It is risky to make a conclusory remark as regards this issue. We will only present two Supreme Court decisions as examples.

In the *Novo* case,[98] the issue was the standing of a foreign enterprise to an international agreement with a Japanese enterprise to challenge a FTCJ decision in the Tokyo High Court. An international agreement between a foreign enterprise, which was a manufacturer and the supplier of a chemical substance, and a Japanese enterprise, which was the exclusive distributor of the product in Japan, whereby the domestic party was obligated to maintain the resale price of the product in Japan and prohibited from selling and manufacturing competing products, was challenged by the FTCJ, and the FTCJ issued an order to the domestic party to cancel the restrictive provisions. The foreign party brought a suit against the FTCJ to have this FTCJ decision cancelled.

The Tokyo High Court, which had the primary jurisdiction in the case, held that the foreign party had no standing to challenge the FTCJ decision, since the mere fact that the FTCJ issued a decision and held an agreement as a violation of the AML did not necessarily mean that the agreement in question was held as unenforceable. The court stated that, since the agreement in question which had been held as a violation by the FTCJ should not necessarily be held as unenforceable as a matter of private law, the foreign party would have a chance to challenge the domestic party in a civil court for a breach of contract and, therefore, the foreign party's contractual interest had not been adversely affected by the FTCJ decision.

Upon appeal by the foreign party, the Supreme Court examined the issue and handed down a decision denying the standing to the foreign party. The Supreme Court reasoned that the domestic party could not utilize the FTCJ decision holding the agreement illegal and ordering the domestic party to cancel the restrictions as a defence in a suit for breach of the agreement if the foreign party brought a suit against the domestic

[98] Decision of the Supreme Court, 28 Nov. 1975, *Minshū*, 19/10 (1965), 1592 *et seq*.

party for such a breach. The Supreme Court drew the conclusion that the decision did not affect the legal position of the foreign party as far as a suit for breach of contract which the foreign party might wish to bring was concerned and, for that reason, the foreign party did not have the standing to challenge the decision of the FTC.

The above decision directly deals with the question of standing rather than the enforceability of an illegal contract. However, the courts' decisions stood on the premiss that an illegal contract was not necessarily deprived of its private law enforceability for the reason of illegality alone.

In the *Miyakawa* case,[99] the issue was whether or not a contract between a financial institution and a borrower of money which was held as a violation of the AML was enforceable as a matter of private law. The financial institution imposed a condition on the borrower that the latter had to maintain a substantial deposit in return for the loan given by the institution. The borrower had to borrow the amount necessary to make this deposit and the effective interest rate was very high. The borrower brought a suit against the financial institution and claimed that the lending contract was unenforceable due to a violation of the AML. The Supreme Court held that the lending contract was a violation of the AML for the reason that it imposed an unreasonable condition on the borrower and consequently amounted to an unfair business practice.

In this case, however, the Supreme Court stated, in *dicta*, that a contract which was in violation of the AML should not immediately be held as unenforceable for the sole reason that it was a violation of the AML unless such a contract was held to be contrary to 'the public order and good morals' as provided for in Article 90 of the Civil Code. Then the Court applied the Anti-Usury Law[100] (which states that interest on a loan in excess of the rate stipulated by the law is null and void and the payment of interest in excess of the stipulated rate is regarded as the payment of capital) to the imposition by the financial institution, stated that the effective interest in this case was excessive, and held that the amount of interest in excess of the maximum provided for in this law was void because of a violation of that law.

Therefore, in this case, the issue was disposed of as that of a violation of the Anti-Usury law. However, the Supreme Court enunciated as a *dictum* that an agreement contrary to the AML is not deprived of its effectiveness as a matter of private law for the reason only that it is a violation of the AML. This *dictum* is often cited as evidence that a private act which is contrary to the AML should not be held as legally unenforceable for that reason alone.

[99] Decision of the Supreme Court, 20 June 1977, *Minshū*, 31/2 (1977), 449 *et seq.*
[100] Risoku Seigen Hō, Law 100, 1954.

It is to be noted that there are some cases in which the courts declared that a contract in violation of the AML was unenforceable. It seems that the issue of enforceability depends on the various factors listed at the outset of this section and the correct conclusion can be reached only by a detailed analysis as to which factors are more predominant in a given case.

4
Industrial Policy

4.1 An Overview

A. WHAT IS INDUSTRIAL POLICY?

Japan has basically a market economy and in a market economy the market mechanism is the most fundamental institution in which enterprises are free to decide the prices they charge, the quantity they produce, and other terms of business, and government regulation of business is kept minimal. However, in every country in the world with a market economy, there are always some measures taken by the government which affect business activities. Even in a market economy in which the market mechanism operates and government intervention should be kept minimal, there is need for supplemental measures to deal with market imperfections. Such market imperfections are sometimes called 'market failures' and include monopolies, externalities, the weak position of small enterprises, trade frictions, the existence of structurally depressed industries, and some other circumstances which necessitate some degree of government assistance and intervention.

The governments of free market economy countries have introduced various measures to assist some sectors of industry, to regulate conduct of enterprises in other sectors, and sometimes to engage in business through the activities of government corporations. In this sense, an accurate picture of every existing free market economy is a mixture of the market mechanism and some kinds of governmental involvement. Each country differs in the extent to which its government is involved in steering the economy. The relative role of the government in assisting and regulating private enterprise is determined by the nation's historical background, its basic political and philosophical orientation, the stage of economic development, and the comparative advantages and disadvantages of industries in the country, and many other factors.

The role of government in controlling the market is greater in Japan than that in the United States and other Western industrialized countries.[1]

[1] Johnson, *MITI and the Japanese Miracle* (Starford, Calif., 1982).

The relatively high degree of government involvement in the economy can be attributed to the following factors. Japan is a relative late-comer to the group of industrialized countries, and the philosophy of 'laissez-faire' was not historically strong. The government–business relationship is more co-operative than adversarial as compared with, for example, the situation in the United States. Also there is a great number of small enterprises in the Japanese economy which play an important role and which cry for some government assistance. Finally, growing protectionism in her trade partners has made it necessary to take some regulatory measures in foreign trade.

Although the term 'industrial policy' appears in newspapers, journals, and academic writings, it has never been officially defined. Once industrial policy was attributed to 'those policies which were exercised by the Ministry of International Trade and Industry [MITI]'.[2] But, of course, MITI is not the only agency which engages in industrial policy. A standard-book on industrial policy entitled *The Industrial Policies of Japan* (*Nihon no Sangyō Seisaku*),[3] defines industrial policies as 'those policies designed to cope with the market failure in the allocation of resources', and includes measures to deal with externalities, anti-competitive structures and conduct, promotion of economies of scale, infant industries, basic research and development, and the elimination of uncertainty in industrial development.

An elaborate definition of industrial policy is probably not necessary. A tentative and yet workable definition of industrial policy should suffice. In the light of this, we may state that the industrial policy is a government policy to supplement the market in the face of market failure and facilitate its performance in the long run, and that it is a set of measures to deal with specific sectors of the economy. This statement roughly corresponds to a definition of industrial policy given by another economist which suggests that industrial policy is: 'the totality of governmental policies undertaken to change the allocation of resources among industries from what it would be otherwise, or to intervene in the industrial organization within a certain individual industry, with an intention to enhance the country's economic welfare if and when unrestricted functioning of the competitive market mechanism is found to fail in achieving that end.'[4] In this respect, industrial policy is distinguished from government measures such as fiscal and monetary policy which may be characterized as 'global steering'. When exercised properly, therefore, industrial policy does not

[2] Kaizuka, *Keizai Seisakuno Kadai* (*Perspective on Economic Policy*) (Tokyo, 1973), 147.

[3] Komiya, Okuno, and Suzumura (eds.), *Nihonno Sangyo Seisaku* (*Industrial Policy in Japan*) (Tokyo, 1984).

[4] See ibid. 3.

go against the market meachanism but supplements its imperfections and facilitates its operations.

B. A BRIEF HISTORY OF JAPANESE INDUSTRIAL POLICY

Since the Meiji Restoration in 1868, the Japanese government has been actively engaged in promoting industry. For the purpose of our study, it suffices if we confine our observation to the period after the Second World War. The period of several years after the end of the Second World War was a period during which the Japanese economic structure was fundamentally reformed. The Occupation Forces brought into Japan the Economic Democratization Policy, which consisted of: (1) agrarian land reform, (2) labour reform, and (3) deconcentration of *Zaibatsu* (the large industrial combines which had controlled major parts of the Japanese economy.[5] Also, the Anti-monopoly Law (the AML) was enacted in 1947 and this law was designed to be the basic framework for Japanese industry. However, as we saw in another chapter, the enforcement of the AML receded from about 1950 and was dormant until about 1960. In the late 1940s, industrial policy exercised by the MITI became the dominant force in the economy.

In the initial stage of industrial policy, measures taken by the government were rather interventionistic, as exemplified by the priority production system (1946–8) in which resources such as funds, foreign exchange, and imported raw materials were allocated to chosen industries, that is, the coal and steel industries. However, since the mid-1950s, the emphasis of industrial policy gradually shifted from direct intervention to measures to provide incentives and information to industries, by, for example, giving tax exemptions and authorizing industry associations.

From 1950 to the mid-1960s, heavy industries such as steel, cars, aluminium, and petro-chemicals were the main objects of industrial promotion and the primary objective of industrial policy at that time was to build up international competitiveness. For this purpose, various incentives such as tax exemptions and subsidies in the form of preferential financing by such organizations as the Japan Development Bank were provided for targeted industries. The MITI also encouraged mergers of large companies. For example, three Mitsubishi industrial companies were merged into Mitsubishi Heavy Industries in 1963 and The Yawata Steel Company and Fuji Steel Company merged into The Japan Steel Corporation in 1969.

Since about the late 1960s, however, there have been changes in the economic conditions which has necessitated a shift of emphasis of industrial policy. Partly because of a heavy emphasis on the growth of

[5] See Bisson, *Dissolution of Zaibatsu in Japan* (Berkeley, Calif., 1954).

the economy in the 1950s and 1960s, environmental problems became serious. Around 1960, an increase in consumer prices became an acute problem and, in early 1970, the Oil Crisis hit the Japanese economy. Also the heyday of the traditional heavy industries passed and high-technology-intensive industries such as computers and semiconductors became important. In the area of foreign trade, an increase of the international competitiveness of Japanese industries aroused concern in her trade partners (especially the United States and the EC) and restrictive trade measures *vis-à-vis* imported products from Japan were taken.

Faced with these new developments, the role of industrial policy, especially that exercised by the MITI, began to change. There was a new emphasis on orderly export, promotion of high technology, and services and knowledge industries, and acknowledgement of a vital need for environmental protection and consumer protection. It is to be noted that this change was only a change in emphasis. Traditional policy regarding conventional industries has continued. It may be more accurate to state that industrial policy by the MITI has become more diversified than before. This new trend still continues today.

In addition to the above, the enforcement of the AML has been revitalized, since the Oil Crisis, when the *Oil Cartel* decisions[6] by the FTCJ and courts established the rule that easy utilization of cartels as tools for industrial policy would not stand up to antitrust scrutinies. Therefore, the MITI has come face to face with the situation that it must take into consideration the impact of the AML when enforcing industrial policy measures and avoid using 'cartels' as tools for implementing industrial policy goals. This requirement has become even more real as a result of the SII between the United States government and the Japanese government in which the Japanese government promised that it would strengthen the enforcement of the AML and refrain from an excessive use of administrative guidance in implementing government policies.[7]

Also, more recently, deregulation of the government control of business activities has become increasingly important and this makes it necessary to define the permissible scope of industrial policy even more narrowly.

C. THE RELATIONSHIP BETWEEN INDUSTRIAL POLICY AND THE MARKET

As above defined, industrial policy should be regarded as a set of government measures designed to supplement the operation of the market

[6] Decision of the Supreme Court, 24 Feb. 1984, *Hanrei Jihō* (1984), 1108, 3 *et seq.*; Decision of the Tokyo High Court, 26 Sept. 1980, ibid. 983 (1980), 22 *et seq.*

[7] Matsushita, 'Structural Impediments Initiative: An Example of Bilateral Trade Negotiation', *Michigan Journal of International Law*, 12/2 (1991), 436 *et seq.*

mechanism. It follows from this that when the government executes industrial policy, certain conditions must be met.

First, measures taken under the industrial policy programme should be limited in time. Measures taken by the government to carry out industrial policy often involve assistance to industries. For example, when the government provides financial assistance to an industry which is suffering from the loss of comparative advantages, such an assistance should be limited in time and scope.

Secondly, measures taken to implement industrial policy should be carried out according to a well-established time-schedule including a plan to phase out the measures.

Thirdly, in implementing industrial policy, the government should try to utilize private initiatives as much as possible. For example, as long as it is practicable, a consortium of private enterprises may be formed to implement the policy rather than direct intervention by the government.

D. THE EFFECTIVENESS OF INDUSTRIAL POLICY IN JAPAN

Industrial policy involves government activities in business, whether promotional or regulatory. A close relationship between government and business is necessary in order for such a policy to be effectively implemented. It is said that industrial policy in Japan is effectively implemented as compared with other countries. Although it is hard to make a general statement that industrial policy in Japan is effectively implemented or vice versa, it is probably true that, at least in some industrial sectors, the MITI's industrial policy in Japan has worked well. There are at least two reasons to explain why the MITI's policy has been successful. First, there has historically been a close relationship between the government and the business community. Since the Meiji Restoration in 1868, the government has been quite active in promoting and helping industry build international competitiveness. Through this historical process, a close co-operative relationship has developed and industries have acquired the habit of working closely with the government under the leadership of the government.[8]

Also, there are informal ties between the government and business as exemplified by 'Amakudari' (descending from Heaven) in which high-ranking government officials become executives of private enterprises when they leave the government and thereby create personal connections between the government and business.

It is to be noted that administrative guidance (of which an account has

[8] Id., 'The Legal Framework of Japanese Industrial Policy', *Brigham Young University Law Review*, 2 (1987), 541 *et seq.*

been made already in a previous chapter) has been an important tool for the government to carry out its industrial policy and the effectiveness of administrative guidance depends on the close co-operative relationship between the government and business as touched upon above.

Industrial policy, as exercised by the MITI, has been successful when its role is that of providing incentive to industries which have some growth potential such as the computer and semiconductor industries. On the other hand, industrial policies have failed when government has tried to assist an industry which had little potential for growth.

Viewed as a whole, the post-war success of Japanese industry should be attributed primarily to the entrepreneurship of industries rather than the industrial polices of the government. Industrial policies, however, have played a significant, though supplemental, role in the industrial growth of the country by providing incentive to industries.

4.2 Basic Research and Development

Although Japan is known as a country of high technology, research and development in Japan have been focused mainly on development research. Research and development can be divided into three categories: (1) basic research, (2) applied research, and (3) development research. In basic research, there is no immediate link between the research and the development of a particular product. Research is conducted only for the purpose of proving a hypothesis. In development research, the direct objective is to embody a technology in the form of a product. Applied research is the intermediary stage between the two.

In Japan, research and development are primarily done by private enterprises and a natural result is that the emphasis is placed on development research which leads to a particular product and profit. On the other hand, the public sector for research and development, such as public research institutions and universities, suffers from lack of funds and from being relatively inefficient. According to a report published by the government in 1983,[9] about 2 per cent of Japan's gross national product was spent in research and development. However, more than 70 per cent of the total amount was spent by private enterprise. Since basic research and development involves large amounts of money and high risk, private enterprises are unlikely to engage in such research unless

[9] Tsūshō Sangyōshō Sangyo Seisakukyoku–Kōgyō Gijutsuin (Industrial Policy Bureau–Industrial Technology Agency, the Ministry of International Trade and Industry), *Sangyō Gijutsu Kaihatsu To Kibangijutsu Kenkyū Enkatsuka Hō* (*Development of Industrial Technology and the Law to Facilitate Research of Basic Technology*) (Tokyo, 1985), 7.

incentives are given. Because developmental research, which produces products, is ultimately derived from basic research, ignoring basic research will eventually weaken the basis of technology.

There has been growing awareness of this possibility, and as a result, some measures for promoting basic research and development have been provided. One such measure is the enactment of the Research Association Law[10] which provides for the establishment of a research association. Basic research involves huge amounts of money and is difficult for a single enterprise to undertake, but if several enterprises pool their money and resources, much can be accomplished. Under this law, private enterprises can form an association for the purpose of carrying out a specific technological task. An association created under this law can apply for a patent on the technology resulting from the joint research. Along with this system of combining resources, tax exemptions of various kinds and governmental subsidies are provided.

Private enterprises can engage in joint research and development in the form of co-operative or joint ventures. For example, private enterprises can form a co-operative under the Civil Code, each member contributes technology and funds, provides research personnel, and jointly engages in research and development of a product. Technology which results from the activities is jointly owned by members and utilized by them. Private enterprises can also form a joint venture company which engages in research and development in a technological area. The joint venture company owns the resulting technology and patents on the technology are licensed to the parent companies.

However, a research association under the Research Association Law has advantages over the above forms of co-operation among enterprises. First, a research association can apply for a patent and own it when granted. Then the patent can be utilized by any member enterprise. Secondly, tax exemptions and other incentives are provided if private enterprises engage in research and development in the form of a research association. Thirdly, often government aid in the form of subsidy or the commissioning of a project is available if private enterprises engage in research and development in the form of a research association under the Research Association Law.

The government sometimes gives subsidies to research associations to carry out a project in the form of monetary grants, and supplies government scientists and engineers. Also, the government sometimes commissions a research association to carry out research for the government. In such areas as super LSI (large-scale integrated circuits) and computers, the device of forming a research association was actively used to

[10] Kōkōgyō Gijutsukenkyū Kumiai Hō, Law 81, 1961.

accomplish the objective. Especially well known is the research association formed by several enterprises to develop basic technology on super LSI. This project was formulated at the suggestion of the MITI and several important enterprises in the field participated. The MITI supplied scientists and engineers, provided financial incentives, and, as a result, important technology in super LSI was created.

However, a research association formed under this law should be temporary and its objective must be specified, such as research in a particular area or on a particular product. For this reason, a research association is suitable when the purpose is to create a basic technology which would not be created by private initiative alone and which should be open to any enterprise after a certain period of time.

There is no provision in the Research Association Law to exempt activities of research associations from the application of the AML. However, they are not likely to be held unlawful under the AML as long as their activities are confined within the area necessary to achieve the objective of the association.

Activities of a research association would create antitrust problems only in some specific situations. If, for example, a research association is utilized as the forum in which to discuss prices of products which are not directly related to the research and development which is the object of the association, this would obviously raise an antitrust problem. Also if a technology created by the research and development activities of a research association is so important that, without this technology, outsiders cannot engage in business, a refusal to grant a licence to outsiders may constitute a monopolization as defined in Article 2(5) of the AML under certain conditions. This is called 'the essential facility doctrine' or 'the bottleneck monopoly doctrine'. Even then, however, the association is allowed to impose different conditions on outsiders in granting a licence, such as difference in royalties from those which are imposed on the members, since to make it obligatory to the research association to treat the members and outsiders equally would deprive the members of the incentive to engage in research and development and would defeat the purpose of creating a research association. Therefore, except for those instances, the activities of a research association are generally held to be lawful under the AML.

There is no conflict between the activities of a research association and the market mechanism since a large-scale project on basic research whose risk is too high for a single enterprise to undertake can be made possible only through the formation of such an association. If there is no research association, nothing is produced, while, on the other hand, a research association may produce some beneficial results.

Another important piece of legislation in this regard is the Basic

Technology Research Facilitation Law,[11] enacted in 1985. Under this law, private enterprises can use government facilities for a small rent when they engage in research and development. Under this law, the Basic Technology Research Facilitation Centre was established which provides funds to private enterprises which are engaged in research and development. Also the Centre itself engages in research and development activities. The Centre also arranges joint research projects among private enterprises and government research institutes and collects and disseminates technological information.

4.3 Depressed Industries

A. POLICIES TOWARDS DEPRESSED INDUSTRIES

It is generally said that there are two kinds of depression. One is cyclical depression and the other is structural depression. A cyclical depression occurs as a process of economic ups and downs. There is a business cycle in the economy which goes through the stages of economic boom, recession, depression, recovery, and boom again. This is a natural cycle of the economy but, when a depression comes, enterprises suffer from slackening business activities, decreasing demand, and consequently shrinking business opportunities.

The frequency and length of a depression varies from one depression to another and from one country to country. In any market economy, however, a depression as a phase of the business cycle occurs inevitably. When a depression comes, appropriate measures which the government should take are measures of global steering such as monetary policy or fiscal policy.

A monetary policy is designed to control the supply of money to the market and when a depression comes the government lowers the discount rate to make it easier for banks to borrow money from the central bank. Thereby banks have greater resources to supply money to enterprises. In fiscal policy, the government utilizes tax policy to affect the economy, and, when a depression comes, the government provides tax reductions and exemptions to various industrial sectors and thereby provides an incentive to enterprises to engage in business activities. Global steering measures as above explained are aimed at controlling the total demand and supply of money and do not in principle interfere with the activities of any one sector of industry or any one enterprise.

Whether the government should extend protection to a specific

[11] Kibangijutsu Kenkyū Enkatsuka Hō, Law 65, 1985. On this law, see n. 9, above.

industrial sector or a group of enterprises when a depression comes is a difficult problem to solve. One the one hand, one may argue that a depression is a good opportunity to weed out inefficient enterprises and, when they are eliminated, the economy is more efficient than before. The remedy applied to inefficient enterprises should be those of social policy, such as unemployment insurance, retraining of workers, and adjustment assistance to the enterprises so that they can shift to other industrial sectors. In the above view, there is no room (or little room if any) for industrial policy in a depression.

However, there is another school of thought which maintains that, when a depression is exceptionally hard, even those enterprises which have a sufficient viability may be eliminated, that it would be an expensive proposition to reconstruct those enterprises again, and that it would not be contrary to the market principle to give such enterprises some protection as an 'emergency relief'.

In Japan, differences of views with regard to what is the proper role of the government in a cyclical depression have not been entirely resolved. However, Article 23.3 of the AML provides for a 'depression cartel' and this is viewed as a measure which enterprises should utilize to weather the storm. As explained later, this article is premissed on the proposition that it is to the benefit of the national economy to give enterprises a temporary relief when they are in a great difficulty in a cyclical depression.

A structural depression poses more difficult problems. A structural depression may be defined as a depression which is specific to one industrial sector and caused by the loss of comparative advantage of the industry *vis-à-vis* that of another country, the lack of competitiveness in relation to competing products, the shift of demand for the product concerned to another product, or some other fundamental changes in the economy or technology which affects that particular industrial sector. Due to its own nature, a structurally depressed industry is in a state of depression whether or not the economy as a whole is in boom or in depression even though a structurally depressed industry will be even more severely affected when a cyclical depression comes as compared with other industries.

A typical structurally depressed industry in Japan is perhaps the coal industry. Once the coal industry was regarded as one of the key industries in the economy. However, due to more inexpensive energy resources, such as petroleum and nuclear power, the viability of the coal industry has declined steadily. Also, the coal industry in Japan has lost the comparative advantages *vis-à-vis* those in foreign countries such as Australia, due to difficult mining conditions, such as deep mining in Japan as compared to strip mining in Australia.

Within this category of structurally depressed industries, there may be another variation. An example is the aluminium and petro-chemical industries in Japan in the 1980s. In those industries, there were sufficient resources in terms of technology and personnel and they were not totally inefficient industries. However, they were hit hard by the Oil Crisis and rising costs of oil which followed the Oil Crisis. In these areas, industries in the United States enjoyed comparative advantages due to lower costs for oil and natural gas. Therefore, those industries in Japan experienced difficulties.

When enterprises are in the state of structural depression, they should exit from this sector, wind up business, or shift to another sector. However, there may be exit barriers. For example, if the industry is characterized as one in which the debt ratio is high, it would create difficulties for enterprises in the industry to exit since debt must first be liquidated and so they may find it difficult to shift to another sector. Also, if mobility of labour is low, it would create an exit barrier.

There is no completely satisfactory answer to the question of whether a structurally depressed industry should be given protection. The general principle is that a structurally depressed industry which in inefficient should not be given protection in a way which makes it possible for it to stay in existence in spite of its inefficiency. However, if a depressed industry is extinguished abruptly, it may cause social disruptions to the area which depends on that industry such as widespread unemployment. In this context, one may argue that a depressed industry should be given a certain time-period to phase itself out gradually. Even if the industry must be phased out, it should be given a 'soft landing' or 'comfortable death'.

Another structurally depressed industry may be revitalized by some government measures. For example, as in the aluminium and petro-chemical industries, they may suffer from excess production capacity and, if given some assistance to reduce this excess capacity by government measures, their conditions may improve and they may regain vitality.

It is probably true that government measures to deal with structurally depressed industries must vary from industry to industry depending on the nature of the problems. Sometimes the measures should aim at phasing out the industry over a certain period of time and at preparing a smooth way out. At other times, the measures should aim at providing some conditions for the industry so that it can remove barriers and difficulties and regain strength.

The OECD coped with this problem by announcing that the policy to deal with a structural depression would be that of a positive adjustment programme (the PAP) in which the government provides temporary assistance to the industry concerned. A reform programme should be formulated by the enterprises concerned and assistance in term of financial aid or otherwise should be given in accordance with the reform programme. Such a reform programme with government assistance should be carried out to a time-schedule. The PAP emphasizes that private initiatives should be utilized as much as possible along with government measures. Therefore, a joint venture of enterprises should be promoted.

B. DEPRESSION CARTEL

Article 24.3 of the AML is designed to provide temporary relief to enterprises when a cyclical depression causes serious injury to industries by allowing enterprises in an industry to agree upon a 'depression cartel' and cut back production. Under this article, when depression lowers price below the average cost of production, thereby causing the majority of enterprises in the affected industry to have difficulties in continuing their operations, and when this depression cannot be overcome by rationalization of enterprises, members of the depressed industry may enter into an agreement to cut back production, utilization of capacity, or sales quantity. If the above measures cannot be taken for some reason or if those measures prove to be ineffective, price-fixing is allowed.

When a depression comes and enterprises in an industry wish to enter into a depression cartel, they must file with the FTC a draft depression cartel agreement. Then the FTC examines the draft in the light of the requirements in Article 24.3 of the AML, and grants a licence to the depression cartel in question for a limited period of time. A depression cartel duly entered into under Article 24.3 of the AML is exempted from the application of the AML. A depression cartel is allowed only to manufacturing industries.

As stated earlier, a depression cartel is allowed only under stringent requirements such as that, in the industry in question, price must be below the average cost of production and there is no means to overcome the difficulty. A relief period is specified in the licence given by the FTC and it is usually quite short, such as a four-month or six-month period. From this, one can see that a depression cartel allowed under Article 24.3 of the AML is designed to deal with a cyclical depression but not a structural depression. Since there is no wording in Article 24.3 of the AML which says that a depression cartel cannot be used for the purpose of dealing with a structural depression, it could be used if parties chose to do so. However, it would be an ineffective tool to be used for this purpose.

C. MEASURES FOR STRUCTURALLY DEPRESSED INDUSTRIES

In Japan, the legislative policy is to extend some forms of government aid to structurally depressed industries, provided that they possess sufficient viability to be restored to competitiveness. The Specific Industries Structure Improvement Temporary Measures Law,[12] which existed between 1984 and 1988, was typical of such legislation. Although this law is defunct now, it serves as a model of measures to deal with structural depression, and the subsequent legislation is partly modelled on it. Therefore, it is worth while to take a brief look at this law and see how it operated.

Under this law, the MITI was authorized to designate an industry as a 'specific industry' which needed measures under this law. Basically there were two measures provided for. One was a type of depression cartel, and the other was a business co-operative arrangement. One cause of the economic difficulty in a structural depression is a surplus of production capacity in relation to effective demand. However, a company operating in the depressed industry tends to be reluctant unilaterally to cut back production capacity, since to do so would cause its market share to shrink if others did not cut back their production as well.

Under this law, the MITI was authorized to issue a directive (administrative guidance) to companies in a specific industry to cut back total production capacity and, in accordance with this directive, the companies entered into an agreement to limit total capacity in the industry and to allocate a quota to each company in cutting back production capacity. This directive was not compulsory but had a *de facto* impact on the industry. When companies in this industry agreed to cut back the excess production facility jointly, the government extended a loan guarantee to the companies to make it easier for the companies to borrow money from banks. This was an authorized cartel arrangement and an agreement to cut back the excess production facility under this law was exempted from the application of the AML.

The other device for dealing with a structurally depressed industry is a business co-operative arrangement. To implement this device, the MITI announced a master plan for reorganization of a designated industry, and the companies in the industry then developed a more elaborate programme including provisions for measures, such as mergers and acquisitions, the establishment of a joint buying or selling agency, and technological co-operation. These arrangements had to be approved by the MITI, and even though the approved arrangement did not technically enjoy exemption from the application of the AML, a negotiation between the MITI and the FTCJ preceded the approval and execution of the programme and this provided assurance that the FTCJ would not take action against an approved arrangement.

The above relief measures were applied in industries such as aluminium,

[12] Sanguyōkōzō Kaizen Rinji Sochi Hō, Law 44, 1983.

petro-chemicals, steel, and wood pulp, and accomplished some degree of success in alleviating the difficulty in those industries. This law expired in 1988 and was not renewed. However, this law may serve as a model for future measures which may be called for in dealing with depressed industries.

In 1987, a law entitled the Specific Industries Reorientation Law[13] was enacted. This legislation will last for nine years. The structure is somewhat similar to that of the previous law although there is no provision for an authorized cartel to cut back the excess production facility. The law shifts the resources of enterprises in a depressed industry to other sectors, which is in sharp contrast to the 1984 law in which an emphasis was placed on the restoration of competitiveness and efficiency in a depressed industry.

4.4 Price Control

A. AN OVERVIEW

As in other countries with a market economy, enterprises in Japan are generally free to set their own prices when they sell products or services. However, there are some situations in which the government interferes with the pricing. Areas such as public utilities (electricity, gas, transportation, and broadcasting) are typical of this public regulation of price. This is a vast field and outside of the scope of the present book. We merely note that the basic principle is that of cost plus fair return, that is, the price should be set at a level at which licensed enterprises can recover the cost of operations and earn a reasonable profit.

In this section, we shall examine two areas in which price control is exerted by the government. One is the price control to be exercised in times of emergency and crisis and the other is the price control which is exercised for the purpose of protecting some industries. They should be regarded as a deviation or abberation from the normal market principle and should be kept at a minimum. As such, however, there are some laws which authorize control and our attention will be focused on them.

B. PRICE CONTROL IN AN EMERGENCY

Owing to circumstances beyond the control of government and private enterprise, prices may rise suddenly, and the whole economy may be in panic. This is what happened in the Oil Crisis. Prices soared as soon as it

[13] Sangyokōzō Tenkan Enkatsuka Rinjisochi Hō, Law 24, 1987.

was learned that the oil supply would be reduced. Panic psychology drove people to buy more and induced merchants to hoard. The result was a catastrophe.

There are four laws to deal with an emergency like the Oil Crisis. One is the Price Control Order,[14] the second is the National Life Stabilization Emergency Measures Law,[15] the third is the Petroleum Products Demand and Supply Stabilization Law,[16] and the last is the Law against Speculation and Hoarding.[17] Except for the first one, all were enacted at the time of the Oil Crisis. Today none of these laws is used. However, they may be used if a crisis comes in the future.

In each of those laws, there are provisions which state that the government can intervene during emergencies and influence prices charged by private enterprise. The forms of intervention are different from one law to another.

The Price Control Order is the most direct form of governmental intervention in the activities of enterprises. Under this law, the government can announce a price freeze with regard to specific commodities during the state of emergency. A price freeze usually takes the form of a maximum price and a violation of it incurs a criminal liability. The Price Control Order was enacted in 1946 to cope with an extraordinary inflation which resulted from the devastation of the Second World War and often utilized in those days to control price hikes. Recently, however, this order has not been used. Even at the time of the Oil Crisis of 1973, the government chose not to utilize this order. It is extremely unlikely, therefore, that this order will be invoked at present or in the near future.

The National Life Stabilization Emergency Measures Law (hereafter referred to as the Stabilization Law) and the Petroleum Products Demand and Supply Stabilization Law are similar in the way in which they are enforced except for the fact that the latter law is applied only with regard to petroleum products. We will concentrate on the former.

The Stabilization Law was enacted in 1973 to deal with the price hike which resulted from the Oil Crisis. Even though this law was enacted too late to be effective as a measure to deal with the Oil Crisis, it is regarded as the prototype of a law which should be used to control price in time of emergency. When there is an emergency, the government sets up the standard price for a designated commodity. The standard price is generally the ceiling price (the maximum price) for the designated commodity. Such a designation can be made on many different kinds of commodity.

[14] Bukka Tosei Rei, Decree 118, 1946.
[15] Kokuminseikatsu Antei Kinkyū Sochi Hō, Law 121, 1973.
[16] Sekiyu Jukyū Tekiseika Hō, Law 122, 1973.
[17] Kaishime Urioshimi Bōshi Hō, Law 48, 1973.

The standard price is nothing but a guideline to be followed by sellers of the commodity, and a violation of it incurs no criminal liability or any other kind of formal sanction. When there is a violation of the standard price, the government publicizes the names of the parties which violated the standard price. Therefore, the effectiveness of this control is supported by the publicity effect of the announcement.

When it is judged that the standard price system has not been effectively enforced, the government can choose to establish the specific standard price. The specific standard price establishes the maximum limit for the price of a designated commodity and, when a seller of the commodity sells it at a price above the specific standard price, the government collects the difference between the two prices as a surcharge, thereby setting off the advantage that the seller made. Therefore, when the specific standard price is established, there is an administrative sanction in the form of a surcharge even if there is no criminal liability.

Beside the above two laws, there is a law entitled 'The Law Against Speculation and Hoarding'. This law is a result of the experiences of the Oil Crisis. In the Oil Crisis, there was a strong expectation on the part of the merchants who sold commodities that the prices of the commodities would go up. Some merchants engaged in hoarding and it pushed up prices even higher. This law was enacted to counteract such moves on the part of merchants who possessed the commodities. Under this law, the government can issue an order to merchants that they should discharge their stockpile when the emergency conditions require it and, in the event of non-compliance, the names of the parties which do not comply are published.

The laws such as the above are obviously emergency measures and if they are invoked lightly, it would seriously disrupt the operations of the market. Therefore, there are safeguards against them being invoked so lightly. First, there is a provision in all such laws that they should be invoked only in emergencies. Secondly, with regard to all those laws, the Cabinet must enact a cabinet decree before the government can issue an order under them. At present, there is no cabinet decree to that effect and, therefore, these laws cannot be invoked.

In the Oil Crisis, the National Diet enacted these laws to stabilize prices. However, in actuality, the government resorted to 'administrative guidance' as explained in an earlier section and it was more effective in stabilizing prices. The Cabinet made a resolution to establish the price reporting system in which each ministry issued a directive (administrative guidance) to enterprises under its supervision that whenever an enterprise wished to raise the price of a designated commodity, it must report to the ministry in charge and obtain the approval of the ministry.

C. PRICE REGULATION TO PROTECT DOMESTIC INDUSTRY

Beside those emergency laws, there are some laws which exert permanent price control in some areas of the economy. Most of them are in agriculture but there are some industrial areas in which there is a system of price regulation. In such areas, the price control is designed to protect specific sectors of the economy such as agriculture. The Food Control Law[18] is a typical example.

Under the Food Control Law, the power to purchase and sell rice is concentrated in the hands of the government. The government purchases rice from farmers and sells it to distributors, and the purchase price and sales price are determined by the government. The purchase price is determined by the government to guarantee that rice farmers recover the costs of production and earn a reasonable profit. The sales price, on the other hand, is determined to guarantee to consumers that it will not be too high. Therefore, the purchase price and the sales price are determined by different principles.

The decision on the purchase price is amenable to political pressures by agrarian groups and until some years ago it kept rising every year. It was impossible to raise the sales price to match the rise of the purchase price and the result was a huge deficit in the rice account of the government. At present, the rise of the purchase price has come to a natural ceiling and the purchase price is either pegged at the level of the previous year or declines.

This price-control system is part of the rice policy exercised by the Japanese government which includes, among other things, a 'setting aside' policy whereby farmers are directed to refrain from planting rice in some specified areas and thereby the amount of production and the prohibition of import of foreign produced rice is controlled. This latter aspect, of course, has created trade issues with the United States.

In other agricultural areas such as meat and dairy products, sugar and raw silk production, the price-stabilization programme operates. We have seen how the price stabilization programme operates in raw silk growing in connection with the *Kyoto Necktie* case[19] in Chapter 1. In other areas, such as meat, dairy products, and sugar production, the price-stabilization programme operates in much the same way. Generally, the Minister of Agriculture establishes the price range with a ceiling and a floor price, and the government or a government corporation engages in selling or buying operations. Whenever the market price goes up above the level of the ceiling, the government sells the commodity in question and makes the price come within the range. When the market price goes below the

[18] Shokuryō Kanri Hō, Law 40, 1942.

[19] See Chap. 1, 1.4, C, above.

range, the government buys the commodity so that the price will rise above the floor price.

Even if price control in emergencies may be justified as long as it is a temporary measure, it would be difficult to justify a permanent price-control system in areas such as agriculture. What makes the system of price support more problematical is the fact that the price-stabilization programme cannot be effectively enforced unless a control of imports is enforced at the same time. Sometimes this import control is executed by way of quantitative restrictions, as exemplified in the Silk Price Stabilization Law, and sometimes it is exercised by way of a differential tariff, in which the tariff equals the difference between the import price and the target price (a price for the domestic market established by the government by setting the ceiling and floor prices of a commodity). If import control is exercised by way of quantitative restriction, it raises the question of whether a restrictive measure is justified for the reason of food national security.

4.5 Protection of Medium and Small Businesses

A. AN OVERVIEW

The protection of medium and small businesses is an important part of industrial policy. The majority of Japanese enterprises are medium and small enterprises and they play an important role in the Japanese economy. They act as suppliers of parts and components, as small shops in local areas, as software houses for computers, as small-scale financial institutions for small business entities, as well as many other things. The sheer number of medium and small enterprises gives them a strong political power.

A 'medium and small enterprise' is generally defined as an enterprise whose employees number 300 or fewer, with capital totalling 100 million yen or less. For the sake of brevity, we will refer to them as 'small enterprises'. The problem of protecting small enterprises arises owing to, among other things, an imbalance in terms of bargaining power between them and large enterprises when they are in transactional relationships, their insufficient competitiveness when they are engaged in competition with large enterprises, and their instability in business operations due to the small-scale of their operations.

It may not always be true that a small enterprise is at a disadvantage in a transaction with a large enterprise or is less competitive compared with large enterprises. However, generally they *are* at a disadvantage in dealing with large enterprises. For example, they often operate as subcontractors to large enterprises, supplying parts and components. In transactions between large manufacturers and small subcontractors, the small subcontractors are generally disadvantaged due to the disparity in bargaining power.

Small enterprises also sometimes compete with large enterprises but again owing to their relative lack of efficiency and competitiveness, they are at a disadvantage.

Protection of small enterprises poses a troublesome problem in a market economy. From a pure market economy viewpoint, there should be no exceptions for small enterprises as far as the operation of the market is concerned, and if small enterprises are eliminated in the process of competition, it promotes efficiency in the economy. On the other hand, there may be an argument that the existence of many small enterprises is the basis of a diverse and pluralistic society. For example, artistic products produced by a small enterprise in one locality may be worth protecting because of their artistic value, even at the cost of some economic efficiency. In this view, the government should protect small enterprises not only for the sake of efficiency but for the promotion of other social values.

There is no clear-cut theory for dealing with the small business problem. Any policy toward small businesses reflects diverse and conflicting objectives and is bound to be a compromise and mixture of ambivalent political, social, and economic goals. Japanese industrial policy toward small businesses is typical of this conflict and confusion.

Laws concerning promotion and protection of small enterprises are many, but they may be classified into laws designed to: (1) promote modernization of small enterprises, (2) organize small enterprises into larger groups, (3) protect small subcontractors subject to large manufacturers, (4) facilitate technological development among small enterprises, (5) aid small enterprises in adjusting to the changing economic environment and in shifting their business to other areas, and (6) secure some business sectors or territories for small enterprises. Among the above, (2) and (6) raise problems in relation to the market principle and the price mechanism. We concentrate on these two aspects.

B. ORGANIZATION OF SMALL ENTERPRISES

There are several laws which authorize small enterprises to form associations or co-operatives of small enterprises. Among them, the important ones are: (1) the Medium and Small Business Organization Law,[20] (2) the

[20] Chūshōkigyō Dantai Hō, Law 185, 1957.

Medium and Small Business Co-operatives Law,[21] and (3) the Environmental Hygiene Law.[22]

The Medium and Small Business Organization Law (hereafter referred to as 'the Organization Law') allows small enterprises to form an association which is characterized as a variation of a depression cartel. As discussed earlier, a depression cartel is allowed under Article 24.3 of the AML. Compared with Article 24.3 of the AML, however, the Organization Law allows a depression cartel in the form of association under more lenient requirements. Also an association formed under the Organization Law can enforce not only measures to overcome depression but also measures for the improvement of management. Under this law, small enterprises can form an industry or commerce association and other related joint restrictions of competition whenever there is 'excessive competition' and 'instability of management' among member enterprises.

Measures that can be exercised by an industry and commerce association include, among others, a restriction of the quantity produced, of the kinds of products to be produced, and joint selling or buying. When those activities are proved to be ineffective in coping with problems of instability of management, price-fixing is also allowed. An industry or commerce association must be licensed by the MITI in order for it to operate lawfully. Activities of an industry or commerce association are exempted from the application of the AML except that unfair business practices are not allowed.

There is a provision in the Organization Law to authorize the MITI to issue an outsider regulation if it is proved that the operation of a commerce and industry association is made ineffective due to the activities of outsiders. An outsider regulation is either an order issued by the MITI to the effect that outsiders should join an industry and commerce association or an order fixing the quantity to be produced, the price to be charged, and other terms of business. To make certain that an order is not invoked too easily, complicated and elaborate procedures are provided, since to invoke it easily would be too supressive of competition.

One criticism raised against this law is that it has been used as a seedbed of cartels among large and small enterprises, since the law only requires that two-thirds of the members of an industry and commerce association be small enterprises and, therefore, large enterprises can join it.

The Medium and Small Business Co-operatives Law (hereafter referred to as 'the Co-operatives Law') authorizes small enterprises to establish a co-operative. The operation of a co-operative is similar but somewhat

[21] Chūshōkigyōtō Kyōdōkumiai Hō, Law 181, 1949.
[22] Kankyō Eisei Hō, Law 164, 1957.

different from an industry and commerce association authorized by the Organization Law, even though there are some overlaps between the activities of the two types of organizations. A small business co-operative is an organization in which members can engage in joint selling, joint buying, joint manufacturing, or other joint activities for the benefit of the members. The purpose of such a co-operative is to accomplish an economy of scale by combining demand, supply, and other resources of the members. For example, if a co-operative composed of 100 small enterprises is engaged in a joint purchasing activity and demand for raw material for 100 enterprises is combined together, the members can enjoy the economy of scale in buying raw materials through a joint purchase.

Also, small enterprises can form a co-operative and engage in joint research and development of technology or in a programme to rationalize management and operations.

When small enterprises are engaged in selling to or buying a product from large enterprises, they may be at a disadvantage *vis-à-vis* the large enterprises due to the difference in terms of bargaining power. In such a situation, small enterprises can form a co-operative and engage in joint selling or buying. This serves as a countervailing power in transactions with large enterprises and makes up the difference in terms of the lack of bargaining power.

Lastly, the federation of small business co-operatives is an important political organization and engages in voicing the views of small enterprises on certain political issues.

Activities of a small business co-operative are exempted from the application of the AML under Article 24 of the AML since activities of a small business co-operative are designed to strengthen the member small enterprises *vis-à-vis* large enterprises and to convert them into a stronger competitive unit. To that extent, there is no conflict between the activities of a small business co-operative and the market principle. However, there may be situations where small enterprises are the dominant force in a particular area and their combined power may be used against consumers by raising the price or against weaker enterprises. Therefore, the exemption from the application of the AML is not given when a co-operative raises prices unreasonably through substantial restraint of competition or utilizes unfair business practices.[23] When a large enterprise joins a co-operative, the FTCJ can order the large enterprise to withdraw from the co-operative.

Another piece of legislation is the Environmental Hygiene Law. The legislative purpose of this law is confused and activities of environmental hygiene associations authorized under this law have been criticized. How-

[23] Art. 24 of the AML.

ever, it still remains as an important piece of legislation in the area of small businesses. The alleged purpose of this law is to promote environmental hygiene. It provides that in order to achieve this objective, small enterprises in the 'hygiene business' may form an 'environmental sanitation association' which can fix prices and other terms of business for the members. Environmental hygiene business is defined in the law as including such businesses as hotels, inns, restaurants, public bathhouses, amusement facilities, shops in which fresh food is sold, and the like. The activities of an environmental hygiene association in fixing prices and other terms of business for the members are exempted from the application of the AML.

The rationale for this legislation is that excessive competition among these enterprises reduces profit, making it difficult for them to provide better environmental hygiene facilities. In this theory, if those enterprises are allowed to form an association and avoid competition among themselves, the greater profit which is earned by this restriction of competition enables them to provide funds to promote better environmental hygiene.

It seems that this legislation has not succeeded in achieving the objective for promoting environmental hygiene. This is probably due to an inherent contradiction involved in the legislation. There is no guarantee that enterprises will use the extra profit earned through restraint of competition to promote environmental hygiene. As shown in the barbershop business, which is designated as one of the environmental hygiene businesses, the higher profit rate made possible by price-fixing attracts more new entries into the market and causes the profit rate to go down. To cope with this situation, an association has to raise prices by price-fixing again, and this turns into a vicious circle.

This legislation is in fact aimed at protecting small enterprises in the name of promoting environmental hygiene. It is fair to say, however, that the legislation has produced more harm than gain to the public in the sense that prices of the services in the environmental hygiene businesses have risen and remain at a high level today. However, due to the great number of enterprises in the environmental hygiene business, environmental hygiene associations possess a strong political influence and this has prevented any change in the law, in spite of much criticism raised against the law and its enforcement.

C. SECURING OF BUSINESS OPPORTUNITIES FOR SMALL ENTERPRISES

There are several laws which secure business opportunities for small enterprises by restricting the new entry of large enterprises into some areas of business. Important laws include (1) the Medium and Small

Business Opportunities Adjustment Law,[24] (2) the Large-Scale Retail Stores Law,[25] and (3) the Retail Business Adjustment Special Measures Law.[26] Those three laws are based essentially on the objective of preserving some business sectors or geographical territories for the exclusive use of small enterprises. The first one deals with manufacturing and wholesale business, the second one is concerned with the retail business. The third one is essentially similar to the other two and will be omitted here.

All such laws have provisions which regulate new entry of large enterprises into the areas covered by the laws. By restricting new entry, these laws restrain competition between large and small enterprises and, for this reason, they pose problems with the competition policy. For the purpose of promoting efficiency, the existence of such laws is problematical. These laws are based not so much on the market principle as on the social policy of protecting weaker members of the business community.

The Medium and Small Business Opportunities Adjustment Law provides for the procedure under which small business organizations (which may be an organization under the Organization Law as discussed above) file a petition with the MITI to regulate new entry of a large enterprise into a field of business in which small business enterprises have been traditionally engaged. The MITI can advise a large enterprise entering the market to delay the new entry, scale down the proposed operations, or take other measures to mitigate the impact on small enterprises in the field. If the advice is not complied with, the MITI can issue an order to the same effect.

The Large-Scale Retail Stores Law establishes the procedure whereby a large-scale retail store (such as a supermarket) must file a report with the MITI when it intends to establish a new store in a local area if the floor space of the store to be established is above 3,000 square metres and to the prefectural government when the floor space is above 500 square metres. The report must first be filed by the person building the store and later by the person who will operate the retail business in it. There are complicated processes in which the newly entering large-scale store must explain its plan of business to local small shopkeepers with a view to obtaining their agreement, and will modify its business plan accordingly.

If the the government decides that small shopkeepers in the locality would be unduly disturbed or suppressed by the entry of the large-scale store, it can recommend that the large-scale retail store intending to enter the market stop entry, reduce the floor space of the store to be built, or

[24] Chūshōkigyō Jigyōbunya Chōsei Hō, Law 74, 1977.
[25] Daikibo Kouri Tenpo Hō, Law 109, 1973.
[26] Kourishōgyō Chōsei Tokubetsusochi Hō, Law 155, 1959.

delay the opening of the store. If the recommendation is not respected, the government can issue an order to the same effect.

It has been the practice in the past that the MITI or the prefectural government advised a newly opening supermarket to negotiate with organizations of shopkeepers in the local market to obtain their agreement. Only after the agreement had been obtained, would the MITI or the prefectural government accept the report by the supermarket.

The Large-Scale Retail Stores Law was a subject of SII negotiation between the United States and Japanese governments. The United States government argued that the restriction of entry of new supermarkets into local markets was an impediment to the access of foreign products into the Japanese market. The reasons are that whereas smaller retailers are often integrated within vertical distribution networks constructed by manufacturers and are not in a position to sell foreign-made products, supermarkets in Japan are relatively independent from large manufacturers and *are* in a position to sell foreign-made products. It argued that to restrict entry of supermarkets into local markets would mean that the sale of foreign-made products in Japan was impeded.

Also, in Japan, some critics have pointed out that this law has impeded the promotion of efficiency and modernization of distribution systems, that it has protected vested interests, that the process of examination and adjustment is so intransparent, and that it has been a barrier to innovative retailers to come into the market.

In response to the claim of the United States government, the Japanese government promised to amend the Large-Scale Retail Stores Law and relax the regulations under this law. Accordingly the examination period was shortened to the maximum of one year. It was provided also that the law would be reviewed after two years (that means in 1993). A separate law was enacted too which provides that when a supermarket intends to establish a space in a building which is solely devoted to selling imported commodities, there is no need to file a report with the government.

It is fair to say that the restriction of new entry by the Large-Scale Retail Stores Law has come to a turning-point. The trend in the future will be towards relaxation of the regulations under this law. As stated before, this law will be reviewed in future and it may be replaced by some legislation which is less restrictive.

Appendix

JAPANESE COMPETITION LAW

ACT CONCERNING PROHIBITION OF PRIVATE MONOPOLY AND MAINTENANCE OF FAIR TRADE

SEPTEMBER 1991

The Fair Trade Commission of Japan

---

1. Act Concerning Prohibition of Private Monopoly and Maintenance of Fair Trade (Act No. 54 of 14 April 1947)

CONTENTS

CHAPTER I: GENERAL PROVISIONS

Sec. 1 [Purpose]

This Act, by prohibiting private monopolization, unreasonable restraint of trade, and unfair trade practices, by preventing excessive concentration of economic power and by eliminating unreasonable restraint of production, sale, price, technology, and the like, and all other unjust restriction of business activities through combinations, agreements, and otherwise, aims to promote free and fair competition, to stimulate the creative initiative of entrepreneurs, to encourage business activities of enterprises, to heighten the level of employment and people's real income, and thereby to promote the democratic and wholesome development of the national economy as well as to assure the interests of consumers in general.

Sec. 2 [Definitions]

(1) The term 'entrepreneur' as used in this Act shall mean a person, who carries on a commercial, industrial, financial, or any other business. Any officer, employee, agent, or any other person who acts for the benefit of any entrepreneur shall be deemed to be an entrepreneur in regard to the application of the provisions of the following subsection and of Chapter III [trade associations] of this Act.

(2) The term 'trade association' as used in this Act shall mean any combination or federation of combinations of two or more entrepreneurs having as its principal purpose the furtherance of their common business interest as entrepreneurs and includes one taking either of the following forms: Provided, That a combination or federation of combinations of two or more entrepreneurs, whose stock or other share capital is owned by the constituent entrepreneurs, and whose principal purpose is to operate and which is actually operating a commercial, industrial, financial, or any other business for profit shall not be included:

(i) Any association incorporated or not incorporated of which two or more entrepreneurs are members (including any position similar thereto).

(ii) Any foundation with or without juridical personality of which two or more entrepreneurs control the appointment or dismissal of directors or managers, the execution or existence of business.

(iii) Any partnership of which two or more entrepreneurs are members, or any contractual combination of two or more entrepreneurs.

(3) The term 'officer' as used in this Act shall mean a director, a partner with unlimited liabilities and executive power, an auditor, or any person with a similar position, a manager, or other employee in charge of business of the main or branch office.

(4) The term 'competition' as used in this Act shall mean a situation in which two or more entrepreneurs do or may, within the normal scope of their business activities and without undertaking any important change in their business facilities or kinds of business activities, engage in any act prescribed in any one of the following paragraphs: Provided, That paragraph (ii) below shall not apply to such competition as provided for in Chapter IV [Stockholding, interlocking directorates, mergers and acquisitions of business]:

(i) Supplying the same or similar goods or services to the same consumers or users.
(ii) Getting supplies of the same or similar goods or services from the same supplier.

(5) The term 'private monopolization' as used in this Act shall mean that any entrepreneur, individually or by combination or conspiracy with other entrepreneurs, or by in any other manner, excludes or controls the business activities of other entrepreneurs, therby restraining, contrary to the public interest, substantially competition in any particular field of trade.

(6) The term 'unreasonable restraint of trade' as used in this Act shall mean that any entrepreneur, by contract, agreement, or any other concerted actions, irrespective of the names, with other entrepreneurs, mutually restrict or conduct their business activities in such a manner as to fix, maintain, or increase prices, or to limit production, technology, products, facilities, or customers or suppliers, thereby restraining, contrary to the public interest, substantially, competition in any particular field of trade.

(7) The term 'monopolistic situation' as used in this Act shall mean that each of the following market structures and undesirable market performances exist in any particular field of business where the aggregate total amount of prices (this term refers to the prices of the goods concerned less a sum equivalent to the amount of taxes levied directly on such goods) of goods of the same description (including goods capable of being supplied without making any significant change to their business facilities or kind of business activities; hereinafter in this subsection referred to as 'particular goods') and those of any other goods having a strikingly similar function and utility thereto, which are supplied in Japan (excluding those exported) or the total amount of prices (this term refers to the prices of the services concerned less a sum equivalent to the amount of taxes levied on the receipient of such services with respect thereto) of services of the same description which are supplied in Japan, during the latest one-year period designated by a Cabinet Ordinance, is in excess of fifty billion yen:

(i) Where the market share (this refers to the ratio accounted for by the aggregate volume) (in case it is not appropriate to be calculated by the quantity, the quantity shall be represented in terms of the amount of their prices; the same shall apply hereinafter in this paragraph) of the particular goods and any other goods having a strikingly similar function and utility thereto or by the volume of the services, which are supplied by the entrepreneur or entrepreneurs concerned, to total volume of those supplied in Japan (excluding those exported) of an entrepreneur exceeds one-half or where the combined market share of two entrepreneurs exceeds three-fourths during a given one-year period.
(ii) Where there exists conditions which make it extremely difficult for any other entrepreneur to be newly engaged in the said particular field of business.
(iii) Where the increase in the price of the particular goods or services supplied by the entrepreneur concerned has been remarkable or the decrease therein has been slight for a considerable period of time in the light of changes occurred in the supply and demand, or in the cost of supplying for such

certain goods or services during such period, and where, in addition thereto, the said entrepreneur has fallen under any one of the following requirements during the said period:

(*a*) that the entrepreneur has earned profit rate far exceeding that which is established by a Cabinet Ordinance as the norm for the class of business designated by such Cabinet Ordinance to which the said entrepreneur belongs; or

(*b*) that the entrepreneur has expended a level of selling costs and general administrative expenses far exceeding one which is considered as the norm for the field of business to which the entrepreneur belongs.

(8) In the event any change has occurred in the economic conditions resulting in a drastic change in domestic industrial shipments and wholesale prices, the amount of prices as prescribed in the preceding subsection may be revised by virtue of a Cabinet Ordinance to reflect such change.

(9) The term 'unfair trade practices' as used in this Act shall mean any act coming under any one of the following paragraphs, which tends to impede the fair competition and which is designated by the Fair Trade Commission as such:

(i) Unjustly discriminating against other entrepreneurs.
(ii) Dealing at unjust prices.
(iii) Unjustly inducing or coercing customers of a competitor to deal with oneself.
(iv) Dealing with another party on such terms as will restrict unjustly the business activities of the said party.
(v) Dealing with another party by unjust use of one's bargaining position.
(vi) Unjustly interfering with a transaction between an entrepreneur who competes in Japan with oneself or the company of which oneself is a stockholder or an officer and another transacting party; or, in case such entrepreneur is a company, unjustly inducing, instigating, or coercing a stockholder or an officer of such company to act against the interest of such company.

CHAPTER II: PRIVATE MONOPOLIZATION AND UNREASONABLE RESTRAINT OF TRADE

Sec. 3 [Prohibition of private monopolization or unreasonable restraint of trade]
No entrepreneur shall effect private monopolization or any unreasonable restraint of trade.

Sec. 4 [Prohibition of particular concerted practices]
Deleted. (Act No. 259 of 1953)

Sec. 5 [Prohibition of private control organization]
Deleted. (Act No. 259 of 1953)

Sec. 6 [Prohibition of particular international agreements or contracts, filing requirement]
(1) No entrepreneur shall enter into an international agreement or an interna-

tional contract which contains such matters as constitute unreasonable restraint of trade or unfair trade practices.

(2) An entrepreneur who has entered into an international agreement or an international contract (limited to only such an agreement or a contract that belongs to the types which are prescribed by the Rules of the Fair Trade Commission as tending to contain such matters as constitute unreasonable restraint of trade or unfair trade practices) shall, in accordance with the Rules of The Fair Trade Commission, file a notification thereof with the Commission, accompanied by a copy of the said agreement or contract (in the case of an oral agreement or contract, a document describing the contents thereof), within thirty days as from the conclusion of such agreement or contract.

Sec. 7 [Elimination measures against private monopolization, unreasonable restraint of trade or particular international agreements or contracts]

(1) In case there exists any act in violation of the provisions of Section 3 [prohibition of unreasonable restraint of trade or unfair trade practices], or Subsection (1) or (2) of the preceding section, the Fair Trade Commission may, in accordance with the procedures as provided for in Division II [procedures], Chapter VIII, order the entrepreneur concerned to file notifications, or to cease and desist from such acts, to transfer a part of his business, or to take any other measures necessary to eliminate such acts in violation of the said provisions.

(2) The Fair Trade Commission may, when it finds it particularly necessary, even when an act in violation of the provisions of Section 3 [prohibition of private monopolization or unreasonable restraint of trade] has already ceased to exist, order the entrepreneurs concerned, in accordance with the procedures as provided for in Division II [procedures], Chapter VIII, to take measures to publicize that the said act has been discontinued and order any other measures necessary to ensure elimination of the said act: Provided, That the foregoing shall not apply to cases where one year has elapsed since the data of ceasing of the said act without recommendation being given to the entrepreneur concerned or without the hearing procedures being initiated with respect to the said act.

Sec. 7.2 [Surcharges]

(1) In case any entrepreneur effects an unreasonable restraint of trade or enters into an international agreement or an international contract containing such matters as constitute an unreasonable restraint of trade, which pertains to the price of goods or services or results in affecting in effect the price of such goods or services by curtailing the volume of supply thereof, the Fair Trade Commission shall order the entrepreneur concerned, in accordance with the procedures as provided for in Division II [procedures], Chapter VIII, to pay to the Treasury a surcharge of an amount equivalent to an amount arrived at by multiplying the sales amount of such goods or services, computed in accordance with the method prescribed by a Cabinet Ordinance, for the period from the date on which the entrepreneur was engaged in the business activities as implementation of such conduct to the date on which the entrepreneur ceased to engage in the business activities as implementation of such conduct (in case such period exceeds three years, the period shall be for three years retroactively from the data on which the

entrepreneur ceased to engage in the business activities as implementation of such conduct; hereinafter referred to as 'period of such implementation') by 6 per cent (or by 2 per cent for retail business or by 1 per cent for wholesale business): Provided, That in case the amount thus computed falls below 500,000 yen, the Commission shall not order the payment of such a surcharge.

(2) In the case of the preceding Subsection, the term '6 per cent' appearing in the preceding Subsection shall be '3 per cent' and the term '2 per cent' shall be '1 per cent', if the entrepreneur falls under any one of the following paragraphs:

(i) Any company whose capital or subscription is not more than 100 million yen and any company or individual whose pay-roll employees are not more than 300 persons, whose main activity is to carry on business in the fields of manufacturing, mining, transportation and other kinds of business (excluding the kinds of business stipulated in paragraph (ii) of this Subsection and the kinds of business stipulated by the Cabinet Ordinance pursuant to paragraph (iii) of this Subsection);

(ii) Any company whose capital or subscription is not more than 10 million yen and any company or individual whose pay-roll employees are not more than 50 persons, whose main activity is to carry on business in the fields of retail trade or services (excluding the kinds of business stipulated in the Cabinet Ordinance pursuant to paragraph (iii) of this Subsection); and any company whose capital or subscription is not more than 30 million yen and any company or individual whose pay-roll employees are not more than 100 persons, whose main activity is to carry on business in the wholesale trade (excluding the kinds of business stipulated in the Cabinet Ordinance pursuant to paragraph (iii) of this Subsection); or

(iii) Any company whose capital or subscription is not more than that specified by the Cabinet Ordinance for each kind of business and any company or individual whose pay-roll employees are not more than that specified by the Cabinet Ordinance for each kind of business, whose main activity is to carry on business in fields specified by such Cabinet Ordinance.

(3) Any person who has received an order under the provisions of Subsection (1) shall pay the surcharges as provided for in Subsection (1) and (2) of this Section.

(4) In case the amount of surchange computed in accordance with the provisions of Subsection (1) or (2) of this Section contains a fraction less than 10,000 yen, such fraction shall be disregarded.

(5) In case the entrepreneur who has committed an act in violation of the provision of Subsection (1) above is a company and if such company has ceased to exist through a merger with another company, the violation of such company shall be considered as a violation of the merging company or consolidated company as a result of the merger, and the provisions of the each preceding Subsection shall apply thereto.

(6) When a period of three years has elapsed from the date of expiration of the period of such implementation (or when a period of one year has elapsed from the date on which the hearing procedures ended in case such hearing procedures had been initiated with respect to such a violation (in case the expiration of the

three-year period following the expiration of the period of such implementation, then the date on which the three-year period expired)), the Fair Trade Commission shall not order such entrepreneur to pay a surcharge for such violation: Provided, That the foregoing shall not apply to cases where the Fair Trade Commission has ordered to pay the surcharge for the said violation to the Treasury under the provisions of Section 48.2(1) [surcharge payment order] and thereafter.

CHAPTER III: TRADE ASSOCIATIONS

Sec. 8 [Prohibited acts of a trade association, filing requirement]

(1) No trade association shall engage in any acts which come under any one of the following paragraphs:

(i) Substantially restraining competition in any particular field of trade.
(ii) Entering into an international agreement or an international contract as provided for in Section 6(1).
(iii) Limiting the present or future number of entrepreneurs in any particular field of business.
(iv) Unjustly restricting the functions or activities of the constituent entrepreneurs (meaning an entrepreneur who is a member of the trade association; hereinafter the same).
(v) Causing entrepreneurs to employ such acts as constitute unfair trade practices.

(2) Every trade association shall, when formed, in accordance with the Rules of the Fair Trade Commission, field a notification thereof with the Commission within thirty days as from the date of its formation.

(3) When any change has occurred to the matters relating to the notification under the preceding subsection, the trade association concerned shall, in accordance with the Rules of the Fair Trade Commission, file a notification thereof with the Commission, within two months after the end of the business year during which such change occurred.

(4) Every trade association shall, when dissolved, in accordance with the Rules of the Fair Trade Commission, file a notification thereof with the Commission within thirty days as from the data of its dissolution.

Sec. 8.2 [Elimination measures against prohibited acts of trade associations]

(1) When there exists any act in violation of the provisions of the preceding section, the Fair Trade Commission may, in accordance with the procedures as provided for in Division II [procedures], Chapter VIII, order the trade association concerned to file a notification, or to cease and desist from such act, to dissolve the said association, or to take any other measures necessary to eliminate the said act.

(2) The provisions of Section 7(2) [measures against already ceased violation] shall apply *mutatis mutandis* to any act in violation of the provisions of Subsection (1)(i), (iv) or (v) of the preceding section.

(3) The Fair Trade Commission may, in accordance with the procedures as

provided for in Division II (procedures), Chapter VIII, in ordering a trade association to take any of the measures set forth in Subsection (1) above or Section 7(2) applied *mutatis mutandis* under the provision of the preceding subsection, when it finds it particularly necessary, at the same time order an officer, manager or constituent entrepreneur (including other entrepreneur when a constituent entrepreneur is acting for the benefit of the entrepreneur; the same shall apply in Section 48 [recommendation] (1) and (2)) of the said association to take measures necessary to ensure the measures provided for in Subsection (1) above or Section 7(2) applicable *mutatis mutandis* under the provision of the preceding subsection.

Sec. 8.3 [Surcharges imposed on constituent entrepreneurs]

The provisions of Section 7.2 [Surcharge] shall apply *mutatis mutandis* to cases where an act is committed in violation of the provisions of Section 8(1) [prohibited acts of a trade association] (i) or (ii) (applying only to such an entrepreneur who is a party to an international agreement or an international contract which contains such matters which constitute an unreasonable restraint of trade). In this case, the term 'any entrepreneur' appearing in Subsection (1) of Section 7.2 shall read 'any trade association', the term 'the entrepreneur concerned' appearing therein shall read 'the constituent entrepreneur (other entrepreneur when a constituent entrepreneur is acting for the benefit of the entrepreneur; the same shall apply hereinafter in this Section) of the trade association concerned and the term 'such entrepreneur' appearing in Subsection (2) of the said Section shall read 'the constituent entrepreneur of such trade association concerned'.

CHAPTER III-II: MONOPOLISTIC SITUATIONS

Sec. 8.4 [Measures against monopolistic situations]

(1) When there exists a monopolistic situation, the Fair Trade Commission may order the entrepreneur concerned, in accordance with the procedures as provided for in Division II [procedures], Chapter VIII, to transfer a part of his business or to take any other measures necessary to restore competition with respect to such goods or services: Provided, That the foregoing shall not apply to cases where the Commission finds that such measures may reduce the scale of business of the said entrepreneur to such an extent that the costs required for the supply of goods or services which such entrepreneur supplies will rise sharply, undermine its financial position and make it difficult for the entrepreneur to maintain its international competitiveness, or where other alternative measures may be taken which the Commission finds sufficient to restore competition with respect to such goods or services.

(2) In issuing an order prescribed in the preceding subsection, the Fair Trade Commission shall give consideration, based on the items prescribed in each of the following paragraphs, to the smooth conduct of business activities by the entrepreneurs concerned, and those associated with them and the stabilization of livelihood for those employed by such enterpreneurs:

(i) Assets, income and expenditures and other aspects of accounting.

(ii) Officers and employees.
(iii) Location of factories, workyards and offices and other locational conditions.
(vi) Aspects of business facilities and equipments.
(v) The substance of patent rights, trademark rights and other intangible property rights and the technological features.
(vi) Capacity for and situations of production and sales, etc.
(vii) Capacity for and situations of obtaining funds and materials, etc.
(viii) Situations of supply and distribution of goods or services.

CHAPTER IV: STOCKHOLDINGS, INTERLOCKING DIRECTORATES, MERGERS AND ACQUISITIONS OF BUSINESS

Sec. 9 [Prohibition of holding company]

(1) No holding company shall be established.

(2) Any company (including a foreign company; hereinafter the same) shall not operate as a holding company in Japan.

(3) The term 'holding company' as used in the preceding two subsections shall mean company whose principal business is to control the business activities of a company or companies in Japan by means of holding of stock (including shares of partnership; hereinafter the same).

Sec. 9.2 [Restriction on total amount of stockholding by a giant non-financial company]

(1) Any stock company whose business is other than financial (this term refers to those engaged in banking, mutual banking, trust, insurance, mutual financing and securities businesses; the same meaning shall apply hereinafter) and whose capital is larger than 10 billion yen or whose net assets (this term refers to the sum of an amount arrived at by deducting the total liabilities from the total assets listed in the latest balance sheet and the amount by which the net assets have increased as a result of an issuance of new stock in accordance with the provisions of Section 280.2 of the Commercial Code (Act No. 48 of 1899) or as a result of an issuance of new stock by the exercise of pre-emptive right endowed by right corporate bonds, or as a result of a merger or the conversion of corporate bonds, if any; hereinafter the same meaning shall apply in this section) are larger than 30 billion yen shall not acquire or hold stock of companies in Japan in excess of its capital or its net assets, whichever is larger (hereinafter referred to as 'the base amount'), if by so doing total amount of acquiring price of such stocks (another price if it is listed so in the latest balance sheet; the same meaning shall apply hereinafter) which it has acquired or holds exceeds the base amount: Provided, That the foregoing shall not apply to the acquisition or holding of such stock in the cases provided for in any one of the following paragraphs;

(i) The acquisition or holding of stock of a company in Japan which has been prescribed by a Cabinet Ordinance and which has been invested in by a juridical person established by the government, a local public authority, or a special law whose total amount of capital is owned by the government or whose liabilities may be contractually guaranteed by the government;

(ii) The acquisition or holding of stock of a company in Japan, as prescribed by a Cabinet Ordinance, engaged in a business contributive to the development of industries and the progress of economic societies, which requires large sum of funds of such a magnitude as to make it difficult to procure by ordinary means;

(iii) The acquisition or holding of stock of a company in Japan whose purpose is to engage in any one or two or more of the following businesses, and which perform business activities pursuant to the objective thereof;
(*a*) Business undertaken outside Japan (including the business undertaken in Japan which is closely connected with, and incidental to, such business);
(*b*) Business of investment or long-term loans to foreign governments or foreign juridical persons (including those businesses which are closely connected with, and incidential to, such businesses, hereinafter referred to as 'investment and financing business');
(*c*) Investment and financing business to the companies provided for in the preceding paragraph; or
(*d*) Investment and financing business to the companies which fall under the purview of this paragraph;

(iv) The acquisition or holding of stock of a company in Japan, as prescribed by a Cabinet Ordinance, engaged in the business provided for in paragraph (ii) above, and in the investment and financing business as provided for in the preceding paragraph;

(v) The acquisition or holding of stock of a company in Japan, established by partially separating the business actually performed by itself, whose issued stock is wholly aquired or owned immediately after the establishment by itself; Provided, That this shall apply only to cases where such stock is held for two years or less from the said company's establishment;

(vi) The acquisition or holding of stock of a company in Japan, established by joint investment with a foreign government, foreign juridical person or foreign national (referred to as 'co-investment company' in Subsection (5) below) when it is particularly necessary for the operation of its business to take the form of such a co-investment company therein; Provided, That this shall apply only to such cases where authorization of the Fair Trade Commission is obtained in advance in accordance with the provisions of the Rules of the Commission;

(vii) The acquisition or holding of new stock aquired or held due to a stockholder allocation or stock dividends on currently held stock (excluding the stock held under the provisions of the paragraphs (i) to (iv) inclusive of the preceding paragraph); Provided, That this shall apply only to cases of stock held for two years or less from the date of its acquisition;

(viii) The acquisition or holding of stock as the result of the enforcement of a lien, pledge, mortgage, or as the result of payment in kind; Provided, That this shall apply only to cases of stock held for a year or less from the date of their acquisition (or for one year or less from the date on which it is decided to conclude rehabilitation procedures, in case the stock is deemed to have been acquired through payment in kind under the provision of Section 265 [special provisions to Section 9.2 or Section 11 of the Act] of the Company Rehabilitation Act (Act No. 172 of 1952)]; or

(ix) The acquisition or holding of stock of a company in Japan for an imperative reason; Provided, That this shall apply only to cases where approval of the Fair Trade Commission is obtained in advance (or without delay after the acquisition of such stock, in case they are acquired under urgent and imperative circumstances) in accordance with provisions of the Rules of the Fair Trade Commission, and where such stock is held for the period or less stipulated by such approval.

(2) If, as a result of a decrease in the base amount of the stock company as provided for in the preceeding subsection, the total amount of the acquisition price of stock held in companies in Japan (excluding the holdings which fall under any one of the paragraphs of the said subsection; the same shall apply in the following subsection) turns out to be in excess of the base amount, the total amount of such acquisition price shall be deemed as the base amount for the purpose of applying the provisions of the preceding subsection during the five years beginning from the date on which the acquisition price exceeded the base amount.

(3) In case the base amount decreases still more during the period under the preceding subsection, the base amount determined prior to such decrease or the total amount of the acquisition price of stock held in companies in Japan as of the date on which the period as provided for in the preceding subsection expired, whichever is the smaller, shall be deemed as the base amount for the purpose of applying the provisions of Subsection (1) above during the five-year period. The same shall apply to cases where the base amount decreased still more during the five-year period immediately following such decrease.

(4) The provisions of the preceding two subsections shall not apply to cases where the base amount has increased beyond the amount which is deemed as the base amount then effective under these provisions.

(5) When the Fair Trade Commission grants authorization under Subsection (1)(vi), it shall, in advance, consult with the Minister of Finance and the competent minister having jurisdiction over the business in which the co-investment company is engaged.

(6) When the Fair Trade Commission grants authorization under Subsection (1)(vi) or approval under paragraph (ix) of the said subsection, the Commission shall, in advance, consult with the minister or ministers who are empowered by virtue of a special statute to make recommendations or give instructions with respect to the financial management of the companies which seek to acquire stock and are subject to such authorization or approval.

(7) In case a company which falls under Subsection (1)(iii) above ceases to become subject thereto, the provision of the said subsection shall not apply to the holding of stock of such company for one year immediately following the date on which such company ceased to fall thereunder.

(8) In case any company acquires stock of another company in Japan under urgent and imperative circumstances subject to an *ex post facto* approval under Subsection (1)(ix) above and fails to obtain such approval, the provision of the said subsection shall not apply to the holding of such stock for one month immediately following the date on which such company failed to obtain such approval.

(9) In the event, as a result of a change in economic conditions, any drastic increase or decrease occurs in the amounts of capital and net assets of the stock companies which rank among the largest two hundred in terms of the size of their capital and net assets (excluding those engaged in financial business; the same shall apply in this subsection), a separate provision may be instituted with respect to the amount stipulated in Subsection (1) by virtue of a Cabinet Ordinance.

Sec. 10 [Prohibition of particular stockholding by a company, filling requirement]

(1) No company shall acquire or hold stock of a company or companies in Japan where the effect of such acquisition or holding of stock may be substantially to restrain competition in any particular field of trade, or shall acquire or hold stock of a company or companies in Japan through unfair trade practices.

(2) Every company in Japan whose business is other than financial and whose total assets (meaning total amount of the assets according to the latest balance sheet; hereinafter the same) exceed two billion yen or every foreign company whose business is other than financial, shall, in case it holds stock of another company or companies in Japan (including the stock held in the form of trust property of pecuniary or security trust of which it is a trustor or beneficiary and can exercise the voting rights or where such trustor can issue instructions regarding the exercise of such voting rights), submit, in accordance with the Rules of the Fair Trade Commission, a report on such stock held in its name or in the name of trustee as of the end of every business year to the Commission within three months therefrom.

Sec. 11 [Restriction on stockholding rate by a financial company]

(1) No company engaged in financial business shall acquire or hold stock of another company in Japan if by doing so it holds in excess of 5 per cent (10 per cent in the case of an insurance company) of the total outstanding stock: Provided, That the foregoing shall not apply to such cases where authorization of the Fair Trade Commission is obtained in advance in accordance with the Rules of the Fair Trade Commission, or to such cases falling under any one of the following paragraphs:

(i) Acquisition or holding of stock as the result of the enforcement of lien, pledge, mortgage, or of payment in kind.
(ii) Acquisition or holding of stock by a company engaging in securities in the course of its business.
(iii) Acquisition or holding of stock in the form of trust property of pecuniary or securities trust; Provided, That this shall apply only to cases where the trustor or the beneficiary of such trust property can exercise his voting rights or where such trustor or beneficiary can issue instructions regarding the exercise of such voting rights.

(2) Any company whose business is financial, being desirous, in the case of paragraphs (i) and (ii) of the preceding subsection, of holding stock of another company or companies in Japan over the period of one year from the date of such acquisition in excess of 5 per cent of the total outstanding stock, shall, in accordance with the Rules of the Fair Trade Commission, obtain authorization in advance from the Commission. The authorization of the Fair Trade Commission

in such case shall be granted with a condition that the company engaged in financial business should promptly dispose of the said stock.

(3) When the Fair Trade Commission grants authorization under the provisions of the two preceding subsections, it shall, in advance, consult with the Minister of Finance.

Sec. 12 [Restriction on acquisition of corporate bonds]

Deleted. (Act No. 214 of 1949)

Sec. 13 [Prohibition of particular interlocking directorates, filing requirement]

(1) Neither an officer nor an employee (meaning in this section a person other than officers in the regular employment of a company) of a company shall hold at the same time a position as an officer in another company or companies in Japan wherever such an interlocking directorate may be substantially to restrain competition in any particular field of trade.

(2) No company shall coerce another company or companies in Japan in competition with it in Japan, through unfair trade practices, to admit one of its officers concurrently to the position of an officer or an employee of the latter company or companies, or to admit its employee, concurrently to the position of an officer of such company or companies.

(3) Every officer or employee of a company who holds concurrently the position of an officer in another company or companies in Japan in competition with it in Japan, shall, in case the total assets of either one company exceed 2 billion yen, file, in accordance with the Rules of the Fair Trade Commission, a notification thereof with the Commission within thirty days as from the date of assuming the position of such an officer.

Sec. 14 [Prohibition of particular stockholding by a person other than a company, filing requirement]

(1) No person other than a company shall acquire or hold stock of another company or companies in Japan whenever such acquisition or holding of stock may be substantially to restrain competition in any particular field of trade, or shall acquire or hold stock of another company or companies in Japan through unfair trade practices.

(2) Every person other than a company shall, in case he has come to hold stock of two or more companies mutually competing in Japan in excess of 10 per cent of the total outstanding stock of the respective company, submit in accordance with the Rules of the Fair Trade Commission, a report on such stock to the Commission within thirty days as from the date of such holding.

Sec. 15 [Prohibition of particular mergers, filing requirement]

(1) No company in Japan shall effect a merger in any one of the following paragraphs:

(i) Where the effect of a merger may be substantially to restrain competition in any particular field of trade.

(ii) Where unfair trade practices have been employed in the course of the merger.

(2) Every company in Japan, which is desirous of becoming a party to a merger shall, in accordance with the provisions of the Rules of the Fair Trade Commission, file a notification with the Commission.

(3) No company in Japan shall, in the cases coming under the preceding subsection, effect a merger until the expiration of a thirty-day waiting period from the date of the issuance of the receipt of the said report: Provided, That the Fair Trade Commission may, when it finds it necessary, shorten the said period, or extend it by an additional period of time not exceeding sixty days with the consent of the companies concerned.

(4) The Fair Trade Commission shall, where it determines to initiate hearing proceedings or makes a recommendation with a view to ordering the necessary measures relating to the merger in question pursuant to the provisions of Section 17.2 [elimination measures against unlawful acts relating to a company], do so before the expiration of a thirty-day waiting period as provided for in the preceding subsection, or of any shortened or extended period under the proviso thereof: Provided, That the foregoing provisions shall not apply in cases where there has been a false statement with respect to important matters in the report specified in Subsection (2) above.

Sec. 16 [Prohibition of particular acquisitions of business, filing requirement]

The provisions of the preceding section shall apply *mutatis mutandis* to an act of a company coming under any one of the following paragraphs:

(i) Acquiring the whole or a substantial part of the business in Japan of another company.

(ii) Acquiring the whole or a substantial part of the fixed assets used for the business in Japan of another company.

(iii) Taking on lease of the whole or a substantial part of the business in Japan of another company.

(iv) Undertaking the management of the whole or a substantial part of the business in Japan of another company.

(v) Entering into a contract which provides for a joint profit and loss account for business in Japan with another company.

Sec. 17 [Prohibition of evasion]

No acts in whatever form or manner shall be committed to evade such prohibitions or restrictions as provided for by Section 9 to the preceding section inclusive [prohibition of a holding company, restriction on total amount of stockholding by a giant non-financial company, prohibition of particular stockholding by a company, restriction on stockholding rate by a financial company, prohibition of particular interlocking directorate, prohibition of particular stockholding by a person other than a company, prohibition of particular merger, prohibition of particular acquisition of business].

Sec. 17.2 [Elimination measures against unlawful acts relating to a company, etc.]

(1) Where there exists any act in violation of the provisions of Section 9.2(1) [restriction on total amount of stockholding by a giant non-financial company], Section 10 [prohibition of particular stockholding by a company], Section 11(1)

[restriction on stockholding rate by a financial company], Section 15(1) [prohibition of particular merger] (including such cases where the said provisions are applied *mutatis mutandis* by Section 16 [prohibition of particular acquisition of business]) or the preceding section, the Fair Trade Commission may, in accordance with the procedures as provided for in Division II (procedures), Chapter VIII, order the entrepreneur concerned to submit a report, or to dispose of the whole or a part of his holding stocks, to transfer a part of his business, or to take any other measures necessary to eliminate such acts in violation of the said provisions.

(2) Where there exists any act in violation of the provisions of Section 9(1) [prohibition of establishment of a holding company] or (2) [prohibition of operation as a holding company], Section 13 [prohibition of particular interlocking directorates], Section 14 [prohibition of particular stockholding by a person other than a company] or the preceding section, the Fair Trade Commission may, in accordance with the procedures as provided for in Division II [procedures], Chapter VIII, order the person violating such provisions to submit a report or file a notification, or to dispose of the whole or a part of his stocks, to resign from his position as an officer in a company, or to take any other measures necessary to eliminate such violation.

Sec. 18 [Measures against the establishment of a holding company or an illegal merger]

The Fair Trade Commission may, in cases where any company has been established in violation of the provisions of Section 9(1) [prohibition of establishment of a holding company] or companies have merged in violation of the provisions of Section 15(2) [filing of merger] and (3) [waiting period of merger], bring a suit to have the said establishment or merger declared null and void.

CHAPTER IV.II: PARALLEL PRICE INCREASES

Sec. 18.2 [Reporting requirement on parallel price increases]

(1) If, in any particular field of business where the total price of goods (this term refers to the price of the goods concerned less an amount equivalent to the amount of taxes levied directly on such goods) of the same description supplied in Japan (excluding those exported; hereinafter the same in this section) or the total prices of services (this refers to the price of the services concerned less an amount equivalent to the amount of taxes levied on the recipients of such services with respect thereto) of the same description supplied in Japan during a one-year period designated by a Cabinet Ordinance, is in excess of 30 billion yen, the ratio of the total amount of such goods or services supplied by the three enterpreneurs, which rank among the three largest entrepreneurs in Japan in terms of volume of supply (this refers to the quantity of goods or services of the same description which one entrepreneur supplied during a given one-year period, and in case it is not appropriate to be calculated by the quantity, the quantity shall be represented in terms of the amount of their prices; hereinafter the same meaning in this section) to the aggregate volume of such goods or services of the same description supplied in Japan during such one-year period (hereinafter referred to as 'the

aggregate volume') exceeds seven-tenths, and if two or more major entrepreneurs (including the largest one) (this term means the five entrepreneurs each of which account for one-twentieth or more of the aggregate volume and rank among the five largest entrepreneurs in Japan; hereinafter the same meaning in this section) raise the price they use as the basis of their transactions in such goods or services of the same description by an identical or similar amount or percentage within a period of three months, the Fair Trade Commission may ask such major entrepreneurs for a report, furnishing a statement of reasons for such a raise in the price of such goods or services: Provided, That this shall not apply to price increases effected by entrepreneurs whose price of such goods or services is authorized or approved by, or filed a notification with, the competent minister in charge of the business in which the said entrepreneurs are engaged (in case such price shall be filed a notification with the competent minister, this shall apply only to such cases where the competent minister has the authority to order a change in such price.)

(2) In the event any change has occurred in the economic conditions resulting in a drastic change in domestic industrial shipment and wholesale prices, the amount of prices as prescribed in the preceding subsection may be revised by virtue of a Cabinet Ordinance in order to reflect such change.

CHAPTER V: UNFAIR TRADE PRACTICES
AMENDMENT OF THIS CHAPTER (ACT NO. 259 OF 1953)

Sec. 19 [Prohibition of unfair trade practices]

No entrepreneur shall employ unfair trade practices.

Sec. 20 [Measures against unfair trade practices]

(1) When there exists any act in violation of the preceding section, the Fair Trade Commission may, in accordance with the procedures as provided for in Division II [procedures], Chapter VIII, order the entrepreneur concerned to cease and desist from the said act, to delete the clauses concerned from the contract and to take any other measures necessary to eliminate the said act.

(2) The provisions of Section 7(2) [measures against already ceased violations] shall apply *mutatis mutandis* to an act in violation of the preceding section.

CHAPTER VI: EXEMPTIONS

Sec. 21 [Natural monopoly]

The provisions of this Act shall not apply to such acts relating to the production, sale, or supply as are done in the proper course of business by a person engaging in railway, electricity, gas, or any other business constituting a monopoly by the inherent nature of the said business.

Sec. 22 [Legitimate acts under special acts and orders]

(1) The provisions of this Act, where there exists a special act concerning a specific industry, shall not apply to legitimate acts of an entrepreneur or a trade

association conducted in accordance with such a special act or an order based upon such an act.

(2) Such special laws as provided for in the preceding subsection shall be specified by a separate act.

Sec. 23 [Acts under intangible property rights]

The provisions of this Act shall not apply to such acts recognisable as the exercise of rights under the Copyright Act, the Patent Act, the Utility Model Act, the Design Act, or the Trademark Act.

Sec. 24 [Acts of co-operatives]

The provisions of this Act shall not apply to such acts of a co-operative (including a federation of co-operatives) which conforms to the requirements stipulated in each of the following paragraphs and which has been formed in accordance with the provisions of a separate act: Provided, That the foregoing shall not apply to such cases where unfair trade practices are employed, or where competition in any particular field of trade is substantailly restrained, resulting in unjust rise of prices:

(i) Its purpose shall be mutal aid among small-scale entrepreneurs or consumers;
(ii) It shall be voluntarily formed; and the participation in and withdrawl from the co-operative shall be voluntary;
(iii) Each member shall possess equal voting rights; and
(iv) If distribution of profits among members is contemplated, the limits shall be stipulated in a law or an order, or in the articles of an association.

Sec. 24.2 [Resale price maintenance contracts]

(1) The provision of this Act shall not apply to legitimate acts performed by an entrepreneur who produces or sells a commodity, the uniform quality of which is easily identifiable and which is designated by the Fair Trade Commission, with another entrepreneur who buys such commodity, in order to fix and maintain the resale price thereof (this term means hereinafter the price at which the latter entrepreneur or a third entrepreneur who purchases from him sells such commodity): Provided, That the foregoing shall not apply if the said act tends to be grossly injurious to the interest of consumers in general or if it is done against the will of the entrepreneur who produces the said commodity, by an entrepreneur whose business is to sell the said commodity.

(2) The Fair Trade Commission shall not designate a commodity under the provisions of the preceding subsection unless it comes under each of the following paragraphs:

(i) The commodity shall be for the daily use by the consumers in general; and
(ii) Free competition shall exist with respect to the commodity.

(3) the designation of a commodity under the provisions of Subsection (1) above shall be made by notification.

(4) Legitimate acts performed by an entrepreneur whose business is to publish copyrighted works or by an entrepreneur whose business is to sell such published works, in order to fix and maintain with another entrepreneur who buys such

works, the resale price thereof, shall be exempted from the application of the provisions of this Act.

(5) The organization formed in accordance with the provisions of any one of the following Acts shall not be included in the term of 'another entrepreneur' who buys commodities or copyrighted works as provided for in Subsection (1) or the preceding subsection: Provided, That the foregoing provisions shall, in the case of the organizations formed under the provisions of any one of the Acts mentioned in paragraphs (viii) and (viii–ii) hereunder, only apply to cases where a business co-operative, a minor business co-operative, a federation of co-operatives, a commercial and industrial association or a federation of commercial and industrial associations purchases such commodity as provided for in Subsection (2) above or copyrighted works as provided for in Subsection (4) above, for the consumption of persons directly or indirectly constituting the said business co-operative, federation of co-operatives, commercial and industrial associations or federation of commercial and industrial associations:

(i) National Public Service Act.
(ii) Agricultural Cooperatives Act.
(iii) National Public Service Mutual Aid Association Act.
(iii.ii) Mutual Aid Association of Public Corporation Employees Act.
(iii.iii) Local Public Service, etc., Mutual Aid Association Act.
(iv) Consumer Cooperatives Act.
(v) Fishing Cooperatives Act.
(vi) Public Corporation, etc. Labour Relations Act.
(vii) Labour Unions Act.
(viii) Small and Medium Sized Enterprise, etc., Cooperatives Act.
(viii.ii) Small and Medium Sized Enterprises Organization Act.
(ix) Local Public Service Act.
(x) Forestry Act.
(xi) Local Public Enterprise Labour Relation Act.

(6) When an entrepreneur as stipulated in Subsection (1) above has fixed the resale price under the said subsection and has entered into a contract for the purpose of maintaining it, he shall, in accordance with provisions of the Rules of the Fair Trade Commission, file a notification thereof with the Commission within thirty days from the date of the conclusion of the said contract: Provided, That the foregoing shall not apply if the Fair Trade Commission stipulates otherwise in its Rules.

Sec. 24.3 [Depression cartels]

(1) Where there exists an extreme disequilibrium of supply and demand for a particular commodity, resulting in circumstances falling under each of the following paragraphs, the provisions of this Act shall not apply to concerted activities of entrepreneurs (including an act of a trade association which causes its constituent entrepreneurs to undertake concerted activities; hereinafter the same) who produce the said commodity or a trade association consisting of such entrepreneurs (hereinafter referred to as 'producers, etc.'), which have obtained authorization under either of the following two subsections: Provided, That the foregoing

shall not apply when they employ unfair trade practices or cause any entrepreneur to employ such acts as constitute unfair trade practices:

(i) The price of the said commodity is below the average cost of production, and a considerable part of the entrepreneurs in the trade concerned may eventually be forced to discontinue production.
(ii) It is difficult to overcome such circumstances as stipulated in the preceding paragraph by the rationalization of individual enterprises.

(2) When circumstances provided for in the preceding subsection exist, those producers, etc. who desire to effect concerted activities relating to restrictions on output or sales, or on facilities or equipments (excluding such as will impede the renovation or improvement of facilities) may, in order to overcome such circumstances, obtain from the Fair Trade Commission authorization of the said activities in advance.

(3) When circumstances provided for in Subsection (1) above exist and if restriction on output of the commodity in a particular trade is found extremely difficult for technical reasons, those producers, etc. who desire to effect concerted activities involving price-fixing may, in accordance with the Rules of the Fair Trade Commission, obtain from the Fair Trade Commission authorization of the said activities in advance. The same shall apply to a price-fixing agreement entered into concurrently with an agreement provided for in the preceding subsection, when the concerted activities have been effected upon authorization under the preceding subsection, and when such concerted activities alone proved to be entirely inadequate to overcome the circumstances stipulated in Subsection (1) above.

(4) The Fair Trade Commission shall not grant authorization as provided for in the preceding two subsections unless the concerted activities applied fall under the conditions provided for in the preceding two subsections and conform with each of the following paragraphs:

(i) That they do not exceed the necessary extent to overcome the circumstances provided for in Subsection (1) above.
(ii) That there is no likelihood of unjustly injuring the interests of the consumers in general, and of related enterpreneurs.
(iii) That they are not unjustly discriminatory.
(iv) That they do not restrict unjustly participation in or withdrawal from such activities.

(5) When the Fair Trade Commission has authorized or dismissed an application for authorization under Subsection (2) or (3) above, or has taken action pursuant to the provisions of Section 66(1) [cancellation or modification of authorization] with regard to authorization under Subsection (2) or (3) above, it shall, without delay, make public the fact showing the reason for the said action.

(6) The producers, etc. engaged in concerned activities after obtaining authorization under Subsection (2) or (3) above shall, without delay, file a notification thereof with the Fair Trade Commission, when they have discontinued the said activities.

(7) The Fair Trade Commission shall, where an objection to authorization

under Subsection (2) or (3) above has been filed, conduct an open summary hearing in accordance with the Rules of the Fair Trade Commission.

(8) The Fair Trade Commission shall, prior to granting such authorization under Subsection (2) or (3) above, or to dismissing an application thereof, consult with the competent minister in charge of the business concerned. The same shall apply when the Fair Trade Commission intends to take action provided for in Section 66(1) [cancellation or modification of authorization] with respect to such authorization under Subsection (2) or (3) above.

Sec. 24.4 [Rationalization cartels]

(1) The provisions of this Act shall not apply to concerted activities of producers who obtained authorization under the following subsection, where they are found particularly necessary for effecting an advancement of technology, an improvement in the quality of goods, a reduction in costs, an increase in efficiency or any other rationalization of enterprises.

(2) Producers, etc. desirous of undertaking concerted activities regarding restrictions on technology or kinds of product, utilization of facilities for storage of raw materials or products or for transportation thereof, or utilization or purchase of by-products, waste, or scrap in the case provided for by the preceding subsection may, in accordance with the provisions of the Rules of the Fair Trade Commission, obtain authorization from the Fair Trade Commission in advance.

(3) The Fair Trade Commission shall not grant authorization under the preceding subsection unless concerted activities applied for fall under the conditions provided for in the preceding subsection, and conform with each of the following paragraphs:

(i) That there is no likelihood of injuring the interests of users.
(ii) That there is no likelihood of unjustly injuring the interests of consumers in general and of related entrepreneurs (excluding customers).
(iii) That they are not unjustly discriminatory.
(iv) That they do not restrict unjustly the participation in or withdrawal from such activities.
(v) That where restrictions on line of product are imposed differently on participants in the concerted activities, such differentiation is not designed unjustly to concentrate production of a particular product in the hands of any specific entrepreneurs.

(4) The provisions of the proviso to Subsection (1) and of Subsections (5) to (8) inclusive of the preceding section shall apply *mutatis mutandis* to the concerted activities as provided for in Subsection (2).

CHAPTER VII: DAMAGES

Sec. 25 [Absolute liability]

(1) Any entrepreneur who has effected private monopolization or unreasonable restraint of trade or who has employed unfair trade practices shall be liable to indemnify the person injured.

(2) No entrepreneur may be exempted from the liability as prescribed in the preceding subsection by proving the non-existence of wilfulness or negligence on his part.

Sec. 26 [Restriction on exercise of the right to claim for damages in court, prescription]

(1) The right to claim for damages as provided for in the preceding section may not be exercised in court until the decision pursuant to the provisions of Section 48(4) [recommendation decision], Section 53.3 [consent decision], or Section 54 [hearing decision] has become final and conclusive or until the decision pursuant to the provisions of Section 54.2(1) [decision to order the payment of surcharge] has become final and conclusive in case no decision has been made pursuant to the provisions above.

(2) The right under the preceding subsection shall, upon expiration of three years from the date on which the decision in the said subsection became final and conclusive, be extinct by prescription.

CHAPTER VIII: FAIR TRADE COMMISSION

Division I: Organization and Power

Sec. 27 [Duty and position]

(1) The Fair Trade Commission shall be established in order to attain the purpose of this Act.

(2) The Fair Trade Commission shall be administratively attached to the Prime Minister.

Sec. 27.2 [Affairs under the jurisdiction of the Fair Trade Commission]

The affairs under the jurisdiction of the Fair Trade Commission shall be as follows:

(i) Matters relating to regulation on private monopolization.
(ii) Matters relating to regulation on unreasonable restraint of trade.
(iii) Matters relating to regulation on unfair trade practices.
(iv) Matters relating to regulation on monopolistic situations.
(v) Doing surveys and research on business activities or actual economic conditions or making coordination of economic laws or orders, relating to regulation on activities which substantially restrain competition in any particular field of trade, regulation on activities which tend to impede fair competition, regulation in order to prevent excessive concentration of economic power or other regulation on unjust restriction of business activities.
(vi) Business which is assigned to the Fair Trade Commission based on a law (including an order based on a law), in addition to those stipulated in any one of the preceding paragraphs.

Sec. 28 [Independence]

The chairman and the commissioners of the Fair Trade Commission perform their duties independently.

Sec. 29 [Organization, appointment of chairman and commissioners and their status]

(1) The Fair Trade Commission shall be composed of a chairman and four commissioners.

(2) The chairman and the commissioners shall be appointed by the Prime Minister with the consent of both Houses of the Diet from among persons whose age is thirty-five or more and who are experts in laws or economics.

(3) The appointment or dismissal of the chairman shall be attested by the Emperor.

(4) The chairman and the commissioners shall be public service officials.

Sec. 30 [Term of office for chairman and commissioners]

(1) The term of office for the chairman and the commissioner shall be five years: Provided, That the term of office for the chairman and the commissioners appointed to fill a vacancy shall be the remainder of the term of office for his predecessor.

(2) The chairman and the commissioner may be reappointed.

(3) The chairman and the commissioner shall retire from the office upon reaching the age of sixty five.

(4) If the term of office for the chairman or the commissioner expires, or a vacancy occurs at the time when the consent of the both Houses of the Diet is unobtainable because the Diet is not in session or the House of Representatives is dissolved, the Prime Minister may appoint the chairman or a commissioner from among such persons having qualifications as provided for in the Subsection (2) of the preceding section. In this case the subsequent approval of both Houses shall be obtained at the earliest session of the Diet after the appointment.

Sec. 31 [Guarantee of status of chairman and commissioners]

The chairman or a commissioner may not, against his will, be removed from office during his term of office, except in the cases falling under any one of the following paragraphs:

(i) When he has been adjudicated incompetent, quasi-incompetent, or bankrupt.

(ii) When he has been dismissed by way of disciplinary punishment.

(iii) When he has been punished for the violation of this Act.

(iv) When he has been sentenced to imprisonment or heavier penalty.

(v) When the Fair Trade Commission has decided that he is incapable of executing his duty on account of his physical or mental breakdown.

(vi) When the subsequent approval of both Houses of the Diet could not be obtained in the case of Subsection (4) of the preceding section.

Sec. 32 [Dismissal of chairman or commissioners]

In the case of paragraphs (i) or (iii) to (vi) inclusive of the preceding section, the Prime Minister shall dismiss the chairman or the commissioner concerned from his office.

Sec. 33 [Chairman]

(1) The chairman shall preside over the affairs of the Fair Trade Commission and shall represent it.

(2) The Fair Trade Commission shall choose in advance a commissioner from among the commissioners who acts on behalf of the chairman in case he is incapacitated.

Sec. 34 [Quorum and voting]

(1) Meetings of the Fair Trade Commission shall not be opened and the decision shall not be made without the attendance of the chairman and two or more commissioners.

(2) All decisions of the Fair Trade Commission shall be made by majority votes of the attending commissioners. In case the votes are evenly divided the chairman shall have the power to decide.

(3) The decision of the Fair Trade Commission under the provisions of Section 31(v) shall, irrespective of the provisions of the preceding subsection, be made with the unanimous concurrence of all commissioners or the chairman except the commissioner or chairman concerned.

(4) For the purpose of applying the provisions of Subsection (1) above, in case the chairman is incapacitated, the commissioner chosen to act on behalf of the chairman pursuant to Subsection (2) of the preceding section, shall be deemed to be the chairman.

Sec. 35 [Executive Bureau, personnel]

(1) The Executive Bureau shall be attached to the Fair Trade Commission for the discharge of its affairs.

(2) Administrative law judges, not exceeding five in number shall be maintained in the Executive Bureau, whose duty shall be to conduct a part of the hearing procedures (excluding the rendering of a decision).

(3) Administrative law judges shall be selected by the Fair Trade Commission from among the personnel of the Executive Bureau who have been found to have the necessary knowledge and experience in law and economics to conduct the hearing procedures and to be capable of making a fair judgement.

(4) A Public prosecutor, private attorney actually practising at the time of the appointment, or a person qualified to be a private attorney shall be included among the personnel of the Executive Bureau.

(5) Duties to be placed upon the personnel who is a public prosecutor under the preceding subsection shall be limited to matters relating to cases in violation of the provisions of this Act.

Sec. 35.2 [Local offices]

(1) Local offices shall be maintained at necessary places as local organizations of the Executive Bureau of the Fair Trade Commission.

(2) The name, location and territorial jurisdiction of each local office under the preceding subsection shall be provided for by a Cabinet Ordinance.

Sec. 35.3 [Administration of personnel]

With regard to the appointment, dismissal, disciplinary measures, and other matters relating to the administration of personnel of the Executive Bureau, the provisions of the National Public Service Personnel Act (Act No. 120 of 1947) shall apply.

Sec. 36 [Salaries of chairman and commissioners]

(1) The salaries of the chairman and the commissioner shall be provided for separately.

(2) The salaries of the chairman and the commissioner shall not be reduced in amount against their will while they are in office.

Sec. 37 [Prohibition of certain activities of chairman, commissioners and personnel]

The chairman, each commissioner and such personnel of the Fair Trade Commission as may be stipulated by an order shall not engage in any one of the following activities while he is in office:

(i) Becoming a member of the Diet or of the legislative assembly of a local public authority, or actively engage in political activities;
(ii) Holding any other remunerative position except as permitted by the Prime Minister; or
(iii) Engaging in commerce or any other business for pecuniary gain.

Sec. 38 [Prohibition of expression of opinion]

The chairman, each commissioner and other personnel of the Fair Trade Commission shall not express their views outside the Fair Trade Commission on the existence or non-existence of facts or application of law with regard to a case of violation: Provided, That the foregoing shall not apply to cases provided for in this Act or where the presentation of the results of study concerning this Act is made.

Sec. 39 [Duty to preserve trade secrets]

The chairman, each commissioner and personnel of the Fair Trade Commission, or any person who once held such position, shall not divulge or make surreptitious use of trade secrets of entrepreneurs which came to their knowledge in the course of their duties.

Sec. 40 [Compulsory powers of inquiry]

The Fair Trade Commission may, if necessary for the performance of its functions, order government agencies, legal entities established by a special act or an order, entrepreneurs, or organizations of entrepreneurs, or their personnel to appear before the Commission, or may require them to submit necessary reports, information or data.

Sec. 41 [Entrustment of research and survey]

The Fair Trade Commission may, if necessary for the performance of its functions, entrust government agencies, legal entities established by a special act or an order, schools, entrepreneurs, organizations of entrepreneurs, or persons of learning and experience to carry out necessary research and survey.

Sec. 42 [Public hearings]

The Fair Trade Commission may, if necessary for the performance of its duties, hold public hearings to obtain views of the public.

Sec. 43 [Publication of appropriate matters]

The Fair Trade Commission may, in order to ensure the proper enforcement of this Act, make public any appropriate matters with the exception of trade secrets of entrepreneurs.

Sec. 44 [Reports to the Diet, submission of opinions]

(1) The Fair Trade Commission shall submit to the Diet, through the Prime Minister, an annual report on the enforcement of this Act. In this case, the report shall contain an outline of the report ordered to be submitted under the provisions of Section 18.2(1) [reporting requirement on parallel price increases].

(2) The Fair Trade Commission may submit to the Diet, through the Prime Minister, its views on matters necessary to attain the purpose of this Act.

Division II: Procedures

Sec. 45 [Report and detection of violation]

(1) Any person may, when he considers that a fact in violation of this Act exists, report the said fact to the Fair Trade Commission and ask for the appropriate measures to be taken.

(2) The Fair Trade Commission, upon receipt of such report as provided for in the preceding subsection, shall make the necessary investigation with respect to the case.

(3) Where any report submitted under the provisions of Subsection (1) above specifies in writing any fact or facts pursuant to the provisions of the Rules of the Fair Trade Commission, and when the Commission decides to take, or not to take, appropriate measures with respect to the case referred to in such report, the Fair Trade Commission shall promptly notify that effect to the person who made such report.

(4) The Fair Trade Commission may, when it considers that a violation of this Act or a monopolistic situation exists, take appropriate measures upon its own authority.

Sec. 45.2 [Procedures for measures against a monopolistic situation]

(1) The Fair Trade Commission shall, if it considers that there exists a fact which falls under the purview of a monopolistic situation, and if it decides to take a measure set forth in Subsection (3) of the preceding section, make a notice of

such action to the competent Minister having jurisdiction over the business in which the entrepreneur concerned is engaged.

(2) In case a notice under the provision of the preceding subsection has been made, the Minister may present to the Commission his view regarding the existence or the absence of such a monopolistic situation and his view regarding other alternative measures which he feels would be sufficient to restore competition as provided for in the proviso to Section 8.4(1) [measures against a monopolistic situation].

Sec. 46 [Compulsory measures for investigation]

(1) The Fair Trade Commission may, in order to conduct the necessary investigation with regard to a case of violation, take any one of the following measures:

(i) Ordering persons concerned with a case, or witnesses to appear for interrogating, hearing their views or collecting report from them;
(ii) Ordering experts to appear to have them give expert testimony;
(iii) Ordering persons holding accounting books, documents and other matters to submit the same, or to retain such submitted matters; or
(iv) Entering any place of business of the persons concerned with a case, or other necessary places and inspect conditions of business operation and property, accounting books, documents and other matters.

(2) The Fair Trade Commission may, when it finds it proper, designate, in accordance with the provisions of an order, investigators from among the personnel of the Fair Trade Commission and cause them to take the measures as provided for in the preceding subsection.

(3) Where an inspection is to be conducted by the personnel in accordance with the provisions of the preceding subsection, they shall be required to carry their identification cards and to show it to the persons concerned.

(4) The authority to take actions pursuant to the provision of Subsection (1) above shall not be construed as one granted for criminal investigation.

Sec. 47 [Record]

The Fair Trade Commission shall, when it has conducted the necessary investigation of a case of violation, keep an investigation record of the main points thereof, and when it has taken any measures as provided for in the preceding section, it shall set out the result thereof.

Sec. 48 [Recommendation to the violator to take corrective measures, recommendation decision]

(1) The Fair Trade Commission may, when it finds that there exists any act in violation of the provisions of Section 3 [prohibition of private monopolization or unreasonable restraint of trade], Section 6(1) [prohibition of particular international agreements or contracts] or (2) [filing requirement of the same], Section 8 [prohibited acts of trade associations], Section 9(1) or (2) [prohibition of holding companies], Section 9.2(1) [restriction on total amount of stockholding by a giant non-financial company], Section 10 [prohibition of particular stockholding by a company], Section 11(1) [prohibition of particular stockholding by a financial

company], Section 13 [prohibition of particular interlocking directorates], Section 14 [prohibition of particular stockholding by a person other than a company], Section 15(1) [prohibition of particular mergers] (including such cases where the said provisions are applied *mutatis mutandis* by Section 16 [prohibition of particular acquisitions of business, etc.]), Section 17 [prohibition of evasion] or Section 19 [prohibition of unfair trade practices], recommend the person who has committed such violations (including the directors and managers of a trade association and its constituent entrepreneurs when the violating act relates to the provision of Section 8) to take the appropriate measures.

(2) The Fair Trade Commission may, if it finds that any act in violation of the provisions of Section 3 [prohibition of private monopolization or unreasonable restraint of trade], Section 8(1) [prohibited acts of trade association] (i), (iv) or (v) or Section 19 [prohibition of unfair trade practices], has already ceased to exist, and if it finds it particularly necessary, recommend to the person who committed such violation (including the officers and managers of such trade association and the constituent entrepreneurs when the violating act relates to the provisions of Section 8(l)(i), (iv) or (v)) to take appropriate measures.

(3) Any person who has received a recommendation under the provisions of the preceding subsection shall notify without delay to the Fair Trade Commission whether or not he accepts the said recommendation.

(4) The Fair Trade Commission may, when the person receiving the recommendation under the provisions of the preceding two subsections has accepted it, render a decision on the line of the said recommendation without resorting to the hearing procedures.

Sec. 48.2 [Procedures for surcharges]

(1) The Fair Trade Commission shall, when it finds there exists a fact as provided for in Subsection (1) [surcharges against entrepreneurs] of Section 7.2 (including cases where this provision is applicable *mutatis mutandis* under Section 8.3 [surcharges against constituent entrepreneurs]; hereinafter the same in this Section), order the entrepreneur or the constituent entrepreneurs of the trade association (or other entrepreneur in case a constituent entrepreneur is acting for the benefit of the other entrepreneur; hereinafter the same in this Section) to pay to the Treasury a surcharge as prescribed in Section 7.2(1) or (2): Provided, That in case hearing procedures have been initiated with respect to such violating act, such order shall not be issued by such time as such procedures have been completed.

(2) An order prescribed in the preceding subsection (hereinafter referred to as 'payment order') shall be made by serving to such entrepreneur a certified copy of such payment order which states the amount of the surcharge to be paid, the basis of computation of such amount, the violating act responsible for such surcharge and the deadline for payment.

(3) The deadline for payment of such a surcharge as prescribed in the preceding subsection shall fall on a date two months after the date on which such payment order is forwarded.

(4) The Fair Trade Commission shall, when it contemplates issuing a payment

order, give in advance, the entrepreneur or the constituent entrepreneur of the trade association concerned, an opportunity to present his views and to submit evidence in support thereof.

(5) If any person is dissatisfied with a payment order, he may, in accordance with the Rules of the Fair Trade Commission and within thirty days from the date on which the certified copy of such order was forwarded, request the Commission to initiate the hearing procedures on the said case.

(6) Except in cases where a decision was rendered pursuant to the provisions of Subsection (4) of the preceding section, Section 53.3 [consent decision] or Section 54 [hearing decision] with respect to the said violating act, a payment order shall be deemed final and conclusive for the purpose of applying the provisions of Section 26 [restriction on exercise of the right to claim for damages in court, prescription], after the lapse of the period prescribed in the preceding subsection.

Sec. 49 [Initiation of hearing procedures]

(1) The Fair Trade Commission may, in the case of Section 48(1) or (2) [recommendation to the violator to take corrective measures] or in the case where there exists a monopolistic situation (excluding the case provided for in the proviso to Section 8.4(1) [measures against a monopolistic situation]. The same shall apply in Section 54(1) [hearing decision].), and if it finds that it would be in the public interest to initiate hearing procedures on the case, initiate hearing procedures on the said case.

(2) When a request as prescribed in Subsection (5) of the preceding section is filed, the Fair Trade Commission shall, except in cases where it rejects the said request as unlawful by a decision, without delay initiate the hearing procedures on the case which is the subject of such request.

(3) In case hearing procedures have been initiated pursuant to the provision of the preceding subsection, the payment order issued relating to such case shall lose effect.

(4) The Fair Trade Commission shall, when it contemplates initiating hearing procedures on a case relating to Section 8.4(1) [measures against a monopolistic situation], consult with the competent Minister having jurisdiction over the business in which such entrepreneur is engaged.

Sec. 50 [Complaints, initiation of hearing procedures]

(1) The complaint shall be made in writing, in which the outline of the case shall be stated, and the chairman and the commissioners participating in the voting of the decision to issue the complaint shall sign it and affix their seal thereto.

(2) The hearing procedures shall be initiated by serving a certified copy of complaint upon a person to be ordered to take such measures (referred to as 'elimination, etc. measures' in Section 52(1) [respondent's defence]) as provided for in Section 7(1) [elimination measures] or (2) [elimination measures against already ceased violations] (including the cases applicable *mutatis mutandis* under the Section 8.2(2) and Section 20(2)), Section 8.2(1) or (3) [elimination measures], Section 8.4(1) [measures against a monopolitistic situation], Section 17.2 [elimination measures] or Section 20(1) [elimination measures] or such person requesting

the initiation of the hearing procedures in accordance with the provisions of Section 48.2(5) [request for initiation of hearing procedures on surcharges] (hereinafter referred to as 'respondent').

(3) The respondent shall be ordered to appear on the date of the hearing proceedings.

(4) The date of hearing proceedings shall be fixed on a day later than thirty days from the date of serving the certified copy of the complaint: Provided, That the foregoing shall not apply when the consent of the respondent is obtained.

Sec. 51 [Answers]

A respondent shall, upon receipt of the certified copy of complaint, submit an answer without delay to the Fair Trade Commission.

Sec. 51.2 [Entrusted proceedings by administrative law judges]

The Fair Trade Commission may, after issuing a complaint, entrust an administrative law judge to conduct a part of the hearing procedures (excluding the decision) in addition to taking the measures under each paragraph of Section 46(1) [compulsory measures for investigation], in accordance with the Rules of the Fair Trade Commission: Provided, That this shall not apply to such person or persons who have performed the duty as the investigator of the said case or those who have intervened in the investigation of the said case.

Sec. 51.3 [Powers of investigators at hearing proceedings]

An investigator designated in accordance with the provisions of Section 46(2) [designation of investigators], may attend hearing proceedings, request evidence to be adopted, and perform other necessary acts.

Sec. 52 [Respondent's or his representative's defence]

(1) A respondent or his representative may, at hearing proceedings, state the reason why an order of the Fair Trade Commission to take elimination, etc. measures or to pay a surcharge under the provisions of Section 7.2(1) [surcharges imposed on entrepreneurs] (including such case when the said provisions are applied *mutatis mutandis* by Section 8.3 [surcharges imposed on constituent entrepreneurs]) in regard to the said case should not be made, submit supporting evidence therefor, request the Fair Trade Commission to interrogate necessary witness, to order expert witness to testify, to order holders of accounting books, documents and other matters to submit them, or to enter the necessary places and inspect the condition of business and property, accounting books and other matters, or may interrogate witnesses or expert witness who are required to attend hearing proceedings by order of the Fair Trade Commission.

(2) A respondent may be represented by an attorney at law or any other appropriate persons approved by the Fair Trade Commission.

Sec. 52.2 [Disclosure of reasons for non-adoption of evidence]

In case the Fair Trade Commission has not adopted any evidence introduced by the investigator, the respondent or his representative, the Commission shall state the reason for not having adopted such evidence.

Sec. 52.3 [Non-appearance of respondents]

The Fair Trade Commission may conduct the hearing proceedings even if the respondent or his representative fails to appear on the date of the said hearing proceedings without a justifiable cause.

Sec. 53 [Hearing proceedings, stenographic record]

(1) All hearing proceedings shall be public: Provided, that when it is found necessary to protect the trade secrets of an entrepreneur, or necessary to the public interest, a hearing proceeding may not be made public.

(2) A stenographer shall attend all hearing proceedings to record statements made therein.

Sec. 53.2 [Qualification for witness, right to refuse testimony, oath, etc.]

(1) The provisions of Sections 143 to 147 inclusive [principles on qualification for witness, relationship between public service secret and witness qualification, criminal responsibility of oneself or close relatives and the right to refuse testimony], Section 149 [qualification for witnesses, the right to refuse testimony], Sections 154 to 156 inclusive [oath of witness, testimony of estimated matters], Section 165 [expert witnesses] and Section 166 [oath of expert witnesses] of the Code of Criminal Procedures shall apply *mutatis mutandis* to the procedures by which the Fair Trade Commission or an administrative law judge, in the course of hearing proceedings, interrogate a witness, or orders an expert to give his testimony.

(2) In such cases as provided for in the preceding subsection, the terms 'court', 'question', and 'defendant' shall read as 'the Fair Trade Commission or an administrative law judge', 'interrogate', and 'respondent' respectively.

Sec. 53.2.2 [Opportunity to state the case directly to the Commission]

In case the Fair Trade Commission has entrusted an administrative law judge to conduct a part of the hearing procedures in accordance with the provisions of Section 51.2 [entrusted hearing proceedings by administrative law judges], if the respondent or his representative so requests, the Commission shall give the respondent or his representative an opportunity to state their views directly to the Commission: Provided, That this shall not apply to a case in which the hearing procedures have been initiated pursuant to the provision of Section 49(2) [initiation of hearing procedures on surcharges] and a decision has been rendered with respect to the violating act of such case pursuant to the provision of Section 48(4) [recommendation decision], the following section [consent decision] or Section 54 [hearing decision].

Sec. 53.3 [Consent decision]

The Fair Trade Commission may, after having determined to initiate the hearing procedures, when the respondent, admitting the findings of fact and the application of law stated in the complaint, submits to the Fair Trade Commission a written statement setting forth that he will accept the decision without resorting to subsequent hearing proceedings, and files a plan setting forth concrete measures which he proposes voluntarily to take in order to eliminate such violation, or to ensure the elimination of such violation, or to restore competition with respect to the goods or services involved in the monopolistic situation, if the Commission finds it appropriate, render a decision on the lines of the concrete measures as stated in such plan without subsequent hearing proceedings.

Sec. 54 [Hearing decision]

(1) The Fair Trade Commission shall, when it finds after hearing proceedings that violation of the provisions of Section 3 [prohibition of private monopolization or unreasonable restraint of trade], Section 6(1) [prohibition of specific international agreements or contracts] or (2) [filing requirement of the same], Section 8 [prohibited acts of trade associations], Section 9(1) or (2) [prohibition of holding company], Section 9.2(1) [restriction on total amount of stockholding by a non-financial giant company], Section 10 [prohibition of particular stockholding by a company], Section 11(1) [restriction on stockholding rate by a financial company], Section 13 [prohibition of particular interlocking directorates], Section 14 [prohibition of particular stockholding by a person other than a company], Section 15(1) [prohibition of particular mergers] (including such cases where the said provisions are applied *mutatis mutandis* by Section 16 [prohibition of particular acquisition of business]), Section 17 [prohibition of evasion] or Section 19 [prohibition of unfair trade practices] exists or that a monopolistic situation exists, order the respondent by a decision to take such measures as provided for in Section 7(1) [elimination measures], Section 8.2(1) or (3) [elimination measures], Section 17.2 [elimination measures] or Section 20(1) [elimination measures] or Section 8.4(1) [measures against monopolistic situations].

(2) The Fair Trade Commission shall, when it finds after hearing proceedings that such act in violation of the provisions of Section 3 [prohibition of private monopolization or unreasonable restraint of trade], Section 8(1) [prohibited acts of trade associations] (i), (iv) or (v) or Section 19 [prohibition of unfair trade practices] no longer exists and if it finds it particularly necessary, order, by a decision, the respondent to take the measures provided for in Section 7(2) [measures against already ceased violations] (including cases to which the said subsection is applied *mutatis mutandis* in Section 8.2(2) and Section 20(2)).

(3) The Fair Trade Commission shall, when it finds after hearing proceedings that such acts or a monopolistic situation as provided for in Subsection (1) did not exist at the time when it issued the complaint, that such acts as provided for in the said subsection or a monopolistic situation existed by the time of the issuance of the complaint, but the said acts or a monopolistic situation have already ceased to exist (excluding decision under the preceding subsection), or that a monopolistic situation exists and falls under the proviso to Section 8.4(1), make clear the said fact by a decision.

Sec. 54.2 [Surcharge payment order]

(1) The Fair Trade Commission shall, when it finds after hearing proceedings a fact as provided for in Section 7.2(1) [surcharges imposed on entrepreneurs] (including cases where this provision is applicable *mutatis mutandis* by Section 8.3 [surcharges imposed on constituent entrepreneurs]), order, by a decision, the respondent to pay to the Treasury a surcharge levied on such violation.

(2) The provisions of Section 48.2(3) [deadline for payment of surcharges] shall apply *mutatis mutandis* to a decision provided for in the preceding subsection.

Sec. 54.3 [Findings based on evidence]

In rendering a decision as provided for in the preceding two sections, the Fair Trade Commission shall, except in the case of facts not challenged by the respondent or known publicly, find the facts in question based on the evidences examined at the hearing procedures.

Sec. 55 [Meetings for decisions]

(1) Decisions shall be made by meeting of the chairman and the commissioners.

(2) The provisions of Section 34(1), (2), and (4) [quorum and voting of the Commission] shall apply *mutatis mutandis* to such meetings as provided for in the preceding subsection.

(3) For a decision ordering the respondent or respondents to take the measures provided for in Section 8.4(1) [measures against monopolistic situations], the decision shall be supported by three or more commissioners or chairman, notwithstanding the provisions of Section 34(2) which are applied *mutatis mutandis* by the preceding subsection.

Sec. 56 [Closed meetings]

Meetings of Fair Trade Commission shall not be made public.

Sec. 57 [Form of decision]

(1) Decisions shall be rendered in writing; and the written decisions shall show the fact found by and the application of law thereto made by the Fair Trade Commission and in the case of the decision under Section 54.2(1) [decisions to order the payment of surcharges], the basis of calculating the surcharge; and the chairman and the commissioners participating in the meeting shall sign it and affix their seal thereto.

(2) A dissenting opinion may be stated in a written decision.

Sec. 58 [Effective date of decision]

(1) A decision shall take effect from the time when the certified copy of the written decision has been served to the respondent.

(2) Any decision ordering the respondent or respondents to take the measures provided for in Section 8.4(2) [measures against monopolistic situations] shall not be enforced unless and until such decision becomes final and conclusive.

Sec. 59 [Interventions of the third parties interested]

The Fair Trade Commission may, if it finds it necessary, cause, on its own authority, a third person interested in the result of the decision, to be a party to the hearing procedures: Provided, That it shall in advance interrogate the respondent and the said third party.

Sec. 60 [Interventions of a govenment agency or public organization]

Any government agency or public organization interested in a case may, if it finds it necessary in the public interest, intervene in the hearing procedures as a party with the approval of the Fair Trade Commission.

Sec. 61 [Opinions of a government agency or public organization]

Any government agency or public organization interested in a case may, in order to protect the public interest, express it views to the Fair Trade Commission.

Sec. 62 [Stay of execution of FTC's order by deposit]

(1) When the Fair Trade Commission has ordered by a decision the cessation of acts constituting violations or any other measures in accordance with the provisions of Section 54(1) or (2) [hearing decision], the respondent may stay the execution of the said order by depositing such bond or securities as may be fixed by the court until the said decision becomes final and conclusive.

(2) The court ruling under the provisions of the preceding subsection shall be made in accordance with the Act of Procedures in Non-Contentious Matters.

Sec. 63 [Forfeitures of deposit]

(1) In a case where a respondent has made the deposit in accordance with the provisions of Subsection (1) of the preceding section and the decision in question has become final and conclusive, the court may, upon application of the Fair Trade Commission, forfeit the whole or a part of such bond or securities deposited.

(2) The provisions of Subsection (2) of the preceding section shall apply *mutatis mutandis* to the court ruling under the provisions of the preceding subsection.

Sec. 64 [Compulsory measures for investigation after decision]

The Fair Trade Commission may, if it considers particularly necessary after a decision rendered in accordance with the provisions of Section 54(1) or (2) [hearing decision], take measures or may cause its personnel to take measures in accordance with the provisions of Section 46 [compulsory measures for investigation].

Sec. 64.2 [A reminder or payment of surcharge and measures against delinquency]

(1) If any person fails to pay a surcharge by the designated deadline, the Fair Trade Commission shall press such person to pay the surcharge by serving a written reminder specifying a deadline therefor.

(2) In case a reminder is served pursuant to the provisions of the preceding subsection, the Fair Trade Commission may collect an arrearage charge computed at a rate of 14.5 per cent per annum of the amount of such surcharge as prescribed in the said subsection for the number of days intervening between the date immediately following the deadline and the date of payment: Provided, That this shall not apply to cases where the arrearage charge involved is less than 1,000 yen.

(3) In case the amount of an arrearage charge, computed in accordance with the provision of the preceding subsection, contains a fraction of less than 100 yen, such fraction shall be disregarded.

(4) In case any person on whom a reminder has been served under the provisions of Subsection (1) fails to pay a surcharge overdue, the Fair Trade Commission may collect such surcharge based on the example of the national tax delinquency procedures.

(5) The claim on a defaulted surcharge as prescribed in the preceding subsection shall have a lien next to those of the national and local taxes, and the prescription on such claim shall be the same as that of the national tax.

Sec. 65 [Dismissal of application for authorization, etc.]

(1) The Fair Trade Commission shall, when an application for authorization under the provisions of Section 9.2(1)(vi) [application for authorization of holding of stock of joint ventures with a foreign person, etc. by a giant company], Section 11(1) or (2) [application for authorization of stockholding by a financial company], Section 24.3(2) or (3) [application for authorization of depression cartels], or 24.4(2) [application for authorization of rationalization cartels] or an application for approval under the provision of Section 9.2(1)(ix) [application for approval of stockholding by imperative reasons by a giant non-financial company] has been filed and if it finds the said application to be groundless, dismiss it by a decision.

(2) The provisions of Section 45(2) [investigation in case of report of a violation] shall apply *mutatis mutandis* to the application for authorization or approval in the preceding subsection.

Sec. 66 [Revocation or modification of authorization, approval or decision]

(1) The Fair Trade Commission may, when it finds, with respect to the authorization or approval as prescribed in Subsection (1) of the preceding section, that the facts required for the said authorization or approval have ceased to exist or have changed, revoke or modify such authorization or approval after hearing procedures.

(2) The Fair Trade Commission may, when it finds that further maintenance of a decision is unreasonable and contrary to the public interest due to the changes in economic conditions and to other reasons, revoke or modify it by a decision: Provided, That the foregoing shall not apply if the interest of the respondent may be injured thereby.

Sec. 67 [Urgent injunction]

(1) The court may, upon application of the Fair Trade Commission, when it finds the matter to be one of urgent necessity, order the person doing an act suspected of violation of the provisions of Section 3 [prohibition of private monopolization or unreasonable restraint of trade], Section 6(1) [prohibition of particular international agreement or contract], Section 8(1) [prohibited acts of trade association], Section 9(1) or (2) [prohibition of holding company], Section 9.2(1) [restriction of total amount of stockholding by a non-financial giant company], Section 10(1) [prohibition of particular stockholding by a company], Section 11(1) [restriction on stockholding rate by a financial company], Section 13(1) or (2) [prohibition of particular interlocking directorates], Section 14(1) [prohibition of particular stockholding by a person other than a company], Section 15(1) [prohibition of

particular mergers] (including such cases where the said provisions are applied *mutatis mutandis* by Section 16 [prohibition of particular acquisitions of business]), Section 17 [prohibition of evasion] or Section 19 [prohibition of unfair trade practices], temporarily to cease the said act, the exercise of voting rights or the execution of duties as an officer in a company, or may rescind or modify such order.

(2) The court may, upon application of the Fair Trade Commission, when it finds the matter to be one of urgent necessity, order the person who has obtained authorization under the provisions of Section 24.3(2) or (3) [authorization of depression cartel] or 24.4(2) [authorization of rationalization cartel], when there is a reason to suspect in view of the provisions of Section 66(1) [revocation or modification of authorization] that conditions necessitating revocation or modification of such authorization under Section 24.3(2) or (3), or 24.4(2) have arisen, temporarily to suspend the said authorized activity, or may revoke or modify such order.

(3) The provisions of Section 62(2) [*mutatis mutandis* application of the Act of Procedures on Non-contentious Matters] shall apply *mutatis mutandis* to the court ruling under the provisions of the preceding two subsections.

Sec. 68 [Stay of urgent injunction]

(1) The execution of an urgent injunction under the provisions of the preceding Subsection (1) or (2), may be stayed by depositing such bond or securities as the court may fix.

(2) The provisions of Section 63 [forfeiture of deposit] shall apply *mutatis mutandis* to forfeiture of deposit under the provisions of the preceding subsection.

Sec. 69 [Access to records]

Any interested person may request to the Fair Trade Commission, after the issuance of a complaint, to peruse or copy the record of a case, or may ask the Fair Trade Commission for a certified copy of a surcharge payment order or a decision or an abridged copy thereof.

Sec. 69.2 [Service]

With regard to the service of documents, the provisions of Section 162 [service agent], Section 169 [place of service, service by meeting], Section 171 [supplementary service, service by leaving] and Section 177 [certificate for service] of the Code of Civil Procedures shall apply *mutatis mutandis*. In this case, the terms 'marshal' and 'court clerk' shall read as 'personnel of the Fair Trade Commission' and the term 'court' shall read as 'the Fair Trade Commission'.

Sec. 70 [Matters to be provided for by order]

Necessary matters with respect to procedures for investigation and hearing proceedings of the Fair Trade Commission, any other matters relating to the disposal of cases as well as those with respect to deposit under Section 62(1) [stay of execution of FTC's order by deposit] and Section 68(1) [stay of execution of urgent injunction by deposit] shall be provided for by a separate order except for such matters as are provided for in this Act.

Sec. 70.2 [Special provisions for appeals]

The decision or any other measures (including the measures effected by an investigator under the provisions of Section 46(2) [designation of and measures by investigators] or by administrative law judges under Section 51.2 [entrusted hearing proceedings by administrative law judges]) that has been rendered by the Fair Trade Commission under the provisions of this Division shall not be appealed under the Administrative Complaint Review Act (Act No. 160 of 1962).

Division III: Miscellaneous Provisions

Sec. 71 [Procedures for designation of unfair trade practices in a specific field of business]

The Fair Trade Commission shall, when it designates specific trade practices in a specific field of business in accordance with the provisions of Section 2(9) [designation of unfair trade practices], first hear the views of entrepreneurs operating in the same line of business as that of the entrepreneurs who employ the said specific trade practices, hold a public hearing to obtain the views of the public and thereupon shall make the designation after due consideration of the views disclosed.

Sec. 72 [Designation of unfair trade pratices by means of a notification]

Designation under the provisions of Section 2(9) [designation of unfair trade practices] shall be made by a notification.

Sec. 72.2 [Public hearing on monopolistic situations]

In case the Fair Trade Commission tries to initiate the hearing procedures on a case as prescribed in Section 8.4(1) [measures against a monopolistic situation], the Commission shall hold a public hearing to obtain views of the public.

Sec. 73 [Accusation, report on non-prosecution]

(1) The Fair Trade Commission shall, when it considers that a crime violating the provisions of this Act exists, file an accusation with the Public Prosecutor General.

(2) The Public Procecutor General shall, when he has taken measures not to prosecute in a case which is the subject of an accusation under the provisions of the preceding subsection, without delay, submit to the Prime Minister through the Minister of Justice a written report stating the said fact and reasons therefor.

Sec. 74 [Public Prosecutor General's request for FTC's investigation, etc.]

The Public Prosecutor General may, when he considers that a crime violating the provisions of this Act exists, notify the Fair Trade Commission of the fact, and request it to investigate and report thereon.

Sec. 75 [Compensation for witnesses or expert witness]

Witnesses or expert witness who have been ordered to appear or to give expert testimony in a hearing in accordance with the provisions of Section 46(1)(i) [FTC's order to witnesses to appear, etc.] or (ii) [FTC's order to expert witnesses to appear, etc.], or (2) [investigator's order to the same effect] or Section 51.2 [administrative law judge's order to the same effect], may claim a travelling allowance and fees as provided for by the order.

Sec. 76 [Rule-making powers of FTC]

The Fair Trade Commission may establish rules with respect to its internal disciplines, procedures for disposing cases and any necessary procedures relating to filing a notification, applications for authorization or approval and other matters.

CHAPTER IX: SUITS

Sec. 77 [Filing of a suit to quash a FTC's decision]

(1) A suit to quash a decision of the Fair Trade Commission shall be filed within thirty days (three months in case of the decision under the provisions of Section 8.4(1) [measures against a monopolistic situation]) from the date on which the decision became effective.

(2) The time-period stated in the preceding subsection shall be peremptory.

Sec. 78 [Transmission of records]

The court shall, upon receipt of a suit, request the Fair Trade Commission without delay, to transmit the records of the case concerned (including interrogation records of persons concerned in the case, witnesses or expert witnesses, stenographic records, and any other matters that may be used as evidences in court).

Sec. 79

Deleted. (Act No. 140 of 1962)

Sec. 80 [Binding authority of FTC's findings]

(1) Findings of fact made by the Fair Trade Commission shall, if established by substantial evidence, be binding upon the court in regard to the suit provided for in Section 77(1) [filing of a suit to quash a decision].

(2) Whether such substantial evidence as provided for in the preceding subsection exists or not shall be determined by the court.

Sec. 81 [Offering of new evidence, reference back of the case to FTC]

(1) A party may plead to the court for offer to introduce new evidences relevant to the case: Provided, That any such offer to introduce evidence relating to the facts found by the Fair Trade Commission shall have the reason which come under any one of the following paragraphs:

(i) Where the Fair Trade Commission failed to adopt the evidence without good cause; or

(ii) Where it was impossible to adduce evidence at hearing proceedings of the Fair Trade Commission, and there was no gross negligence on the part of the party in failing to adduce such evidence.

(2) In the cases prescribed in proviso to the preceding subsection, the onus shall be on the party concerned to show either of the reasons provided for in the preceding subsection.

(3) When the court finds there is a reason for offer to introduce evidence under proviso to Subsection (1) and it necessary to examine such evidence, it shall refer the case back to the Fair Trade Commission and order to take the appropriate measures after examining such evidence.

Sec. 82 [Quashing decisions]

The court may quash a decision of the Fair Trade Commission if the decision falls under any one of the following paragraphs:

(i) If the facts on which the decision is based are not established by substantial evidence; or

(ii) If the decision is violating the Constitution, or other laws or orders.

Sec. 83 [Reference back of a decision]

The court may, when it finds it necessary that further hearing proceedings shall be conducted in a case where it shall quash a decision of the Fair Trade Commission, refer the case back to the Fair Trade Commission giving the reasons therefor.

Sec. 84 [Request for FTC's opinion on amount of damages]

(1) When a suit for indemnification of damages under the provisions of Section 25 [absolute liability] has been filed, the court shall, without delay, request the opinion of the Fair Trade Commission with respect to the amount of damages caused by such violation as provided for in the said section.

(2) If a counter claim for indemnification of damages under the provisions of Section 25 is made in court proceedings for the purpose of offsetting the other claim, the provisions of the preceding subsection shall apply *mutatis mutandis*.

Sec. 85 [Original jurisdiction]

Original jurisdiction over any suit coming under any one of the following paragraphs shall lie in the Tokyo High Court:

(i) A suit concerning a decision of the Fair Trade Commission;

(ii) A suit concerning indemnification of damages under the provisions of Section 25 (absolute liability); or

(iii) A suit concerning offences as provided for in Sections 89 to 91 inclusive.

Sec. 86 [Exclusive jurisdiction of the Tokyo High Court]

Any case stipulated in Section 62(1) [stay of execution of FTC's decision by deposit], Section 63(1) [forfeiture of deposit] (including cases where the said provisions are applied *mutatis mutandis* by Section 68(2) [forfeiture of deposit for stay of execution of urgent injunction]), Section 67(1) and (2) [urgent injunction], Section 97 [administrative fines for contraventions of decisions] and Section 98 [administrative fines for contraventions of urgent injunction] shall be under the exclusive jurisdiction of the Tokyo High Court.

Sec. 87 [Special panel in the Tokyo High Court]

(1) A panel of judges invested with the jurisdiction to hear exclusively the suits provided for in Section 85 [original jurisdiction] and such cases as stipulated in the preceding section shall be established within the Tokyo High Court.

(2) The number of judges in the panel under the preceding subsection shall be five.

Sec. 88 [Suit for the cancellation of authorization of depression cartel or rationalization cartel]

A suit for the cancellation of authorization under the provisions of Section 24.3(2) or (3) [authorization of depression cartels], or Section 24.4(2) [authorization of rationalization cartels] may not be filed unless and until a ruling on the objection to the authorization has been rendered.

Sec. 88.2 [Special provisions for suits relating to FTC's decisions]

With respect to a suit relating to a decision of the Fair Trade Commission, the provisions of Section 6 [Minister of Justice's guidance, etc. to administrative agencies on suits] of the Act concerning the Authority of the Minister of Justice over the Suits in which Interests of State Are Involved (Act No. 194 of 1947) shall not apply.

CHAPTER IX.II: MISCELLANEOUS PROVISIONS

Sec. 88.3 [Interim measures]

In case any Cabinet Ordinance or Rules of the Fair Trade Commission is instituted, amended, or repealed in accordance with the provisions of this Act, necessary interim measures (including those relating to penal provisions) may be provided for by virtue of such Cabinet Ordinance or rules of the Fair Trade Commission to the extent deemed reasonably necessary as a consequence of such institution, amendment, or repeal.

CHAPTER X: PENAL PROVISIONS

Sec. 89 [Penalties against private monopolization or unreasonable restraint of trade]

(1) Any person committing one of the following offences shall be punished by penal servitude for not more than three years or by a fine of not more than 5 million yen:

(i) Any person who, in violation of the provisions of Section 3 [prohibition of private monopolization or unreasonable restraint of trade], effected private monopolization or unreasonable restraint of trade; or

(ii) Any person who, in violation of the provisions of Section 8(1) [prohibited acts of trade association] (i), effected substantial restraint of competition in any particular field of trade.

(2) An attempt to commit an offence falling under the preceding subsection shall be punished.

Sec. 90 [Penalties against prohibited international agreements or contracts, prohibited acts of trade association, or non-observance of final and conclusive decision]

(i) Any person who, in violation of the provisions of Section 6(1) [prohibition of particular international agreements or contracts] or Section 8(1)(ii) [prohibition of particular international agreements or contracts by a trade association] entered into an international agreement or an international contract which contains such matters as constitute unreasonable restraint of trade;

(ii) Any person who violated the provisions of Section 8(1)(iii) [limiting the number of entrepreneurs by a trade association] or (iv) [restriction on function or activity of the constituent entrepreneur by a trade association]; or

(iii) Any person who failed to comply with the decision as provided for in Section 48(4) [recommendation decision], Section 53.3 [consent decision] or Section 54(1) or (2) [hearing decision], after it has become final and conclusive.

Sec. 91 [Penalties against holding company, unlawful stockholding or interlocking directorates, etc.]

Any person committing one of the following offences shall be punished by penal servitude for not more than one year or by a fine of not more than two million yen:

(i) Any person who, in violation of the provisions of Section 9(1) [prohibition of establishment of a holding company], established a holding company, or violated the provisions of Subsection (2) [prohibition of operation as holding company] of the said section;

(ii) Any person who, in violation of the provisions of Section 9.2(1) [restriction on total amount of stockholding by a giant non-financial company], acquired or held stock;

(iii) Any person who, in violation of the provisions of the first part of Section 10(1) [prohibition of particular stockholding by a company], acquired or held stock;

(iv) Any person who, in violation of the provisions of Section 11(1) [restriction on stockholding rate by a financial company], acquired or held stock; or who, in violation of the provisions of Subsection (2) of the said section, held stock;

(v) Any person who, in violation of the provisions of Section 13(1) [prohibition of particular interlocking directorates], held concurrently positions as an officer of a company;

(vi) Any person who, in violation of the provisions of the first part of Section 14(1) [prohibition of particular stockholding by a person other than a company], acquired or held stock; or

(vii) Any person who, in violation of the provisions of Section 17 [prohibition of evasion], comitted such prohibitions or restrictions prescribed in the paragraphs above.

Sec. 91.2 [Penalties against failure to file notifications, etc.]

Any person committing one of the following offences shall be punished by a fine of not more than two million yen:

(i) Any person who, in violation of the provisions of Section 6(2) [filing requirement of a specific international agreement or contract], failed to file a notification, or filed a false notification;

(ii) Any person who, in violation of the provisions of Section 8(2) to (4) inclusive [filing requirement of a trade association], failed to file a notification, or filed a false notification;

(iii) Any person who, in violation of the provisions of Section 10(2) [filing requirement of stockholding by a company], failed to submit a report, or submitted a false report;

(iv) Any person who, in violation of the provisions of Section 13(3) [filing requirement of interlocking directorates], failed to file a notification, or filed a false notification;

(v) Any person who, in violation of the provisions of Section 14(2) [filing requirement of stockholding by a person other than a company], failed to submit a report, or submitted a false report;

(vi) Any person who, in violation of the provisions of Section 15(2) [filing requirement of mergers] (including cases where the said provisions are applied *mutatis mutandis* by Section 16 [filing requirement of acquisitions of business], failed to file a notification, or filed a false notification;

(vii) Any person who, in violation of the provisions of Section 15(3) [waiting period of mergers], effected registration of the establishment of a company by merger or the registration of change in the previously registered entry;

(viii) Any person who, in violation of the provisions of Section 15(3) [waiting period of mergers] which are applied *mutatis mutandis* by Section 16 [restriction on acquisitions of business], carried out an act coming under any one of the paragraphs of Section 16;

(ix) Any person who, in violation of the provisions of Section 18.2(1) [filing requirement of a report on parallel price increases], failed to file a report, or filed a false report; or

(x) Any person who, in violation of the provisions of Section 24.2(6) [filing requirement of resale price contracts], failed to file a notification or filed a false notification.

Sec. 92 [Concurrent punishment]

Any person committing any one of the offences stipulated in Sections 89 to 91 inclusive [violations of prohibition of private monopolization, prohibition of unreasonable restraint of trade, prohibited acts of trade association, prohibition of particular international agreement or contract, non-compliance of final and conclusive decision, prohibition of particular stockholding, etc.] may, according to the circumstances, be punished by both penal servitude and a fine.

Sec. 92.2 [Penalties against perjury]

(1) Where any witness or expert witness, who testified in accordance with the provisions of Section 53.2 [qualification for witness or expert witness, the right to

refuse testimony, oath, etc.], made a false statement or expert testimony, he shall be punished by penal servitude from not less than three months to not more than ten years.

(2) Where a person committing an offence under the preceding subsection confesses his crime prior to the termination of the hearing proceedings and before the discovery of such offence, the penalty for such offence may be commuted or remitted.

Sec. 93 [Penalties against divulging secrets]

Any person who violated the provisions of Section 39 [duty to preserve trade secrets] shall be punished by penal servitude for not more than one year or by a fine of not more than 100,000 yen.

Sec. 94 [Penalties against interference with inspection, etc.]

Any person who refused, obstructed or evaded the inspection as provided for in Section 46(1)(iv) [inspection by entering by the Fair Trade Commission] or (2) [measures by investigator], or Section 51.2 [measures by administrative law judge], shall be punished by penal servitude for not more than six months or by a fine of not more than 200,000 yen.

Sec. 94.2 [Penalties against non-compliance with compulsory measures]

Any person coming under any one of the following paragraphs shall be punished by a fine of not more than 200,000 yen:

(i) Any person who, in violation of such orders as provided for in Section 40 [compulsory measures for inquiry], failed to appear or to submit a report, information or data, or submitted a false report, information or data;

(ii) Any person concerned with a case or any witness who, in violation of the order issued to him under the provisions of Section 46(1)(i) [interrogation of persons concerned with a case or witnesses by the Commission] or (2) [measures by investigators], or Section 51.2 [entrusted proceedings by administrative law judge], failed to appear or to give testimony, or gave a false testimony, or failed to submit a report, or submitted a false report;

(iii) Any person who, in violation of the order issued to an expert witness under the provisions of Section 46(1)(ii) [FTC's order to make expert testimony, etc.] or (2), or Section 51.2, failed to appear or to give expert testimony, or gave a false expert testimony;

(iv) Any person who, in violation of the order issued to the holder of the objects under the provisions of Section 46(1)(iii) [FTC's order to submit documents, etc.] or (2), or Section 51.2, failed to submit the same; or

(v) Any person who, in violation of the order issued to a witness or an expert witness under the provisions of Section 154 (oath of witnesses) or Section 166 (oath of expert witnesses) of the Code of Criminal Procedures which are applied *mutatis mutandis* in Section 53.2 [oath of witnesses or expert witnesses], refused to take the oath.

Sec. 95 [Double punishment]

(1) When a representative of a juridical person, or an agent, an employer or any other person in the service of a juridical person or of an individual, committed

a violation as provided for in Section 89 [violation of prohibition of private monopolization or unreasonable restraint of trade, or substantial restraint of competition by a trade association], Section 90 [violation of prohibition of particular international agreements or contracts, limiting number of entrepreneurs in a particular field of business, or non-compliance of final and conclusive decision, etc.), Section 91 [violation of prohibition of holding company, prohibition of particular stockholding, etc.] (excluding (v)), Section 91.2 [violation of filing requirements] or Section 94 [interference with inspection], the said juridical person or the said individual shall be punished by such fine as provided for in each section in addition to the punishment of the offender.

(2) Where a representative, a manager, an agent, an employee or any other person in the service of a non-juridical organization has, with regard to the business or property of the said organization, committed a violation of Sections 89, 90 91(i) [violation of prohibition of a holding company], (vi) [violation of prohibition of particular stockholding by a person other than a company] or (vii) [violation of evasion] (limited to only those relating to (i) or (vi)) or Section 91.2(i), (ii), (v) or (ix), the said non-juridical organization shall be punished by such fine as provided for in each section in addition to the punishment of the offender.

(3) In cases specified in the preceding subsection, the provisions of the Code of Criminal Procedure pertaining to the litigation wherein a juridical person is in the defendant or the suspect shall apply *mutatis mutandis* in addition that the representative or manager shall represent the organization in the litigation concerned.

Sec. 95.2 [Punishment of representatives of juridical persons who failed to prevent violation]

In case of a violation of Section 89(1)(i) [violation of prohibition of private monopolization or unreasonable restraint of trade], Section 90(i) [violation of prohibition of international agreements or contracts relating to unreasonable restraint of trade] or (iii) [non-compliance of final and conclusive decision] or Section 91 [violation of prohibition of a holding company, prohibition of particular stockholding, etc.] (excluding (v)), the representative of a juridical person (excluding those who come under trade associations in case of violation of Section 90(i) or (iii) who failed to take necessary measures to prevent such violation knowingly of the existence of such a plan or who failed to take necessary measures for the rectification of such violation knowingly of the existence of such violation, shall also be punished by such a fine as provided for in the relevant sections.

Sec. 95.3 [Punishment of directors, etc. of trade associations who failed to prevent violation]

(1) Where a violation of Section 89(1)(ii) [substantial restraint of competition by a trade association], or Section 90 was committed, a director or any other officer or a manager of a trade association or its constituent entrepreneurs (including another entrepreneur who was acted for by a constituent entrepreneur) who failed to take the necessary measures to prevent such violation knowingly of the existence of such a plan or who failed to take the necessary measures to rectify

such violation knowingly of the existence of such violation shall be punished by such a fine as provided for in the relevant sections.

(2) Where a director or any other officer or a manager of a trade association or its constituent entrepreneurs as prescribed in the preceding subsection, is a juridical person or any other organization, the provision of the said subsection shall apply to such director or any other officer or a manager of the said organization.

Sec. 95.4 [Dissolution of trade associations]

(1) The court may, when it considers that the sufficient grounds exist, declare a trade association to be dissolved simultaneously with the imposition of a penalty as provided for in Section 89(1)(ii) [substantial restraint of competition by a trade association], or Section 90 [violation of prohibition of particular international agreement or contracts, limiting number of entrepreneurs by a trade association, non-compliance of final and conclusive decision, etc.].

(2) When the dissolution has been declared in accordance with the provisions of the preceding subsection, the trade association shall be dissolved by such declaration, notwithstanding the provisions of any other law or order, or articles of association, or any other stipulations.

Sec. 96 [Exclusive accusation by the Fair Trade Commission]

(1) Any offence under Sections 89 to 91 inclusive [violation of prohibition of private monopolization or unreasonable restraint of trade, prohibited acts of a trade association, prohibition of particular international agreements or contracts, non-compliance of final and conclusive decision and prohibition of particular stockholdings, etc.] shall be considered only after an accusation of the Fair Trade Commission has been filed.

(2) The accusation under the preceding subsection shall be made in writing.

(3) The Fair Trade Commission, in filing the accusation under subsection (1), may, when it considers it appropriate that the declaration under subsection (1) of the preceding Section or Section 100(1)(i) [revocation of patent rights or patent licenses] should be made with respect to an offence under the accusation, state the said effect in the said accusation.

(4) The accusation under subsection (1) shall not be withdrawn after public prosecution has been instituted.

Sec. 97 [Administrative fines for contraventions of decisions]

Any person who contravened a decision under Section 48(4) [recommendation decision], Section 53.3 [consent decision] or Section 54(1) or (2) [hearing decision] shall be liable to an administrative fine of not more than five hundred thousand yen: Provided, That the foregoing shall not apply when the said act shall be punished under the penal provisions.

Sec. 98 [Administrative fines for disobeying urgent injunctions]

Any person who disobeyed a ruling of the court under the provisions of Section 67(1) or (2) [urgent injunction], shall be liable to an administrative fine of not more than three hundred thousand yen.

Sec. 99 Deleted. (Act No. 214 of 1949)

Sec. 100 [Revocation of patent rights or patent licences and exclusion from government contracts]

(1) The court may, in a case coming under Section 89 [violation of private monopolization or unreasonable restraint of trade, substantial restraint of competition by a trade association] or Section 90 [violation of prohibition of particular international agreements or contracts, limiting number of entrepreneurs by a trade association, and non-compliance of final and conclusive decision, etc.], according to circumstances, make the following declaration simultaneously with the sentence of penalties: Provided, That the declaration under paragraph (i) hereunder shall be made only when the said patent right, or exclusive or non-exclusive licence for a patented invention belongs to the offender:

(i) That the patent under patent right, or the exclusive or non-exclusive licence for the patented invention to which the offence relates shall be revoked; or

(ii) That the offender shall be barred from becoming a party to a contract with the government for a period of not less than six months and not more than three years after the date when the judgment became final and conclusive.

(2) When a judgment with the declaration as provided for in paragraph (i) of the preceding subsection becomes final and conclusive, the court shall transmit the certified copy thereof to the Director General of the Patent Office.

(3) The Director General of the Patent Office shall, upon receipt of the certified copy of the judgment under the provisions of the preceding subsection, revoke the patent right, or the exclusive or non-exclusive licence for the patented invention.

2. Unfair Trade Practices

(June 18, 1982; Fair Trade Commission Notification No. 15)

In accordance with the provisions of Section 2(9) of Act Concerning Prohibition of Private Monopoly and Maintenance of Fair Trade (Act No. 54 of 1947), Unfair Trade Practices (the Fair Trade Commission Notification No. 11 of 1953) shall be totally amended as follows and put into force on September 1, 1982.

Unfair Trade Practices

(Concerted Refusal to Deal)

1. Without proper justification, taking an act specified in one of the following paragraphs concertedly with another entrepreneur who are in a competitive relationship with oneself (hereinafter, referred to as a 'competitor'):

(i) Refusing to deal with a certain entrepreneur or restricting the quantity or substance of a commodity or service involved in the transaction with a certain entrepreneur; or

(ii) Causing another entrepreneur to take an act which comes under the preceding paragraph.

(Other Refusal to Deal)

2. Unjustly refusing to deal, or restricting the quantity or substance of a commodity or service involved in the transaction with a certain entrepreneur, or causing another entrepreneur to take any act which comes under one of these categories.

(Discriminatory Pricing)

3. Unjustly supplying or accepting a commodity or service at prices which discriminate between regions or between the other parties.

(Discriminatory Treatment on Transaction Terms, etc.)

4. Unjustly affording favourable or unfavourable treatment to a certain entrepreneur in regard to the terms or execution of a transaction.

(Discriminatory Treatment in a Trade Association, etc.)

5. Unjustly excluding a specific entrepreneur from a trade association or from a concerted activity, or unjustly discriminating against a specific entrepreneur in a trade association or a concerted activity, thereby causing difficulties in the business activities of the said entrepreneur.

(Unjust Low Price Sales)

6. Without proper justification, supplying a commodity or service continuously at a price which is excessively below cost incurred in the said supply, or otherwise unjustly supplying a commodity or service at a low price, thereby tending to cause difficulties to the business activities of other entrepreneurs.

(Unjust High Price Purchasing)

7. Unjustly purchasing a commodity or service at a high price, thereby tending to cause difficulties to the business activities of other entrepreneurs.

(Deceptive Customer Inducement)

8. Unjustly inducing customers of a competitor to deal with oneself by causing them to misunderstand that the substance of a commodity or service supplied by oneself, or terms of the transaction, or other matters relating to such transaction are much better or much favourable than the actual one or than those relating to the competitor.

(Customer Inducement by Unjust Benefits)

9. Inducing customers of a competitor to deal with oneself by offering unjust benefits in the light of normal business practices.

(Tie-in Sales, etc.)

10. Unjustly causing the other party to purchase a commodity or service from oneself or from an entrepreneur designated by oneself by tying it to the supply of another commodity or service, or otherwise coercing the said party to deal with oneself or with an entrepreneur designated by oneself.

(Dealing on Exclusive Terms)

11. Unjustly dealing with the other party on condition that the said party shall not deal with a competitor, thereby tending to reduce transaction opportunities for the said competitor.

(Resale Price Restriction)

12. Supplying a commodity to the other party who purchases the said commodity from oneself while imposing, without proper justification, one of the restrictive terms specified below:

(i) Causing the said party to maintain the sales price of the commodity that one has determined, or otherwise restricting the said party's free decision on sales price of the commodity; or

(ii) Having the said party cause an enterpreneur who purchases the commodity from the said party to maintain the sales price of the commodity that one has determined, or otherwise causing the said party to restrict the said enterpreneurs free decision on sales price of the commodity.

(Dealing on Restrictive Terms)

13. Other than any act coming under the preceding two paragraphs, dealing with the other party on conditions which unjustly restrict any transaction between the said party and his other transacting party or other business activities of the said party.

(Abuse of Dominant Bargaining Position)

14. Taking any act specified in one of the following paragraphs, unjustly in the light of the normal business practices, by making use of one's dominant bargaining position over the other party:

(i) Causing the said party in continuous transaction to purchase a commodity or service other than the one involved in the said transaction;

(ii) Causing the said party in continuous transaction to provide for oneself money, service or other economic benefits;

(iii) Setting or changing transaction terms in a way disadvantageous to the said party;

(iv) In addition to any act coming under the preceding three paragraphs, imposing a disadvantage on the said party regarding terms or execution of transaction; or

(v) Causing a company which is one's other transacting party to follow one's direction in advance, or to get one's approval, regarding the appointment of officers of the said company (meaning those as defined by Subsection 3 of Section 2 of the Act Concerning Prohibition of Private Monopoly and Maintenance of Fair Trade).

(Interference with a Competitor's Transaction)

15. Unjustly interfering with a transaction between another enterpreneur who is in a domestic competitive relationship with oneself or with the company of which one is a stockholder or an officer and its other party to such transaction, by

preventing the formation of a contract, or by inducing the breach of a contract, or by any other means whatsoever.

(Interference with Internal Operation of a competing company)

16. Unjustly inducing, abetting, or coercing a stockholder or an officer of a company which is in a domestic competitive relationship with oneself or with a company of which one is a stockholder or an officer, to take an act disadvantageous to such company by the exercise of voting rights, transfer of stock, divulgence of secrets, or any other means whatsoever.

Index